Microhistories: demography, society and culti
1930 uses a local study of the Blean area
and early twentieth centuries to explore some of the more significant societal changes of the modern western world. Drawing on a
wide range of research techniques, including family reconstitution
and oral history, Barry Reay aims to show that the implications of
the microstudy can range way beyond its modest geographical
and historical boundaries. Combining cultural, demographic, economic and social history in a way rarely encountered in historical
literature, Dr Reay examines a fascinating range of topics. He
extends the parameters of the fertility transition, sketches out a
medical–social history of nineteenth-century rural England, charts
the contours of family labour and the complexities of class,
questions orthodoxies about kinship and the nuclear family, and
explores the contexts of Victorian sexuality and the meanings of
popular literacy.

This book demonstrates the challenging potentials of microhistory, and makes a central contribution to the 'new rural history'. It
will be of interest to family and oral historians, as well as historical
anthropologists, demographers, geographers and sociologists.

Microhistories: demography, society, and culture in rural England, 1800–1930

Cambridge Studies in Population, Economy and Society in Past Time 30

Series Editors

ROGER SCHOFIELD

ESRC Cambridge Group for the History of Population and Social Structure

RICHARD SMITH

ESRC Cambridge Group for the History of Population and Social Structure

JAN DE VRIES

University of California at Berkeley

PAUL JOHNSON

London School of Economics and Political Science

Recent work in social, economic and demographic history has revealed much that was previously obscure about societal stability and change in the past. It has also suggested that crossing the conventional boundaries between these branches of history can be very rewarding.

This series exemplifies the value of interdisciplinary work of this kind, and includes books on topics such as family, kinship and neighbourhood; welfare provision and social control; work and leisure; migration; urban growth; and legal structures and procedures, as well as more familiar matters. It demonstrates that, for example, anthropology and economics have become as close intellectual neighbours to history as have political philosophy or biography.

For a full list of titles in the series, please see end of book

Microhistories: demography, society and culture in rural England, 1800–1930

BARRY REAY

University of Auckland

CAMBRIDGE
UNIVERSITY PRESS

Published by the Press Syndicate of the University of Cambridge
The Pitt Building, Trumpington Street, Cambridge CB2 1RP
40 West 20th Street, New York, NY 10011–4211, USA
10 Stamford Road, Oakleigh, Melbourne 3166, Australia

First published 1996

Printed in Great Britain at the University Press, Cambridge

A catalogue record for this book is available from the British Library

Library of Congress cataloguing in publication data
Reay, Barry.
Microhistories: demography, society and culture in rural England,
1800–1930 / Barry Reay.
p.   cm. – (Cambridge studies in population, economy and society
in past time: 30)
Includes bibliographical references.
ISBN 0 521 57028 x (hc)
1. Family reconstitution – England – Kent – History.
2. Demography – England – Kent – History.
3. Kent (England) – Statistics – History.
4. Kent (England) – Social conditions.
I. Title.   II. Series.
HQ759.98.R43   1996
301'.09422'3–dr20   95–26140   CIP

ISBN 0 521 57028 x hardback

CE

*To Athina Tsoulis, and Alexa
and Kristina Tsoulis-Reay*

Contents

Conclusion

    Bibliography   263
    Index   283

Maps and plates

Figures

Tables

Preface

The basis for much of what follows is family reconstitution, pioneered in France by Louis Henry, in England by E. A. Wrigley and the Cambridge Group for the History of Population and Social Structure, and used with great effect by John Knodel in his work on eighteenth- and nineteenth-century Germany.[1] This technique – the linking together of life events recorded in the registers of baptisms, marriages, and burials – allows a depth of demographic analysis simply not possible at the macro level. Family reconstitution, in the words of Knodel, 'has vastly expanded the horizons of historical demography'.[2] 'No other technique', write Wrigley and R. S. Schofield, 'offers comparable range or richness of material.'[3] Yet there is a dearth of such studies for nineteenth-century England. The Cambridge Group's family reconstitutions – for totals varying from thirteen to twenty-six parishes –

---

[1] For some important English family reconstitution studies (mostly for the early-modern period), see: E. A. Wrigley, 'Mortality in pre-industrial England: the example of Colyton, Devon, over three centuries', *Daedalus*, 97 (1968), pp. 546–80; D. Levine, *Family formation in an age of nascent capitalism* (New York, 1977); R. Schofield and E. A. Wrigley, 'Infant and child mortality in England in the late Tudor and early Stuart period', in C. Webster (ed.), *Health, medicine and mortality in the sixteenth century* (Cambridge, 1979), ch. 2; E. A. Wrigley and R. S. Schofield, 'English population history from family reconstitution: summary results 1600–1799', *Population Studies*, 37 (1983), pp. 157–84; C. Wilson, 'Natural fertility in pre-industrial England, 1600–1799', *Population Studies*, 38 (1984), pp. 225–40; C. Wilson, 'The proximate determinants of marital fertility in England 1600–1799', in L. Bonfield, R. M. Smith and K. Wrightson (eds.), *The world we have gained* (Oxford, 1986), ch. 8; K. Wrightson and D. Levine, 'Death in Whickham', in J. Walter and R. Schofield (eds.), *Famine, disease and the social order in early modern society* (Cambridge, 1989), ch. 3; R. T. Vann and D. Eversley, *Friends in life and death* (Cambridge, 1992); J. Landers, *Death and the metropolis: studies in the demographic history of London, 1670–1830* (Cambridge, 1993). John Knodel's work on Germany is seminal: J. E. Knodel, *Demographic behavior in the past* (Cambridge, 1988).

[2] Knodel, *Demographic behavior*, p. 6.

[3] Wrigley and Schofield, 'English population history', p. 183.

mostly stop by 1800.[4] The bulk of Richard Vann and David Eversley's important study of the Quakers finishes at 1849.[5] John Landers' innovative work on London mortality covers the period up to 1830.[6] This book is the first concentrated study to apply the technique of family reconstitution to a group of English communities over the whole of the nineteenth century.

Although the combined population of the three parishes was small, it generated a large number of life events and a substantial amount of historical data: more than 6,000 baptisms, the marriages of over 2,600 individuals, and at least 3,500 burials. The reconstituted family lies at the core of this study. As with all reconstitutions, the sizes of the sets of data vary. The completed family reconstitution forms, FRFs, provide the ages at marriage for over 1,600 people (more than 800 women). But the most useful set of FRFs is that of the 401 families for whom we have reconstituted life histories, from the marriage of family heads, through the births (and often the marriages and deaths) of their children, if they had any, to the dissolution of their partnerships, usually through death.[7] They form the basis for the fertility and mortality calculations which follow. The numbers involved are a respectable size by Cambridge Group criteria. The fertility chapter draws on a total of more than 1,600 woman years in the age group 30–34. (Chris Wilson's work on English natural fertility was based on parish totals which ranged from 614 to 3,841 woman years in age group 30–34, over the much longer period 1600–1799. The famous Colyton contributed 1,323 woman years.[8]) A further sub-set of 289 marriages remained intact until the woman reached the end of her potentially fertile age span, defined here, as in other studies, as the age of 45; they are what are known as 'completed families' and were used

[4] *Ibid.* (based on thirteen parishes); C. Wilson, 'Marital fertility in pre-industrial England: new insights from the Cambridge Group family reconstitution project' (paper prepared for the Conference on Demographic Change in Economic Development, Hitotsubashi University, Tokyo, December 1991) (based on twenty-six parishes).

[5] Vann and Eversley, *Friends in life and death.*

[6] Landers, *Death and the metropolis.*

[7] I have followed the conventions of family reconstitution set out by E. A. Wrigley, 'Family reconstitution', in Wrigley (ed.), *An introduction to English historical demography* (New York, 1966), ch. 4; and Knodel, *Demographic behavior.* There were nonconformists in the area in the second half of the century – Wesleyans and Primitive Methodists – but many of them used the Church of England for their rites of passage and there are also surviving Methodist registers of births which I drew on. Vaccination registers provided dates of birth for part of the period. So it was possible to complete forms for some nonconformist families, those who would normally escape the net of family reconstitution. Coordination with the decadal census returns for individual parishes provided some added confirmation of births and deaths.

[8] Wilson, 'Natural fertility', p. 227.

to calculate completed family size. Those completed families with children – 273 in all – provide the data for age at last birth and for birth or confinement intervals. Again this is a substantial number of cases by reconstitution standards. (The influential studies of Bottesford, Colyton, Shepshed and Terling drew on respective data bases of 146, 162, 252 and 67 cases of age at last birth, stretching over two hundred years.[9])

One of the weaknesses of family reconstitution is that it misses the mobile sections of the population. By covering three adjoining parishes this study lessens the penalty of geographical mobility felt so keenly in single-parish reconstitutions. Most mobility was short-range, so a number of moving families were picked up in the registers of the two neighbouring parishes. The FRFs can be divided into marriage cohorts representing particular time periods, or grouped into parish and socio-occupational categories.

But this book goes further than family reconstitution. It develops the newer technique of 'total reconstitution' by linking the reconstituted families to other historical records. It is based not just on the thousands of linkages between baptisms, marriages and deaths, but on the coordination of the family reconstitution files with information held in a variety of other sources: court, school, tithe, newspaper, poor relief, probate and census. The result of the total reconstitution approach is to inject some class analysis and cultural context into the picture, thus overcoming a major criticism of earlier reconstitution studies.[10]

I also draw upon oral history for the late nineteenth- and early twentieth-century sections of the book. The oral accounts provide a perspective of material and social life simply not available in any other source. It would have been very difficult to have written the chapter on the social economy without the rich oral evidence. If used carefully, the oral account can throw light on aspects of life in earlier times too, by using it as a foil for more fragmentary evidence: what the French historian Marc Bloch termed the 'regressive method'.[11]

It is important to stress what this book is and is not. It is not a comprehensive history of life in the Blean in the nineteenth and early twentieth centuries; as even a glance at the table of contents will indicate, there are whole areas of social life not dealt with or touched upon only lightly. The power of authorial intent should not be mini-

---

[9] *Ibid.*, p. 236.

[10] See A. Macfarlane, S. Harrison and C. Jardine, *Reconstructing historical communities* (Cambridge, 1977); P. Sharpe, 'The total reconstitution method: a tool for class specific study', *Local Population Studies*, 44 (1990), pp. 41–51.

[11] P. Burke, *Popular culture in early modern Europe* (London, 1978), pp. 81–7.

mized. The sources speak, and we listen and respond; but it is the historian who asks the questions and determines the agendas. My guiding unit of enquiry and analysis has been social class. Had I focused on gender, for example, I would have written a very different book.[12]

If it is not an *Annales*-aspiring account of every aspect of life in a community (or communities) over a century or more, neither is this book traditional local history of the English sort. Rather it is an extended exercise in microhistory, where the local becomes the site for the consideration of much wider issues.[13] *Microhistories* focuses on life in the Blean area of Kent during the nineteenth and early twentieth centuries, but uses the particular to explore some of the more significant societal changes of the modern western world, and, it should be stressed from the outset, to engage with important historiographical issues.

The focus continually shifts over the period, both in terms of subject matter and time. The emphasis is on the nineteenth century, but some chapters are wider ranging, including material up to the 1920s. I have attempted to breach some of the barriers between qualitative and quantitative history, to draw on the widest possible range of source material, and, in line with the aims of this series, to traverse the boundaries between cultural, demographic, economic and social history. The reader can judge how successful this has been. Some of the chapters cross less than others. Chapter 2 is resolutely demographic: chapter 4 will be easily recognizable to social historians. But most chapters defy easy classification, spilling out across perimeters, making use of a variety of local sources.

In sum, the aim of this book is to show that the implications of the microstudy can range way beyond modest geographical and historical boundaries. Whether in extending the parameters of the fertility transition (chapter 2), sketching out a medical–social history of nineteenth-century rural England (chapter 3), charting the contours of the social economy (chapter 4) and the complexities of class (chapter 5), questioning orthodoxies about kinship and the nuclear family (chapter 6) or exploring the contexts of Victorian sexuality (chapter 7) and the meanings of popular literacy (chapter 8), I hope that this book will demonstrate the exciting and challenging potentials of microhistory.

---

[12] For the potentials of a gendered approach to communities, see P. Sharpe, 'Gender-specific demographic adjustment to changing economic circumstances: Colyton 1538–1837' (University of Cambridge Ph.D. thesis, 1988); N. G. Osterud, *Bonds of community: the lives of farm women in nineteenth-century New York* (Ithaca, 1991); C. Daley, 'Gender in the community: a study of the women and men of the Taradale area, 1886–1930' (Victoria University of Wellington Ph.D. thesis, 1992).

[13] See chapter 9 for a discussion of microhistory.

Acknowledgements

This book grew out of research which I began for an earlier publication, *The last rising of the agricultural labourers* (1990). One of my aims in that book was to place a rising – a moment of labouring protest – in its community context, and to do that I began detailed work in the local archives. In many respects, *Microhistories* is a continuation of the introductory section of that earlier work: sentences became pages, single paragraphs ended up as whole chapters. As the reader will discover, the technique of family reconstitution has made this possible. I can still remember those tentative steps in a demographic direction. Maureen Molloy showed me a family reconstitution form; Kenneth Lockridge spent time discussing the conventions and techniques of reconstitution; Vivien Brodsky patiently checked my earliest efforts. This was in the early or mid 1980s (I am vague about the precise date), and these people have doubtless long forgotten their role; I am grateful nonetheless. I would also like to thank Eilidh Garrett, Roger Schofield and Chris Wilson of the Cambridge Group for their encouragement when – many years later – I arrived at 27 Trumpington Street with a bundle of tables and graphs, and John Knodel (of the Population Studies Center at the University of Michigan) for reading an initial version of chapter 2 and saving me from some potential mistakes.

Many individuals have been supportive, reading and commenting on what have become various sections of the book. I am extremely grateful to Frazer Andrewes, Meg Arnot, Linda Bryder, Raelene Frances, Eilidh Garrett, Bridget Hill, Rab Houston, Alun Howkins, David Kertzer, John E. Knodel, Colin Lankshear, John Leckie, David Levine, Deborah Montgomerie, Charles Phythian-Adams, Jean Robin, Bruce Scates, Roger Schofield, Keith Snell, W. B. Stephens, Simon Szreter, Athina Tsoulis, David Vincent, Adrian Wilson, Michael Winstanley, Keith Wrightson and Philippa Wyatt. Jan Kelly, of the

Department of Geography at the University of Auckland, was good enough to provide technical advice on map-making.

Although it faltered towards the end, the University of Auckland's Research Committee has been generous in its responses to requests for financial assistance. I would also like to thank the Leave Committee for granting me the leaves in 1988 and 1992 which made the research for this book possible.

I owe a great deal to the staff of the Centre for Kentish Studies at Maidstone, the Canterbury Cathedral Archives, the Public Record Office, the Newspaper Library at Colindale, the Templeman Library of the University of Kent, and Somerset House. The staff of Auckland University Library have been consistently cheerful and efficient; Rainer Wolcke has been particularly helpful.

Colleagues in one's own department are frequently taken for granted (or worse), but they are an important source of intellectual and emotional support. I am especially indebted to Frazer Andrewes, Greg Bankoff, Malcolm Campbell, Caroline Daley, Raewyn Dalziel, Rae Frances, Paul Husbands, John Leckie, Deborah Montgomerie, Philip Rousseau, Bruce Scates, Hans van Dyk and Philippa Wyatt.

I also owe a great deal to people living in and near Boughton, Dunkirk and Hernhill, or with links to that area. Sandys and Lesley Dawes and Harold and Marian Kay have been wonderfully hospitable. Tommy Boorman and Harold Kay provided access to their rich photographic collection (the Harold Kay collection). Arthur Percival has kept me in touch with the work of local historians. And Ann Bones, Tommy and Lydia Boorman, the Dawes family, Leonard Godden, Dorrie Hadlow, Percy Judges, Harold Kay, Percy Saddleton, Jean Sell, Hubert and Dorothy Tong, Emily Wade and Harry Wheeler have shared their knowledge and experiences with a stranger from New Zealand.

Needless to say, I owe most to my partner, Athina Tsoulis, and our children, Alexa and Kristina Tsoulis-Reay. They have always exhibited a healthy scepticism towards my various projects; with gratitude (and in quiet revenge) this one is dedicated to them.

Material in four chapters has appeared before. Chapter 2 was published in *Continuity and Change*. Chapter 6 was in a recent issue of *Journal of Family History*. Chapter 7 is a considerably revised version of an article in *Rural History*. Chapter 8, in an earlier form, was published in *Past and Present*. However, much of what follows is new.

Abbreviations

CCA   Canterbury Cathedral Archives, Canterbury
CKS   Centre for Kentish Studies, Maidstone
PRO   Public Record Office, Kew
PP   *Parliamentary Papers*
TL   Templeman Library, University of Kent, Oral History Project:
       Life in Kent before 1914

Introduction

Plate 1 Horsemen at work in Hernhill, early this century.

1

Place and people

I

Boughton-under-Blean, Dunkirk and Hernhill, the three adjoining parishes which are the focal point of this study, are situated in England's south east in the Blean area of Kent, about midway between the towns of Faversham and Canterbury. They have seldom featured in the history books. The district had a brief moment of infamy in 1838 when a messianic figure, the self-styled Sir William Courtenay, led an abortive rising of agricultural labourers which was crushed with some savagery by the military.[1] A London lawyer, sent out in the wake of the massacre to examine life in these parishes, was struck by the beauty of the place: 'The scenery of this district is peculiarly English. Gently rising hills and picturesque vales, covered with a rich herbage, or bearing the show of a minute and skilful husbandry, succeed to each other. Fields of waving corn are interspersed with gardens, hop-grounds and orchards.' He thought it particularly tragic that the 'moral condition of the inhabitants of so fair a spot should stand ... in such mournful contrast with its order and beauty'.[2] The land that so impressed our observer was part of the 'foothill' area of Kent, the county's main grain district and a centre for hops and fruit.[3] But the area was not all 'gently rising hills and picturesque vales'. It bordered the marshes, malaria country, habitat of mosquitoes as well as sheep. The outsider was taken with the orderly patchwork of orchards and fields, yet much of the land was wooded. Indeed the vast bulk of Dunkirk – four out of every five acres – was woodland, providing a

[1] See B. Reay, *The last rising of the agricultural labourers* (Oxford, 1990).
[2] F. Liardet, 'State of the peasantry in the county of Kent', in *Central Society of Education, third publication* (London, 1968), pp. 88–9 (first published 1839).
[3] A. Everitt, *Landscape and community in England* (London, 1985), p. 67.

3

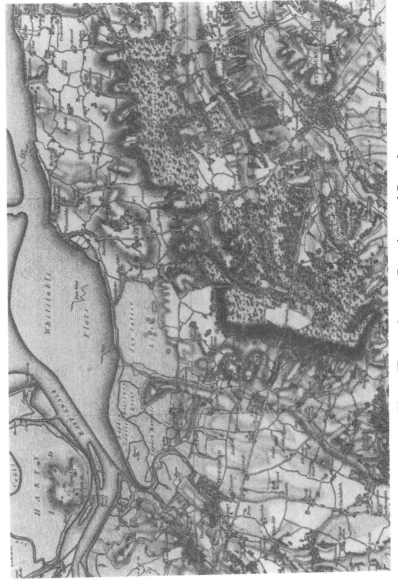

Plate 2 The area between Faversham and Canterbury

steady profit for its owners and a hard living for the assortment of wood-workers and wood-stealers who harvested the oaks and chestnut underwood.

Although we may delude ourselves that we are stepping back in time whenever we leave the motorway and wind our way down a narrow hedged lane, the rural world of the past is truly a vanished country. So many visual markers have gone: the windmilled village sky-line, the wells, smoking chimneys, wash- and bake-houses, vault privies and cesspools, the small shops (the butcher's with its freshly killed meat hanging outside), the ubiquity of wood as a raw material. At the start of our period, we have to imagine an environment without the motor, where the horse and horseman ruled. It is a world we glimpse fleetingly in the story of the two seasoned draught horses who came cantering like colts at the sound of the voice of their waggoner, long-absent with pneumonia, wrenching the plough from the hands of his astonished stand-in, pushing one another to get to the old man first: 'you could hear them crying almost because they was so pleased to see their master, and the poor old boy stood and cried, he just stood and wept because his horses knew him'.[4] Then came the traction engines, mechanical mammoths which groaned between the narrow hedgerows until petrol replaced steam. But motorized vehicles were scarce in the early decades of this century and children could play on country roads. Now motorways cut huge grey swathes through the Blean countryside, covering old hop-fields and orchards with bitumen and cement. The children have vanished from the lanes. Petroleum is king.

The sounds were different too. We can no longer hear the dull 'thud, thud' of the flail echoing throughout the Blean, the repetitive 'clang' of the smithy, the never-ending sawing which drifted over the meadows and orchards from the Dunkirk woods. Even the language of the inhabitants has changed. Who hears these days of 'clung' (dull), 'cotchering' (gossiping), 'dunty' (stupid), 'ernful' (lamentable), 'feasy' (whining), 'flammed' (deceived), or 'glincey' (slippery)?[5]

Of course we pretend a link with the past when we stand outside the former home of a nineteenth-century craft family or admire an eighteenth-century farmhouse. But the threads are tenuous. Apart from a few substantial cottages built by a philanthropic landlord in the mid to late Victorian period, the homes of the labouring population have long

[4] Hernhill Oral History, A. Bones, b. 1912. The Hernhill Oral History Tapes are interviews which I carried out in 1991–2 as part of my research on the Blean area of Kent.

[5] W. D. Parish and W.F. Shaw, *A Dictionary of the Kentish Dialect and Provincialisms in use in the County of Kent* (London, 1887) (Kraus reprint, Vaduz, 1965).

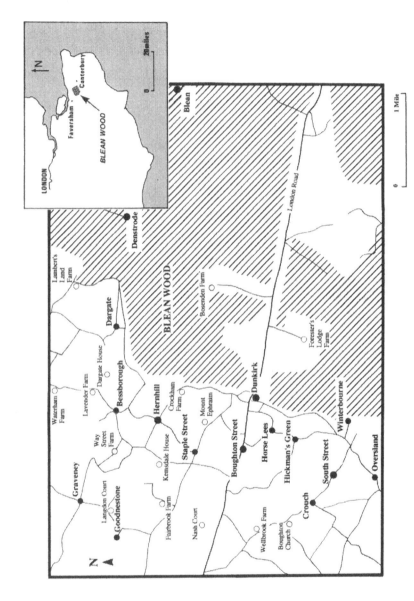

Map The hamlets and settlements of the Blean in the mid nineteenth century.

6

Plate 3 Richardson's Mill, Boughton Street.

Plate 4 A Staple Street butcher, early this century.

Plate 5 The Forge, Preston Street.

Plate 6 Traction engine in Canterbury, late nineteenth century.

since disappeared. What we read as our architectural heritage is merely the surviving houses of farmers, some trades and crafts families and the landed gentry: it is a material image of our past which renders the majority of the population invisible. The example of Dargate's Dove beerhouse encapsulates the dangers of visual distortion. No doubt the handsome, late nineteenth-century, red-brick Dove public house tells us something of the wealth of Victorian brewers. But it provides little sense of the nineteenth-century Dove, the plaster-and-thatch beerhouse which preceded its brick descendant and which provided a living for the Goodwin family and momentary escape for labouring folk for the best part of a hundred years.

At least the names of the hamlets, farms and small villages are much the same – though only the old people know where 'Sluts Hole' is. The main unit of settlement was the hamlet, the rural equivalent of the urban neighbourhood. Hernhill parish contained four main hamlets: the houses and cottages around the church ('Hernhill village'), Staple Street, Dargate and Bessborough or the Forstall. In the 1870s Staple Street consisted of about thirty houses or cottages and had a population of just under 200. But there were other smaller groups of cottages around farms such as Waterham, Way Street and Crockham. Each hamlet had wells (Staple Street had nine) and often a public house or beershop: the Red Lion opposite the church, the Three Horse Shoes at Staple Street, Noah's Ark at Bessborough and the Dove at Dargate.

Dunkirk consisted of scattered settlements on the edge of the Blean woods and along the main road. There were hamlets at Denstrode, Winterbourne and at the bottom and top of Boughton Hill. Boughton's main settlements were at Boughton Street (a long row of trades and crafts and labouring households on either side of the London Road), South Street, Horse Lees, Hickman's Green, Oversland and Crouch; there were other collections of dwellings around Boughton pottery and at Fairbrook, Wellbrook and other farms.

It is difficult to know how the occupants of such rural areas perceived their communities. Although the church would have encouraged those involved to think of a Hernhill, a Boughton or (from the 1840s) a Dunkirk, the parish was an administrative unit which did not necessarily signify any sense of identity. Indeed Dunkirk did not have a church for the first third of the nineteenth century and Boughton's church was situated some distance from the parish's largest concentration of inhabitants at Boughton Street, an absence recognized by the Methodists (Wesleyan and Primitive) who had chapels at each end of the Street. Moreover, several hamlets cut across parish boundaries. Denstrode was half in Dunkirk and half in Blean parish; Dargate was

Plate 7 The Dove beerhouse, Dargate, *c.* 1870s.

Plate 8 The Dove, Dargate, *c.* 1890.

Plate 9 The Dove in the early twentieth century.

Plate 10 Hernhill from the church tower at the turn of the century.

Plate 11 Berkeley Lodge (on the left at the top of the hill) and Boughton Hill, *c.*
1840s. The sketch disguised the steepness of Boughton Hill so that prospective
purchasers of Berkeley Lodge would not be discouraged.

Plate 12 Boughton Street, early this century.

partly in Hernhill and partly in Dunkirk; the Boughton pottery settlement was on the Hernhill border; Horse Lees was both in Dunkirk and Boughton.

It is likely that many rural inhabitants would have identified most immediately with a few cottages on the edge of a wood ('Thornden Wood cottages') or a handful of dwellings near a farm ('Brenley cottages'). Albert Packman lived at Crockham in Hernhill, less than a mile from the 'village', but he recalled a feeling of childhood isolation: 'we were never allowed to go up there to play with the others'; 'just absolutely dopey living down there in those three houses, never see nothing, never go anywhere'.[6] Although the presence of a compulsory parish-centred school system at the end of the century helped mould parish identification and loyalty, this was not true in the preceding years. The parish is merely a useful means of classification which will be employed as such throughout this book; we should not mistake such usage for a declaration of community identity.

II

However, it is the people rather than the places of the Blean with which this book is most concerned. There were 1,581 women, men and children in the three parishes at the start of the nineteenth century and 3,337 when the census was taken in 1891 – an increase over the century of 111 per cent. The most rapid period of local population growth occurred during the first three decades of the century, reflecting the national population increase which formed a back-drop to the introduction of the New Poor Law. The population of the three parishes rose by over 50 per cent in the period 1801–31. The age balance of the population was totally different to present-day distributions. If late twentieth-century observers could be transported back in time to the Victorian village, they would immediately notice the large numbers of youngsters in and around the cottages, lanes and farms: at mid century 40 per cent of the population was under 15 years of age, compared with half that number today. There was also a lower proportion of elderly people. In 1851 only one in ten people was aged 60 or above: today there would be twice that number.[7]

The profile of the elite changed during the century. In the early decades of the nineteenth century the big landlords were a rather remote force, content, for the most part, to receive their rents from the

[6] TL, A. Packman, b. 1892.
[7] Reay, *Last rising*, pp. 10–12. The population figures for 1891 come from the census: PRO, RG 12/712.

farmers or to rely on their agents, the bailiffs and stewards, to look after their interests. Almost 80 per cent of land in Hernhill and 98 per cent of land in Dunkirk (most of it woodland) was owned by outsiders. Just over half of Dunkirk was the property of two of these non-resident landowners, the Dean and Chapter of Canterbury and Sir Edward Dering, who were among the largest landowners in Kent, with scores of holdings in a great many parishes. Surveys during the 1820s and 1840s show other prominent Kent landowners with investments in the Blean: all were absentee owners. Indeed George Gipps, the proprietor of Bosenden Wood, the scene of the massacre of agricultural labourers in 1838, was a governor of the colony of New South Wales.[8]

The gentry were thickest on the ground in Boughton. Yet the most cartographically imposing estate in the area, the Knatchbulls' Nash Court, stood empty for the first half of the century. Mount Ephraim – Hernhill's equivalent to Nash Court – was a comfortable but comparatively modest residence at mid century, occupied by the vicar of Hernhill.[9] In Dunkirk, as an observer complained of its labouring population in the 1830s, there was no-one above the status of farmer, 'neither gentry, clergyman, surgeon, nor anybody above their own condition to connect them with the civilization of the higher classes'.[10]

By the end of the century, however, the landowners had a tangible presence in the parish. Nash Court housed the Milles-Lades, one of the largest resident landowning families in the area and owners of a third of Boughton in 1910.[11] Mount Ephraim had been rebuilt, its architecture and topography proclaiming that it was the residence of the proprietor of a large slice of the surrounding country. Its owner, Sir Edwyn Sandys Dawes, was a shipping magnate and pioneer of the frozen meat industry whose portfolio before his death in 1903 included a controlling interest in the New Zealand Shipping Co., chairmanships of the Australasian United Steam Navigation Co., the Austral Freezing Works, the South African and Australasian Meat and Cold Storage Co. and British India Associated Steamers, and directorships of both the

[8] PRO, MPZ 26, Reference Book or Terrier to the Plan of the Ville of Dunkirk 1827–8; PRO, IR 29/17/178, Hernhill Tithe Apportionment Award 1840; PRO, IR 29/17/41, Boughton Tithe Apportionment Award 1840. I obtained information on the wider holdings of the large landowners from Roger Kain's 'Data files for tithe surveys: Kent landowners *c.* 1840', held at the University of Exeter.

[9] See census returns. Unless otherwise stated, the information relating to the censuses comes from the Census Enumerators' Books (1841, 1851, 1861, 1871, 1881, 1891) for the parishes of Hernhill, Boughton-under-Blean and Dunkirk: PRO, HO 107/466/5; HO 107/471/11; HO 107/473/12; HO 107/1626; RG 9/525; RG 10/976–7; RG 11/966–7; RG 12/712.

[10] Liardet, 'State of the peasantry', p. 133.

[11] CKS, IR 4/37/1, Valuation Book 1910, Boughton.

British India Co. and the Suez Canal.[12] In 1910 his son W. C. Dawes owned a quarter of Dunkirk and Hernhill, landlord of at least eight farms, two potteries, almost seventy cottages and ten houses.[13] Then there was Kemsdale, an impressive house built probably in the 1840s, which was the home of Charles Wharton, civil engineer and railway constructor, and his wife, Lucy Wharton, landowner of 500 acres. (W. C. Dawes lived there briefly at the end of the century.) Even Dunkirk had its big house, Berkeley Lodge (*c.* 1840), on Boughton Hill, built by a prosperous Liverpool mercer and haberdasher, with gazebo, 50-foot observatory, views on every side for 50 miles around, including the French coast and London and a 14-acre garden of terraced walks and grottoes, complete with model ships, telegraph, windmill and lighthouse. 'Neither words nor painting can do it adequate justice.'[14]

Architecture proclaimed the configurations of class in the three communities; the occupants of the big houses changed, there were renovations here and there, but the buildings remained as monuments to hierarchy and privilege. The difference between the early and late Victorian Blean was that those with controlling local interests were increasingly likely to occupy these houses. The gentry were of the parish rather than unknown outsiders; they dispensed charity and held community festivities. And so the notion of the big house acquired more meaning. The local school would even grant holidays to mark events in the gentry's lives: the marriage of a Dawes daughter, the funeral of Lucy Wharton.[15]

Hernhill labourers would not have known that Edwyn Dawes left effects (movable goods) worth £300,000, or that a coal mine in New Zealand, one of many business interests, was bringing William Dawes a cool £3,000 or £4,000 a year. They were unlikely to be aware that Dawes spent more on his motor car in 1908 (a Siddeley) than any one of them was likely to earn in twenty to twenty-five years; that his shooting costs in 1906 would have supported 600 labouring families for a week; or that even his annual dog-biscuit bill was the equivalent of the yearly wage of two agricultural labourers.[16] But the inequalities were there on the door step, so to speak, for all to see. As Hernhill-born

[12] J. T. Critchell and J. Raymond, *A History of the Frozen Meat Trade* (London, 1912), pp. 361–3; Somerset House, Will of Sir Edwyn Dawes, 1904.

[13] CKS, IR 4/37/1, Valuation Book 1910, Boughton, Dunkirk, Hernhill.

[14] *Kelly's Directory* (Canterbury, 1882), p. 185; CKS, TR 2804/2, Sale catalogue for Berkeley Lodge.

[15] CKS, C/ES 183/1/1, Hernhill Church of England School Log Book, 1872–1959, pp. 182, 229.

[16] Somerset House, Will of Sir Edwyn Dawes, 1904; Collection of Sandys Dawes, Mt Ephraim, Hernhill, W. C. Dawes, Ledger Book 1905–9 and Cash Book, 1910–13.

Plate 13 Nash Court, Boughton.

Plate 14 Kemsdale Lodge at the turn of the century.

Albert Packman put it, the Dawes family 'were very rich and they seemed to own practically all of Kent'.[17]

III

Yet much of the day-to-day exercise of local power was in the hands of the more substantial farmers. The census returns from 1851 to 1881 provide a rough guide which undoubtedly underestimates small-holders but gives a fair indication of the number of the larger farmers residing in the three parishes. There was a total of about seventy farms in the three parishes at any one time in the nineteenth century.[18] Of those, from eleven to seventeen ranged from 100 to over 700 acres in size, large, though not huge, by Kent standards. Some of these farmers were men of substance. Thomas Carter esq. of Dargate House (*c.* 1851 to 1888) was listed as a farmer and hop-grower in the census and he farmed from 200 to 400 acres with the help of a bailiff. He had servants and gentry connections and left an estate worth some £25,000.[19] Fairbrook Farm was owned by the gentry-aspiring George Francis esq. and then by Robert Neame, farmer and grazier (700 acres), member of an influential Kent family. Walter Berry, whose parents owned and farmed the 50- to 70-acre South Street Farm during the nineteenth century, was farming (mostly as tenant) nearly a third of Boughton by the early twentieth century.[20] From the point of view of the labouring population, such people would have been virtually indistinguishable from the major landlords.

There were owner-occupiers in the area: two generations of Edward Stevens Brownings owned and farmed Cherry Orchard or Coleman's Land Farm in Hernhill. But the majority of substantial farms were either run by bailiff or tenant. Bailiffs came and left, so it was the tenant farmers who provided the family and class continuity in the area: the Alexanders at Way Street and the Curlings at Crockham and Yorkletts (200 to 700 acres) in Hernhill; the Saddletons at Forester's Lodge Farm (200 to 400 acres) and the Curlings at Lambert's Land (200 to 400 acres) in Dunkirk; the Owens at Boughton Farm (100 acres) and the Ashbees at Clockhouse Farm in Boughton.

Farmers included women as well as men. Sophia Curling ran Crockham with her sons for a number of years after her husband's

[17] TL, A. Packman, b. 1892.
[18] That is, households headed by a farmer according to the censuses of 1851 and 1881. The census of 1891 does not provide information on farm size.
[19] Somerset House, Will of Thomas Carter, 1888.
[20] CKS, IR 4/37/1, Valuation Book 1910, Boughton.

death. Stephen Butcher's wife, Jemima, was left the farm so that, as his will stated, she could continue 'my business ... for her support and maintenance and for that of my six children'.[21] Matilda Coe continued to run Brenley Farm as a widow, without the help of sons, although she did employ a bailiff. She was listed as a farmer of 250 acres in the census of 1881. Mary Ann Berry farmed Boughton Street Farm with her son Walter. Presumably these women were involved sufficiently in the running of their farms to assume responsibility when their husbands died.

Below what I have termed the more substantial farmers there was a group of medium-sized farms, those from 25 to 99 acres. These were farms like Lavender Farm in Hernhill (30 to 40 acres), purchased in the early 1800s for £1,330, which went through a variety of owners and tenants.[22] Another example is Bosenden Farm in Dunkirk (60 acres), owned by George Gipps in the 1820s and by W. C. Dawes in 1910, but rented by a succession of farming families: Culver, Saddleton, Gorham. There were from nine to thirteen of these medium-sized farms at any given moment, that is from 20 to 25 per cent of those designated as farming households in the various censuses.

The farmers were the 'little kings' of village life, a kind of pseudo-gentry in many nineteenth-century rural parishes.[23] They were the power brokers of local society with whom the labouring population had most contact. They were the major employers. The ratio was about one man per 20 acres on average when the census was taken in April (not the busiest time of the year) or, if we include boys, one labourer per 15 or 16 acres. The medium-sized farms were employing from two to six men and perhaps a woman and a couple of boys. The more substantial holdings had usually from eight to thirty men as well as women and up to a dozen boys. At the extreme end of the scale, the Neames of Fairbrook employed more than forty labourers and William Carter, farmer, grazier and hop-planter, had a work force of sixty men and twelve boys when the Boughton census was taken in 1861. During the harvests, the larger employers would take on several hundred hands. Harry Ash's father, who was bailiff to Barnes of Berkeley, took on 150 families for the hops, or about 500 workers.[24] The fate of the farmers therefore had ramifications for the welfare of the labouring population. The Boughton school log book recorded 'numerous' with-

[21] CKS, PRC, 32/70/141, Will of Stephen Butcher, 1834.
[22] Title deeds in possession of Harold Kay, Hernhill, 'Abstracts of the title ... to a farm and land called Lavender at Hernhill', 1859.
[23] W. Howitt, *The Rural Life of England* (Shannon, 1971), p. 88 (first published in 1838).
[24] TL, H. Ash, b. 1898.

drawals when the estate of a leading farmer changed hands and parents had to leave the village to seek a living elsewhere.[25] In Hernhill the farmers dominated the vestry and thus the positions of local office: they were the churchwardens, the guardians, the overseers, the surveyors.

Like the mansions of the gentry, the larger farmhouses were part of what has been termed the 'iconography of social division'.[26] Though once again their owners or occupants changed, their very endurance through time (from the eighteenth, seventeenth, sixteenth centuries) declared the social position of the landed employer. They could visually dominate a hamlet, standing out among the small cluster of cottages which housed the farmer's workers. And often farm and hamlet would have the same name: Way Street, South Street, Fairbrook, Waterham, Lambert's Land, Yorkletts, Crockham, Bessborough, Dargate, High Street. These farms were important markers in the labouring population's mental maps of their community, points of reference which still recur in interviews with elderly residents.

IV

This leaves the small farmers, the real peasantry of the nineteenth and early twentieth centuries. As Alun Howkins has explained, there is no way of locating the extent of these smallholdings except at the local level.[27] Farm sizes are notoriously difficult to gauge and it is foolhardy to try to map rates of wealth and status or even to establish subsistence levels from acreages. Fifty acres of pasture is not equivalent to 50 acres of hops or fruit or to 50 acres of woodland. National and county levels do not necessarily make sense at a local level. Mick Reed has suggested 100 acres as the defining limit of the small family producer; J. M. Neeson and Howkins have argued for a figure of 50 acres.[28] But in the Blean, 25 acres seems a far more likely cut-off point. All the Boughton, Dunkirk and Hernhill farmers who were described as employers of labour in 1881 had properties of more than 25 acres. All of those who

[25] CCA, U3/221/25/13, Boughton-under-Blean School Log Book, 1864–95, p. 433.

[26] C. Rawding, 'The iconography of churches: a case study of landownership and power in nineteenth-century Lincolnshire', *Journal of Historical Geography*, 16 (1990), p. 157.

[27] A. Howkins, *Reshaping rural England: a social history 1850–1925* (London, 1991), p. 39.

[28] M. Reed, 'The peasantry of nineteenth-century England: a neglected class?', *History Workshop*, 18 (1984), pp. 53–76; J. M. Neeson, *Commoners: common right, enclosure and social change in England, 1700–1820* (Cambridge, 1993), p. 306; A. Howkins, 'Peasants, servants and labourers: the marginal workforce in British agriculture, c. 1870–1914', *Agricultural History Review*, 92 (1994), pp. 49–62. For an important study of smallholders, see A. Hall, *Fenland worker-peasants: the economy of smallholders at Rippingdale, Lincolnshire, 1791–1871* (*Agricultural History Review*, Supplement Series vol. I, 1992).

did not employ labour had farms of 25 acres or less. Holdings below 25 acres relied heavily upon family labour, were less likely to hire labour than the larger farms and were often dependent on some other form of activity to contribute towards the household economy – a craft or trade, or the sale of their own labour to larger farmers in return for cash or as exchange for specialist help on their farms.

There were from sixteen to twenty-seven such holdings in the three parishes according to the census returns, or about 40 to 50 per cent of those described as farmers. But the true number of smallholdings must have been much greater, for it would have included those to whom the enumerator ascribed some other primary occupation: craftsmen, dealers, shopkeepers, woodmen, labourers. In Hernhill and Dunkirk in the mid nineteenth century, for example, land surveys indicate a total of just over ninety occupiers of land holdings in the range of 1 to 24 acres.[29] This would include land held but not worked as well as holdings which formed part of estates in other parishes, but the discrepancy between the land survey and census suggests that the latter's figures for small farmers may have to be adjusted upwards. Over 60 per cent of those who rented land of 1 acre or more in Dunkirk and Hernhill in 1840 and 1866 occupied plots of this smallholding size (over 70 per cent if we stretch our definition to 50 acres).[30]

Hernhill's small farmers at mid century included Alex Foad, who farmed 8 acres of his own land at Dargate (arable and hops); John Hadlow, who rented 4 acres at Dargate and who earned a living variously as bailiff at Lavender Farm and as a butcher and grocer; and William Curling, farmer of from 6 to 10 acres, who worked regularly for his uncle Edward Curling of Crockham Farm. The small farmer predominated in Dunkirk; and they were *small* farmers. Those described as farmers in the censuses of 1841 and 1851 occupied or owned properties as small as 2 or 3 acres. It must have been precarious living on these tiny plots, with perhaps an acre of hops, an acre of arable, a few pigs, possibly some woodland. Family labour was important, including the work of the farmer's wife. Almost all the small farmers in the three parishes were married at some stage; few remained single.[31] Such households would have been hard to distinguish from those of the cottagers, agricultural labourers and woodmen who inhabited the area. Many of these smallholders actually owned their patches of land,

[29] PRO, IR 29/17/178, Hernhill Tithe Apportionment Award 1840; CKS, U 11772 O24, Dunkirk Land Survey, 1866.
[30] *Ibid.*
[31] File of sixty-six small farmers (25 acres or less) based on censuses for the three parishes, 1851–81. Sixty-three of the sixty-six were married.

carved up, squatter-style, when the commons, wastes and woods of the Blean were settled during the Napoleonic Wars. But they must have been heavily mortgaged by the time they had erected their cottages and outhouses on their newly acquired ground. Their relationship with the larger farmers was one of unequal dependency. The more substantial farms used the skills and labour of the smallholders, but the small farmers needed the equipment and even the organized labour of the larger farms. The Crockham Farm account book shows that the Curlings dried hops, threshed wheat, ploughed, harrowed and carted for smaller farms in the area. They ploughed land for Alex Foad, for example: 8 acres at 15s. an acre. They fetched fish for manure and hop-poles for William Curling's small hop-ground.[32]

We should not draw a rigid distinction between family labour and hired labour as the defining characteristic of small farming. Situations varied with individual circumstance, the type of farming (hops were more labour intensive) and the family's position in the household cycle. Small farmers of less than 25 acres employed outside help when family labour power was not sufficient; indeed 40 per cent of small farmers in the three parishes during the period 1851 to 1891 were employing some kind of labour – men, boys or female servants – at the time of the census (60 per cent employed sons or had sons over the age of 15 in the house who had no other given occupation). Smallholders could sell their own labour power as well, or could combine their farming with other pursuits. Almost 30 per cent of the area's small farmers had some other kind of occupation that was declared in one of the censuses: general dealer, wood-dealer, fruiterer, wheelwright, publican, woodman, agricultural labourer, miller or grocer. Other members of the household could contribute in the same way: 27 per cent of small farming families had daughters at home who were described as dressmakers, or sons who earned a living as labourers or in the crafts and trades.[33]

The smallholder survived into the twentieth century. The parish agricultural returns for the three parishes for 1910 imply a minimum of thirty-eight holdings of from 1 to 4 acres and forty-two from 5 to 50 acres (there were at least twenty-three holdings of more than 50 acres). In other words, of those returning schedules of their farms or holdings, just under 80 per cent conformed to Howkins' and Neeson's definition of a peasant holding.[34]

[32] Collection of Sandys Dawes, Mt Ephraim, Hernhill, Farming Account Book of Crockham Farm 1837–46.
[33] Small farmer file: see footnote 31 above.
[34] PRO, MAF 68/2412/11, Agricultural Returns: Parish Summaries, Kent, 1910.

V

One recent account of the rural social structure has placed the crafts and trades in 'the middle ground between the farmers and labourers'.[35] But in fact the trades and crafts ran the whole scale from farmer to labourer in their range of status and social condition. They included the substantial employer, the small master with one or two helpers, the self-employed with no help other than family (like the archetypal small farmer) and the man (or woman) who worked at a trade or craft for someone else. There were from 130 to 150 such households in the three parishes in the nineteenth century (22 or 23 per cent of household heads). Some 170 to 200 males earned a living in the trades and crafts (18 to 20 per cent of total male occupations in the censuses of 1851 and 1891). Hernhill and Dunkirk offered little in the way of goods and services. But in Boughton in 1851 over a quarter of the working male population was employed in a trade or craft: as shoemakers, carpenters, wheelwrights, butchers, grocers, blacksmiths, thatchers, charcoal and lime burners, sawyers, brick and tile makers, plumbers and glaziers, millers, bakers, victuallers, blacksmiths, bricklayers, tailors, dealers of various sorts, drapers, builders, potters, weavers and as a harnessmaker, hairdresser and perfumer, watchmaker and chemist. Boughton's women included laundresses, at least some of whom must have been self-employed entrepreneurs, seamstresses, milliners, dressmakers, a tailoress, a grocer and draper, a milliner, a shoebinder and a female blacksmith who employed two male workers.

Some of these households farmed as well. In Hernhill at mid century, the farmer/publican Noah Miles owned a 14-acre farm and rented an equivalent amount of land; he also rented the Three Horse Shoes at Staple Street and Noah's Ark, a Bessborough beershop, run by Miles's son. The parish's carpenter, wheelwright, blacksmith and shoemaker all farmed smallholdings as well. Because much of the work in a public house or beershop could be undertaken by the women of a household, victualling was frequently combined with farming or a craft. A wheelwright ran South Street's King's Arms in 1851 and a blacksmith kept the Fox beerhouse in Oversland. Harry Ash (born 1898), who grew up in nearby Harbledown early this century, recalled that the publican of the Plough Inn had a wood business and kept a few sheep.[36]

The craft and trade elite included the Woolright family at Berkeley

---

[35] J. H. Porter, 'The development of rural society', in G. E. Mingay (ed.), *The agrarian history of England and Wales*, vol. VI, *1750–1850* (Cambridge, 1989), p. 855.

[36] TL, H. Ash, b. 1898.

Lodge, whom we have already encountered, and the Boughton builder, William Judges, who had over thirty workers. However, employers were in a minority, even at a more humble level. The census of 1891 allows a calculation of the status of household heads. The trades and crafts made up a significant proportion (41 per cent) of the employer class, but the trades and crafts as a group were divided between employer (23 per cent of craft and trade household heads in 1891), employed (34 per cent) and self-employed (42 per cent).[37] While those at the top sat comfortably in the village elite, the majority of men and women in the trades and crafts worked for themselves or others.

Oral history accounts by people born in the Blean area in the late nineteenth or early twentieth centuries give an idea of the lives in some of the more modest households. B. H. Fagg was a blacksmith, born near Chartham in 1894, but living and working in Harbledown during the early decades of this century. His father was a craftsman too, a wheelwright, carpenter and undertaker whose shop in Lower Harbledown was just across the street from the forge where Fagg junior started work in 1908 at the age of 14. Fagg described his father's work radius as about three or four miles and he would walk to a job with an old hand-cart for his material and tools. Like craftsmen everywhere, Fagg senior catered for the various needs of the local economy. He made carts and waggons – four-wheeled waggons, dung carts, timber tugs, tradesmen's vans (which he also painted) and small traps to take the children to the fields for fruit-, hop- and potato-picking – as well as ploughs – Kent ploughs and little wooden ones used by cottagers for furrowing and planting potatoes. He made gates and fences, ladders for the orchards and troughs for bakers. Nor was he above a bit of plumbing work and general household repair: his son recalls roof-tiling, wall-papering and carpet-laying. Finally, he was the local under-taker, measuring the corpse, constructing the coffin, which took about a day, as well as organizing the bearers and the digging of the grave.

The younger Fagg's work as a blacksmith was somewhat more specialized. But in his time he made tools (hoes, chisels, forks), fitted handles to spades and shovels, set scythes ('Practically every different man had a different way of swinging a scythe, so you had to set the scythe to suit him, not to suit yourself'), tended to the various metal fittings of ploughs, hop-washers, carts and waggons and did a bit of iron fencing and plumbing. The bulk of his work involved caring for horses. He made and fitted shoes, curing, as an unofficial 'animal doctor', ailments such as swollen feet or rotting hooves; he could

---

[37] See tables 5.1 and 5.2 below.

describe the anatomy of a horse's hoof and the intricacies of 'frost nailing' in the winter or shoeing for 'drop foot'. Fagg plied his trade in an arc not unlike that of his father: from Harbledown down to St Dunstans and then up to Dunkirk at the top of Boughton Hill and across to Chartham Hatch. He did not cover the village of Blean because there was a blacksmith there – 'you didn't step on his ground'.[38]

Although they seldom get any recognition in the census, women played an important role in such small businesses. Mrs E. Clark (born 1885), daughter of a Badlesmere shoemaker, said that her mother did all the cooking for her father's five apprentices as well as embroidering flowers around the button-holes on the women's shoes.[39] Fanny Rigden (later Dadson), born in Faversham in 1895, recalled that her father, a cabinet-maker, decorator and upholsterer, 'used to go about gentlemen's houses with my mother, she used the machine, he cut the material out and my mother used to put it together. I was always taken along to hold the work, to keep it straight ... We had a very useful time as a child, we was helping dad in everything ... I think I used to know as a child every wood there was by smell, and I've still got the smell of mahogany in my nose.' He made coffins; Fanny's mother did the linings. Apart from helping her husband, Mrs Rigden took in needlework as well as running the home and bringing up the children. She baked her own bread and seldom bought food.[40]

VI

The bulk of the employable male population in Boughton, Dunkirk and Hernhill worked as labourers and agricultural labourers, throughout the century: 54 per cent and 62 per cent in 1851 and 1891 respectively (see figure 1.1). If we include farm servants, the proportions were 62 and 64 per cent. They ranged in age from 10 year olds to the over-eighties, for the nineteenth-century work force lacked the tidy specificity of modern times – people started work and stopped work at widely differing ages. The modern meaning of retirement makes little sense in this world. All were involved in farmwork of some sort or found employment in the vast tracts of woodland. Because of the agricultural diversity of the area, there was, as we shall see, a variety of different work available; but seasonal employment predominated and consequently required a reserve army of labour – female and male, adult and child – for harvesting.

[38] TL, B. H. Fagg, b. 1894.   [39] TL, E. Clark, b. 1885.   [40] TL, F. Dadson, b. 1895.

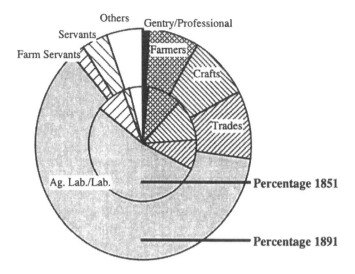

Figure 1.1 Male occupations in 1851 and 1891 (combined parishes).

Farmworkers in the nineteenth century defy neat classification. Contemporaries (and historians) usually draw a distinction between farm servants and other workers, but differ in their definition of farm service. Some confine it to those who actually lived with their employers. Others extend the term to include those workers on yearly contracts, even if they did not live with their 'master'. Waggoners, for example, who were often married men, could live in an employer's cottage, rent their own home, or live in the farmhouse with a farmer or bailiff. They could be farm servants or ordinary farmworkers, depending upon one's definition. W. A. Armstrong has divided farmworkers into farm servants, regular outdoor labourers and casual labourers. And so long as these are not treated as hard-and-fast categories, they are a useful starting point for discussion.[41]

The decline of the farm servant in this part of the country is not in doubt. Few males were employed as farm servants in 1851, fewer still in 1891. The proportions dropped from 8 per cent to 2 per cent, or from a total of seventy-two men and boys so described, to a mere nineteen. What is questionable is the timing of the demise of the farm servant. The Blean was in England's south east, where, it used to be historical orthodoxy, 'the system of indoor service had declined to near extinc-

---

[41] W. A. Armstrong, 'Labour I', in Mingay (ed.), *Agrarian history*, p. 671.

tion by the early 19th century'.[42] Yet we should not exaggerate the
rapidity of the decline of the farm servant even here. The census misses
the subtleties of the life-cycle of employment. Farm service was a
transitional phase, mostly for the younger members of society, a period
of training in skills which they would later use, either on their own
land or on the land of employers. Because it was a stage in the life of a
farmworker, often spent outside the parish of his birth, it is difficult to
reconstitute the families of these men: the sources conspire against it.
But it is likely that at mid century many men spent part of their lives as
farm servants. In Boughton, Dunkirk and Hernhill in 1851, farm
servant was the most important occupation after agricultural labourer
and labourer for unmarried males aged 15 to 24 (see table 1.1). When
we focus on this sex and age group, then, farm service assumes a
significance masked by broader occupational structures. Indeed there
was one farm servant for every 1.3 labourers in that age group. As
Mick Reed and Brian Short have found of parts of Sussex, farm service
was far from extinct in the formative work culture of young labouring
men in the 1850s, men, in many cases, who would continue to work on
farms as agricultural labourers throughout the century.[43]

In past centuries the institution had offered a schooling for the
children of farmers. In her influential study of early-modern servants
in husbandry, Ann Kussmaul was unable to determine the social
complexion of farm servants, but she concluded (on the available
evidence) that service 'was not simply a temporary extension of the
agricultural proletariat into the household of farmers. Servants were
not all children of poor labourers, destined to become labourers when
they left service.'[44] In fact this would be a reasonable description of the
situation in the Blean in the nineteenth century. Of just over fifty
young farm servants whose background is known (*c.* 1841 to 1891), 71
per cent were the sons of agricultural labourers and 27 per cent were
from farming families.[45] This suggests that the sons of farmers still
made use of farm service in the homes of their social equals, but that
the principal clientele was the labouring population.

The majority of farmworkers were hired by the day or the week or

[42] M. Reed, 'Indoor farm service in 19th-century Sussex: some criticisms of a critique',
      Sussex Archaeological Collections, 123 (1985), p. 225.
[43] Reed, 'Indoor farm service'; B. Short, 'The decline of living-in servants in the transition
      to capitalist farming: a critique of the Sussex evidence', *Sussex Archaeological Collec-
      tions*, 122 (1984), pp. 147–64.
[44] A. Kussmaul, *Servants in husbandry in early modern England* (Cambridge, 1981), pp.
      77–8.
[45] The children of couples married in Boughton, Dunkirk and Hernhill and whose
      households were present in the immediate area for three or more censuses during the
      period 1841–91 (the same group of households used in chapter 6: Families).

Table 1.1 *Occupations of unmarried males aged 15 to 24, combined parishes, 1851*

	Number	Percentage
Farmers	13	5.9
Trades/crafts	41	18.5
Ag. Lab./Lab.	83	37.4
Farm servants	62	27.9
Servants	10	4.5
Others	6	2.7
No occupation	7	3.1

Total of 222 males. The farmers include two sons of farmers, and the trades and crafts include two sons of men who were tradesmen or craftsmen.

engaged to do piece-work. But here we need to distinguish between the few 'constant men' and the vast bulk of casual labour. The 'constant man', employed by the same farmer (or several farmers) on a regular basis, or perhaps on a yearly contract, could live quite comfortably. This elite, the 'aristocrats of rural labour',[46] was comprised of men with particular skills or expertise – waggoners, ploughmen, cowmen, shepherds – or those with a wide range of abilities – hedging, ditching, thatching, working with horses, hop-drying and so on. The account book for Hernhill's Crockham Farm shows that there was a wide range of regular work for a few skilled men: harrowing potatoes, beans and wheat and shimming hops in April, carrying hop-poles in May, shimming beans, peas and potatoes in June, carting hay in July, carrying and threshing wheat in August and September, ploughing up potatoes and carting potatoes and beans and drying hops in October, ploughing and threshing in November and work on hops from December to March.[47] Those who (along with their families) worked more or less permanently for the Curlings at Crockham earned from £35 to £57 a year in day work plus £4 to £14 extra for the harvest and hopping, that is, from 15s. to 25s. a week. William Curling, a nephew, described by his boss as a 'capital labourer', was earning £50 a year in the late 1830s (or 19s. a week). He was also a small farmer of 10 acres – a further reminder of the elasticity of categories. Marshall Brunger, described as a farm labourer in the census of 1851, earned about £48 a year, or 18s. 6d. a week, but this included the help of his wife and their son.[48]

[46] Armstrong, 'Labour I', p. 675.
[47] Farming Account Book of Crockham Farm.
[48] Liardet, 'State of the peasantry', p. 107.

They were the labouring elite; the experience of the majority was radically different. When the census of 1851 was taken in March and April and farmers were asked how many men they employed, the total number that they gave for the three parishes was 54 per cent of the number of men and boys described as agricultural labourers or farm servants. The implication is that about half the male labouring population were out of work in the spring and presumably even more in the winter.[49] If there was such a thing as a typical agricultural worker, the occasional or casual labourer has a strong claim.

This is not the place for a detailed discussion of labouring incomes and budgets. Work was irregular for most labourers; many would be laid off in the winter months, therefore weekly rates of pay give little indication of annual income. Alternatively, we need to take into account the earnings of other members of the family as well as extra money at harvest time. Roughly speaking, one balanced the other. So it is not too much of a distortion to think in terms of an ordinary farmworker's wage of 13s. 6d. a week or £35 a year at mid century in this part of Kent and 15s. a week or £39 a year as the 1900s approached.[50]

Len Austin, born in 1902 in Chartham, son of a farm labourer and farmworker himself, who worked and lived in the Boughton hamlet of South Street, provides a perspective of life at the labouring level. Both Austin and his father worked for a man whom we have already encountered, Sir Walter Berry of Gushmere Court (Selling), a businessman and large-scale farmer. Austin began his career as the lowest of the low, a back-house boy: 'That was wait on the servants, wait on the mistress, wait on everybody. Hand and foot.' There he learned that hierarchy reached down to the meanest level, for the servants would be placed in order around the table. 'I used to sit at the bottom, opposite the cook, down at the bottom': the cook would serve herself first; 'I came last'.

Apart from this brief employment (the house boy was always replaced each year with a younger recruit), Austin was an agricultural labourer for his entire working life, a highly experienced one, who could describe the complexities of work with horses and the care of sheep, the skills associated with harvesting and the threshing machine and with hop and fruit growing, as well as the intricacies and hidden struggles of piece-work. He had started young – when the horses which he led looked 'as big as elephants' – and was able to do anything.

[49] See also Reed, 'Indoor farm service', p. 228.
[50] Reay, *Last rising*, pp. 52–4; TL, L. Austin, b. 1902.

[Y]ou was expected to do anything. When you went to work, a proper farmworker was supposed to be able to do anything there was on that farm ... Look after bullocks today, pigs tomorrow, get two horses to go to harrow tomorrow, next day perhaps go and help the brick layer, mix up cement, next help the chap on the roof doing the guttering. Don't matter what you do, stacker, thatcher, anything. Hop drier, you had to learn to do anything. If you was on that farm long enough.

'You had to do anything and as you lived on, worked on a farm from a boy, seeing your father and other people do it, you kind of got it ingrained into you.'

He set out the pecking order at the labouring level. If you started as a shepherd's boy you would progress to shepherd. Or you could begin as a yard boy, then help around horses so that you could become a waggoner's mate or second boy, the aim being to proceed to waggoner (usually as a married man: a wife was needed because the mate would often board with the waggoner). On larger farms the bailiff followed the farmer, 'the boss', in rank, but in the absence of a bailiff the waggoner or (on sheep farms) the shepherd could be classed as 'the top man of the farm', 'the big man'. If there were several waggoners, they would be divided into first waggoner, second waggoner and so on. An alternative track, which both Austin and his father followed, was to concentrate on general labouring. Austin consciously avoided positions of responsibility. Thatchers, for example, were paid more than ordinary agricultural labourers, but 'if anything went wrong you had to carry the can for about five or six other chaps'. It was not worth it for the small extra amount that was paid.[51]

VII

It would be misleading to convey the impression that work was a male prerogative. At the labouring level of society all women worked, regardless of their invisibility in the censuses. Whether it was a girl looking after younger children while her mother earned some money weeding or tying hops, children gleaning with their mother, or a wife keeping poultry and rabbits, all were making a contribution to the family economy just as legitimately as the male householder who earned a few shillings a day when he could and who was recorded in the census as an agricultural labourer.

When we think of women's work we should think of two economies: the formal market, the capitalist economy, with the wage at its centre and the informal economy, non-wage-based, located in the family and

[51] TL, L. Austin, b. 1902.

dominated by the labour of women and children just as the other was ruled by men.[52] The census recorded participation in the formal economy, but it was notoriously sex- and age-biased, failing to recognize those who worked part-time or whose labour became conveniently subsumed under that of the household head. Eliza Packman did not work according to the local census returns for Dunkirk. But we know that she helped her stepfather in the woods, dragging the poles that he cut, for it was there that he raped her in 1848.[53] Beerhouses were nearly always listed under the occupation of the man, frequently a labourer, yet it was the women of the family who served in the tap room during the day and baked the bread sold with the beer. The men would work in the fields during the day and serve beer at night. We will see later that the work of both women and children was central to life in the communities of the Blean and will explore (in Chapter 4) the 'informal economy' in some detail. But we can pause now to set out some parameters and to discuss the more obvious role of women.

According to the census definition of 'occupation', the majority of women in the three parishes were earning a living as servants in March and April of 1851 and 1891. Indeed at a national level, service was an important occupation for young women right up until the Second World War.[54] They were the general servants, maids, domestic servants, cooks, housekeepers, barmaids and household nurses who made up 57 per cent and 61 per cent of female occupations at the middle and end of the century (see figure 1.2). Eighty-eight per cent of unmarried women aged 15 to 24 who were assigned an occupation in the census of 1851 were listed as servants of some type (see table 1.2). Young women also moved out of their parish to take up service. All the single female emigrants from Dunkirk and Hernhill, located in the census of 1851 in surrounding parishes, were house servants, maids, housekeepers and general servants. Although the stereotype is of service in the large household of the gentry or prosperous upper middle class, the majority of servants (in 1851 and 1891) were in the households of farmers and the trades and crafts (see figure 1.3). The 'typical' servant household was not one of a hierarchy and multiplicity of servants, but of one or two general or household servants. Just

---

[52] D. Gittins, 'Marital status, work and kinship, 1850–1930', in J. Lewis (ed.), *Labour and love* (Oxford, 1986), p. 251; E. Higgs, 'Women, occupations and work in the nineteenth-century censuses', *History Workshop*, 23 (1987), p. 60.

[53] CKS, Q/SBe 191, East Kent Quarter Sessions, January 1848.

[54] P. Taylor, 'Daughters and mothers – maids and mistresses: domestic service between the wars', in J. Clarke, C. Critcher and R. Johnson (eds.), *Working class culture* (London, 1979), ch. 5.

Table 1.2 *Occupations and household backgrounds of unmarried females aged 15 to 24, combined parishes, 1851*

	Number	Percentage
Without occupations		
Farmers (daughters or relatives)	20	12.1
Trades/crafts (daughters or relatives)	24	14.5
Ag. Lab./Lab. (daughters or relatives)	27	16.4
Others	13	7.9
Total	**84**	**50.9**
With occupations		
Servants	71	43.0
Others	10	6.1
Total	**81**	**49.1**

Total of 165 females.

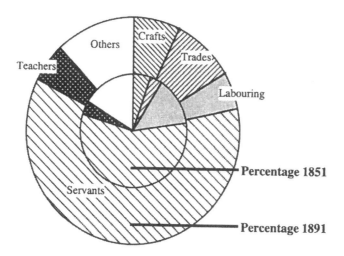

Figure 1.2 Female occupations in 1851 and 1891 (combined parishes).

Introduction

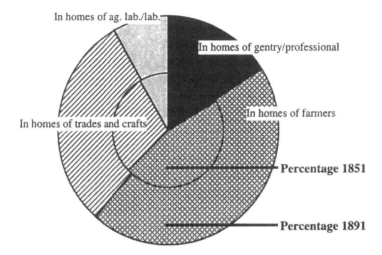

Figure 1.3 Distribution of servants (including farm servants) in 1851 and 1891 (combined parishes).

under 70 per cent of female servants in the three parishes in 1851 were general servants or house servants. Nearly 80 per cent of female servants were in households with from one to three servants; 40 per cent were in houses where they were the only servant. Only 15 per cent worked in houses with five or more servants and in many cases most of the other servants were male farm servants. Nor was there any guarantee that service was a formal, paid contractual arrangement between employer and employee. At least 18 per cent of female servants in the 1851 sample were relatives of the household head and may well have been providing unpaid or very poorly paid labour.

Service could be a rather isolating experience. In the words of V. Turner, who worked as a 'general', a lone servant in a farming household, 'it was lonely to be in service'. She worked from 6 a.m. to 8 p.m. every day, with only Thursday afternoons (2 p.m. to 6 p.m.) and Sunday evenings (6 p.m. to 8 p.m.) off. There was nowhere for her to go during her leisure hours: only 'roaming the country roads' or to church. Her daily duties involved cleaning, lighting the fires, helping to prepare breakfast, lunch and supper, caring for a baby (and then a young child), washing its clothes, doing the family ironing (their washing was sent out to a local woman) and taking the child for a walk every afternoon. They were 'nice people to work for', but life was very restrictive. She had to wear appropriate clothing: a black dress when she took the child out, a white apron and cap for serving, a blue apron for scrubbing. She had to be in by certain times and was not to talk to 'anyone' – that is, male farmworkers – while walking the child. Her wage was 3s. 6d. a week.[55]

Although it is not a subject often broached in oral histories, sexual harassment must have been a risk that many women ran.[56] I talked to a Boughton woman whose first job had been general servant in a household in a nearby parish. She had been constantly harassed by males in the family; as she put it, girls of that young age group and position were considered 'fair game'. Her strategy was one of avoidance – she could not tell her parents and it was impossible to complain to her employers because they were the ones at fault – but the strain was immense. She left within the year, telling her parents that the work was too hard. I had been talking to her for over an hour about a variety of subjects, including women's work and sexuality, yet she had not mentioned her time in service. It was only after the conclusion of our talk, when the tape had been switched off, that we got onto the subject and the details emerged. Clearly the experience had been extremely traumatic. She told me that she had pushed it right out of mind until our conversation had forced her to rethink that aspect of her past.

The pie charts of female and male occupations indicate that there was roughly the same proportion of women listed as servants as there was men occupied as agricultural labourers or labourers (see figures 1.1 and 1.2). The relationship was closer than one of mere functional equivalence. Although young women from the families of farmers and those in the trades and crafts worked in other households as servants, service was work that the children of rural labourers did. The oral accounts of those who grew up in the late nineteenth and early twentieth centuries are insistent on this: 'That's all the girls had to do, go in service. Nothing else'; 'That's all there was for girls then'; 'When I was young there was nothing for girls to do except go into service'; '[P]ractically any girl that had got any go at all was in service.'[57] Of fifty-five female servants in my total reconstitution dossier for the nineteenth century, forty-three (78 per cent) had fathers who were labourers. Some women with fathers who worked in a craft or trade conveyed a sense that service was preferable to farm or rural factory

[55] TL, V. Turner, b. 1896.

[56] For the nineteenth century, see J. Barber, ' "Stolen goods": the sexual harassment of female servants in west Wales during the nineteenth century', *Rural History*, 4 (1993), pp. 123–36.

[57] TL, G. Post, b. 1896; V. Turner, b. 1896; E. Burgess, b. 1890; L. Austin, b. 1902.

work. 'Oh my mother wouldn't have us working anywhere else only service ... You see if you worked on the fields you was looked down on. So of course we all had to go ... everybody went to service'; 'When you go to service, and live with another gentleman's family, you see a lot, you learn a lot, which to me is a finishing education to every working man's daughter.' It 'was an interesting life because you could learn how to be a good housewife as you grew to be a young lady. The money was not much.'[58] But we have seen that there was no guarantee that a young woman would end up in a gentleman's house, and the children of farmworkers are less likely to have shared the prejudice against field work.

Edward Higgs has noted that the census enumerators differed in their recording of women's occupations.[59] We are fortunate that William Bailey, the enumerator for a large subdivision of Boughton, was particularly inclusive in his returns for 1861, which allows a more detailed examination of the census material at a local level. Of 267 women aged 15 and over in the Boughton subdivision, 40 per cent were working (that is, assigned an occupation). The figures take on a different complexion if we break them down further to take account of the woman's marital status. Over 70 per cent of unmarried or widowed women were classified as working; whereas the figure for married women was only 18 per cent. More specifically, the households of labourers and agricultural labourers (containing women over the age of 15), were divided roughly equally between those where a female member of the family worked – as agricultural labourers mainly, but also as servants, laundresses, charwomen and a tailoress – and those where she did not. Of those households whose women were not assigned any occupation, a half had a child under the age of 4 and the others were divided between those with a working son and/or a lodger and those where the women concerned were over 60 years old.

Even by the census's limited criteria, it could hardly be argued that Boughton women did not work in the 'formal economy' – and this for a time when seasonal employment was scarcely at a premium. The rules seem straightforward. Single women worked. Married women worked in full-time work outside the home when they were able, but had to consider the effects of their absence. With a young child in the house, and without older children to assume childcare responsibilities,

[58] TL, V. Turner, b. 1896; F. Dadson, b. 1895.
[59] Higgs, 'Women, occupations and work', p. 63. For an important study of women's work in London, using the 1881 census, see the recent article by A. August, 'How separate a sphere? Poor women and paid work in late-Victorian London', *Journal of Family History*, 19 (1994), pp. 285–309.

it must have made more sense to stay at home with the child. If a son was working and living at home, the better strategy was probably to devote time to aspects of household survival other than simple wage labour. Or work could be found at home with the tasks involved with taking in a lodger or boarder. J. W. Manuel (born 1903) said that his father's first wife died: 'Then you see, him being a horseman, he had to have a wife to run a home, because he had to have a lodger, because of his mate, with the horses. So he had to chase round quick and get settled down again. Get started again. I think that a lot of that was economics you know, to keep up his position.'[60]

VIII

There are those who claim to be able to detect occupational division by sight or even smell. Walter Rose (born 1871) said that he was able to tell the gait and stoop of a cowman from that of the 'four-square set' of the horseman. Those who worked the fields were brown like the soil they cultivated and they tied their trousers under the knee. Builders wore corduroy trousers. Painters favoured cloth. The odours of work clung to the garments of workers: to move from stable to cow-house 'was to enter another world altogether. Instead of the strong ammoniated smell of the stable, one became conscious of a pervading essence of meadows; the laxative quality of green grass in semi-fluid manure, and sweet smelling milk.' Builders had the scent of lime, carpenters of wood, saddlers and shoemakers of leather and wax.[61] Some of us may be sceptical of such visual and olfactory skills, but there is no doubting the importance of occupation as a source of identity and social division and classification. The 'main indicator of an individual's location in social space', Andrew Miles and David Vincent have written, 'has always been occupation'.[62] The occupations of rural people, their work and the way they earned a living are central to the analysis in this book.

[60] TL, J. W. Manuel, b. 1903.
[61] W. Rose, *Good neighbours* (Cambridge, 1942; reprinted Green Books, Bideford, 1988), pp. 14, 17, 35, 37–8, 43–4.
[62] A. Miles and D. Vincent (eds.), *Building European society: occupational change and social mobility in Europe 1840–1940* (Manchester, 1993), p. 3.

PART I

Demography

Plate 15 Children at Chartham Hatch, early this century.

2

Fertility

I

It is generally acknowledged that one of the fundamental social transformations in our past was the decline in European fertility in the late nineteenth and early twentieth centuries. It is unfortunate, then, that one of the greatest gaps in English population history is the immediate back-drop to the 'fertility transition', the period from 1800 to 1880. There is scholarly material available for the years before and after these dates. The Cambridge Group provides a detailed account to 1799.[1] The macro studies of British fertility decline resume the picture in the last two or three decades of the nineteenth century.[2] But the years in between, a crucial slice of our demographic past, are hidden from history.

It is a question not just of a shortage of studies of England's fertility transition, but of the type of work that is available. Whether based on aggregative counts from parish registers or the published census data available from the second half of the nineteenth century, the macro studies are unable to answer some important demographic questions. They can inform about long-term, aggregated shifts in population but can tell us little about the individual, class and community dynamics

---

[1]   E. A. Wrigley and R. S. Schofield, 'English population history from family reconstitution: summary results 1600–1799', *Population Studies*, 37 (1983), pp. 157–84; C. Wilson, 'Natural fertility in pre-industrial England, 1600–1799', *Population Studies*, 38 (1984), pp. 225–40; C. Wilson, 'The proximate determinants of marital fertility in England 1600–1799', in L. Bonfield, R. M. Smith and K. Wrightson (eds.), *The world we have gained* (Oxford, 1986), ch. 8.

[2]   M. S. Teitelbaum, *The British fertility decline* (Princeton, 1984); R. I. Woods, 'Approaches to the fertility transition in Victorian England', *Population Studies*, 41 (1987), pp. 283–311; M. R. Haines, 'Social class differentials during fertility decline: England and Wales revisited', *Population Studies*, 43 (1989), pp. 305–23.

of fertility. One way around this problem is detailed work at a micro level, using the technique of family reconstitution.

Recently published surveys of European population history have highlighted the lack of information on English fertility patterns during the nineteenth century and the thinness of material dealing with the early stages of the fertility transition. We have a list of assumptions, based on trends before and after this period, and an even longer list of gaps in our knowledge. As Robert Woods has put it:

> The origins of the secular decline of marital fertility in Britain, as in much of western Europe with the exception of France, are to be found in the second half, but especially the last quarter of the nineteenth century. This much at least is clear from the available vital statistics, but there are many aspects of this fundamental change in demographic structure that remain obscure. By what means was the size of families limited? Why did marital fertility decline from this period and not earlier or later? Were the reasons economic or social in origin, of necessity or through the choice of fashion? Who controlled their fertility first and did others learn from their behaviour? Hypotheses abound, but the evidence remains tantalising in its vagueness or insecurity.[3]

Michael Anderson has also outlined some of the problems:

> In England, marital fertility appears remarkably constant between 1600 and 1800 ... The picture after 1800 is obscure in the absence of adequate numbers of reliable reconstitutions; this is particularly unfortunate given the birth rate surge of this period. By 1851 marital fertility was still around the late-eight-eenth-century level, but the possibility remains that a temporary rise had played some role in the rapid population growth of the previous fifty years. On present evidence, however, changes in marital fertility were not important in English population changes in our period.[4]

These are intriguing issues. There is virtual agreement that nupti-ality, a drop both in female marriage ages and the proportion of women not marrying, was the driving force behind England's popula-tion explosion in the eighteenth century, but its role thereafter is obscure.[5] There is an orthodoxy, outlined in Anderson's comments above, that marital fertility was remarkably uniform in England from the sixteenth to the nineteenth centuries, varying little over time or between regions. It is also argued that although English fertility was of a modest level compared to other natural fertility regimes, it was indeed natural fertility; there is little or no evidence of family limitation

---

[3] R. Woods, *The population of Britain in the nineteenth century* (London, 1992), p. 46.

[4] M. Anderson, *Population change in north-western Europe, 1750–1850* (London, 1988), pp. 41–2.

[5] *Ibid.*, pp. 49–52; M. Anderson, 'The social implications of demographic change', in F. M. L. Thompson (ed.), *The Cambridge social history of Britain 1750–1950* vol. II, *People and their environment* (Cambridge, 1990), pp. 32–4.

until the late nineteenth century.[6] The impression conveyed is of rather sudden change from the 1870s, when natural fertility gives way to family limitation. Chris Wilson and Robert Woods write that fertility in England 'remained at levels analogous to those of the pre-industrial era until the 1870s, when a widespread and remarkably homogeneous decline set in'.[7] This initial reduction in English marital fertility was achieved, it is claimed, though the evidence comes from Germany rather than from England, by means of 'stopping', the cessation of childbirth before the end of the woman's fertility, rather than by the deliberate lengthening of the intervals between births.[8] Finally, there is the issue of which social group initiated the transition in Britain. The old interpretation of the social diffusion of fertility limitation from the middle classes down has been challenged, but critics have yet to present a convincing alternative. 'The picture is still confused on these matters'.[9] In other words, even when we set aside the whole issue of explaining why the decline occurred when it did and limit our discussion to the actual mechanics of the transition, there are many interesting uncertainties and questionable assumptions. This study, and others like it, cannot deal with every doubt, but they can begin to undermine our ignorance of the background and early stages of England's fertility transition.

II

A fall in female marriage ages is believed to be one of the main forces behind the growth of England's population in the eighteenth century. Although the figures vary from study to study, the work of the Cambridge Group suggests that female ages at first marriage dropped from a mean of 26.2 years for marriages during the second half of the seventeenth century to 23.4 at the beginning of the nineteenth century.

[6]   Wilson, 'Natural fertility', pp. 239–40; Woods, 'Approaches', p. 283; C. Wilson and R. Woods, 'Fertility in England: a long-term perspective', *Population Studies*, 45 (1991), pp. 399–400. For a recent restatement of the orthodoxy, see T. W. Laqueur, 'Sexual desire and the market economy during the Industrial Revolution', in D. C. Stanton (ed.), *Discourses of sexuality: from Aristotle to Aids* (Ann Arbor, 1992), pp. 192–200.

[7]   Wilson and Woods, 'Fertility', p. 399.

[8]   Woods, *Population,* p. 48; W. Seccombe, 'Starting to stop: working-class fertility decline in Britain', *Past and Present*, 126 (1990), p. 153; Woods, 'Approaches', p. 291. The means of deliberate control were abortion (about which we have little statistical information), coitus interruptus or withdrawal, abstinence and contraceptive devices (probably rarely used in the nineteenth century): Woods, 'Approaches', p. 291; Seccombe, 'Starting to stop', *passim;* Woods, *Population,* p. 49; A. McLaren, *A history of contraception* (Oxford, 1990), ch. 6.

[9]   R. Woods, 'Working-class fertility decline in Britain', *Past and Present*, 134 (1992), pp. 201–2.

Table 2.1   *Mean age at first marriage by parish*

Year of marriage	Boughton Female	Boughton Male	Dunkirk Female	Dunkirk Male	Hernhill Female	Hernhill Male	All parishes Female	All parishes Male
1800–34	22.6	25.9	(21.9)	(25.4)	21.6	24.2	22.1	25.1
1835–49	23.1	(26.0)	21.9	25.9	22.1	25.6	22.4	25.8
1850–64	23.0	26.1	23.3	25.5	22.5	(24.9)	23.0	25.6
1865–80	23.9	25.2	22.4	25.3	23.3	25.3	23.4	25.2
Change 1800–34 to 1865–80	+1.3	−0.7	+0.5	−0.1	+1.7	+1.1	+1.3	+0.1

Results in parentheses are based on 30–49 cases.

The result was an increase in the period of women's total, potential, marital fertility. Male marriage ages, not as important for fertility, declined from 28.1 to 25.3 over the same period.[10]

Female marriage ages for our three Kent parishes, 22.1 for the combined cohort of 1800–34, certainly support the nationwide trend of a reduction in ages from early-modern levels (see table 2.1). They were even lower than the Cambridge Group's means, although in keeping with several other early nineteenth-century reconstitution figures.[11] Male ages – 25.1 – were similar to those of the Cambridge Group. Female means then rose gradually over the century, reaching 23.4 for those married in the years 1865–80. Male means rose slightly after 1834, perhaps in response to the New Poor Law, framed to discourage support for large families among the poor, but were only 25.2 by the 1870s. These movements do not seem to follow Roger Schofield's suggested rapid rise in marriage ages after the introduction of the New Poor Law.[12]

Means, however, do not tell us much about age distribution. Figure 2.1 sets out distributional changes for the combined Kent parishes over the century. Apart from initial movement after 1834, male ages did not change greatly. The majority of men first married when they were aged between 20 and 24, but about a third, throughout the century, married aged 25 to 29. Though the proportion halved from 1800 to 1880, few married in their teens. The changes in distribution of female first marriages were far more marked. Over the century there was a decline

---

[10]   Wrigley and Schofield, 'English population history', p. 162; E. A. Wrigley and R. S. Schofield, *The population history of England 1541–1871* (Cambridge, 1989 edn), p. 255.

[11]   See the summary Table 7 in D. R. Mills, *Aspects of marriage: an example of applied historical studies* (Open University Social Science Publications, Milton Keynes, 1980), p. 21.

[12]   R. Schofield, 'English marriage patterns revisited', *Journal of Family History*, 10 (1985), pp. 8–9, 19.

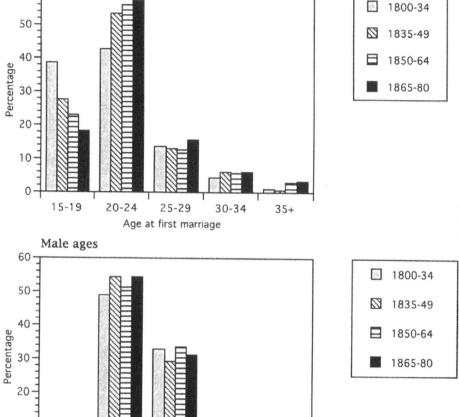

Figure 2.1 Distribution of age at first marriage by year of marriage for combined parishes, 1800–80.

in extremely young marriages and a rise in the proportion married aged 20–24. Nearly 40 per cent of female brides in the 1800–34 cohort were teenage brides: by 1865–80 the proportion aged from 15 to 19 had halved to 18.2 per cent. Even so, throughout the century, 75 to 80 per cent of women who married for the first time were 24 or younger.

Table 2.2   *Mean age at first marriage by occupational group of groom*

Year of	Trades/Crafts		Farmers		Ag. Lab./Lab.	
marriage	Female	Male	Female	Male	Female	Male
1800–34	22.3	24.6	22.2	25.2	22.1	25.3
1835–49	24.0	25.5	23.4	–	21.8	25.6
1850–80	23.9	25.4	27.6	27.1	22.4	25.1
Change 1800–34						
to 1850–80	+1.6	+0.8	+5.4	+1.9	+0.3	−0.2

Results based on fewer than twenty cases are omitted

The later marriage registers give details of the occupations of grooms, and the technique of total reconstitution provides similar information for earlier marriages, so it is possible to consider socio-economic differences which may be disguised in these means and distributions. The numbers for some of the categories are rather small but the results are worth noting. Female and male mean marriage ages at the labouring level were stable throughout the period at around 22 and 25, whereas those of the trades and crafts rose from 22.3 to 23.9 and from 24.6 to 25.4 respectively. Far more dramatic was the rise in ages for farming couples. Female means moved from 22.2 to 27.6; male's from 25.2 to 27.1 (see table 2.2). These differences are reflected in the distribution graphs in figure 2.2. Twenty-seven to 37 per cent of women who married labourers and agricultural labourers were younger than 20 years, at any stage during the century.[13] The proportions in that age group who married men in the trades and crafts and farming were very similar in the early nineteenth-century cohort. However, they fell in the succeeding cohorts (to as low as 10 per cent for young women marrying craftsmen and shopkeepers); by 1880 a teenage farming bride must have been a rarity.

It is clear that the statistical averages for the combined populations concealed some important socio-economic variations. We can rule out marriage ages as a significant factor in any changes in fertility at the labouring level in this part of England during the nineteenth century. For farming families the picture is very different. Farmers' wives reduced their potential childbearing span by an average of over five years; age at marriage could have been as important in reducing this group's fertility in the nineteenth century as it had been in increasing that of their ancestors in the eighteenth. The sample size is extremely

[13] If we were to use the age of 20 rather than 19 as a cut-off point the proportion of young brides would be even higher: 40 to 50 per cent of brides at the labouring level were aged 20 or younger.

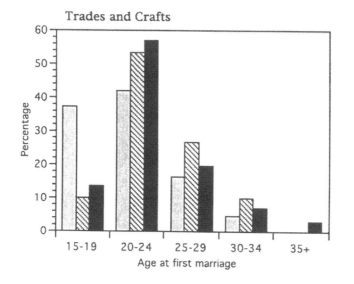

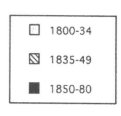

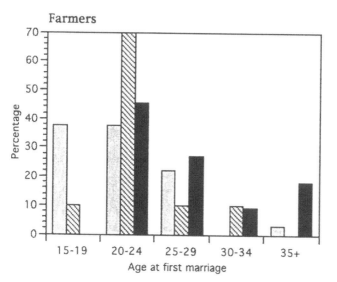

Figure 2.2 Distribution of female ages at first marriage by occupation of groom
and year of marriage

small but the farming community was a small section of the population
anyway. My figures for the farmers should be treated with caution but
they raise possibilities for future research. The other surprising finding,
in the light of Schofield's comments about the New Poor Law (mentioned earlier), is that it was the trades and crafts and farming groups
rather than the agricultural labourers which showed the greatest
response, nuptiality-wise, immediately after 1834. If one of the inten-
tions of the legislation of 1834 had been to remove the incentives to
early marriage, the message was lost on the labouring population of
the Blean.[14]

---

[14] Of course they may have responded by not marrying at all. But because of
geographical mobility it is impossible to calculate meaningful celibacy rates at the
parish level. The impact of social and economic developments upon nuptiality is
something of a scholarly minefield. For an introduction, see R. M. Smith, 'Fertility,
economy, and household formation in England over three centuries', *Population and
Development Review*, 7 (1981), pp. 595–622; D. R. Weir, 'Rather never than late:
celibacy and age at marriage in English cohort fertility, 1541–1871', *Journal of Family
History*, 9 (1984), pp. 340–54; J. A. Goldstone, 'The demographic revolution in
England: a re-examination', *Population Studies*, 49 (1986), pp. 5–33; D. Levine,
Reproducing families (Cambridge, 1987); B. Hill, 'The marriage age of women and the
demographers', *History Workshop*, 28 (1989), pp. 129–54.

III

One of the main benefits of the technique of family reconstitution is that it permits the calculation of marital fertility rates, crucial to debates about population change. We may recall the picture of stability and homogeneity in English marital fertility levels into the nineteenth century: the tendency to assume, in the absence of any evidence to the contrary, that what the Cambridge Group found of the late eighteenth century prevailed for much of the nineteenth. The figures for age-specific marital fertility for our rural Kent parishes, set out in table 2.3 and figure 2.3, come as something of a surprise. Not only are the levels of age-specific marital fertility much higher than one might anticipate from the Cambridge Group's natural fertility levels, but they also indicate change over the period, the possibility that age-specific marital fertility rather than marriage age was an important mechanism behind population change in the nineteenth century.

Table 2.3 raises something of a challenge to the statement that 'marital fertility ... varied little over time and space until the post-1870 secular decline'.[15] It is interesting to compare the Kent village 'natural fertility' level – my description for the first cohort (1800–34) – with levels for the Cambridge Group's reconstitutions, those for German village populations in the nineteenth century, and with recent data for the nineteenth-century Quakers (see figure 2.4). The Kent parish rates are closer to those of these other populations than they are to the Cambridge Group's low fertility norms. The comparison between the Quakers, the Kent parishes and the English reconstitutions is another argument against the homogeneity of the English experience.

Table 2.3   *Age-specific marital fertility (combined parishes)*

Year of marriage	20–24	25–29	30–34	35–39	40–44	45–49	TMF30+/ TMF20+
1800–34	429	412	355	275	184	38	0.503
1835–49	474	380	334	282	154	17	0.480
1850–64	481	361	315	260	162	20	0.473
1865–80	506	413	316	205	112	18	0.415
Percentage change 1800–34/1865–80	+18	+0.2	−11	−25	−39	−53	−17

The age-specific fertility rates are per 1,000 married women and all are based on more than 100 woman years per five-year period. TMF = total marital fertility (see p. 53).

[15]   Wilson and Woods, 'Fertility', p. 414.

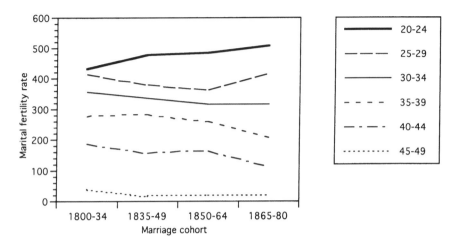

Figure 2.3 Age-specific marital fertility by marriage cohort for combined parishes. (The age-specific fertility rates are per 1,000 married women and all are based on more than 100 woman years per five-year period.)

Indeed the similarities between age-specific marital fertility in rural Kent and Germany are striking. What Knodel has observed of his German villagers was equally true of the people of the Blean represented in figure 2.3 and table 2.3. There were two distinct trends in marital fertility: 'toward higher fertility among younger married women and toward lower fertility among older women'. The first may well represent an increase in underlying fertility. The second 'undoubtedly reflects an increasing practice of deliberate family limitation'.[16]

IV

There are various ways of exploring fertility levels. M is one index that is frequently employed. It is the age-specific rate at age 20–24 for the subject cohort, expressed as a ratio of the rate for the same age group in Coale and Trussell's model natural fertility schedule (derived from data for a variety of natural fertility populations). As Knodel has explained, M can serve, 'under some circumstances, as an indicator of the underlying level of natural fertility':

---

[16] J. Knodel, 'Demographic transitions in German villages', in A. J. Coale and S. Cotts Watkins (eds.), *The decline of fertility in Europe* (Princeton, 1986), p. 358.

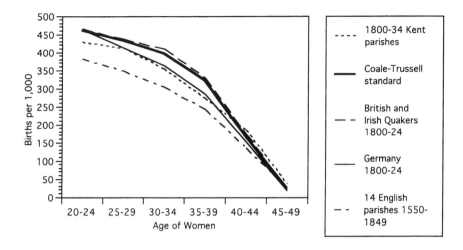

Figure 2.4 Age-specific marital fertility of Kent parishes (natural fertility cohort) compared with other studies. (The German data comes from J. E. Knodel, *Demographic behavior in the past* (Cambridge, 1988), p. 257, Table 10.2; information on the Quakers from R. T. Vann and D. Eversley, *Friends in life and death* (Cambridge, 1992), p. 132, Table 4.1. I used the Coale–Trussell natural fertility schedule given in J. Knodel, 'Family limitation and the fertility transition: evidence from the age patterns of fertility in Europe and Asia', *Population Studies*, 31 (1977), p. 223, n. 12. The Cambridge Group figures comes from Wilson, 'Natural fertility', p. 228, Table 2.)

It is based on the assumption that even when family limitation is common, the fertility of younger married women is unlikely to be influenced since such women are at the early stages of family-building and have not reached the number of children they do not want to exceed. The M index is constructed so that it will equal 1.00 when the underlying level of natural fertility is the same as the level embodied in the standard natural fertility schedule. Deviations from 1.00 indicate the proportionate deviation from that level.[17]

The M index for the Kent villages increases from 0.93 to a high of 1.10. It is considerably higher than the indexes for the fourteen English parishes with non-adjusted rates in the 0.8 range;[18] and it increases over the nineteenth century to a rate higher than the natural

[17] J. E. Knodel, *Demographic behavior in the past* (Cambridge, 1988), p. 261.
[18] See Wilson, 'Natural fertility', pp. 233–4. The highest is Bottesford with 0.90.

Table 2.4 *Coale–Trussell index of natural fertility (M) by year of marriage
in the three Kent parishes*

	1800–34	1835–49	1850–80
By place			
Boughton	0.90	1.06	1.06
Dunkirk	(0.96)	(1.03)	(0.94)
Hernhill	0.95	(1.00)	(1.20)
All parishes	0.93	1.03	1.07
By occupation			
Trades/Crafts	(0.91)	(0.80)	(1.04)
Farmers	1.02	–	(1.41)
Ag. Lab./Lab.	0.92	1.02	1.06

Results in parentheses are based on fewer than 100 woman years for the age
group 20–24; those based on fewer than 20 woman years are not included.

fertility model. Table 2.4 gives the Coale–Trussell indexes for three
marriage cohorts, by parish and by occupational group. The trends are
consistent (apart from the Dunkirk figures). The natural fertility levels
increased over the century in two of the three parishes and for the
three main occupational groups. By 1850–80 the levels in Hernhill were
higher than in the adjoining villages and hamlets; farmers were the
most fecund of the socio-occupational groups.

One of the weaknesses of M as an index is that it can be distorted
by high levels of prenuptial pregnancy which inflate the age-specific
rates. However, it is possible to adjust the marital fertility rates to
correct the distortion caused by bridal pregnancy rates of from 40 to
45 per cent for the three parishes (see table 2.5).[19] The adjusted
parameters are lower but still show a rise from 0.86 (slightly above
the mean of the Cambridge Group's adjusted Ms) to 0.99. In other
words, even the adjusted rates indicate a 15 per cent rise in the
natural fertility level from the 1800–34 marriage group to the 1865–80
group. The levels are slightly lower than in Knodel's Germany;
otherwise the trends are very similar for our respective reconstitutions.[20] The apparent increase in the underlying marital fertility of
younger women raises intriguing parallels with similar findings for
rural Germany and Switzerland during the same century. The

[19] I used the method outlined in Wilson, 'Natural fertility', p. 232. My adjustments
were different, of course.
[20] See J. Knodel and C. Wilson, 'The secular increase in fecundity in German village
populations', *Population Studies*, 35 (1981), p. 60, Table 2; Knodel, *Demographic
behavior*, p. 268, Table 10.4.

Table 2.5 *Percentage of women pregnant at time of marriage and index of underlying fertility level adjusted for prenuptial pregnancy (combined parishes)*

Year of marriage	Percentage prenuptially pregnant	Adjusted M	Unadjusted M
1800–34	41.7	0.86	0.93
1835–49	39.6	0.92	1.03
1850–64	40.0	0.97	1.05
1865–80	45.1	0.99	1.10
Percentage change 1800–34/1865–80	+8.2	+15	+18

These calculations are drawn from the same data base as that used for constructing age-specific marital fertility in table 2.3 above.

problem is that there is no convincing explanation for these changes.[21]

V

We can now return to the other aspect that we observed in the age-specific marital fertility rates – the likelihood of deliberate family limitation as the century progressed. For age-specific marital fertility rates can also be used to examine the issue of fertility control. The Coale and Trussell index of *m* compares the age structure of the subject age-specific marital fertility against a calculated standard or model natural fertility schedule.[22] A value of *m* that is less than 0.2 (including minus values) is generally taken to indicate little or no family limitation; values above 0.5 show fertility control. 'In addition', as Knodel has put it, 'steady rises in the value of *m* (such as occurred in many European populations during the historic decline in fertility during the last half of the nineteenth century and the first decades of the twentieth) are almost certainly indications of increasing practice of family limitation even though each successive increment was often small in size' (see table 2.6).[23]

[21] Knodel and Wilson, 'Secular increase'; Knodel, *Demographic behavior*, pp. 284–6; R. Netting, *Balancing on an alp* (Cambridge, 1981), pp. 145–68.

[22] J. Knodel, 'Family limitation and the fertility transition: evidence from the age patterns of fertility in Europe and Asia', *Population Studies*, 31 (1977), pp. 223–4.

[23] J. Knodel, 'Natural fertility in pre-industrial Germany', *Population Studies*, 32 (1978), p. 489.

Table 2.6   *Coale–Trussell index of fertility control (m) by year of marriage*

	1800–34	1835–49	1850–80
By place			
Boughton	0.01	0.87	0.38
Dunkirk	−0.09	0.06	0.10
Hernhill	−0.16	0.29	0.55
All parishes	−0.08	0.26	0.36
By occupation			
Trades/Crafts	0.09	(−0.03)	0.24
Farmers	−0.14	–	(0.68)
Ag. Lab./Lab.	−0.09	0.23	0.38

Results in parentheses are based on an average of fewer than 100 woman years per five-year age group within the 20–49 range; those based on averages of fewer than 20 woman years are not included.

Table 2.7   *Index of fertility control adjusted for prenuptial pregnancy (combined parishes)*

Year of marriage	Adjusted m	Unadjusted m	Difference
1800 – 34	−0.19	−0.08	0.11
1835 – 49	0.11	0.26	0.15
1850 – 64	0.22	0.33	0.11
1865 – 80	0.26	0.41	0.15

The Coale–Trussell m index is by no means unproblematic. Vann and Eversley have recently questioned its applicability to pre-industrial populations.[24] Like the M index it can be distorted by high levels of pre-marital pregnancy, although few studies make any adjustments to compensate for this error. Table 2.7 provides the adjusted rates for the combined parishes.[25] The adjustments depress the indexes considerably, bringing them within the range associated with prevailing natural fertility and lack of family limitation. Yet there is still evidence of the upward move mentioned by Knodel as a sign of increasing family limitation. The adjusted values from 1835–49 onwards are higher than almost all the rates for the Cambridge Group's fourteen English parishes, taken by Wilson as providing 'scant evidence of family limitation'.[26] Even if we make the required downward mental adjustments, table 2.6 indicates that sections of the

[24]   R. T. Vann and D. Eversley, *Friends in life and death* (Cambridge, 1992), pp. 178–85.
[25]   Following the procedure outlined by Wilson, 'Natural fertility', p. 232.
[26]   *Ibid.*, p. 234.

community were beginning to limit their fertility. There were local differences in these neighbouring parishes: Boughton and Hernhill were more advanced than Dunkirk. Furthermore, the figures for the labouring population suggest that those at the bottom of society were moving towards fertility control in the nineteenth century; they were not awaiting an urban, middle-class lead in the early twentieth century. In short, while the shifts in adjusted rates are far from dramatic and may be interpreted by some as falling within the pattern of natural fertility, the general upward movement in the index of fertility control implies adjustments in reproductive behaviour before the period normally associated with the fertility transition.

Another indicator of the transition from natural to limited fertility is the ratio of total marital fertility over the age of 30 to total marital fertility over the age of 20. Total marital fertility or TMF is the number of births that a woman would experience (for the age-specific rates in question) if she completed her reproductive span. The lowering of TMF 30+/TMF 20+ is one of the signs of family limitation. In natural fertility cohorts values are close to 0.50; Wilson's fourteen English populations were all within the range of 0.47 to 0.53.[27] As table 2.3 shows, the ratios for Kent drop below the Cambridge Group's natural fertility ratios; the drop of 17 per cent from 1800 to 1880 is close to the decline of 15 per cent in Knodel's German villages during the period 1800–99.[28]

In populations where there are efforts at fertility control, the age-specific rates tend to decline more rapidly with age than they do in purely natural fertility regimes. Shifts in the pattern of marital fertility over time, then, which can be demonstrated graphically, could indicate moves towards fertility control.[29] Figure 2.5 captures movement over the century. The decline in fertility with age is even more noticeable when the rates are plotted for women who were less than 25 years old when they married, that is the vast bulk of the married population at all stages during the course of the nineteenth century. When the values are indexed with the rate for age group 20–24 as 100, the downward curve is obvious (see figure 2.6) The graphs provide convincing evidence of fertility change over the nineteenth century. The downward dip with age in the marital fertility of the later marriage cohorts is in keeping with a decline in fertility.[30] The downward curve after 1835 may well reflect direct response to the New Poor Law. That the

---

[27] *Ibid.*, p. 230.

[28] Knodel, *Demographic behavior*, p. 257, Table 10.2.

[29] J. Knodel, 'Natural fertility: age patterns, levels and trends', in R. A. Bulatao and R. D. Lee (eds.), *Determinants of fertility in developing countries* (2 vols., New York, 1983), vol. I, pp. 65–70.

[30] Compare with the graphs in Knodel, *Demographic behavior*, p. 256, Figure 10.1.

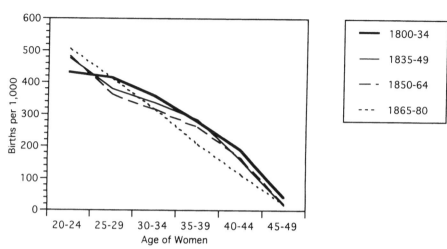

Figure 2.5 Age-specific marital fertility by year of marriage for combined parishes.

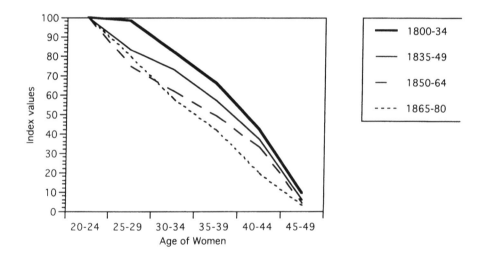

Figure 2.6 Age-specific fertility of women married aged under 25 years, indexed with rate for age group 20–24 being 100 (combined parishes)

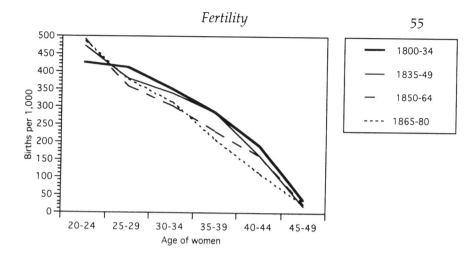

Figure 2.7 Age-specific marital fertility at the labouring level by year of marriage (combined parishes).

wives of agricultural labourers and labourers were involved in these trends is clear from their age-specific fertility rates plotted in figure 2.7; it reiterates the point that they were not awaiting some later lead from their social superiors.

Finally, a comparison with German fertility levels reinforces the claim that family limitation had arrived in nineteenth-century Kent. Figure 2.8 plots the German natural fertility and family limitation cohorts against the Kent village cohorts for 1800–34 (natural) and 1865–80 (limitation). The age-specific fertility rates are for women married in the same age group, 20–24. The correspondences between the respective natural and limitation cohorts are very close.

To summarize, the marital fertility rates suggest two competing trends. The demographic transition in rural England was a dual transition. And at the risk of labouring the point, it is worth re-emphasizing the parallel with Germany. Not only are the moves towards family limitation similar but there are comparable rises in natural fertility. In other words, the early stages of the transition to fertility control were carried out in these rural parishes, as in village Germany and fertility transitions today, in the face of an increasing natural fecundity.[31]

---

[31] T. Dyson and M. Murphy, 'The onset of fertility transition', *Population and Development Review*, 11 (1985), pp. 399–440; Knodel, *Demographic behavior*, pp. 284–6.

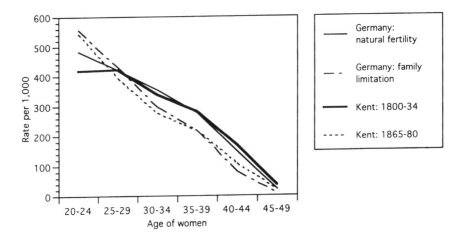

Figure 2.8 Age-specific fertility of Kent and Germany compared (women married aged 20–24). (The German rates come from Knodel, *Demographic behavior*, p. 373, Table 13.7.)

VI

There are suggestions of a start of the fertility transition in rural Kent. But how was fertility being controlled? There are two possibilities that are usually discussed in this context: spacing and stopping.[32] They can be practised separately or in conjunction. In spacing, or nonparity-specific limitation, couples prolong the intervals between births, that is space out the births. Stopping behaviour, or parity-specific limitation, occurs when couples avoid having children after they have a certain number, that is stop. The onset of parity-specific limitation or stopping behaviour is the easiest to detect in family reconstitutions. Indeed one of the traits associated with control by stopping is the sort of age-specific fertility pattern shown in figure 2.6 where there is a steepening decline in marital fertility as age increases. Another sign of stopping behaviour is a decrease in the age of women at the birth of their last child. In natural fertility populations the mean age at last birth is around the age of 40 (depending on average age at marriage). The mean age at last birth for the fourteen English parishes studied by Wilson was 39.6; in the German villages the average was 40.3 for the

---

[32] Yet again I depend upon the work of Knodel: Knodel, 'Demographic transitions'; Knodel, *Demographic behavior*, ch. 12. See also the discussion in D. L. Anderton and L. L. Bean, 'Birth spacing and fertility limitation', *Demography*, 22 (1985), pp. 169–83.

Table 2.8   *Age of mother at last birth by year of marriage*

	1800−34	1835−49	1850−64	1865−80
By place				
Boughton	39.3	38.4	39.1	(38.9)
Dunkirk	41.3	42.0	(41.1)	−
Hernhill	41.9	37.8	(39.1)	(38.2)
All parishes	40.7	39.5	39.7	38.4
By occupation				
Trades/Crafts	38.7	(38.5)	40.3	(36.0)
Farmers	42.3	−	−	−
Ag. Lab./Lab.	41.1	40.2	39.1	39.2
By age group				
Women married aged <20	41.5	41.5	37.6 (for 1850–80)	
Women married aged 20–24	40.0	39.3	39.4	38.7
Women married aged 25–29	41.2	39.3	38.8 (for 1850–80)	

Results in parentheses are based on fewer than twenty cases; those based on fewer than ten are omitted.

1750–99 marriage cohort and 39.8 for that of 1800–24.[33] A reduction in the age at last birth over successive marriage cohorts – provided that changes in marriage age are taken into account – is an indication of the presence of the stopping strategy. Table 2.8 sets out ages at last birth for the Kent parishes.

The trends are consistent: a reduction of about two years over the cohorts, with the exception of Dunkirk and (although it is not shown) the farmers. There are contrasts in levels. The wives of those employed in the trades and crafts finished childbearing at earlier ages than labouring women; even when the latter had reduced their ages at last birth, their mean was higher than that of the trades and crafts at the start of the century. The fall in means is not dramatic. In fact most still lie within 38 and 41, the averages of non-controlled, natural fertility, populations. But the means were reduced, a sign, as Knodel has observed of a similar trend in pre-transition Germany, 'that the under-lying behavioral pattern was also beginning ... to change, and that the behavioral mechanisms which were eventually to reduce fertility to much lower levels were already emerging'.[34] That adjustments were

[33]   Wilson, 'Natural fertility', pp. 234–6; Knodel, *Demographic behavior*, p. 291, Table 11.2.
[34]   Knodel, *Demographic behavior*, p. 293.

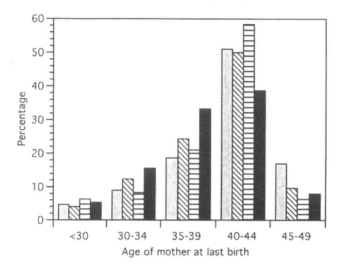
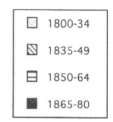

Figure 2.9 Distribution of age at last birth by year of marriage for combined
parishes (percentages).

being made comes out more clearly with the distribution of the age of
women at their last births shown in figure 2.9. Clearly there was a
reduction in the proportion of women giving birth after the age of 40
and an increase in the numbers who ceased childbearing while still in
their thirties.

Stopping behaviour also reveals itself demographically in birth
spacing. In the early stages of family limitation, when couples are
trying to stop having children without effective contraception, there
will be accidental pregnancies or changes of heart when personal
circumstances change. So one of the signs of the introduction of
stopping is an increase in the last birth interval as what was intended
to be the last child became the second to last child. Birth spacing
patterns are set out in table 2.9 and (visually) in figure 2.10.[35] There are
some inconsistencies: the women with 7–10 confinements who indicate
stopping behaviour in the 1835–49 and 1850–65 cohorts but not in that
of 1865–80 and the women in the marriage group for 1850–64 with 3–6
intervals who increased their spacing and then dropped back to an
earlier level. However, the interconfinement intervals tend to support

[35] Following Knodel, I have divided the sample into final numbers of confinements per
woman and have calculated the intervals *per woman*. This avoids swamping the
sample with the intervals of women with large families and avoids obscuring those
with smaller completed families who may well have been practising some form of
family limitation.

Table 2.9 *Mean last interconfinement interval and mean of all preceding intervals (in months) for combined parishes by year of marriage*

	Final number of confinements per married woman			
	3–6	7–10	11+	Total
Last interval				
1800–34	40.9	41.4	(35.9)	40.3
1835–49	41.0	51.4	(37.5)	45.8
1850–64	(41.9)	(50.0)	(29.6)	43.3
1865–80	(56.7)	(40.4)	(33.1)	48.2
All preceding intervals				
1800–34	32.3	30.3	(24.9)	30.0
1835–49	34.7	28.6	(24.5)	30.1
1850–64	(40.1)	(27.3)	(23.3)	32.2
1865–80	30.6	(27.3)	(22.6)	28.4

Results in parentheses are based on fewer than twenty cases. The intervals are for women with at least three confinements and are calculated per woman rather than by each pooled interval.

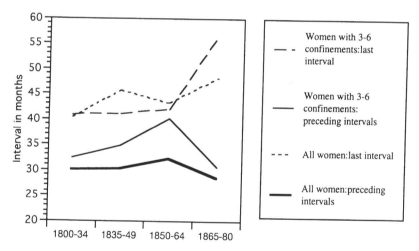

Figure 2.10 Mean last interconfinement interval and mean of all preceding intervals (in months) by year of marriage (combined parishes).

the introduction of stopping as a means of controlling fertility. The last interval has increased by the last marriage cohort, particularly for those women with modest-sized families (those with 3–6 confinements) – a pattern consistent with stopping or parity-specific limitation. The other intervals (those excluding the last) show little movement and thus little indication of spacing or nonparity-specific control. In fact these

Table 2.10   *Distribution of birth intervals for women with three or more*
confinements for combined parishes by year of marriage (percentages)

	Final number of confinements per married woman		
Year of marriage	3–6	7–10	11+
1800–34	29.4	53.9	16.7
1835–49	35.5	48.4	16.1
1850–64	43.2	40.9	15.9
1865–80	48.4	35.5	16.1

intervals actually narrow over the cohorts, reinforcing my earlier claims for an increase in the underlying fertility level.

It is also important to note that the proportion of women with smaller families – those probably limiting family size – increases over time. As table 2.10 shows, those women with 3–6 confinements comprised just under 30 per cent of the cohort in 1800–34; by 1865–80 they were nearly half. Those with very large families, who patently were not limiting their fertility at all, always formed about 16 per cent of the sample. This would seem to imply that the early stage of the fertility transition was characterized by an increasing proportion of women willing to modify their behaviour, living alongside a group who did not change their behaviour at all. If representative of other English communities, this would somewhat modify the stereotype of a massive sea-change in 1870.

But there is still the possibility of social variation. Table 2.11 and figure 2.11 show that the totals do indeed hide some differences at the labouring level. Stopping behaviour is confirmed by the increase in the last interval. But there is the possibility that births were spaced too; the wives of agricultural labourers and labourers with smaller families (3–6 confinements) increased their birth intervals over the century despite an increase in their underlying fertility. We saw earlier that it is assumed that stopping behaviour was the sole mechanism of control in Britain's fertility transition. But Eilidh Garrett has discovered that young Yorkshire workers in a nineteenth-century textile town may have spaced their children early on in marriage.[36] The experience of the Kent and Yorkshire workers suggests that spacing should not be

---

[36]   E. M. Garrett, 'The trials of labour', *Continuity and Change*, 5 (1990), pp. 121–54. Simon Szreter will be arguing something similar in a forthcoming re-analysis of the 1911 fertility census. Vann and Eversley have raised the possibility of spacing behaviour among newly-married Quakers in pre-industrial southern England: Vann and Eversley, *Friends*, p. 162.

Table 2.11   *Mean last interconfinement interval and mean of all preceding intervals (in months) for women at the labouring level (by year of marriage)*

	Final number of confinements per married woman			
	3–6	7–10	11+	Total
Last interval				
1800–34	(45.6)	43.7	(32.9)	42.8
1835–49	(40.3)	55.7	(37.5)	47.3
1850–80	53.4	(46.7)	(26.7)	46.4
All preceding intervals				
1800–34	(30.8)	31.4	(29.3)	30.9
1835–49	(34.8)	30.1	(24.8)	30.8
1850–80	38.8	(27.4)	(23.1)	31.5

Results in parentheses are based on fewer than twenty cases. The average preceding intervals are calculated per woman rather than by each pooled interval.

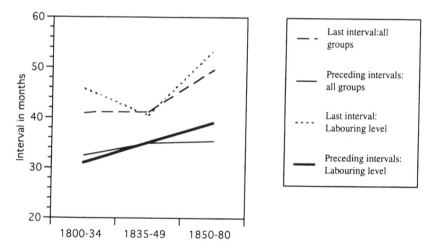

Figure 2.11 Mean last interconfinement interval and mean of all preceding intervals for women at the labouring level with 3–6 final confinements.

dismissed too readily as a means of regulating nineteenth-century fertility.

VII

When we examine the completed family sizes of our marriage cohorts we can see a decline over the century (see table 2.12). People were reducing their family sizes during the nineteenth century. Women who

Table 2.12   *Mean completed family size (number of children per family) for combined parishes and occupational groups by year of marriage*

	1800–34	1835–49	1850–64	1865–80
All parishes	7.6	6.5	6.1	5.9
Trades/Crafts	6.3	(5.2)	5.9 (for 1850–80)	
Farmers	8.8	–	(4.1) (for 1850–80)	
Ag. Lab./Lab.	7.6	6.8	6.5	6.1

Results in parentheses are based on fewer than twenty families; those based on fewer than ten are omitted. Note also that the completed family size includes those with no children.

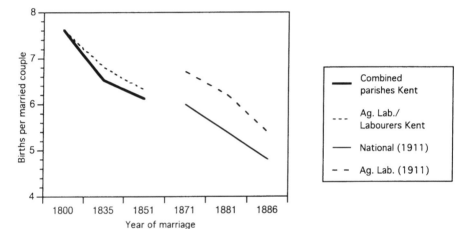

Figure 2.12 Number of children per family for combined parishes compared to 1911 national census data. (The 1911 figures come from Anderson, 'Social implications', p. 43, Table 1.4.)

married between 1865 and 1880 could expect to bear an average of 5.9 children, compared to the 7.6 of the generation married before 1835. The wives of agricultural labourers reduced their family sizes from 7.6 to 6.1. These averages are not vastly different from the national numbers calculated retrospectively from the 1911 census. Women married in 1871–80 had an average of 6.0 children; agricultural labourers had a mean of 6.7. Those marrying at the national level during the period 1886–91 would reduce their respective family sizes to 4.8 and 5.4; presumably the Blean parishes followed a similar path (see figure 2,12).[37]

[37]   The 1911 material comes from the figures provided in Anderson, 'Social implications', p. 43, Table 1.4.

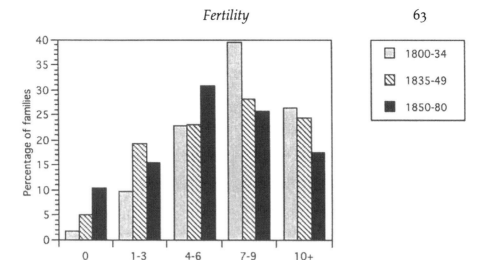

Figure 2.13 Distribution of completed family size by marriage cohort (combined parishes).

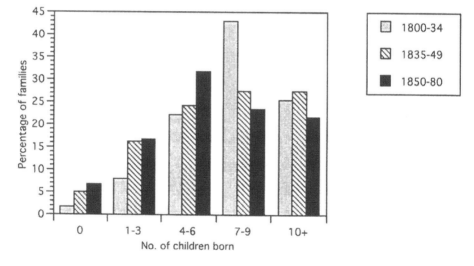

Figure 2.14 Distribution of completed family size by marriage cohort for labouring families (combined parishes).

The movement in means is not as informative as the figures which show shifts in distribution (see figures 2.13 and 2.14). At the start of the century the most common family size (number of children) was nine; by the last part of the century it had fallen to five. The full implications of England's population increase in the 'long' eighteenth century reveal themselves in the family sizes of the 1800–34 cohort: two-thirds (66 per cent) of all families had seven or more children; under a third produced completed family sizes of from one to six children. Those couples marrying from 1850–80, however, had reduced the proportion with seven or more children to 43 per cent; nearly half (46 per cent) experienced family sizes of from one to six.

VIII

This chapter has been schematic, deliberately so, establishing parameters rather than attempting explanations. None the less, it has clear ramifications for several current demographic orthodoxies.

The most significant fall in family size occurred in the period immediately following the institution of the New Poor Law of 1834, which raises the possibility that the transition may have begun earlier than has previously been thought. Indeed we have tended to concentrate on the contrasts between the 'natural' fertility cohort of 1800–34 and the later cohorts of 1850–80 or 1865–80, yet many of the significant changes in the various fertility indicators occurred in the marriage cohort of 1835–49 – those couples marrying immediately after the introduction of the New Poor Law (see table 2.13). For the index of fertility control (m), the final birth interval, and completed family size, the most substantial changes occurred between the cohorts of 1800–34 and 1835–49. The changes in age at last birth and percentage with 3–6 birth intervals were larger later in the century, but they were still significant after 1834. It was only female mean marriage ages which showed the least change for that cohort. Of course I have not canvassed other variables. One would need to chart economic fluctuations: depression in the rural sector for much of the period before 1850; improvement in the 1850s and 1860s; depression in the 1870s and 1880s. A host of pressures could have affected demographic developments during that period. But there is at least a prima facie case for re-thinking the role of the institution of the New Poor Law.

Knodel's detailed and wide-ranging demographic analysis of German village populations in the eighteenth and nineteenth centuries found little social variation in marital fertility: 'Perhaps the most striking feature for couples married between 1750 and 1849 is the general lack of substantial occupational differentials'.[38] However, it would be rash to generalize from these findings in the absence of English occupational detail in the Cambridge reconstitutions. The

---

[38] Knodel, 'Demographic transitions', p. 373.

Table 2.13   *Summary of indicators of fertility: changes from cohort to cohort (in points)*

	m index	Age at marriage	% with 3–6 births	Final birth interval	Age at last birth	Completed family size
1800–34	−0.08	22.1	29.4	40.3	40.7	7.6
Change	+0.34	+0.3	+6.1	+5.3	−1.2	−1.1
1835–49	0.26	22.4	35.5	45.8	39.5	6.5
Change	+0.06	+0.6	+7.7	−2.5	+0.2	−0.4
1850–64	0.33	23.0	43.2	43.3	39.7	6.1
Change	+0.08	+0.4	+5.2	+4.9	−1.3	−0.2
1865–80	0.41	23.4	48.4	48.2	38.4	5.9

demographic data base of the Blean study is small compared to that of the German villages and the Cambridge Group, but it does at least raise the possibility that marital fertility in the English natural fertility regime was not as 'homogeneous' as has been assumed.[39] The labouring population, farming families and couples involved in trading and the crafts had different levels of marital fertility. Knodel found 'more pronounced' occupational differences after 1850 as the various sectors of society began to take part in the fertility transition.[40] Here the Kent evidence would support the German village experience. Although all groups were beginning to participate in what would become known as the fertility decline, once again my findings suggest social or occupational variation, particularly when other demographic variables are taken into account. By the last marriage cohort of 1850–80, farming couples were marrying far later than the other main occupational groups, presumably in response to agricultural crisis, and had thereby reduced their completed family size to just over four.

This study has suggested that marital fertility played a role in English demographic history. In a recent summary of English population growth, E. A. Wrigley observed:

The matter is greatly simplified by the fact that there is no evidence suggesting any change in the level of marital fertility (that is the fertility of women once married) between the reigns of Elizabeth and Victoria. Age-specific marital fertility rates derived from family reconstitution studies do not change over time, nor do they differ from the marital fertility measures inferred from the mid-nineteenth century data collected in the early decades of civil registration.

---

[39]   By J. Cleland and C. Wilson, 'Demand theories of the fertility transition: an iconoclastic view', *Population Studies*, 41 (1987), p. 16.
[40]   Knodel, 'Demographic transitions', p. 373.

It follows that the increase in fertility must have been principally due to change in nuptiality: in the age at which women married and in the proportion who were never married.[41]

The findings for rural Kent do not challenge the importance of nuptiality as a driving force in the population history of England; indeed they confirm the low marriage ages for the early nineteenth century and the upward rise as the century progressed. But the Blean reconstitutions do suggest that demographers may have been somewhat premature in their willingness to slide quickly from 1800 to the 1870s, and with their assumptions that marital fertility was a constant in the fertility equation. The underlying level of marital fertility rose in the villages and hamlets of the nineteenth-century Blean and fertility control was carried out in the face of this increasing fecundity. Whether this was part of an English-wide change, reflected in the rising national marital fertility index for 1871, is worthy of further consideration.[42]

Findings from a few rural parishes will probably make little dent in the orthodoxy surrounding a topic the size of the British fertility decline. At one level it could be argued that the Kent parishes demonstrate the strength of the natural fertility regime, right to the eve of the fertility transition in the late nineteenth and early twentieth centuries. The fertility adjustments were relatively minor. But adjustments were made and it is instructive to see the transition in terms of a longer perspective. I have been at pains to stress that the nuanced changes in averages over the century mask rather more interesting and significant distributional shifts which, one assumes, reflect adjustments in fertility. The origins of the transition – in rural England at least – lay in the gradual adjustments of a small, gradually increasing, number of couples who were controlling their fertility. The tempo of fertility control intensified from the 1880s onwards, if the national figures are correct, and later in some areas of Britain, but the transition had begun a generation earlier. Michael Teitelbaum was incorrect when he set 'the onset of fertility decline' in 'the 1870s and later'.[43]

This does not overturn any notion of more rapid demographic change from the 1880s, but it does suggest that the orthodoxy of an almost overnight change in mentality and behaviour needs to be rethought. When, over ten years ago, John Knodel and Etienne van de Walle summarized the dynamics of Europe's demographic revolution,

41 E. A. Wrigley, 'Population growth: England, 1680–1820', *ReFresh*, 1 (1985), p. 3.
42 See Teitelbaum, *British fertility decline*, ch. 6. He seemed eager to explain away the rise.
43 *Ibid.*, p. 225.

they wrote of a 'shift from natural fertility to family limitation' which 'reflected a radical change in the reproductive behaviour of couples and societies. It was sudden and proceeded irreversibly until much lower levels of fertility were reached.' It represented a 'radical change in attitudes toward childbearing'. It 'occurred rapidly' and was 're-markably concentrated in time'. In England 'the starting date of the decline lay between 1890 and 1900 for almost all the 40 counties and for London as well'. A 'close communication network, combined with cultural homogeneity, made for almost simultaneous acceptance of family limitation throughout the country despite widely varying levels of urbanization and economic development'. Van de Walle and Knodel linked the decline to the 'spread of a new mentality – an openness to the idea of manipulating reproduction'. Again and again, they empha-sized the absence of deliberate fertility control before the transition, the sudden adoption of birth control and the rapidity of the transition.[44] The experience of the Blean contradicts almost all these assumptions. There was not a rapid break from natural fertility to family limitation so much as a series of adjustments within the natural fertility regime until family limitation began to dominate.[45] No change in *mentalité* need have occurred, merely more and more couples showing a will-ingness to control their family sizes through abortion, withdrawal and abstinence, the methods used (oral history indicates) well into the twentieth century. The demographic transition in the Blean, whenever it was completed, had a history which stretched back at least to the early nineteenth century; it did not come out of a clear sky in 1880 or 1890.

---

[44] E. van de Walle and J. Knodel, 'Europe's fertility transition: new evidence and lessons for today's developing world', *Population Bulletin*, 34 (1979), pp. 1–43. Woods, 'Approaches', p. 309, also stresses the rapid change in England in the 1870s, 1880s and 1890s.

[45] My chapter can also be read as part of a wider literature which is starting to question the uniformity of the European fertility decline as presented by the demographers of the Princeton European Fertility Project: see J. and P. Schneider, 'Demographic transitions in a Sicilian rural town', *Journal of Family History*, 9 (1984), pp. 245–72; D. Levine, 'Recombinant family formation strategies', *Journal of Historical Sociology*, 2 (1989), pp. 89–115; K. Ittmann, 'Family limitation and family economy in Bradford, west Yorkshire 1851–1881', *Journal of Social History*, 25 (1991–2), pp. 547–73; J. R. Gillis, L. A. Tilly and D. Levine (eds.), *The European experience of declining fertility: a quiet revolution, 1850–1970* (Oxford, 1992). As Levine has put it, we should think of 'multiple paths', 'not one but many fertility declines': D. Levine, 'Moments in time: a historian's context of declining fertility', in Gillis, Tilly and Levine (eds.), *European experience of declining fertility*, p. 329.

3

Health

In June 1838 the bodies of men killed by the military in England's last rising of agricultural labourers were interred in the churchyards of Hernhill and Boughton-under-Blean. The dead leader of the abortive insurrection, an imposter, the self-styled Sir William Courtenay, was buried on the morning of 5 June. His followers, all men from the Blean area of Kent, followed him to their graves in the afternoon: three men in their twenties, two in their early thirties, two in their forties and one aged 62. (Poor relief paid for five of the coffins.) Newspaper reporters had an opportunity to observe, first-hand, the impact of these losses on the local community. They wrote, poignantly, of a people in grief. A woman sat outside a cottage in Hernhill, the last in a row of 'neat' labourers' dwellings: 'Her back was to the road, and her eye fixed on the house, while every moment her body could be observed shaking and trembling as if she were struggling against some frightful emotion'. 'In walking through the village I heard the voice of wailing in almost every house'. 'Another woman I heard singing most dolefully to a young child she held in her arms, and ever and anon breaking off to bewail her dear, dear husband.' A week later, a reporter attended Hernhill church to assess the mood of the congregation. It was as if 'some great national calamity' had occurred. Labouring men, with black crape on their hats, gathered in the churchyard. The women were 'dressed in deep mourning'. In Boughton, too, 'there was a gloom on the faces of a larger portion of the labouring classes'.

Such a swath of mortality among men of that age was unusual in the rural world of early Victorian England – hence the desolation described by the newspapers. This is not to say that death was a stranger to the inhabitants of the Blean. But it was the death of the very young that

Plate 16 Cemetery and public house (Red Lion) in Hernhill at the turn of the century.

marked the mortality regime which governed their lives. Many of those who turned out in the Hernhill rising had lost children in infancy or early childhood. William Rye, an agricultural labourer killed in 1838, had lost three of his eight children as infants. Edward Wraight, another fatality, had six surviving children out of a total of eleven (three had perished as infants and two as children).[1]

Oral histories reveal similar experiences of young death. Harold Kay (born 1921), from a small farming family, was the second of thirteen children, two of whom died at birth. His father was from a family of nine, but four had died at birth or shortly thereafter. Harold recalled the tiny coffins of the parish young, so small that they were merely carried under the arm of the undertaker, the local wheelwright and carpenter.[2] Lydia Boorman (born 1916) came from a family of 'about thirteen children, only eight survived'.[3] Elsie Foster (born 1908) lost a 5-year-old brother, scalded to death before she was born. She could also remember the death of her eldest sister's 2-year-old child when

---

[1] See B. Reay, *The last rising of the agricultural labourers* (Oxford, 1990), pp. 132, 157–9.
[2] Hernhill Oral History, H. Kay, b. 1921. The Hernhill Oral History Tapes are interviews which I carried out in 1991–2.
[3] Hernhill Oral History, L. Boorman, b. 1916.

Elsie herself was only 4. He 'lay there in his coffin and they couldn't keep me out of the room. I sat beside him for hours':

> I believe he was the only one I ever saw when I was young. But it fascinated me, they couldn't keep me out; when they couldn't find me there was I sitting there holding his hand. He was two and I was four ... Yes, I can see him there now, laying there. Pretty little boy he was. My mother used to say he was too pretty to live, too good to live; he was a nice little boy.[4]

The people of the Blean and other parts of rural England lived with such young deaths into the 1920s and 1930s. Today in England only about 1 to 2 per cent of children are dead by the age of 5; in early Victorian England the figure was from 25 to 28 per cent. Even as late as 1921 the rates were from 11 to 13 per cent.[5] This slow demographic transition, from high to low mortality, is one of the great transformations of the modern world.

Yet we know remarkably little about health and mortality in the rural areas of nineteenth-century England. As with so many areas of that century's social history, the focus has been on the towns.[6] Even the relatively well-researched field of the history of infant mortality has little to say about rural experiences and trends. We are told that infant mortality rates were lower in rural than in urban areas and that they declined earlier than the 1899–1900 turning point for the national decline in infant mortality.[7] As for other aspects of rural health and mortality, most accounts go little further than to note the relatively high life expectancy of the agricultural labourer.[8] In short, rural health does not rate highly on the agenda of either medical or rural historians and its limited literature conveys a rather optimistic impression. The

---

[4] Hernhill Oral History, E. Foster, b. 1908.

[5] M. Anderson, 'The social implications of demographic change', in F. M. L. Thompson (ed.), *The Cambridge social history of Britain 1750–1950*, vol. II, *People and their environment* (Cambridge, 1990), p. 27, Table 1.2.

[6] This applies to the basic texts, F. B. Smith, *The people's health 1830–1910* (London, 1979) and A. S. Wohl, *Endangered lives: public health in Victorian Britain* (London, 1983), as well as the best recent monograph on nineteenth-century diseases, A. Hardy, *The epidemic streets: infectious disease and the rise of preventive medicine 1856–1900* (Oxford, 1993).

[7] R. Woods, 'The effects of population redistribution on the level of mortality in eighteenth- and nineteenth-century England and Wales: revisited and revised' (paper prepared for the Conference on Demographic Change in Economic Development, Hitotsubashi University, Tokyo, December 1991, a revised version of an article which first appeared in *Journal of Economic History*, 45 (1985)); Woods, 'Infant mortality in Britain, 1850–1950: variation in levels and the process of change' (a paper prepared for the Workshop on the Decline of Infant Mortality in Europe, 1850–1950, Florence, April 1992).

[8] A. Armstrong, *Farmworkers: a social and economic history 1770–1980* (London, 1988), pp. 140–1. Alun Howkins' otherwise admirable book has nothing at all on rural health: *Reshaping rural England: a social history 1850–1925* (London, 1991).

aim of this chapter is to sketch out some possibilities for a medical–
social history of nineteenth-century rural England and to raise the
prospect of a somewhat more pessimistic interpretation.[9]

[9] Most of the English family reconstitution studies which deal with mortality focus on
the early-modern period: see E. A. Wrigley, 'Mortality in pre-industrial England: the
example of Colyton, Devon, over three centuries', *Daedalus*, 97 (1968), pp. 546–80;
D. Levine, *Family formation in an age of nascent capitalism* (New York, 1977); R. Schofield and E. A. Wrigley, 'Infant and child mortality in England in the late Tudor and
early Stuart period', in C. Webster (ed.), *Health, medicine and mortality in the sixteenth
century* (Cambridge, 1979), ch. 2; E. A. Wrigley and R. S. Schofield, 'English population history from family reconstitution: summary results 1600–1799', *Population
Studies*, 37 (1983), pp. 157–84; K. Wrightson and D. Levine, 'Death in Whickham', in J.
Walter and R. Schofield (eds.), *Famine, disease and the social order in early modern society*
(Cambridge, 1989), ch. 3; R. T. Vann and D. Eversley, *Friends in life and death*
(Cambridge, 1992), ch. 5; J. Landers, *Death and the metropolis: studies in the demographic
history of London, 1670–1830* (Cambridge, 1993). See also Knodel's important work on
Germany: J. E. Knodel, *Demographic behavior in the past* (Cambridge, 1988). I have
followed the conventions of family reconstitution set out by E. A. Wrigley, 'Family
reconstitution', in Wrigley (ed.), *An introduction to English historical demography* (New
York, 1966), ch. 4; Wrigley, 'Mortality in pre-industrial England'; and Knodel,
Demographic behavior. The calculations of infant and child mortality, probability of
dying by occupation of father, and birth intervals are based on family reconstitution.
However, I employed the technique of aggregative analysis to obtain the figures for
the seasonality of burials: see D. E. C. Eversley, 'Exploitation of parish registers by
aggregative analysis', in Wrigley (ed.), *Introduction to English historical demography*, ch.
3; M. Drake (ed.), *Population studies from parish registers* (Matlock, 1982). The burial
registers after 1813 provide information on the age at death, so it makes the
calculation of burial seasonality by aggregative analysis relatively easy. The endo-
genous rate for the three parishes in the second half of the nineteenth century (those
dying before the age of one month) was 28.7 per 1,000 births, encouragingly similar to
the Registrar General's breakdowns at mid century (see E. A. Wrigley, 'Births and
baptisms', *Population Studies*, 31 (1977), p. 302). For calculations of infant mortality at
the occupational and hamlet level it was necessary to use the family reconstitution
data. The problem here is that because there was a delay between birth and baptism,
often of two months in this part of the country, there will be an under-registration of
infant deaths in the reconstitutions – infant deaths never linked to the appropriate
parents because the infant died before it could be baptized. To compensate for this
under-registration I have adjusted the reconstitution infant mortality rates by the
ratio:

parish infant mortality rate by aggregative analysis
parish infant mortality rate by family reconstitution

that is, by the ratio 1.325. (The correction ratio used by Wrigley and Schofield in their
calculations for 1750–99 was 1.241: Wrigley and Schofield, 'English population
history', p. 178.) The aggregative analysis rate was calculated from the baptisms in the
Church of England and Methodist registers (to get the number at risk) and burials
recorded by the Church of England (to get the number dying). The Methodists in the
area (Wesleyan and Primitive) baptized their infants both in the established church
and in their own chapel; they used the Church of England for burials. It is possible
that there is still a slight under-estimation of infant mortality. One of my oral history
informants in Boughton (Harry Wheeler, b. 1912) told me that it was not unheard of
for premature and unbaptized infants to be handed to one of the local undertakers, a
builder, for burial. He recalls that people who purchased the builder's property, many
years later, encountered bones every time they dug in the garden. A man from

II

Let us start with infant and child mortality which are usually treated as proxies for wider standards of living: as Richard Vann and David Eversley have put it, 'quality and quantity of life come close together'.[10] Table 3.1 sets out trends in infant and child mortality in our three (combined) parishes over the nineteenth century. Our current view of infant mortality in nineteenth-century rural England depends almost entirely on the work of R. I. Woods and (as we saw) his theme is one of contrasting urban and rural experiences: rural rates were lower and fell earlier than the national decline after 1900. Although rates rose in the towns over the century, there was a long-term decline in rural infant mortality from 1701 to 1911.[11] It is clear from table 3.1 and figure 3.1 that infant mortality in our hamlets and villages moved in the opposite direction to Woods' national rural trend, increasing by 60 per cent from the birth cohort of 1800–34 to that of 1865–80. The rate for 1865–80 is higher than his estimated figure of 125 infant deaths per 1,000 live births for rural areas in 1881.

There are also clear age differentials. The mortality rate for children aged 1–4 rose until mid century and then fell. The rate for those aged 5–9 rose initially and then fell; and the mortality of older children (10–14) declined steadily. As Knodel found of nineteenth-century German villages, infant and child mortality followed 'divergent paths'.[12] The probability of dying by age 5 and by age 10 increased over the nineteenth century by 44 per cent and 31 per cent respectively (see table 3.2), due largely to the rise in infant mortality. Expectation of life at birth was 50 years for the family reconstitution cohort of 1800–34; for those of 1835–49, 1850–64 and 1865–80 it was 47.5 years.[13]

It is possible that the figures for the combined parishes mask some local variations. Table 3.3 charts parish differences in infant mortality. The rates converge for the last cohort, but until then there was a wide range of parish mortality levels. Clearly infants were more at risk if they lived in the parish of Dunkirk. But life chances were even more localized than this. By linking family reconstitutions to the parish listings for consecutive censuses, it is possible to determine where

Hernhill (Harold Kay, b. 1921) said that one of his sisters, born prematurely, was buried in the garden of his father's house.

[10] Eversley and Vann, *Friends*, p. 186.

[11] Woods, 'Effects'; Woods, 'Infant mortality'.

[12] Knodel, *Demographic behavior*, p. 40.

[13] Estimated by matching infant and child mortality rates against the Model West Life Tables in A. J. Coale and P. Demeny, *Regional model life tables and stable populations* (New York, 1983), pp. 47–8.

Table 3.1   *Infant and child mortality (rate/1,000) by date of birth for combined parishes, 1800–80*

Age	Date of birth			
	1800–34	1835–49	1850–64	1865–80
Infant	87.8 [694]	100.8 [552]	109.4 [484]	140.6 [396]
1–4	62.1	96.2	108.8	77.8
5–9	33.7	48.5	23.1	23.3
10–14	27.2	25.9	13.6	8.8

The figures in parentheses indicate the number of infants at risk for each cohort.

Table 3.2   *Probability of dying by age 5 and age 10 (combined parishes), 1800–80*

Date of birth	1800–34	1835–49	1850–64	1865–80
5 q 0	0.144	0.187	0.206	0.208
10 q 0	0.173	0.226	0.224	0.226

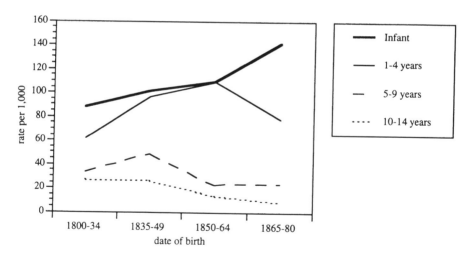

Figure 3.1 Infant and child mortality trends (rate/1,000) for combined parishes, 1800–80.

Table 3.3   *Infant mortality (rate/1,000) by parish, 1800–80*

	Date of birth			
	1800–34	1835–49	1850–64	1865–80
Boughton	86.1	72.3	76.3	148.8
Dunkirk	–	128.2	148.2	131.2
Hernhill	110.8	102.8	112.8	134.9
All	87.8	100.8	109.4	140.6
Total at risk	694	552	484	396

families lived when their children were born and growing up. This can bring analysis down to the hamlet level. Table 3.4 sets out the infant and child mortality rates for families living in the hamlet of Staple Street in Hernhill and for the settlements of Horse Lees and Boughton Common (on the boundary of Dunkirk and Boughton). The mortality of infants and very young children is high. The infant mortality rate for rural Horse Lees is more in keeping with figures for nineteenth-century Liverpool than with the benign rural rates that we have been led to expect.[14] The rates for 1–4 year olds in Staple Street and Horse Lees would not look out of place in twentieth-century Nepal or Bangladesh.[15] Almost a third of the children in late nineteenth-century Horse Lees did not live to the age of 5. While infant mortality levels in the Blean did not conform to national rural experience at a macro level, the microhistory of the Blean certainly reinforces another of Woods' themes: the sheer range of mortality experience in nineteenth-century England.[16]

Locality clearly influenced mortality levels, but what of social variation? The probability of dying, by occupation of father, is set out in table 3.5. These aggregates hide trends over the century. The mortality of the infants of labouring families was 140.4 per 1,000 for the cohort 1865–80, while the rate for the trades and crafts was only 96.7. But in the period 1800–34 the infants of men earning a living in the trades and crafts had been dying at the rate of 131.7 per 1,000. Over the century, then, the infant mortality of trades and crafts families

[14] Woods, 'Effects', p. 4, Table 3.
[15] S. O. Rutstein, *Infant and child mortality*, World Fertility Survey Comparative Studies, vol. XLIII (pamphlet, 1984), p. 17, Figure 2.
[16] R. Woods, 'Mortality patterns in the past', in R. Woods and J. Woodward (eds.), *Urban disease and mortality in nineteenth-century England* (New York, 1984), ch. 2. See also, C. H. Lee, 'Regional inequalities in infant mortality in Britain, 1861–1971: patterns and hypotheses', *Population Studies*, 45 (1991), pp. 55–65. The same was true of the period 1600–1799: Wrigley and Schofield, 'English population history', pp. 178–9.

Table 3.4 *Infant and child mortality (rate/1,000) at the hamlet level,*
1840–80

	Infant	1–4	5–9	10–14
Staple Street	132.5	119.7	29.1	10.5
Horse Lees/Boughton				
Common	215.0	117.6	37.3	27.6

The total numbers of infants at risk were small: 130 for Staple Street and 228 for Horse Lees.

Table 3.5 *Probability of dying, by occupation*
of father (combined parishes), 1800–80

	5 q 0	10 q 0
Trades/Crafts	0.198	0.210
Farmers	0.156	0.175
Ag. Lab./Lab.	0.185	0.217

declined while that of labourers rose. So there were some social differences. As table 3.5 shows, the children of farming families certainly stood a better chance of survival.

Yet it is the local variation which stands out. Our figures would seem to indicate that place rather than occupation exerted the more telling influence on mortality in these parishes.[17]

III

Another way of approaching health in the past is through patterns in the seasonality of mortality. As in other communities, the seasonality of mortality varied with age.[18] A comparison between figures 3.2 and 3.3 shows the importance of providing an age breakdown in discussions of the seasonality of death. The basic pattern of figure 3.2

---

[17] Knodel, *Demographic behavior*, p. 71; E. Garrett and A. Reid, 'Satanic mills, pleasant lands: spatial variation in women's work, fertility and infant mortality as viewed from the 1911 census', *Historical Research*, 67 (1994), pp. 156–77. My intention is not to deny class differentials in infant mortality, but simply to suggest that they may have been more muted (at some levels) in the villages. For class variations, see R. I. Woods, P. A. Watterson and J. H. Woodward, 'The causes of rapid infant mortality decline in England and Wales, 1861–1921 Part I', *Population Studies*, 42 (1988), pp. 363–5. And for a fascinating case study of the interaction between environment and class, see N. Williams, 'Death in its season: class, environment and the mortality of infants in nineteenth-century Sheffield', *Social History of Medicine*, 5 (1992), pp. 71–94.

[18] Schofield and Wrigley, 'Infant and child mortality'.

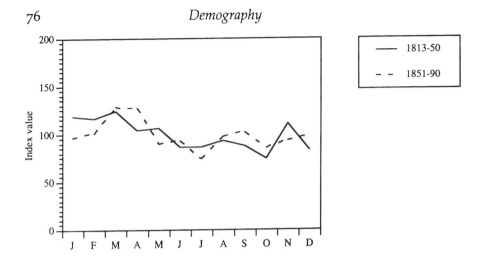

Figure 3.2 Indexed total burial seasonality (all age groups), combined parishes, 1813–90.

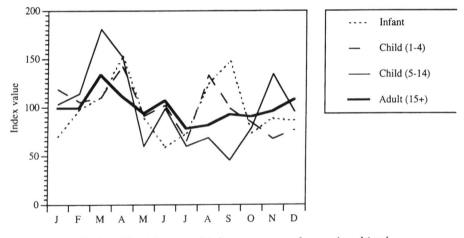

Figure 3.3 Indexed burial seasonality by age group, 1851–90 (combined parishes).

(combined burials) clearly obscures the complexity of age differentials set out for the second half of the century in figure 3.3.

The contrast in figure 3.3 between younger and older children is clear. The very young (1–4) exhibit a similar pattern to infants, with twin peaks in late summer–autumn and spring mortality; they, like infants, were susceptible to the diarrhoeal infections of the warm weather (more of which later) and to the respiratory ailments of the late winter and spring. It is probable that these twin peaks reflect some deaths from malaria, a disease which afflicted all age groups but which proved more fatal to the young.[19] The parishes, particularly Hernhill, bordered the marshes, malarial country, and mosquitoes must have thrived in the ill-drained, cesspool conditions which, as we will see, characterized some of the hamlets. The Medical Officer of Health noted in 1884 that:

the heat of the weather in the summer months developed a large amount of Malaria with the effect that Malarious Fever became very prevalent. In olden times these fevers were designated "low fever" both by the public, and by the profession, but they are now distinguished as Enteric, Typhoid, Gastric &c. &c. but mostly in this locality derive their origin from Marsh Malaria, and spread by contagion when suitable cases come in contact with persons suffering from the disorder.

In 1886 he observed deaths in Hernhill and Boughton from fever which 'probably owed its origin to malaria'.[20] The total mortality pattern for the three parishes conveyed in figure 3.2 is not the same as that charted by Mary Dobson for malaria parishes, so it is unlikely that this part of the Blean was a major malarial area.[21] But infant and child seasonality conforms to the malaria mortality highs of autumn and spring, so the disease probably had some effect. Contained too in figure 3.3, though it would be difficult to locate the seasonality with any accuracy, would be deaths due to diseases which particularly hit children and infants under 5 – whooping cough, scarlet fever, measles and (to a lesser extent) diphtheria – which, as we will discuss, were present in the area. Indeed Anne Hardy has argued that measles mortality helped to sustain the death rate of the under-fives in the decades up to 1900.[22]

The mortality of older children (5–14) forms an exaggerated image of the adult pattern: low in late summer and autumn, at a maximum in winter and spring. Again the winter and spring peak reflects the results of respiratory infections. Influenza was particularly active in the first half of the year. A Faversham diarist recorded the combination of cold and ill-health in his entry for 24 April 1837:

[19] M. Dobson, '"Marsh fever" – the geography of malaria in England', *Journal of Historical Geography*, 6 (1980), p. 375.

[20] PRO, MH 12/5068, Ministry of Health Poor Law Papers, Faversham Correspondence, Report of Medical Officer of Health of Rural District for 1884; PRO, MH 12/5069, Report of Medical Officer of Health of Rural District for 1886.

[21] Compare Dobson, '"Marsh fever"', p. 381, Figure 13.

[22] C. Creighton, *A history of epidemics in Britain*, vol. II (London, 1965 edn), pp. 664, 672, 729, 742–3; Smith, *People's health*, pp. 104–11, 136–52; Hardy, *Epidemic streets*, pp. 28, 59; A. Hardy, 'Rickets and the rest: child-care, diet and the infectious children's diseases, 1850–1914', *Social History of Medicine*, 5 (1992), pp. 392–5.

The first warm day this spring, the white-thorn buds did not open until about the 18th. inst. From October [1836] the thermometer ranged from 32 degrees freezing to 45 deg.; seldom higher; the wind nearly the whole of this time north east with frequent cold rains and showers of sleet or snow. This was followed with so unhealthy an atmosphere that the influenza raged in consequence; scarcely a family escaped without some of its members being affected; in others, the whole of them, and many deaths were the result.[23]

But the peak would also include mortality caused by the main child-hood diseases. Although measles, diphtheria and scarlet fever were to be found during most parts of the year, sickness was concentrated in the winter and spring. Mortality was often due not to the disease itself but to secondary pneumonia and this was more likely in the colder months.[24]

IV

But it is the seasonal pattern of infant mortality that is of most interest. Not only was infant mortality increasing over the century, but figure 3.4 shows that the increase was accompanied by a remarkable change in the pattern of mortality as its seasonality shifted radically in the second half of the century. The autumnal peak – first in August and then in September – is clear and forms the classic pattern of diarrhoea mortality.[25] It also raises an intriguing parallel with developments in Germany where there was a similar change in the seasonality of mortality.[26] Attempts to explain the German phenomenon have focused on breastfeeding, suggesting that the changes in seasonality reflect a change in feeding patterns to earlier weaning or increased supplemental feeding and that this shift may have arisen in response to 'the increasing demands made on women's time by agricultural activities such as harvesting'.[27] Rudolph Bell's research on rural Italy found local peaks in infant mortality – in July and August in some parts and in August, September and even November in others – which

---

[23] CKS, FA/Z 41/2, E. Crow, 'Historical Gleanings Relative to the Town of Faversham and Parishes Adjoining', p. 114.

[24] Smith, *People's health*, p. 143; L. Bradley, 'An enquiry into seasonality in baptisms, marriages and burials. Part 3: burial seasonality', in Drake (ed.), *Population studies from parish registers*, p. 89; Hardy, *Epidemic streets*, p. 45.

[25] See Williams, 'Death in its season', pp. 85–6, Table 1 and Figure 6. See also, G. Mooney, 'Did London pass the "sanitary test"? Seasonal infant mortality in London, 1870–1914', *Journal of Historical Geography*, 20 (1994), pp. 158–74.

[26] Knodel, *Demographic behavior*, p. 63. Compare my figure 3.4 with his Figure 3.6.

[27] Knodel, *Demographic behavior*, p. 66. For a Swedish perspective on the complexity of the subject, see A. Brandstrom, 'The impact of female labour conditions on infant mortality: a case study of the parishes of Nedertornea and Jokkmokk, 1800–96', *Social History of Medicine*, 1 (1988), pp. 329–58.

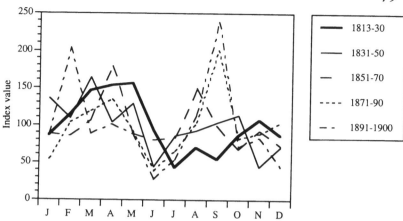

Figure 3.4 Indexed seasonality of infant burials by year of birth, 1813–1900 (combined parishes).

he linked to 'maternal absence' at specific harvests (wheat, figs, olives and mushrooms).[28]

Medical experts in the Blean area were convinced of a connection between infant deaths and feeding practices. The Medical Officer for the rural area around Faversham observed in his annual report for 1881 that 'many of the infants in this locality are fed from bottles and often left for hours while the mothers are at work in the brickfields & factories &c'.[29] A report from the urban sanitary authority noted the way in which 'diarrhoea and many other intestinal diseases … decimate infant life' and attributed the extensive mortality to bacteria and decomposing milk in the long-tubed bottles favoured in Faversham.[30] Another report in 1885 wrote of the 'injudicious feeding' within the jurisdiction of the urban authority; 'hand feeding is common and the use of starchy foods for young infants almost universal with the less educated classes'.[31] And in 1886 a large imbalance of deaths in the rural district for the third quarter of the year (July, August, September) was attributed 'largely' to diarrhoea: 'a peculiar state of the atmosphere existed rendering "milk" rapidly putrid, and hence those children brought up with cow's milk became attacked with sickness and diarrhoea, and rapidly succumbed'.[32]

[28] R. M. Bell, *Fate and honor, family and village: demographic and cultural change in rural Italy since 1800* (Chicago, 1979), pp. 35–41.
[29] PRO, MH 12/5067, Report of Rural Sanitary Authority for 1881.
[30] *Ibid.*, Report of Urban Sanitary Authority for 1881.
[31] PRO, MH 12/5069, Report of Medical Officer of Health of Rural District for 1885.
[32] *Ibid.*, Report of Medical Officer of Health of Rural District for 1886.

We know from the demographic data that the women of the Blean weaned their children earlier than in the Cambridge Group's eighteenth-century English parishes and than in those areas of rural Germany where breastfeeding was extensive.[33] Indeed the demo-

---

[33] Family reconstitution provides what John Knodel has described as 'indirect evidence' of breastfeeding patterns through the calculation of birth intervals. 'The rationale is based on the well-established finding that breastfeeding typically postpones the resumption of ovulation in women following birth and thus extends the postpartum period when a woman is not susceptible to conception. As a result, breastfeeding lengthens the average interval to the next birth' (Knodel, *Demographic behavior*, p. 545). The debate about the effects of breastfeeding on ovulation is complicated and lactation's supposed contraceptive role appears to depend on a number of variables: the duration and amount of feeding, whether supplementary feeding takes place. One study has calculated that 'it is in the period from ten to twenty months after giving birth that lactation would do the most to prevent a further conception'. Even without breastfeeding – taking into account a period of post-birth amenorrhea, the potential of miscarriage, and the time required for the next conception – birth intervals could last an average of 21 months (Eversley and Vann, *Friends*, pp. 147, 166–8). However, women who nursed their babies extended the interval; Knodel found that in breastfeeding villages the intervals could be as high as 30 months, whereas in places where the practice was least extensive intervals were down to just under 20 months (Knodel, *Demographic behavior*, pp. 542–9). In short, in natural fertility regimes the postpartum non-susceptible period is longer for populations where breastfeeding is common. Historical demographers test for breastfeeding patterns in the past with two basic measurements: the calculation of the difference between the interval between the first and second confinements and the interval to first birth (that is the difference between a possibly breastfed interval and an obviously non-breastfed one); and the difference between the interval where a child survives beyond age 1 (where the mother could be lactating) and that when the child dies before age 1 (where the mother is unlikely to be breastfeeding beyond a year). The figures for the Kent villages are set out below.

Measurements of changes in the postpartum non-susceptible period (NSP) in months

(a) *Estimated NSP (i)*

Year of marriage	Interval to first birth	Interval between first and second births	Difference (est. NSP) in months
Combined parishes			
1800–34	21.1	25.7	4.6
1835–49	(21.4)	(27.5)	(6.1)
1850–80	16.4	25.6	9.2
Boughton			
1800–34	(23.1)	(25.4)	(2.3)
1835–49	(25.8)	(28.5)	(2.7)
1850–80	(16.7)	(26.9)	(10.2)
Hernhill			
1800–34	(18.0)	(26.4)	(8.4)
1835–49	(18.5)	(27.5)	(9.0)
1850–80	(15.7)	(24.4)	(8.7)

Note: for women whose first child was baptized more than 8 months after marriage and with at least two confinements; results based on less than 100 cases are in parentheses and those on less than 20 are omitted.

graphic measurements of the extent of breastfeeding match those described by Knodel as 'least extensive' and 'intermediate' in his table for nineteenth-century German villages.[34] This would correspond neatly to later local oral history evidence which places weaning at around 6 or 8 months. Whether weaning was voluntary or because of working mothers' inability to lactate we have no real way of knowing. Ian Buchanan has certainly argued that involuntary cessation of breastfeeding was a factor in the coalfield areas at this time.[35]

What we do not have is direct evidence that bottle-feeding was favoured by field workers. Harold Kay could not remember any bottle-feeding in Hernhill until the 1940s. Babies were breastfed until they went on to solids at about 8 months. He could recall having 'often' seen women in the fields breastfeeding; they would take prams into the fields for pea-picking, for example.[36] Dorothy Tong, who was born in 1912, said that in the Boughton–Dunkirk area most of the women breastfed until the infant was 6 or 8 months, 'and then we used to cook the food and mash it all up'. She could also remember babies being

(b) Estimated NSP (ii)

Year of marriage	Child born at onset of interval dies before age 1	Child born at onset of interval survives	Difference (est. NSP) in months
Combined parishes			
1800–34	(22.1)	27.4	5.3
1835–49	21.3	(30.2)	8.9
1850–80	(18.5)	24.6	6.1

Note: final birth intervals are omitted; results based on less than 100 cases are in parentheses and those on less than 20 are omitted.

Chris Wilson has explained the modest marital fertility rates in his pre-1800 English parishes as the result of extended breastfeeding: mothers probably suckled their children for at least a year, possibly for as long as 16 months (C. Wilson, 'The proximate determinants of marital fertility in England 1600–1799', in L. Bonfield, R. M. Smith and K. Wrightson (eds.), *The world we have gained* (Oxford, 1986), pp. 219–24). The short Kent NSPs – shorter than the 12-month averages for the Cambridge Group's reconstitutions – suggest that either breastfeeding for extended periods was confined to small sections of the community, that breastfeeding was for shorter periods, or that supplemental feeding was introduced to the child at an early stage in its development. The NSP results may explain the relatively high fertility of the Kent reconstitutions in comparison to the Cambridge Group parishes (see chapter 2), but they do not seem to reflect any movement away from breastfeeding in Kent during the nineteenth century. If anything, change was in the other direction, as witnessed by the increase in NSP after 1850 for Boughton where it is possible that women were returning to nursing.

[34] Wilson, 'Determinants', pp. 219–24; Knodel, *Demographic behavior*, pp. 542–9, esp. p. 546, Table F.1.

[35] I. Buchanan, 'Infant feeding, sanitation and diarrhoea in colliery communities 1880–1911', in D. J. Oddy and D. S. Miller (eds.), *Diet and health in modern Britain* (Dover, New Hampshire, 1985), pp. 155–7.

[36] Hernhill Oral History, H. Kay, b. 1921.

taken out into the fields in trucks or trolleys. Dorothy considered breastfeeding more compatible with field work than the bottle. 'Most of them breastfed out there, because it was such a bind if you'd got to take a bottle'.[37] Nor is there any demographic evidence for a mid nineteenth-century reduction in durations of breastfeeding of a kind that would account for the trends in seasonal infant mortality. The lack of extended breastfeeding which characterized the parishes of the Blean was as true of the 1800s as it was of the 1880s.[38]

But if mothers were not reducing their periods of breastfeeding to meet the demands of agricultural work and may not have been bottle-feeding when they did, it is still possible that some were timing their weaning to coincide with particular harvests. It is the September peak in mortality that is prominent in the second half of the nineteenth century, and September was the month of hopping, so vital to the household economies of labouring families in the area until well into the twentieth century.[39] It may well have been that rather than forcing women to early bottle-feeding – as happened with regular factory work – seasonal agricultural work merely encouraged some of those with infants of weanable age to move them off the breast before harvesting began (the comments of Dorothy Tong notwithstanding). They were weaned and possibly left with older sisters or relatives, or simply wheeled out into the fields when the risks of infection from contaminated food and drink were at their height. The more refined infant mortality patterns for the second half of the nineteenth century, set out in figure 3.5, are certainly compatible with such an interpretation. The September peaks in mortality of children of weanable age in the second half of the nineteenth century may mirror an increase in the importance of hops in the local economy.[40]

However, there is a further factor. In an important study of infant feeding and sanitation in late nineteenth- and early twentieth-century mining communities in Wales and northern England, Buchanan discovered a similar peak in autumnal mortality due to endemic diarrhoea. This, he argued, was due mainly to the role of the house-fly, with breeding habits determined by earth rather than air temperature

---

[37] Hernhill Oral History, D. Tong, b. 1912.
[38] See footnote 33.   [39] See chapter 4.
[40] The total acreage of hops in the three parishes almost doubled between 1840 and 1870 – from 370 to over 700 acres – and then remained stable through to 1890. My calculations are based on the tithe and agricultural returns: PRO, IR 29/17/41, Boughton Tithe Apportionment Award 1840; IR 29/17/178, Hernhill Tithe Apportionment Award 1840; MAF 68/246/13, Agricultural Returns: Parish Summaries, Kent, 1870; MAF 68/702/17, Agricultural Returns: Parish Summaries, Kent, 1880; MAF 68/1272/17, Agricultural Returns: Parish Summaries, Kent, 1890.

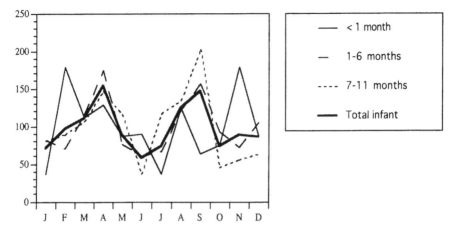

Figure 3.5 Infant sub-group burial seasonality, 1851–90 (combined parishes).

and therefore more active in the autumn. A change in weather at the end of the century, combined with poor sanitation, rather than any significant increase in artificial feeding (although artificially fed infants were more vulnerable), explained the endemic diarrhoea and the correspondingly high total infant mortality rates of up to 244 per 1,000 live births.[41]

The ingredients for a similar scenario were present in the parishes of Boughton, Dunkirk and Hernhill. As we have seen, infants were weaned at a relatively early age and were therefore vulnerable to infection from contaminated food or drink. Summers were dry and hot in the latter part of the nineteenth century – this has already been established and linked to rising infant mortality in the urban areas at a national level.[42] Sanitation was poor. Diarrhoea was directly linked to sanitation – whether it was contaminated water, or food or drink infected by the ubiquitous fly, the vector linking humans to the bacteria found on household and animal waste. And we know that conditions were deteriorating in parts of the nineteenth-century Blean. Drainage in the rural districts was generally of the cesspool system, though there were open drains in Boughton. Houses, or groups of houses, would have a cesspool for drainage, a midden for household refuse, a vault privy (simply a hole sunk into the ground) and a well for their water supply. Over time the filth and pollution of cesspool, privy and midden could find their way into the water course and the nearby

[41] Buchanan, 'Infant feeding'.
[42] Woods, Watterson and Woodward, 'Causes', p. 362.

well. There were moves to improve the water supply, to clean up rubbish, to replace the vault privy with the disposable earth or pail closets and to improve drainage, but little was accomplished in the nineteenth century.[43]

An outbreak of diphtheria in Hernhill in 1878–9 prompted an enquiry into sanitary conditions in the hamlet of Staple Street, a fortunate coincidence for the historian for this was one of the hamlets with high infant mortality. A total of nine wells in the hamlet supplied thirty-two houses and a population of 190: all the wells were found to be polluted by sewage percolation. The report considered that the principal source of contamination was agricultural refuse (manure and other decaying matter) in the surrounding fields and farms which had polluted 'the whole substratum of water percolation'; 'local causes' were thought to be only a contributory factor – 'such as manure heaps, cesspools & refuse matters "always found more or less in all back yards"'.[44] Some of the most heavily polluted wells were closed, but the problem remained. In the late 1890s the water of Staple Street was still being described as 'polluted to a very great extent' and notice was served on landlords to provide wholesome water to their tenants.[45] There is no reason to suppose that Staple Street was unique in its deteriorating sanitation – it merely came under the spotlight because of a diphtheria epidemic which, one assumes, had little to do with polluted wells. Our interest lies with the conditions described in the wake of the epidemic: manure pits, seeping cesspools, stinking privies, pig sties close to houses, badly drained sheds and stables, polluted wells. This was the ideal environment for fly-borne, endemic diarrhoea. These local black-spots in sanitation also help to explain the importance of the locality as a determiner of infant mortality levels.

To conclude, breastfeeding patterns did not change dramatically in the nineteenth century in a way that would account for the trends in seasonal infant mortality traced in the burial registers. Infant feeding practices – the lack of extended breastfeeding – certainly made the increase in mortality possible but they do not seem to have changed markedly during the nineteenth century. I would favour a multi-causal

---

[43] PRO, MH 12/5066, Report of Medical Officer for Third District for 1878 and Reports on an outbreak of diphtheria at Staple Street, Hernhill; PRO, MH 12/5073, Reports of Medical Officer of Health of Rural District for 1896–8; PRO, G/F NPS 3, Faversham Rural Sanitary Authority Report Book, 1883–5.

[44] PRO, MH 12/5066, Rural Sanitary Authority, Faversham, Report on an outbreak of diphtheria at Hernhill, 27 July 1879.

[45] PRO, MH 12/5073, Report of Medical Officer of Health of Rural District for 1897 and Notices served on owners of Staple Street wells, 1898.

explanation for the rise in infant mortality and its accompanying shift in seasonality. Poor sanitation and polluted water, a series of hot summers, seasonal weaning in response to the hop harvest, and lack of extended breastfeeding all contributed to the harvest of infant death in the latter decades of the nineteenth century.

V

Seasonal patterns of mortality are useful as a guide to the health of infants and the very young, but they are less sure for older children. We are fortunate for the second half of the century in having another source for the health of children of school age (those aged 5 to 14), the school log book. Because of the concern of teachers with student attendance, the log book, when kept assiduously, recorded a week-by-week chart of sickness, work and weather, the three things which kept students away from the classroom. Log books have been exploited for the light that they throw on child labour; they have not been much used for child health. When used in conjunction with another useful source, the District Medical Officers' reports, the log books provide a useful survey of the communicable diseases of the latter part of the nineteenth century.

A whole range of ailments are recorded in these rural log books: mumps, skin disease, sore throats, chickenpox, coughs, colds and bronchitis, influenza, whooping cough and the rare case of smallpox. But the main, constantly recurring, childhood diseases, all major killers in nineteenth-century England, were diphtheria, scarlet fever and measles.[46] The local pattern which emerges is of a continuous background morbidity, punctuated by several epidemics every decade – 1878–9 (diphtheria), 1881–2 and 1885 (scarlet fever), 1887 (measles), 1895–6 (diphtheria, scarlet fever and measles), 1897–8 (diphtheria and scarlet fever) – in which large numbers of school-age children became sick and some died. That the epidemics were just the tip of the iceberg of general sickness is clear from the list of references to absences due to illness: measles in Boughton in 1871, Hernhill and Boughton in 1874, Hernhill 1876, Boughton 1877, Boughton 1880, Hernhill 1881, Boughton 1882, Boughton and Hernhill 1886 and 1887, Hernhill 1896; diphtheria in Hernhill in 1878–9 and 1887, Boughton and Hernhill in 1890 and 1896, Hernhill in 1897 and 1898; scarlet fever in Boughton and Hernhill in 1881, Hernhill in 1882, Boughton 1885, Hernhill 1890, Boughton 1892, Hernhill 1894, 1896 and 1897.[47]

[46] Smith, *People's health*, p. 136.
[47] CKS, C/ES 183/1/1, Hernhill Church of England School Log Book, 1872–1959; CCA,

The first epidemic for which we have details is the diphtheria epidemic in Hernhill in the years 1878–9. Diphtheria, once common in Britain but now rare, is a disease of young children spread by droplets from the throat, nose or skin, particularly through contact in the classroom and home. It starts with rather general symptoms, which can include a headache and sore throat and is characterized by the development of a membrane in the pharynx or larynx (though there are other types of diphtheria). The toxins produced in diphtheria can result in cardiac arrest, paralysis or suffocation.[48] The first references to the epidemic in the Hernhill log book are to the sickness of thirteen children and the death of two in early November 1878 and to irregular attendance at the end of that month due to the wet weather and fear of diphtheria (an average of 88 children attended out of a possible 136). On 19 December 'Dr Dring ordered the school to be closed on account of the number of children sick'. The school was opened a month later, but only 62 returned to school. The last mention of the epidemic occurred in February 1879, with reference to the return of diphtheria and to cleansing with sulphur.[49] The District Medical Officer wrote that there had been an epidemic of sore throats in Hernhill before the onset of 'true diphtheria', which had begun in the hamlet of Staple Street in the household of the landlord of the Three Horse Shoes public house and then in adjoining cottages. All those infected in this initial phase drew water from the same well.[50] This threw suspicion on the water supply (which we have seen was polluted) but infection was almost certainly spread by direct contact, for the families concerned would have socialized and played together. Another report, printed in 1880, provided more detail. Before the diphtheria deaths, throat illness had been widespread among the children not only of Staple Street but in Waterham and Forstall, other Hernhill hamlets, and in South Street in Boughton, and Sheldwich. Fatal cases were registered variously as 'acute laryngitis', 'diphtheria and croup', 'inflammation of the lungs' and 'diphtheria'. The impact on Hernhill was dramatic. In that parish there had been seventy cases of throat illness with eight deaths; in Staple Street alone, there had been fifteen cases of diphtheria and three deaths in the space of a few weeks. William Hadlow, a Staple Street carpenter, lost three children in the epidemic.[51]

U3/221/25/13, Boughton-under-Blean School Log Book, 1864–95. Unfortunately the Dunkirk Log Book has not survived.

[48] A. B. Christie, *Infectious diseases* (London, 1980), ch. 34: 'Diphtheria'.
[49] CKS, C/ES 183/1/1, pp. 71–2, 74, 75.
[50] PRO, MH 12/5066, Report on outbreak of diphtheria in Hernhill, 13 January 1879.
[51] *Ibid.*, Mr. W. H. Power's Report to the Local Government Board on Diphtheria at Hernhill, 1880. The information on the Hadlows comes from family reconstitution.

This is not the place to discuss all the outbreaks, but one other is worth mentioning in some detail. The measles epidemic of 1887 is of interest because it provides the opportunity to see a highly contagious disease in action. Measles was in the area before the onset of the epidemic; there are references to it for both 1886 and early and mid 1887.[52] However, the Medical Officer for the district pinpointed the start of the outbreak to September 1887, claiming that a more virulent strain of measles was brought into Boughton by hoppers from Whitstable (outside the district). For a while it was confined to the Boughton farms where the hop-pickers were staying, but in October, presumably with the return of the children to school, 'it burst forth in a widespread epidemic' and more than a hundred children were afflicted with the illness within days. The Boughton Church of England and Wesleyan schools were shut in October–November. Hernhill school reported wholesale absences and it closed for a month in November–December. The epidemic then moved eastwards through the Blean to Dunkirk, Harbledown and Canterbury. (Graveney, Goodnestone and Faversham – to the west of Boughton and Hernhill – were not affected.) The gap between morbidity and mortality is clear from the district figures: there were five deaths out of more than 500 cases.[53]

Sometimes the major diseases of childhood would strike together. There were diphtheria deaths in Hernhill in 1887 during the measles epidemic and the school shut in early 1890 because of the simultaneous appearance of scarlet fever and diphtheria. From 1896 to 1898 the Hernhill school was battered by a succession of illnesses: scarlet fever and diphtheria in April 1896, measles in May (when the school closed), an outbreak of diphtheria from August to November 1897 (when again the school closed and several children were sent to the isolation hospital), whooping cough in November and diphtheria in January 1898.[54] Scarlet fever and diphtheria, often associated with each other, the former distinguishable by its characteristic rash and peeling skin, were also present in Boughton and Dunkirk in 1896 and 1897. The District Medical Officer again blamed the hop-pickers and pointed also to the role of the classroom: 'I almost despair of this malady being stamped out, many of the cases being of a mild character, the children after a few days are sent to school with the result that a large outbreak occurs'. Over forty children from Boughton, Dunkirk and Hernhill

[52] CKS, C/ES 183/1/1, pp. 142, 143, 150; CCA, U3/221/25/13, p. 400.
[53] PRO, MH 12/5069, Report of Medical Officer of Health of Rural District for 1887; CKS, C/ES 183/1/1, p. 152; CCA, U3/221/25/13, p. 412.
[54] CKS, C/ES 183/1/1, pp. 147, 148, 167, 225, 226, 229, 241–4; PRO, MH 12/5073, Report on outbreak of diphtheria in Hernhill, November 1897.

were admitted to the isolation hospital in 1897 suffering from diphtheria and scarlet fever.[55] The burial registers record eleven deaths of children from Hernhill in a little over a year from 1896 to 1897. The oldest was 11.[56] In 1898 there were nearly 200 official notifications of cases of scarlet fever and diphtheria for the rural district which contained our parishes.[57]

We have barely scraped the surface of the history of childhood illness and mortality, but a few observations can be made. Clearly mortality should not be confused with morbidity: childhood death is but a pale reflection of general conditions of health. Sickness stalked the schools of the nineteenth-century Blean. J. C. Riley has described this period in Europe as 'a transition from an age of death to an age of sickness'; our part of rural England was no exception.[58] The other interesting factor to emerge is the role of the classroom. The incidence of diphtheria and scarlet fever was highest among children of school age and it is tempting to relate the impact of such infectious diseases in the late nineteenth century to the rise of school attendance. Compulsory schooling, with the increasing likelihood that young children would be together in close proximity for long periods of time, must have provided the ideal environment for contagion. The classroom could convert isolated outbreaks into epidemics.[59]

VI

We know relatively little about adult health in the rural areas. The focus on child and infant mortality should not detract attention from adult deaths in the nineteenth century. In 1861, 38 per cent of women and 45 per cent of men died between the ages of 25–65 compared to 15 or 16 per cent today.[60] We know from the family reconstitutions of those married in Boughton, Dunkirk and Hernhill between 1800 and 1880 that from a quarter to a third of marriages were broken by the death of one of the partners before the woman reached the age of 45. Women faced the risk of maternal mortality at a level of 6.1 per 1,000 live births in this part of the nineteenth-century Blean and possibly as high as 12.3 per 1,000 in Boughton in the early twentieth century.[61]

55 PRO, MH 12/5073, Report of Medical Officer of Health of Rural District for 1897.
56 CCA, Parish Church of Hernhill, Hernhill Register of Burials, 1870–1924.
57 PRO, MH 12/5073, Report of Medical Officer of Health of Rural District for 1898.
58 J. C. Riley, *Sickness, recovery and death: a history and forecast of ill health* (London, 1989), p. 192.
59 See Smith, *People's health*, pp. 147–8; Hardy, *Epidemic streets*, pp. 44, 88.
60 Anderson, 'Social implications', p. 27, Table 1.2.
61 Based on family reconstitution for the marriage cohorts 1800 to 1880. The parish

(The rate in England in the 1850s was 4.6 per 1,000. In 1980 it was 0.1.)[62]

In contrast to infant mortality, there was little change in the seasonality of adult deaths during the nineteenth century (see figure 3.6). The relative flatness of the adult pattern also contrasts with those of the youngest age groups. There is a low for late summer and autumn and a high in winter and spring. It is generally recognized that this basic pattern, stable over long periods of time for many parts of north west Europe, reflects the importance of winter and spring respiratory diseases as a cause of adult death.[63] Influenza, bronchitis and pneumonia were common ailments. Tuberculosis or consumption (phthisis), was a killer too. A 'large proportion' of patients at the Kent and Canterbury Hospital in the 1830s were 'in some stage or other of pulmonary consumption'. 'We have to hope that as time goes on', the health report for the Faversham rural district observed in 1886, 'this large death rate from phthisis will diminish. The gradual improvement in the dwellings of the people, their better ventilation and freedom from damp walls, & floors must in time do much to lessen the mortality from this cause'.[64] Winter was a difficult period for a population which depended heavily upon agricultural labour: work was lost through wet weather and snow or simply because there was little to be done at that time of the year.[65] Household resources dwindled and as families tightened their belts they must have been particularly vulnerable to the ravages of illness. Oral accounts this century speak of winter desperation and of a recognition that those

breakdowns are 5.2/1,000 for Dunkirk and Hernhill and 7.6/1,000 for Boughton. Of 2,131 mothers at risk in the combined parishes, thirteen died within forty-two days of the baptism of their child: that is, a rate of 6.1/1,000. A Boughton Midwife's Register of Cases for 1904–9 and 1915–16, in the possession of Harry Wheeler of Boughton (her grandson), records two maternal deaths out of 163 deliveries. This suggests a rate of 12.3/1,000, though of course the numbers are small. Definitions vary. Knodel defines maternal mortality as deaths within the first forty-two days following childbirth; Schofield uses sixty days as the cut-off point; Wrigley and Schofield take as a maternal death that 'within ninety days of a child's birth (baptism)': Knodel, *Demographic behavior*, p. 104; R. Schofield, 'Did the mothers really die?', in Bonfield, Smith and Wrightson (eds.), *World we have gained*, p. 248; Wrigley and Schofield, 'English population history', p. 181. I have used the shortest estimate to allow for the possible two-month delay between birth and baptism in these parishes, which would tend to inflate the rates slightly. But if I had used sixty days as the measurement, the figures would not have been very different.

[62] Schofield, 'Did the mothers really die?', p. 231.
[63] E. A. Wrigley and R. S. Schofield, *The population history of England 1541–1871* (Cambridge, 1989 edn), p. 296.
[64] A. Lochee, *A Descriptive and Tabular Report of the Medical and Surgical cases treated in the Kent and Canterbury Hospital ... 1838 to 1840* (Canterbury, 1841), p. 36; PRO, MH 12/5069, Report of Medical Officer of Health of Rural District for 1886.
[65] See chapter 4.

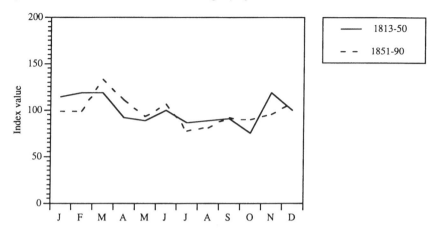

Figure 3.6 Indexed seasonality of adult burials, 1813–90 (combined parishes).

were the difficult months to get through. 'After Christmas ... yes, winter time ... I think that was the worst time'. Dorothy Tong recalled that her mother used to say, 'the falling of the leaf is going to tell whether he's going to live'; if a sick or elderly person could survive the period after November, then they would be all right.[66]

National figures for the middle of the nineteenth century and the early twentieth century point to the longevity of the rural labourer in comparison to other workers.[67] But this does not mean that it was a life free from ill-health and pain. A report from the Kent and Canterbury Hospital – which treated men and women from the Blean as both in-patients and out-patients – wrote in 1841 of the 'prevalence of chronic diseases here'. 'The truth is, that the great majority of the disorders encountered here are *chronic*, in every sense of the word':

In this part of the country, where the working classes are chiefly field labourers, atmospheric changes, and constant exposure to cold and wet, though acting imperceptibly on habituated constitutions for a time, never fail, in the end, to determine the character of the resulting diseases: thus we have, in abundance, inflammatory affections of the pleura, the lungs, and the air-passages; obstinate rheumatisms of muscular parts; and neuralgic affections from cold, sometimes amounting to complete paralysis. But, at the Hospital, we rarely get these cases in the acute or primary stages: the patient waits, and

[66] Hernhill Oral History, D. Tong, b. 1912.
[67] Armstrong, *Farmworkers*, p. 140; R. Woods and J. Woodward, 'Mortality, poverty and the environment', in Woods and Woodward (eds.), *Urban disease and mortality*, p. 27; Wohl, *Endangered lives*, pp. 280–2; M. R. Haines, 'Conditions of work and the decline of mortality', in R. Schofield, D. Reher and A. Bideau (eds.), *The decline of mortality in Europe* (Oxford, 1991), ch. 10.

waits, in the hopes of natural amendment; or, perhaps, on a Saturday night, he takes a dose of physic, and *'gets bled'*, the *'res angustae domi'* preventing him from seeking further relief, or from 'laying up', until absolutely obliged. He then comes to us, at last, with an hepatised lung, or an adherent pleura, or a thickened bronchial membrane, almost irrevocably loaded with puriform secretion, the effect of long-standing, sub-acute inflammation; and his sojourn in the hospital and the amount of benefit received are in proportion to the previous delay, which has rendered his complaint obstinate. Most of these persons cannot afford to pay for the continued attendance of a medical man, and the 'Unions' will not grant even medical relief, whilst they are 'in work': so that, if seized with an acute inflammatory attack, it frequently runs on entirely unchecked, or is only partially relieved by the tardy assistance afforded.[68]

As we saw, our parishes were on the margins of a malarial area and although the disease did not kill large numbers of adults, it contributed to the morbidity of the district. Fever, 'continued', 'intermittent' and 'remittent', 'more prevalent in spring and autumn than at other seasons of the year', was one of the main complaints of patients in the Kent and Canterbury Hospital in the late 1830s.[69]

Rheumatism – a result of cold and damp living and working conditions – was another prevalent ailment, for both sexes, though more men than women attended the hospital for treatment. Chronic rheumatism was found in older adults (the average age of such patients was 47 for males and 49 for females), but people in their twenties suffered from acute rheumatic pain.[70] A 20-year-old carpenter had 'Pain, swelling and redness, from acute rheumatism, in all of the large joints, and also of the hands and knuckles: the skin of the parts affected is intensely hot, with effusion into both knee joints, and *oedema of both legs and feet!* Sweats profusely; is entirely helpless'.[71] Rheumatic pains, though not necessarily with such crippling symptoms as those of the young carpenter, must have been commonplace in the rural areas. One of the doctors at the Kent hospital complained of a readiness to consult local healers, 'wise women' and 'knowing men'. He was aghast at a celebrated local remedy for rheumatism, the juices of a decomposed toad (left to rot on a dung-heap): 'And with this delicate product of animal and vegetable decomposition, the affected parts are to be diligently rubbed before a good fire.' The doctor's own recommendation for chronic rheumatism was the outward application of mustard several times a day and the internal use of quinine and opium.[72]

Such routine ailments – and leg ulcers were another common

[68] Lochee, *Descriptive and Tabular Report*, p. 19.   [69] *Ibid.*, pp. 8, 10, 17, 55.
[70] *Ibid.*, pp. 9, 11.   [71] *Ibid.*, p. 28.   [72] *Ibid.*, pp. 20, 36.

complaint[73] – rarely figure in medical histories. They cannot compete with the drama of epidemics. Yet they affected the lives of large numbers of people. They were endured, no doubt, as part of normal living, but must have been particularly worrying for a population which earned its living by labour. Although it is impossible to quantify the material, applications for poor relief give some insight into the daily battle against ill-health and the ramifications of sickness for the family economy. The illness or injury of a man could remove a wage earner. The incapacity of a woman could remove a household manager as well as another contributor of income. The sickness of a child could sabotage an important cog in the family economy quite apart from providing added strain on the household purse. Man, woman and child all played a vital role in the social economy of labouring families and the temporary or permanent incapacity of one or more of these family members could spell disaster to those fragile economies.[74] The Faversham Poor Law Union Relieving Officer's Application and Report Book chronicles the desperation of ill-health, whether by sickness or injury, which forced families and individuals to seek poor relief: continuing fevers, consumption, lameness of the arm or leg, fractures, burns, shoulder or side injuries, ruptures, hand infections or injuries, abscesses and unspecified illnesses and infirmities.[75]

Many injuries would have been work-related. This is a much neglected area of research, though the oral accounts provide information for the early twentieth century. Twelve-year-old J. W. Manuel (born 1903) was committed to the workhouse for medical assistance when his face was injured in an explosion while bird-scaring, a relatively common accident among rook boys.[76] Two traction engine drivers who operated in the Blean provided a somewhat laconic account of other possibilities when they were interviewed by the historian Michael Winstanley:

Accidents, an uncle, he got blown up and killed. One got his leg in the doings, he had his leg chewed off didn't he? Uncle Arthur, yes. Uncle Arthur. He said his foot slipped down in the casing and went down in the gears and chewed his leg up. Another one had a boiler burst and blew the old man up, didn't it. Uncle Walt. Uncle Walt. Blew him out the engine, just minor things, you know. Just minor things. That was the end of him.

Their father 'ran over a bloke' and gave the widow half a crown in compensation.[77] Most work-related injuries in the period before farm

[73] *Ibid.*, pp. 13, 15.   [74] See chapter 4.
[75] CKS, G/F RA 12–14, Faversham Union Relieving Officer's Application and Report Books, 1859–61.
[76] TL, J. W. Manuel, b. 1903.   [77] TL, S. Baldock, b. 1895 and J. Baldock, b. 1916.

mechanization would have been more mundane, if still disabling: the ruptures, fractures, sprains and cuts encountered daily by the Poor Law relieving officers.

VII

In November 1881 a traction engine rattled through Dunkirk. As it passed the church, the engine's pilot, who walked in front of the steam machine with a flag, called out to onlookers 'Don't you know to-day Mother Shipton prophesied the end of the world? What will you charge to bury me?' Shortly afterwards the man was crushed by his own engine.[78] Death could come at any time to the inhabitants of the Blean. And yet, as we have seen, death was not entirely capricious. It had its parameters, its biases. It stalked the very young; it was attracted to particular seasons, localities and environmental conditions.

It is important to remember the context of health care in this and other parts of rural England. The only doctor for the three parishes was at Boughton. But as such practitioners were fully aware, consulting a doctor or hospital was a last resort, normally during epidemics or for serious injuries. Of those who did visit a doctor, many relied on credit (as with the grocer), and one twentieth-century oral informant can remember the practice of settling the year's debt after hopping (the 'measle bill') so that the family would get treatment during the following months. 'And if you didn't pay it this year, you didn't get any treatment next year. You could lie and die next year. Till you went hop-picking again.'[79] Even for the early twentieth century, oral informants are agreed, 'you never called the doctor unless it was absolutely essential because you just couldn't afford to pay'.[80] 'Oh no, you never had the doc. You had toothache and your face out but you didn't have anything'.[81] For their part, it was 'a constant cause of complaint with many of the country practitioners, that they are obliged to suit their prescriptions to the domestic necessities and avocations of their patients, rather than to the actual symptoms of their diseases'.[82] Some potential patients, as now, went direct to the chemist.[83] Some turned to local healers, like the old woman at Staple Street, early this century, who earned a living taking in washing and dispensing 'all sorts of old-fashioned

[78] *Faversham Mercury*, 19 November 1881.
[79] Hernhill Oral History, E. Wade, b. 1908.
[80] Hernhill Oral History, H. Kay, b. 1921.
[81] Hernhill Oral History, E. Wade, b. 1908.
[82] Lochee, *Descriptive and Tabular Report*, p. 19.
[83] Hernhill Oral History, H. Kay, b. 1921, T. Boorman, b. 1920; TL, F. Pack, b. 1897.

cures'.[84] But the most widespread form of healing must have been self-medication. Oral accounts of the early decades of the twentieth century provide the detail: mustard, linseed and bread poultices, honey and vinegar or blackcurrant jam and hot water for sore throats, oil of cloves for toothache, goose fat or mustard oil on brown paper, applied to the chest for colds.[85] Harry Matthews (born 1890), who lived in the Brents at Faversham, said that his mother pulled out her own teeth.[86]

The medical world that we have been traversing can never match the horror of life in the big cities. The work-related illnesses and injuries of the rural labouring population pale in comparison with industrial accidents and health conditions and urban disease. However, the Blean was certainly no pastoral paradise, and its experience provides an added perspective to the medical history of nineteenth-century England. From the institution of the New Poor Law in 1834 to the year 1880, expectation of life at birth was 47.5 years, a long way from Woods and Woodward's suggested 56 years for rural labourers.[87] (The national rates today are in the upper sixties and mid seventies.) Endemic diarrhoea ensured that infant mortality levels climbed in this part of rural England to levels comparable to those of modern-day Bangladesh and Pakistan.[88] The experience of Horse Lees infants matched that of many nineteenth-century British cities. And it was an age of sickness for the children of the Blean. Though the mortality of school-age children declined in the second half of the century, morbidity did not. Epidemics of diphtheria, scarlet fever and measles flourished in the schools. The health experience of agricultural labourers may have been better than that of other occupations, relatively speaking, yet for many it was a life of suffering and pain still insufficiently explored by historians.

[84] Hernhill Oral History, A. Bones, b. 1912.
[85] TL, G. Post, b. 1896, J. W. Manuel, b. 1903; Hernhill Oral History, H. Tong, b. 1909, D. Tong, b. 1912, E. Wade, b. 1908.
[86] TL, H. Matthews, b. 1890.
[87] Woods and Woodward, 'Mortality, poverty and the environment', p. 26.
[88] Rutstein, *Infant and child mortality*, p. 16, Table 3.

PART II

Society

Plate 17 Hop-pickers at Langdon Court Farm, Graveney.

4

Social economy

I

Steve Tremeere was born in 1897 and grew up in Dover in the early decades of this century.[1] His father was a fisherman. His mother was the daughter of a master shoemaker (or snob as shoemakers were known then): 'my mother was a little more upper class than what we were'. She was committed to an asylum when Steve and his brother and sister were very young and his father decided that he would give up the sea and look after the children himself rather than sending them to relatives. 'With the aid of an old woman he looked after us, the wickedest whelp that was ever born she was.' Life was not easy. When Tremeere was 6, his 8-year-old brother died after being kicked in the stomach at school. By the time he was 10, he and his sister of 14 were being left alone while their father, now a fitter's mate, went on four-day trips to France working on a paddle steamer. (The old woman was no longer looking after them.)

Steve left school in his early teens: 'As soon as we got 14 we had to go earn something.' He worked in a variety of jobs: as a milk boy, up at 5 a.m., selling milk from a two-gallon bucket; driving a pony and cart for a fruit shop, starting at 4 a.m. three mornings a week to be

[1] TL, Steve Tremeere, b. 1897. The 'Life in Kent Project' was carried out by Michael Winstanley in the mid 1970s and formed the basis for his book, *Life in Kent at the turn of the century* (Folkestone, 1978); and his 'Voices from the past: rural Kent at the close of an era', in G. Mingay (ed.), *The Victorian countryside* (London, 1981), reprinted in Mingay (ed.), *The vanishing countryman* (London, 1989). Chapter 14 of *Life in Kent*, 'A Dover childhood', is based on the Tremeere interview; however my emphasis in what follows is somewhat different. I draw heavily on the Kent Oral History archive and I am most grateful to Dr Winstanley and the archivist of the collection, Derek Whittaker, for making this material available. I also use interviews which I carried out in 1991–2 as part of my research on the Blean area of Kent, hereafter referred to as Hernhill Oral History.

early at market; as a pony boy in the pits. Then he joined the army and fought in the Great War. Invalided home from the Dardanelles, he walked into the house unannounced after an absence of several years; 'The old man just looked at me and said, are you back again? I said, yes. He said what do you want for tea? I said, bloaters.' Tremeere senior earned 15s. a week, his son recalled, and he worked from 6 a.m. to 6 p.m. five days a week and to midday on Saturdays. Their rent was 4s. 6d. Steve remembered this clearly because he was paid 5s. a week when he worked as a fruit boy and gave 4s. 6d. of this to his father for the rent. His sister worked locally as a servant as soon as she turned 14; she was paid 1s. a week and got her food free but she returned home each night at 7 p.m. to look after Steve. Their household economy varied according to the stage reached in the family's cycle; times were far harder when the children were young and their father had to pay the woman to look after them. Things were easier when the children were in full-time work – it was a necessity that they found waged work at the earliest possible time.

But what really comes through in this story of urban survival in the early twentieth century is not so much the wage as the thousand and one other ways of making ends meet. Paid work is only part of a much wider economic picture. The role of the wife and mother is at the centre of this picture, as we shall see in due course. In the case of the Tremeeres, her absence contributed to their predicament. Steve was acutely aware of the difference that the presence of his mother would have made to what has been termed, so aptly, that 'economy of expedients'. 'Of course if we'd had a mother here, she would have been able to put it out a bit more wouldn't she?' ('put it out' meaning make the wage stretch). In the absence of a mother, their father coordinated the household's 'strategies for survival'. The children also played an important part.[2]

It was vital to know all the economies that could be made. Stale bread was cheaper, so they 'never bought a new loaf of bread'. It was possible to buy cracked eggs at a lower price if you took a basin with you. On Saturdays, if you went to the covered market you could procure 'two pennorth of pork loins. Big armful. Bring them home, the old man would chop them all up, they went in a big iron saucepan.' Much of this scavenging was done by the children. At dinner-time, when they had to fend for themselves, the young Tremeeres would go

---

[2] For the 'economy of expedients', see O. Hufton, 'Women and the family economy in eighteenth-century France', *French Historical Studies*, 9 (1975–6), p. 22. For 'strategies for survival', see D. Vincent, *Poor citizens: the state and the poor in twentieth-century Britain* (London, 1991), p. 4.

to the soup kitchen where they could get the watered-down left-overs for 1d. There was skill involved in knowing how to make the meagre rations spread. They had giblet pie at Christmas, tasty and economical. When 'we got very hard up we'd go down to the poultry keepers and ask them for chicken heads. Get a pile of them, poke them in some boiling water, scalded them. Then all you had to do was to pick all the feathers off them and all the skulls went back with soup powder in it and made a nice stock for supper.'

And there was a finely developed sense of the cost of things which remained with Tremeere in the 1970s. Margarine (they could not afford butter) was 4d. a pound. An outlay of 2d. for stewing meat, 1d. for potatoes, 1d. for 'pot herbs' (carrots, turnips, onions), would provide the ingredients for a stew. Expenditure, through economic necessity, was always in what to the modern eye seems minuscule amounts, certainly not the most economical way of buying things. Breakfast could be bought in the morning at the local shop: a 'farthingsworth' ($\frac{1}{4}$d.) each of tea and sugar and a 'ha'porth' ($\frac{1}{2}$d.) of condensed milk. The Tremeeres were well aware of their financial boundaries. It was possible to buy rabbits for 8d. or 9d., 'if you had the money'. One could get a half a leg of mutton for 18d. if you went to the butcher late at night on Saturday when he sold off the meat that would not keep until Monday: but 'Eighteen pence was a bloody lot you know then.' However, a ha'porth of rice and a half pint of milk (also $\frac{1}{2}$d.) was within their range and could provide a filling meal.

The children played an important role in the household economy well before they were old enough to bring in a steady wage. Steve ran errands for the street prostitutes and would get the odd $\frac{1}{2}$d. or $\frac{1}{4}$d. Sailors were always good for a bit of cash. They 'would chuck you a penny to get them some fags or some more beer'. Or 'some old girl', one of the regulars at the pawnshop ('uncles'), would send him to the broker on Monday mornings to pawn 'the old man's' suit for 'two bob or half a crown' and then later in the week get him to redeem the ticket and pay the 2d. or $1\frac{1}{2}$d. interest. Steve's profit from this circulating community economy of poverty was his commission of $\frac{1}{2}$d. He managed to acquire a pair of pram wheels and a sugar box to make a barrow and he would cart coke for his customers (usually old women) for $\frac{1}{4}$d. a bag; 'that got you 1d'. 'Then I used to go to the Cause is Altered pub with my little barrow, and I used to take all the bottles of stout and the beer to the old girls in the Gorley alms houses, their weekly orders'. They had little themselves but would pay a farthing sometimes. More often, they paid in kind with cakes. But Tremeere could still end up with $2\frac{1}{2}$d. by Saturday afternoon.

Of course there were less honest ways of managing. The young Tremeere was adept at these strategies. Fresh fruit could be had from orchards or fruit-stalls. He had a coat with a missing pocket-lining, specially fashioned for such forays. 'Always had a coat like that ... No pocket in it, your hand went like that, your hand was in your pocket, it was picking something, your hand was still in your pocket, but the fruit was underneath it.' Meat could be stolen from the butcher's: 'They lost many a bit of meat when they was poking around serving somebody up that end, and somebody would have a bit off [this] end.' When Tremeere worked as a fruit boy he had to sell fruit from a market stall and he would keep some of the takings for himself, putting them in his shoe in case his pockets were checked. Earlier, when he went carol singing for the church, he would hold back a few pence. 'You put 2d. in your pocket and give your teacher 2d. Couldn't have it all could she? Not for charity. We was singing for ourselves, not for them. Singing for our supper.' There was no sense of remorse, no indication that he thought that his behaviour was morally wrong. He viewed his actions, and presumably the actions of others, in terms of survival. Indeed he was philosophical about his situation: 'We didn't thieve it. There was one motto we always learnt at school, that was ... God helps those who help themselves. So we used to help ourselves, thinking he would help us. I don't know whether he did or not, he didn't say nothing. We ate it alright. Oh dear, oh dear.' His teachers would have been horrified at this interpretation of the dominant ideology.

This fascinating piece of oral history, recorded in the 1970s by Michael Winstanley, is much more than the life story of a man who thought that the Labour leader, James Callaghan, was 'no more labour than what my cat is'. It is a finely etched portrait of making ends meet in a working-class community, a remarkable tale of survival, and it provides an evocative introduction to the subject of this chapter. The economic world we will be traversing has been called a variety of things: the economy of the poor, the economy of makeshifts, an economy of expedients, the neighbourhood economy, the hidden economy. I have termed it the 'social economy' because I feel that this best conveys the sheer range of the economic activity involved in getting a living, and because it covers all the interstices of an economic life which was also, very firmly, a social life.[3] Previous discussions of this milieu have tended to follow the contours of urban and industrial England, concentrating on London and the northern towns. Yet the

---

[3] The term 'social economy' is used by J. Walter, 'The social economy of dearth in early modern England', in J. Walter and R. Schofield (eds.), *Famine, disease and the social order in early modern society* (Cambridge, 1989), ch. 2.

social economy had a rural as well as an urban dimension. This chapter provides a somewhat different focus: small town and village Kent.

II

There is no denying the importance of the male wage for nineteenth- and twentieth-century working-class households. Oral history informants invariably knew what their fathers had earned, even though they were looking back to their own childhoods. Men could trace average earnings over long periods of time. They were aware of skilled and unskilled differentials and they often had detailed knowledge of piece-work or task-related earnings. One man, whose father was a brick-moulder in turn-of-the-century Faversham, could list off the rates paid in the brickfields: barrow-loaders got $2\frac{1}{2}$d. per thousand; the boy who pushed them out got $3\frac{1}{2}$d. per thousand. A barrow loader (boy) loading 50,000 a week would take home 10s. 5d., a good sum for a youngster. The man who cut and shaped the bricks got $5\frac{1}{2}$d. or 6d. an hour; the moulder, the aristocrat of brickmaking, earned 10d. an hour.[4] Len Austin, who lived in the hamlet of South Street in Boughton-under-Blean, recalled that his father, a farmworker, got 15s. a week before the First World War. During the war his wages came up to 20s. and were 47s. immediately after 1918. In 1921, 'when the slump set in ... he was lucky if he got 25 bob a week'. Austin remembered farm wages of 32s. 6d. in 1924 with the first Labour government; at the start of the Second World War they were some 40s. per week.[5] These rates are very close to the averages mapped out in Alan Armstrong's tables of farmworkers' wage trends.[6]

It needs to be said that there are immense problems with the nominal wage as a gauge of household income. At one and the same time it both underestimates and overestimates earnings. A. L. Bowley signalled the former when he distinguished between 'wages' of 14s. 6d. and 'earnings' of 16s. 4d. for Kent in 1892 in his chart of agricultural labourers' wages.[7] The male wage rate does not normally include extra harvest earnings, piece-work or perquisites. Nor, as we shall see, does it reflect the earnings of women and children, either as independent workers or in assisting the adult male in piece-work. The percentages

[4] TL, H. Adley, b. 1886.   [5] TL, L. Austin, b. 1902.
[6] A. Armstrong, *Farmworkers: a social and economic history 1770–1980* (London, 1988), pp. 121, 167, 184.
[7] A. L. Bowley, *Wages in the United Kingdom in the nineteenth century* (Cambridge, 1900), table at end of book.

varied according to the internal family structure, but a survey of over 500 labouring families in rural Norfolk and Suffolk in the 1830s found that about half the income of an average family came from the husband's day work and piece-work, about a third from the earnings of the wife and children (including gleaning), and 15 per cent in harvest wages, which presumably would also include (as may have the husband's piece-work earnings) the labour contribution of women and children.[8]

Wage security could not be taken for granted in the labouring world. The down side of the nominal wage is that it assumes constant weekly employment throughout the year when in fact it was quite usual for rural workers to be without paid work in the winter months or to be on lower wage rates. They would lose pay when rain or frost or snow made work impossible or when they were sick. In the 1870s, a Kent union activist, Alfred Simmons, asked some agricultural labourers to keep a tally of the days lost on account of inclement weather. Their replies showed an average loss of eighty-five days (excluding Sundays) or about three months' worth of weekly wages per year.[9] Over the year, this would reduce the weekly wage of 15s. 6d. during the 1900s to just over 11s. 6d. a week for the year. Simmons had a political point to make and may have exaggerated his case, but even if we allow for distortion the substance of his claim remains. One has only to consult the poor law records to see the pronounced seasonality of relief (see figures 4.1 and 4.2). Seventy per cent of applications for assistance from the Faversham Poor Law Union in the late 1850s were made in the period from December to June. And of those males who stated their occupations, 90 per cent were agricultural labourers.[10] Oral accounts also testify to the winter desperation of labouring homes. Frank Pack's father was out of work for a 'couple of months' each winter. He never forgot those times when 'we were all out of work': 'And we were starving, there's no doubt about it'.[11]

Work in the towns could also be seasonal. The lucrative Faversham brickmaking stopped in the winter. A few key men were retained to prepare for the next season; some trekked to London to work in the gasworks for the winter, taking lodgings and returning home to see

[8] J. P. Kay, 'Earnings of agricultural labourers in Norfolk and Suffolk', *Journal of the Royal Statistical Society*, 1 (1838), calculated from the summary table on p. 183.
[9] F. Carlton, '"A substantial and sterling friend to the labouring man": the Kent and Sussex Labourers' Union 1872–1895' (University of Sussex M. Phil. thesis, 1977), p. 31.
[10] That is those from Boughton, Dunkirk and Hernhill who applied for relief. The figures are calculated from CKS, G/F RA 12–14, Faversham Union Relieving Officer's Application and Report Books, 1859–61.
[11] TL, F. Pack, b. 1897.

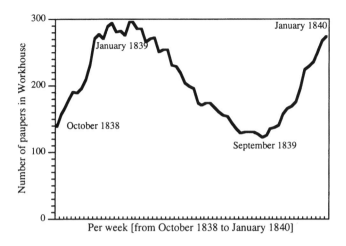

Figure 4.1 Weekly numbers of paupers in the Faversham Workhouse, 1838–40.

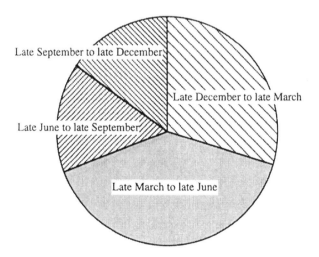

Figure 4.2 Poor relief applications from Boughton, Dunkirk and Hernhill, 1859–61 (male and female applicants – per person per quarter).

their families every fortnight or so. Others attempted to eke out a living in and around Faversham, perhaps loading and unloading barges, or they would try their hands at field work if it was available. The majority of brickmakers were out of steady work for most of September, October, November and December. Such was the environment of Harry Matthews. The Matthews family went hopping in September and then Harry's mother went wurzel-pulling at 10s. an acre. The men did potato-picking; and they sometimes got a few shillings beating for a Christmas shoot at one of the big houses. His father would set off along the creek at 6 a.m. and perhaps get a job on a barge for a few days; or he broke granite by hand for 15s. a ton. He also worked at a local pub as a cellarman. This constant round of getting by during the winter was referred to as 'scheming'. Matthews said that they managed to keep out of the workhouse because his father was always able to 'nip round and scheme three or four bob now and then'.[12]

It is clear from the adult male wage rates quoted earlier that there must have been large sections of the labouring population where the nominal income of the household's principal male wage earner was insufficient to support a family. Len Austin's father's 15s. was well below the calculated poverty lines of pre-war England: that is the estimated 18s. 4d. (rural) and 21s. 8d. (urban) required to keep a man, a woman and three children in 'physical efficiency'.[13] As Syd Twist told Michael Winstanley:

there was a lot of casual labour in those days. The brickfields and the field work was all casual. And of course, if parents, the father was at sea or barging, then the income was intermittent, he'd get an advance when he started and then if he was away for three or four weeks, there would be no more money coming in till he came home. There was that sort of thing, see, the standard of living of a lot of them was very low. There's only those in regular work that had got a sustained standard.[14]

The economic role of other family members was crucial in such households.

III

A further weakness of using wage rates as a guide to the working economy is that such accounts do not take sufficient cognisance of

---

[12] TL, H. Matthews, b. 1890. See also, TL, H. Adley, b. 1886; S. Twist, b. 1899; and Winstanley, *Life in Kent*, ch. 13.
[13] P. H. Mann, 'Life in an agricultural village in England', *Sociological Review*, first series, 1 (1904), p. 169.
[14] TL, S. Twist, b. 1899.

those who were not formal wage earners. The oral histories mention the range of possibilities almost *en passant*, as if such activities, so much a part of the social landscape (particularly in towns), were merely taken for granted and not worthy of note. There were the street entertainers: the Russian bear man in Tremeere's childhood Dover; men with monkeys. 'Grinners', who usually lived in lodging houses, would go around the town, pulling faces for halfpennies or pennies. In the 1900s, street traders came to Faversham each weekend for the market, selling concoctions which purported to cure corns or colds. Their stalls offered just about anything. 'Didn't matter what it was, they'd have a go at selling it.'[15] Rag-and-bone men, fish-sellers, the muffin man 'was always round shouting their wares at that time'. People would sell from baskets or they would walk around with fish on a string or a tray. Faversham petty traders would hawk stuff from barrows 'if there was a glut of sprats or fruit'. Men lived off shrimping; they would catch them in the morning and sell them in the streets in the afternoon for 2d. a pint.[16]

Twist and Matthews, who knew the social environment of early twentieth-century Faversham intimately, spoke of the people of the Tanner Street lodging houses who seemed to survive on next to nothing. They would carry luggage for a few coppers or get a couple of pence holding farmers' horses for them while they went about their business in Faversham. It was said that some of these men slept in a lodging-house passage, propped up against a rope; they could not afford the price of a bed. In the morning, the proprietor would slacken off the pulley which held the rope 'and let them all down and they'd go out'. 'It was remarkable how they lived'; 'they weren't rowdy people, well they hadn't got enough money to be'.[17] People were adept at making the most of the left-overs from a larger economy. London rubbish was carted to Faversham by the barge-load for use in brick-making and a few pence could be made in 'totting', sifting through the refuse for bones, coppers, bottles, jars, metal, anything of small value.[18]

Dealers are another group closely linked to labouring culture, yet they have a somewhat shadowy place in labour historiography, despite their immortalization in H. E. Bates's *The Darling Buds of May*.[19] Those involved in dealing defy easy classification, traversing the boundaries between wage labouring, petty trading and (in many cases)

---

[15] TL, S. Tremeere, b. 1897; H. Matthews, b. 1890.
[16] TL, S. Twist, b. 1899; H. Matthews, b. 1890.
[17] TL, S. Twist, b. 1899.
[18] TL, A. Wise, b. 1894; H. Adley, b. 1886; H. Matthews, b. 1890.
[19] H. E. Bates, *The Darling Buds of May* (London, 1958).

subsistence farming, a segment of the population who were wage-dependent for only part of the year. Yet they were an important and noticeable part of rural economy and society, these men and their families who cobbled together a living through a bewildering variety of means and with vastly varying degrees of success.

Frank Kemsley (born in 1887) came from one such family in Molash, not many miles from the Blean. Kemsley's father was a horse dealer who supplied tradespeople in Faversham and Canterbury and the general area. He was also a chicken dealer and had contracted to supply Canterbury poulterers with chicken, which he presumably bought in the neighbourhood and then sold for a profit (he sent the old hens to London). The Kemsleys had a small farm; they would buy horses from London, rest them up and train them for farm work, and then sell them to farmers. They started with 1 acre and eventually acquired 30 acres. They worked hard and saved: 'mother worked, worked hard, we all worked hard and ... didn't spend 3d. when 2d. would do'. They were entrepreneurs. They bought a four-wheeled waggon which they hired out as a local taxi. They would buy whelks in Whitstable, boil them up, and sell them at fairs in the district for 1d. a plate. They sent mole-skins and rabbit-skins (presumably poached) to London. Kemsley senior organized shooting competitions at a Boughton pub; he would take a load of chickens and sell tickets to shoot to compete for the prize of a chicken. They would get the runts of the pig-litters cheap, fatten them up, kill them, 'and sell it out round the village'. They purchased bullocks, used by the local farmers for manure, and then drove them to Ashford market. Kemsley junior also had a milk-run, going out each morning with milk from his father's cow, sold by the pint or half-pint. At some stage, his mother took over a small shop which had become bankrupt and she got the agency for the local post office – his sister delivered the letters.

The Kemsley family is not typical in terms of its success and seemingly inexhaustible enterprise. But their example captures the essence of the dealer milieu. The Kemsleys were not in big money. Frank knew when to buy cheap meat from the butcher; he knew that stale bread made a good bread pudding. He worked for his father for much of his life; when he got married in 1912 his father paid him 16s. a week. When he was a child, his mother felt it necessary to go hop-picking and his father would mow barley for a neighbour at 6s. an acre. Frank's verdict was that his father 'got a living, that's all that mattered wasn't it?' The work of women and children was vital to such family economies. The whelk-selling business of the Kemsleys was a family effort. The father bought the whelks; the children took them out of the shells after they had been boiled; and the mother did the selling at the fair. (Father 'was always round the dealer boys, having some beer'.) When Kemsley's father mowed barley, his wife would bind it and the children would stand the shocks upright.[20]

There were dealers in Boughton, Dunkirk and Hernhill: general dealers and dealers in wood or fruit. Percy Saddleton (born 1907) knew them this century. 'Buy anything, yes. Crop of potatoes, or anything, field of spuds, they'd buy, get casual labour and come and pick 'em up.' 'They'd be like small farmers They might have a small holding of their own, you know, just keep a few chicken or pigs or something, just to keep themselves going in winter.' 'They'd scratch a living somehow.'[21] Len Godden (born 1890), a Boughton dealer, was over 100 years old when I met him. His mother had been a dressmaker and his father had been a bricklayer. One of his grandfathers was a charcoal burner, the other a brickmaker. He went to Dunkirk school, but left at the age of 12 or 14 (he was a little unclear) to start work as a rook boy. He drove a horse for a builder's yard for a number of years, but while still in his teens did his first deal, buying and selling cherries. He had kept pigs and the money that he got from them staked him for this first transaction. His memory was fading: his daughter had to elaborate from time to time. But his eyes would light up whenever he mentioned deals done and prices paid. Indeed his memory seemed structured in terms of such deals and any question asked seemed always to return to the subject. His dealing grew out of the penny capitalism of his youth: when he went hop-picking with his aunt, instead of labouring he would be off with a man selling lemonade. As an adult, Godden dealt in horses and pigs; 'buy something of everything'. He bought apples and sold them in Dover and Folkestone. He delivered coal in winter. 'Always chopping and changing.' Sometimes the transactions must have hovered on the border of legality: during the First World War he bought blankets from the soldiers and resold them. The idea was to always have an eye open for the main chance; 'always' down the pub with the 'dealer boys', the 'good old boys'. He bought cherries or peas by the acre and paid labourers to pick them – his future wife was a picker on one of his cherry fields. He kept bees and sold the honey in pots which he had scavenged. He sold potatoes. He went round with a pony and cart on September evenings to sell food to the hop-pickers. He took pigs to market for the local publican.[22]

[20] TL, F. Kemsley, b. 1887.
[21] Hernhill Oral History, P. Saddleton, b. 1907.
[22] Hernhill Oral History, L. Godden, b. 1890.

Finally, at the bottom of the scale, were the transients. Some of the inhabitants of Faversham's west-end accommodation houses were permanent residents, but many were men on the tramp, looking for work; 'men that had left their families away and was walking to find a job. If they found a job they'd bring their families here'. They would purchase their food in minute quantities each day from the nearby grocer's and public house.[23] Matthews used to see people on the tramp checking into the workhouse in the late afternoon; before they left in the morning, they had to do some washing if they were women or break granite if they were men, as payment for the night's bed and food. Some of them hid their few possessions outside in a hedge or behind a wall before they went into the workhouse, picking them up the next day.[24]

The court records of the nineteenth century occasionally provide glimpses into this almost unrecorded world. Two men and a boy were apprehended after they had approached the house of Hernhill's vicar in 1867, asking for bread. The three had been in the workhouse and were 'very hungry'. When the constable searched the men, he discovered a total of 6d. – 'I asked them how they got into the Union [workhouse] with that money?'– and tickets for a shirt and tools pawned in Peterborough. One of the men still had some shoemaking tools; the boy was carrying an empty basket.[25] Matilda Clark, 'a masculine-looking woman' who appeared before the Sittingbourne Police Court in 1878 charged with drunkenness, said that 'she made Bexley her home in the summer and Ashford in the winter, but she generally went to Chatham in the meantime. She worked in the fields in the summer, and hawked goods in the winter'. Both she and her companion, Henry Clark, 'a cripple', had pedlar's licences.[26] Tramping could be a permanent rather than temporary way of life. Walter Scott, arrested in rural Ospringe in 1873 for vagrancy and begging, went from door to door presenting a note which claimed that he was both deaf and dumb. A shoemaker's wife related that Scott 'presented a card written on it deaf and dumb. I shook my head and he then swore at me'. This swearing mute aroused suspicion and Walter Scott (if indeed that was his real name) left his historical imprint.[27] But most of these transients have vanished without a trace, save for the occasional entry in the parish burials, like the one in the Boughton-under-Blean

[23] TL, S. Twist, b. 1899.   [24] TL, H. Matthews, b. 1890.
[25] CKS, PS/US 11, Upper Division of the Lathe of Scray Petty Sessions 1864–8, 15 July 1867.
[26] *Faversham Mercury*, 18 May 1878.
[27] CKS, PS/US 13, Upper Division of the Lathe of Scray Petty Sessions 1871–6, 8 July 1873.

register for 28 June 1890: 'A man unknown found by the side of the road near Brenley Corner. Age: about 50.'[28]

IV

It would be little exaggeration to see the history of the social economy as the history of women's work. Nowhere is this truer than in the households of rural labourers. There is an orthodoxy, only recently challenged, that women were being forced out of the agricultural work force in the nineteenth century.[29] Keith Snell has certainly demonstrated the declining participation of women in farm work in the corn lands of eastern England.[30] But there were important regional variations and the fruit and hops of Kent ensured an ongoing role for women in the cycle of employment. This much is clear from the parliamentary surveys of the nineteenth century and the oral life stories of the twentieth, both of which attest to the prevalence of agricultural work for women (usually married women) in Kent.

A parliamentary report in the 1860s noted that 'in the hop-growing parishes, almost any woman can work (if she will) during a considerable part of the year'.[31] And it is the hop which figures most strongly in accounts of married women's work in the early twentieth century. September hop-picking became part of the labouring culture of this part of rural England and indeed of dockland and working-class London, with women and children descending upon the hop-grounds year after year, joined by their menfolk on weekends.[32] The Kent schools closed; schoolmasters acted as tallymen. The whole family could take part in hop-picking. With payment by the bushel, all hands counted. A good picker could pick about 20 bushels in a day; a child of 12 years a little over half that amount again. Women were considered better pickers than men. The hops offered other work too. Hop-poling was done by men but with help from women and boys who positioned

---

[28] Canterbury Cathedral Archives, Boughton-under-Blean Register of Burials, 1875–1907.

[29] See the discussions in Armstrong, *Farmworkers*, pp. 123–4; H. Bradley, *Men's work, women's work* (Cambridge, 1989), ch. 4; A. Howkins, *Reshaping rural England: a social history 1850–1925* (London, 1991), pp. 101–8, 203–5.

[30] K. D. M. Snell, *Annals of the labouring poor: social change and agrarian England 1660–1900* (Cambridge, 1985), ch. 1.

[31] *Second Report of the Commissioners on the Employment of Children, Young Persons, and Women in Agriculture*, PP, 1868–9, vol. XIII, p. 81.

[32] Most of the informants in the TL collection mention hop-picking, as do those interviewed for the Hernhill Oral History project. See also, M. Lewis (ed.), *Old days in the Kent hop gardens* (Maidstone, 1981). G. O'Neill, *Pull no more bines: an oral history of east London women hop pickers* (London, 1990), deals with memories of picking as late as the 1970s.

the poles – 'a wife with a boy can double a man's wages, at least, by getting the poles ready for him'.[33] Women also did piece-work on their own account: hop-tying was done by the acre, almost exclusively by women. As one nineteenth-century commentator somewhat romantically put it, 'the soil is handled and subdued by the man; the plant is tended and trained by the woman; in the gathering are united all – man, woman and child'.[34] It was estimated in the 1850s and 1860s that women with work in the hop areas could add about £7 to the family coffers, 'to their means of subsistence for the winter'. 'Women's earnings are here a great help to a working family, especially in summer; hop picking is looked forward to to pay off old debts and rents and the woman here is the chief contributor.'[35] The *Morning Chronicle* survey of the rural districts in 1850 was well aware of the importance of hops in the social economy of families in the southern counties:

the hop-picking season is generally looked forward to by many of them with considerable anxiety, as being the turning-point as regards their means for the year. It interposes like a screen between many of them and the workhouse; and if it fails them, they have, too frequently, no alternative but to throw themselves upon the union for the winter. It is seldom, indeed, that you find them relying upon this alone for obtaining the necessaries of life. But they do almost universally rely upon it for supplying them with the means of meeting all the extra expenses to which they have been put, or may still be put, during the remainder of the year, such as for medical attendance, shoes, change of raiment, &c. ... The past year was of grievous disappointment to thousands of them, in consequence of the almost universal failure of the hops. The great majority of those whom I met in deep distress in Kent attributed much of the privation which they were enduring to having had their calculations falsified in respect to the usual earnings of the hop-picking season. In some portions of Surrey, where the yield was good, they were not disappointed.[36]

The generations born in Kent in the period 1890–1930 stressed the importance of hop money for settling old debts run up over the winter, paying the doctor's bill and for providing shoes and clothes for the children. Just how important this money could be in the struggle for survival is illustrated by the memory of Harold Kay (born 1921), one of many children in a Hernhill small-farming household during the Depression, of the year when his mother suffered a miscarriage and could not go hop-picking: 'We were literally starving that Christmas'.[37]

Labour by the task was common in Kent and so it was often the man

[33] *PP*, 1868–9, vol. XIII, p. 277.
[34] *Reports of Special Assistant Poor Law Commissioners on the Employment of Women and Children in Agriculture, PP*, 1843, vol. XII, p. 150.
[35] *Morning Chronicle*, 13 February 1850: 'Labour and the poor: The rural districts'; *PP*, 1868–9, vol. XIII, pp. 273, 279.
[36] *Morning Chronicle*, 13 February 1850.   [37] Hernhill Oral History, H. Kay, b. 1921.

of the labouring household who 'employed' his wife and children to help him fill his contract. At harvest time he could contract to reap by the acre and husband and wife would work together using the sickle or he would use a bagging hook and she would tie the sheaves after him. Working like this they could earn together between 16s. and 36s. a week. The diversification of this part of Kent offered other opportunities. For 1s. to 2s. a day in piece-work or day wages, women could work in their own right: rag-cutting, pole-shaving, bean-planting, weeding, mangold-thinning, fruit-picking, hay-making, harvesting, potato- and turnip-picking, as well as hop-tying and hop-picking.[38] Macnade Farm, near Faversham, provided evidence to the Agricultural Commission of 1867, outlining some of the potentials of the contributions of women and children. This 300-acre farm, large by local standards, paid some £500 in one year for the work of women and children around the farm. It kept 12 women, 8 girls and 8 boys in somewhat fitful work outside harvest and hopping and employed 360 women and children during the hop-picking. Individual women earned £3 a year on average (the most earned by one woman was £5 10s. 9d.), girls £2 7s. and boys £3.[39] But this did not include harvest earnings or the income from hops. When the contribution of these wage-earners is taken into account, a working wife and child, through yearly labour and hopping, could add a further £12 or so to the household economy, an average of around 4s. 6d. a week.

Women and children formed a vast reserve army of labour, there to be called upon during periods of peak activity, hence the hostility of farmers in the nineteenth century to legislation attempting to restrict child labour. One of the qualifications of an employable agricultural labourer was that he had a wife willing and able to work on the farm; this was as true of the early twentieth century as it had been in the nineteenth. Harry Ash (born 1898), son of a Harbledown bailiff, said that women had to work. Farmers would hire men with wives so that they had the extra labour. 'Practically it was the only way to get engaged, working sometimes'.[40] J. W. Manuel's father was a horseman. His mother 'had to go out to work in the fields, it was really compulsory, women on the farm were expected to go to work ... They used to get smothered in mud and dirt the women, they had to do all the lot you know, heavy work and all that, there was no question.'[41]

Stanley Marsh was born in Blean in 1901 and started school on his fourth birthday; 'Most of the children started school at four years of

[38] See B. Reay, *The last rising of the agricultural labourers* (Oxford, 1990), pp. 45–7.
[39] PP, 1868–9, vol. XIII, pp. 281–2.
[40] TL, H. Ash, b. 1898.   [41] TL, J. W. Manuel, b. 1903.

age, for the simple reason that their parents, both father and mother, needed to have some sort of employment in the village in order to maintain themselves above the poverty line.' He remembered that men and women worked side by side at the corn and hay harvests in the 1900s. The men cut in gangs with scythes; the women collected the corn and lay it in sheaves; the sheaves were tied by men.[42] A. Austin recalled women picking fruit: blackcurrants, gooseberries, redcurrants, raspberries and strawberries. They also picked peas from 7 a.m. until 5 p.m. for 18d. a day at the turn of the century, exactly what they would have earned over a generation earlier in the 1860s. For this they had to walk miles there and back just to get to work, 'dragging them little kids behind them'.[43] Women in Hernhill in the early 1900s picked strawberries from 4.30 a.m. to 7.30 a.m. to be sent by train to the London market. 'All the prams, all the babies all wheeled up there.'[44] Dorothy Tong (born 1912), who lived in nearby Dunkirk, could remember the babies in 'trucks' (boxes with hoods and handles) and all the children in the fields with their mothers when she went picking fruit and training hops. She 'started out on the fields' when her own four children were 'old enough to be left' and worked as a farmworker until she was in her sixties. Her husband, Hubert, was a ladder-maker but business was slack in the winter so her work was crucial for the family's survival: 'I used to go out here owing, to earn some money to keep us.'[45] Elsie Foster's (born 1908) mother worked 'out in the fields fruit picking, picking up potatoes, picking peas, she worked jolly hard. She had to in them days, to bring up all of us.'[46] One of the early Prudential agents, selling 1d. a week life insurance policies at the turn of the century, used to work only in the evenings during the summer because all the women in the rural districts were out in the fields during the day.[47] Violet Turner (born 1896) had to work in the fields after she got married – 'my husband's money wasn't good enough to keep us on'. She worked in the hop-fields, picking, training, cutting and burning hop-bines; she planted and picked potatoes; picked fruit, beans and parsley; she worked in the beetroot fields; and cut cabbage and picked brussels in winter ('I've had to knock the snow off them').[48] There is not much evidence here for a decline in the rural female labour force.

---

[42] Canterbury Library, S. Marsh, 'An account of Blean and surrounds', unpublished typescript.
[43] TL, A. Austin, b. 1889.   [44] TL, A. Packman, b. 1892.
[45] Hernhill Oral History, D. Tong, b. 1912; H. Tong, b. 1909.
[46] Hernhill Oral History, E. Foster, b. 1908.   [47] TL, E. Burgess, b. 1890.
[48] TL, V. Turner, b. 1896.

V

It must be clear by now that the work of children was a linch-pin of the social economy. Mr Edward Stanhope's report to the Parliamentary Commission of 1867 outlined the nature of child labour in agricultural districts: 'The labour of children is of two sorts; (1) where they are hired directly by the occupier of the farm, and (2) where they are employed by their parents on gardens or allotments, in assisting in gleaning or other family work, in collecting fuel or woo[d], and in gathering blackberries or mushrooms in the lanes.'[49] The records of Kent schools chart the seasonal ebb and flow of the labour of school-age children during the late nineteenth century, either working directly for wages or helping a father or mother with piece-work: bark-stripping and hop-tying in April and May; pea-picking, hay-making and fruit-picking in June and July; harvesting in August; fruit-picking and hopping in September; the harvest of vegetables in October and November; field work, bird-scaring, wood-cutting and hop-pole-shaving during the winter. Boys were employed in an extremely wide range of tasks – indeed most of the jobs done by men and women. The work of girls tended to reflect that of women, for that was how the skills of one generation were handed on to the next.[50]

The peak period for children's labour in the rural areas was May to September (inclusive). To argue for a lack of jobs for children from a census taken in March or April is thus somewhat beside the point, but Hugh Cunningham does demonstrate that when we write of child employment (or unemployment) during the nineteenth century, we are effectively writing about children aged 10 and over.[51] Eight year olds did work for wages on the farms, but they were a tiny minority. As the farmer Mr F. Neame stated, in opposition to measures to curb juvenile labour:

I do not see the necessity of any Act to prohibit it, for in agriculture the children will not be of much use under 10 years of age, neither will they be of much use if they are kept without work much over that age, for it is by early and good training that the habits of industry are formed. Between 10 and 13 or 14 is a time of life when the children are unable to obtain a situation away from home, a time when they are a heavy and increasing expense to their parents, and a time when they require better living than perhaps the wages of their parents can afford, without the assistance of some earnings from their children.[52]

---

[49] *PP*, 1868–9, vol. XIII, p. 89.

[50] See chapter 8 below. See also, J. Kitteringham, 'Country work girls in nineteenth-century England', in R. Samuel (ed.), *Village life and labour* (London, 1975), pp. 75–138.

[51] H. Cunningham, 'The employment and unemployment of children in England *c.* 1680–1851', *Past and Present*, 126 (1990), pp. 115–50.

[52] *PP*, 1868–9, vol. XIII, p. 282.

Those who did work were paid about 6d. a day or 3s. 6d. a week, though they could earn more than this during the various harvests. H. J. Ward, who was born in Charing in 1868 and who left school at the age of 10, wrote that the children in labouring households had to leave school if a job came up; 'if there was a job going at any wage though very small we had to try for it even at 2d. or 3d. per day'.[53]

By the 1900s the cumulative effects of parliamentary legislation had forced the threshold of the effective working age of children upwards from 10 towards 14. Fourteen was the upward cut-off point: the oral sources are agreed on this. In the labouring households of the villages and hamlets of Kent, the rule was that as soon as the child turned 14 it was agricultural labour for the boys and domestic service for the girls, a pattern which remained into the 1930s. 'Get out and get on with it' was the attitude.[54] Some left earlier. J. W. Manuel was 'only too glad' to leave school at 12 'to earn a few shillings'. He said that children younger than this could get work on a farm, helping their mother with the fruit or working for a labourer who had contracted to pick potatoes.[55] Mrs E. Burgess went into service when she was 12: 'I had to get away from school as soon as I could help bring a little bit for living'; 'when I was young there was nothing for girls to do except go to service'.[56] Violet Turner (then Grey) went off to service when she was 14. She got 3s. a week. Her mother and brother walked with her the long walk to Chilham station and her mother bought the ticket. 'I said to my mother, only a single ticket mother, don't I have to have a return one, aren't I coming home? No, she said, I don't want you home yet a while, you've got to earn your living now. Oh I cried, I got on the train, I sat and cried.'[57] Len Austin left school when he was young too. His father wanted him to get out and work: 'Work. Just work. That's why I had to leave school before I was 13 to work. I only got four bob a week when I left.'[58]

It is clear from the interviews with the generation born in the 1890s and the 1900s that the little money they earned was not seen as their own. We may recall that Tremeere's wages paid for the rent (though he did hold back 'earnings' that his father was unaware of). Hubert Tong (born 1909) worked in the Dunkirk–Boughton area as an agricultural labourer when he was 14; he handed his 8s. a week to his mother and she gave him 1s. back.[59] Most saw themselves as earning for the family

---

[53] Ashford Library, H. J. Ward, 'My early recollections of Charing since 1868', unpublished typescript, 1933, p. 8.

[54] TL, Mr and Mrs Arnold, b. 1907 and 1910.

[55] TL, J. W. Manuel, b. 1903.   [56] TL, E. Burgess, b. 1890.

[57] TL, V. Turner, b. 1896.   [58] TL, L. Austin, b. 1902.

[59] Hernhill Oral History, H. Tong, b. 1909.

economy, though they did not phrase it precisely in those terms. A brick-moulder's son put it quite simply: 'Us being a large family, as soon as I was able I left school for work. The four shillings I earned the first year would go into the pool.' And when he recounted the potential earnings of young barrow-loaders in the brickfields, he observed that the boy might get 5d. of the 10s. 5d. that he earned a week and his mother would get the 10s.[60] A. Austin was given 6d. a week out of his wage when he first worked. Albert Packman was paid 8d. a day for his first job on a farm, 4s. a week, which he handed over to his mother. 'Mum give me a penny for myself.' 'It was more than my four bob to keep me.'[61] Violet Turner's first paid work was as a servant in a local household, so she remained at home. Her mother kept all of her 2s. a week. One of her brothers, who worked with their father, did not get paid anything at all (he eventually joined the army).[62] Dorothy Tong told me at one point in the interview that her mother gave her 6d. a week, which she spent on dancing. It later transpired that the 6d. which her mother 'gave' her was in fact part of the £1 a week that Dorothy (she was then Dorothy Coombs) earned at the Chartham paper mill.[63] Syd Twist explained that attitudes were different then; children were pleased to be able to contribute to the survival of the family: 'You know, you knew that every penny helped.'[64]

The second type of child labour outlined by Stanhope in 1867 was unwaged work. As Anna Davin has put it, the labouring household was 'an economic unit in which all members but the very youngest played a part', contributing unpaid labour as well as any earnings.[65] Harold Kay recalls that he was effectively earning money for the family from the age of 9. In the summer he would be out at 4 a.m. helping his father pick blackberries and mushrooms from the lanes and hedgerows to sell. He worked with his mother in the hop-fields, both picking and hop-training, 'to make money to keep the family going'. His mother also went pea-picking but was unable to do too much lifting because she was often pregnant, so Harold did the heavy work. She contracted to pull wurzels (beets) in the autumn and would work during the day while her son and husband took over in the evenings, 'when it was moonlight', to help her fill the quota ('I can still see very good in the dark'). 'This was more money for the family.'[66]

---

[60] TL, H. Adley, b. 1886.   [61] TL, A. Austin, b. 1889; A. Packman, b. 1892.
[62] TL, V. Turner, b. 1896.   [63] Hernhill Oral History, D. Tong, b. 1912.
[64] TL, S. Twist, b. 1899.
[65] A. Davin, 'When is a child not a child?', in H. Corr and L. Jamieson (eds.), *Politics of everyday life* (London, 1990), p. 39.
[66] Hernhill Oral History, H. Kay, b. 1921; and H. Kay, personal correspondence, 6 March 1993.

Children would gather fuel. Packman used a sugar box on wheels to get pine cones for the copper.[67] Harry Matthews would be up before school in the winter, sometimes before light, scouring the tips for cinders and pieces of wood for the family fire.[68] Children chopped wood and roots, fetched water from the well, collected rabbit food or acorns for the pig.[69] The young Matthews scavenged weekend left-overs of food from a middle-class woman whom he did odd jobs for.[70] Both boys and girls helped around the house; they looked after the younger children or they made sure that the fire was lit and there was a pot of tea for their mother when she returned from work in the late afternoon.[71] They would run errands. Nine-year-old Matthews went to the pub at 7 a.m. on summer mornings to fetch his brickmaking father his first pint for the day.[72] Children would go shopping or do a preparatory reconnaissance of the shops in the nearest town on Saturday mornings, seeking out the cheapest bargains so that their parents need not waste time looking when they went shopping on Saturday nights.[73] The school log books of the late nineteenth century indicate that girls would be kept at home to help with domestic chores, on washing days for example, or to look after the very young members of their families and free their mothers for work in the fields. Boughton youngsters sometimes remained at home on the day before a market to pick produce in their parents' gardens.[74]

Children would also go gleaning with their mothers. A recent study of gleaning found that gleaning was worth from £1 to £3 a year for labouring families in the period before 1850 or 3 to 14 per cent of those families' average income. Kay's 1838 survey of the earnings of agricultural labourers in Norfolk and Suffolk was at the bottom end of the margin: a consistent 3 per cent of annual earnings, an average annual value of just over £1.[75] But as we have seen, a pound was a significant amount in that penny economy. In the corn-lands where there was little prospect of other subsidiary earnings or means of gathering free food, the gleanings must have been extremely important for the family economy, particularly where there was winter unemployment. In such areas gleaning no doubt fulfilled the function that hopping did in Kent, with the same disastrous impact on the makeshift family economy should the woman of the house be unable to carry out this annual task.

[67] TL, A. Packman, b.1892.   [68] TL, H. Matthews, b. 1890.
[69] TL, J. W. Manuel, b. 1903; A. Packman, b. 1892; G. Post, b. 1896.
[70] TL, H. Matthews, b. 1890.   [71] TL, A. Packman, b. 1892.
[72] TL, H. Matthews, b. 1890.   [73] TL, E. Burgess, b. 1890.   [74] See chapter 8.
[75] P. King, 'Customary rights and women's earnings: the importance of gleaning to the rural labouring poor, 1750–1850', *Economic History Review*, 44 (1991), pp. 461–76; Kay, 'Earnings'.

This does not mean that people did not glean in the Blean. Cases appear in the court records for the nineteenth century. A woman was gleaning in a Dunkirk field in 1836 when she saw some men with dogs and guns hunting for partridges on the farmer's land. In the same area in 1841 three women and their children were gleaning for barley when a man came up to them, asked them what they were doing and hit one of them in the face. In Boughton in 1861 a dispute between some gleaning families ended up in the courts. In all three cases the events occurred in September – at the end of the harvest – and those carrying out the gleaning were women and children.[76] We know little about the fate of gleaning during the late nineteenth and early twentieth centuries, but the fact that it is rarely mentioned in the oral evidence (in stark contrast to hopping) suggests that its role in subsistence had probably declined.

Stanhope should have listed a third type of children's work: penny capitalism.[77] Like Steve Tremeere in Dover, Harry Matthews squeezed the most out of the local economy. He could bring in 9d. to 18d. a day 'totting', that is sifting through Faversham waste for bones and bottles. He dealt with other boys, offering them 1d. each for the silver ferrules found on broken smoking-pipes, knowing where he could get 3d. for them. He bought herrings from a local pub at $\frac{3}{4}$d. each and sold them for 1d. 'I can't ever remember being what we call broke, because I'd always got something. I could buy or sell anything, I could, I reckon.'[78] The opportunities for such childhood dealing were far greater in the towns.

VI

We saw that theft played an important role in Tremeere's repertoire of survival; it was also important the villages. And yet theft does not loom large in social histories of the British working class, even though it is clear from many of the oral histories and the earlier court records that stealing was part of the economy of makeshifts. We are dealing here with a rather amorphous subject, ranging from perks to petty theft, regular or occasional, and more organized, large-scale thieving.

The records of the nineteenth century permit us to look a little more closely at crimes of subsistence, for that is what most of them were:

---

[76] CKS, Fa/JP 7/1, Faversham Petty Sessions/Upper Division of the Lathe of Scray Petty Sessions 1832–9, 29 September 1836; CKS, PS/US 10, Upper Division of the Lathe of Scray Petty Sessions 1839–45, 2 September 1841; *Faversham Mercury*, 7 September 1861.

[77] For penny capitalism, see J. Benson, *The penny capitalists* (Dublin, 1983).

[78] TL, H. Matthews, b. 1890.

theft of peas, beans, grain, rabbits, fowls, fruit, potatoes, cabbages, turnips, fuel. Two Hernhill labourers were in trouble in 1870 for stealing potatoes. One was reputed to have said, 'old Gough has got some bloody nice potatoes here let's have some of them'; he 'had a string tied round his trouser bottom and his trousers' leg full of potatoes'.[79] It must have been a question of luck, for there is no doubt that those actually caught were but the tip of a vaster undeclared 'dark figure of crime'. Many were stealing to eat – the man with the potatoes down his trousers had the vegetables for his dinner. Or they were getting household fuel, a potentially large item of expenditure. William Mears, a 47-year-old labourer who found himself in the courts in 1852 for stealing 8d. worth of coal, said in his defence that he 'had got no work, no money, nor no victuals and no firing'.[80] However, we know that some were selling rather than consuming the items that they stole. Goods stolen in Kent villages were pawned in Canterbury or sold in nearby beershops.[81] There were complaints of semi-organized thefts of foodstuffs from the rural areas for sale in markets in the towns. Returns to a Royal Commission in 1837 reported that stolen articles were 'sold regularly in the streets as vegetables, rabbits, fowls, fish, fruit, &c.'[82] In 1885 it was alleged that greens taken from Hernhill fields were finding their way to Whitstable for sale.[83]

Theft may have been the principal means of support for some individuals. A father and son, arrested in the winter of 1890–1 for wood-stealing in Dunkirk, were notorious offenders. It was said in the police court that these men 'did not seem to do anything for a living but steal this wood, which they converted to various purposes such as handles for blacksmiths' hammers ... they might almost put over their door "Stealers of Underwood"'. James senior had asked their apprehender to 'let him have a few to get a loaf with': the man replied, 'no, he had had loaves enough from there already'.[84] One can safely assume that other rural communities had their Jameses.

Len Austin made no bones about the situation in many labouring homes in the first part of this century: 'If you couldn't get it you'd pinch it. Well, I don't care what anyone says, if they speak the truth they did, they pinched all they could, they had to or else they'd starve'.[85] Several

[79] CKS, PS/US 12, Upper Division of the Lathe of Scray Petty Sessions 1868–71, 11 July 1870.
[80] CKS, Q/SBe 209, East Kent Quarter Sessions, 2 July 1852.
[81] Reay, *Last rising*, p. 71.
[82] PRO, HO 73/9, Royal Commission to inquire at the best means of establishing an efficient Constabulary Force, 1836–8, pt 2.
[83] *Faversham Mercury*, 9 May 1885.   [84] *Faversham Mercury*, 7 February 1891.
[85] TL, L. Austin, b. 1902.

of those interviewed in the 1970s spoke of youthful indiscretions, such as picking up turnips from the fields on the way to school and eating them, stealing potatoes and cooking them on an open fire, or fruit stealing (Manuel said that the only fresh fruit that they got they stole).[86] Others talked about the perks of farmwork; of potatoes put into pockets, of handfuls of beans or peas taken while threshing, of hop-pockets finding their way into cottages as curtains.[87] The attitude of the farm labourer was that small quantities taken from the place of work for personal consumption, or to feed chickens, rabbits or pigs, was a perk. (Horsemen frequently helped themselves to extra food for their teams.) In their eyes, this was different from theft. 'Well I mean to say, if you grew cabbages or potatoes, well that's what you call perks. You wasn't allowed to take them home, but you did. There it was ... If you looked after the horses you could always get hold of a bit of corn for your chickens, that kind of thing.' The farmer knew what was going on but 'he didn't say anything like'.[88] The attitudes of farmers varied. We know from the nineteenth-century records that some took their employees to court for theft. Others probably turned a blind eye to small amounts. Percy Saddleton, who farmed in Hernhill in the 1920s and 1930s, knew that his workers took his corn to feed their chickens: 'We used to feed the chicken; I know that.' But he did not do anything about it other than making sure that his workers had nothing bigger than a chicken or rabbit to feed. 'We knew they hadn't got anything, poor devils.'[89]

'Scrumping' was a local term which covered this sort of activity. Strictly speaking, 'scrumping' was the gathering of windfall apples, but people in Hernhill and Boughton used it in a much more general way to describe activity encompassing gleaning, 'perks' of the sort just discussed and pilfering from those other than one's employer. This attachment of a name to activity with an almost deliberate indefinitude seems to have been a means of self-justification for the labouring community. 'Well, we didn't pinch, we just took them didn't we ... But then that's scrumping wasn't it?'[90]

Poaching was rife in the rural areas. The large poaching gangs have gained the most attention, but the most typical offenders were labouring men operating alone or in small groups, snaring, tracking, hunting with dogs and guns. Poaching was what has been called a

[86] TL, Mr and Mrs Arnold, b. 1907 and 1910; J. W. Manuel, b. 1903.
[87] TL, F. Pack, b. 1897; Hernhill Oral History, E. Wade, b. 1908.
[88] TL, G. Post, b. 1896; V. Turner, b. 1896.
[89] Hernhill Oral History, P. Saddleton, b. 1907.
[90] Hernhill Oral History, E. Wade, b. 1908.

'social crime', enjoying the sympathy, if not the open sanction, of large sections of the labouring population.[91] Frank Kemsley said it was all right to catch rabbits – 'they were our perks' – but not pheasants. 'Everybody' would poach rabbits in the woods.[92] Len Austin used wires, though he knew how to catch a rabbit with a stick of bramble; he said that the poachers used ferrets. His family relied on rabbits for meat – 'if we didn't get rabbit we didn't get nothing else' – and would also sell them for 9d. ('an hour and a half's pay practically').[93] Men poached for the same reasons that they stole – to supplement their diet or their modest incomes. Whether the goal was food or money, the ultimate goal was the same: to make ends meet. 'Theft' was an integral part of the social economy.

VII

Income, whatever the source, and whether in cash or kind, formed only part of the labouring family economy. Expenditure and distribution were just as important. Indeed labour history should be as much about budgeting as the male wage and organized labour.[94] Here we come back to the role of women in the social economy. In the words of David Vincent, 'Any understanding of the strategies which were adopted to cope with poverty, and the costs which they entailed, has to begin with those around whom everything seemed to revolve.'[95]

Budgeting was a fine art. Earnings were unpredictable. There was an awareness of the seasonality discussed earlier, the major income fluctuations over the year. But there were waves within waves, so to speak, for it was difficult to know when illness or injury would strike or when a bad crop or bad weather would undermine the fragile margin between survival and destitution. There were the longer, life-cycle fluctuations too: many labouring families could expect a period of deeper poverty before their children were old enough to make a substantial contribution to the family economy. Middle-class observers were critical of the lack of planning in labouring households and of the

[91] See J. G. Rule, 'Social crime in the rural south in the eighteenth and early nineteenth centuries', *Southern History*, 1 (1979), pp. 135–53; A. Howkins, 'Economic crime and class law: poaching and the game laws, 1840–1880', in S. Burman and B. E. Harrell-Bond (eds.), *The imposition of law* (New York, 1979), ch. 15.
[92] TL, F. Kemsley, b. 1887.   [93] TL, L. Austin, b. 1902.
[94] See L. H. Lees, 'Getting and spending: the family budgets of English industrial workers', in J. M. Merriman (ed.), *Consciousness and class experience in nineteenth-century Europe* (New York, 1979), ch. 8. See also Ellen Ross's marvellous chapter, 'Feeding a family', in Ross, *Love and toil: motherhood in outcast London 1870–1918* (New York, 1993), ch. 2.
[95] Vincent, *Poor citizens*, p. 6.

lack of awareness (by the keeper of the household budget) of average yearly earnings. If these critics had swapped places with the subjects of their attention, they would have realized the impossibility of so-called rational calculation. The strategy of the poor really was the only one available to them. As we shall see, they used credit as a way of evening out some of the fluctuations, but the bulk of their calculations had to be made on a day-to-day basis.

The aim was to feed at the least possible cost; to fill stomachs rather than providing nutrition and variety. Bread and potatoes were the staples. Household budgets drawn up in the various nineteenth-century surveys show that from 40 to 60 per cent of the male wage was spent on bread or flour. In the mid nineteenth century, a family of two adults and four children would be spending about 5s. a week on flour out of an adult male wage of some 13s. Those with larger families, though not necessarily higher wages, would be spending even more. Some women baked their own bread – it is probable that bakehouses were shared in much the same way as wells – but many purchased it, probably because of the lack of cooking facilities, the cost of fuel and the amount of time involved in baking for a large family (even if it was done just once a week). As we have seen, some would get stale bread to economize.

By the end of the century the dietaries indicate that the percentage spent on bread or flour dropped as diets became more varied, but bread can still be described as the basic food item in labouring households.[96] As Twist put it, 'Bread was the major, the basic diet, bread was, bread and potatoes, no question of that.'[97] The oral histories all mention the ubiquity of bread. 'Marvellous what we did live on. Mostly bread and jam. Bread and potatoes. Potatoes and onion pasty usually we had to take to work. Bread and cheese mostly.' Kemsley recalled that bread and jam was 'pretty near all they lived on, bread and jam, poor people. Well poor, good honest working people, the kids used to always take bread and jam to school, had nothing else to take. No butter, never think about kids having butter. Dripping – used to have dripping sometimes.'[98] Manuel summarized his childhood diet in similar terms:

---

[96] See the discussions in E. H. Hunt, *British labour history 1815–1914* (London, 1988), pp. 81–8; and D. J. Oddy, 'Food, drink and nutrition', in F. M. L. Thompson (ed.), *The Cambridge social history of Britain 1750–1950*, vol. II, *People and their environment* (Cambridge, 1990), ch. 5. Compare the budgets in E. C. Tufnell, 'The dwellings and general economy of the labouring classes in Kent and Sussex' [1841], in J. Simon, *Report on the sanitary condition of the City of London* (London, 1853), with the later budgets in M. F. Davies, *Life in an English village* (London, 1909).
[97] TL, S. Twist, b. 1899.   [98] TL, L. Austin, b. 1902; F. Kemsley, b. 1887.

I suppose up to a point we was like these peasants that I used to read of later in China and the far east where they had a bowl of rice a day. Well we had a little more, when you come to weigh it up. We had more slightly, we had porridge every morning, or bread and marge, and in the evening I suppose more bread and marge or something, cheese. Nothing else.[99]

'We lived plain' was the retrospective verdict.[100] Of course bread was not the only food item. Vegetables were grown in cottage gardens in the villages and in allotments in the towns. Informants spoke of fathers digging their own plots after a day's labour.[101] The Faversham brickyards provided space for horticulture.[102] Pigs, rabbits and chicken could all provide a supplement to rural diets. People would raise them themselves or they would purchase their various products in small quantities from their neighbours. Several people spoke of sharing an egg between two or three children as a treat on Sundays.[103] Horace Adley's family kept pigs: 'A man what used to live up there used to kill them, then he used to cut them up and all the people buy. Anybody out of work give them the head.'[104] The oral informants remember jams, pickles, puddings (much of their food was boiled rather than baked), soups, stews, meats (mainly offal) and fish. Parents would wait until the butcher's was about to close and buy a few pence worth of pieces.[105] The brickmakers of Faversham had the reputation of being big consumers of meat.[106] But the overriding impression is of the enforced vegetarianism of numerous labouring households in both the nineteenth and early twentieth centuries: 'It was all vegetables ... vegetables and cabbage and potatoes was your limit'.[107]

Nor should we get carried away by childhood memories of cottage-garden self-sufficiency and rabbit stew. It is true that garden-grown potatoes and greens meant less money spent in the weekly budget. B. S. Rowntree and M. Kendall found in their study of rural labouring families in 1913 that a majority supplemented the food purchased with produce from their own gardens. But they cautioned against overrating the value of the garden. On average, about a twelfth of the food consumed by these families was home-grown.[108] An agricultural labourer pointed out that an average garden would not have kept a decent-sized family for long. At most, it was a help; people still had to buy or steal the bulk of their vegetables. 'Used to have to buy potatoes

---

[99] TL, J. W. Manuel, b. 1903.   [100] TL, S. Twist, b. 1899.
[101] TL, E. Burgess, b. 1890; Hernhill Oral History, E. Foster, b. 1908.
[102] TL, H. Adley, b. 1886.   [103] TL, E. Burgess, b. 1890; G. Post, b. 1896.
[104] TL, H. Adley, b. 1886.   [105] TL, E. Burgess, b. 1890; F. Pack, b. 1897.
[106] TL, S. Twist, b. 1899.   [107] TL, J. W. Manuel, b. 1903.
[108] B. S. Rowntree and M. Kendall, *How the labourer lives* (London, 1913), p. 307.

or pinch them.'[109] There was also a limit to the number of rabbits that a labouring family could raise for meat – usually two or three in hutches – and they would hardly provide fare for the weekly pot, unless they were supplemented by poaching.[110]

Mothers and wives had to 'make something out of nothing', in Emily Wade's apposite phrase.[111] It was the wife and mother's task to purchase, procure, distribute, calculate and decide on priorities. She often did so at her own expense. Laura Oren has warned against assuming that all members of a family shared the same standard of living. Like society at large, experiences were determined by gender and age.[112] It was common practice for wage-earning males to enjoy a better diet than other members of the family. If meat was consumed in any quantities, the chances were that it went to the father and the elder wage-earning males. Meat, as Rowntree and Kendall wrote, was used as a flavouring rather than as a substantial course. And it was for the man only.[113] All too often it was the wife and mother who scrimped on her own food to make sure that her children would not go without. 'We never went without did we? We went very short, but we didn't go without.' 'Well our mothers went without that was why.' 'My family used to say to me, mother, why do you always have the head of the rabbit, and why do you always have the parson's nose of a chicken. I used to say that was all that was left time I'd fed ten of us a chicken or a rabbit, there wasn't much left.'[114]

The pressures of making do devolved upon the women. Elsie Foster, daughter and wife of agricultural labourers, described the double jeopardy of wet weather:

If they got a wet day and couldn't go to work, they used to go up the pub, put it on the slate, what they owed, you see, and then when they had their week's money, they had to take that lot out and pay their debts, and the poor old mother had to have what was left. Yeh, they was a bit hard times for women in them days. That's why mother had to go out to work.

She said that her mother looked after the money because she was more thrifty than her father.[115] Village women would walk to the nearest

---

[109] TL, L. Austin, b. 1902.
[110] TL, H. Adley, b. 1886; H. Ash, b. 1898.
[111] Hernhill Oral History, E. Wade, b. 1908. For 'making do', see E. Hostettler, ' "Making do": domestic life among East Anglian labourers, 1890–1910', in L. Davidoff and B. Westover (eds.), *Our work, our lives, our words* (London, 1986), ch. 2.
[112] L. Oren, 'The welfare of women in labouring families: England, 1860–1950', *Feminist Studies*, 1 (1973), pp. 107–25.
[113] Rowntree and Kendall, *How the labourer lives*, pp. 308–9.
[114] Hernhill Oral History, E. Wade, b. 1908; A. Bones, b. 1912.
[115] Hernhill Oral History, E. Foster, b. 1908.

town because that was where the bargains could be found.[116] Mothers had to enforce the fine rules of economy that kept families afloat. Packman's father was a bailiff so he lived more comfortably than many. Nevertheless, there were economies to be observed. You:

couldn't have bread and butter if you had jam, you didn't have butter, if you had cheese you didn't have butter. If you had butter you didn't have nothing else with it. You couldn't have the lot together, and that was the first thing when I left home, I thought oh this is smashing, I sat down and had bread, butter and jam, bread, butter and cheese, cor.[117]

But it is an interview with a Kent woman in 1850 which provides the best picture of the wife's role in the household economy. There were ten in the family, but the eldest daughter was in service and a boy worked to maintain himself ('minus his clothes'). There were still eight dependent on the wages of her husband, a farm labourer, who earned 13s. a week. A quarter of this went on rent, 3d. on school fees for three children, a few pence on clothing and coal clubs. This left a total of 9s. 6d. for food. She spent up to 7s. on bread and the remainder went on vegetables and cheese. The woman said that she had to provide over 100 meals a week for 9s. 6d. (her interviewer noted that in fact the number was 168). The proper management of food was crucial; when she was confined to her bed during childbirth, the bread had not lasted because the nurse who had been brought in to look after her and the family 'did not know how to cut it right'. 'My husband often comes home very tired ... and thinks it very hard sometimes that he can't have a bit of butcher's meat for supper. But then I tell him that if he works with his hands, I work with the head and hands too, so that there's not much difference between us.'[118]

Food was not the only demand on the family purse. Economies could be made through making or repairing items that would normally have to be bought. Mats were made out of rags.[119] Beds would be filled with chaff at threshing time.[120] Women would make their families' shirts, frocks, nightgowns, quilts and sheets.[121] Boots and shoes were mended with the leather from old saddles. Hop sacking was used for curtains.[122] There were other ways of saving pennies. Clothes were handed down in the family; those bought were always at least a size too big.[123] Ward wrote that 'Clothes were nearly all home

---

[116] TL, F. Pack, b. 1897.　　　[117] TL, A. Packman, b. 1892.
[118] *Morning Chronicle*, 30 March 1850.
[119] TL, H. Adley, b. 1886, F. Pack, b. 1897, A. Packman, b. 1892; Hernhill Oral History, E. Wade, b. 1908.
[120] TL, A. Packman, b. 1892; V. Turner, b. 1896.
[121] TL, A. Austin, b. 1889; V. Turner, b. 1896.
[122] Hernhill Oral History, E. Wade, b. 1908.　　　[123] TL, L. Austin, b. 1902.

made or made by a tailoress cut out or down, boys of fathers, girls of mothers ... your clothes were always made large enough to hand down to your next brother or sister, we looked more like scarecrows than youngsters.'[124]

VIII

Credit lay at the heart of the social economy.[125] Indeed, given the fluctuations in income and demand discussed earlier, labouring families would not have survived without it. Pawning – to Tremeere's 'man with the three brass balls' – served this function in the towns. A report from Liverpool in 1909 described the resort to the pawnshop as 'a sort of retrogressive saving. In bad weeks clothes and furniture are pledged and debts incurred. In good weeks the surplus is spent in getting straight again.'[126] The inhabitants of villages and hamlets did not have such easy access to the pawnshop, so credit there was more direct: they went into debt to the landlord, shopkeeper, publican and doctor. The only way they survived, according to Frank Pack, was by credit. If they got behind with the rent they would pay it after the harvest; the same with the shopping.[127] Len Austin said that it was possible to get credit in all the local shops. 'They liked it. They'd rather have what they call, what you call it, tailed up as they call it, they liked that, because they knowed they'd got your trade, they didn't mind if you paid or not because they knew they'd still got your trade coming in.' In the pubs, drink could be put on the slate, although this was usually cleared at the end of the week. People would get into debt to the doctor too – 'practically everybody in the village owed him money'. Austin could also remember a variety of traders who came out to the villages selling clothing which could be purchased for a shilling a week.[128] Harry Wheeler's parents ran a pub and then a shop in Boughton. Credit was an accepted part of business, particularly during the winter months. He explained that credit was two-edged: shopkeepers were reluctant to refuse credit for fear of losing trade and once they had given it it was difficult to stop because if they did they might never be paid. It was a case of assessing the credit-worthiness of individuals, easier no doubt in smaller face-to-face communities. The expectation in the hopping areas was that debts would be cleared after

---

[124] Ward, 'Early recollections', p. 8.
[125] See M. Tebbutt, *Making ends meet: pawnbroking and working-class credit* (Leicester, 1983); P. Johnson, *Saving and spending: the working-class economy in Britain 1870–1939* (Oxford, 1985), ch. 6.
[126] Quoted in Johnson, *Saving and spending*, p. 178.
[127] TL, F. Pack, b. 1897.   [128] TL, L. Austin, b. 1902.

picking.[129] The Faversham brickies would go into debt for bread and groceries and 'square it all in the summer'.[130]

There were various loosely organized, self-help schemes to facilitate the saving of a few pennies and shillings. Many labouring households belonged to coal clubs – often run from pubs. Subscribers paid so much a week and coal was bought in bulk and shared out among contributors. Boot or shoe and clothing clubs consisted of time-payments (that is, savings) for specific items of clothing.[131] Matthews ran a 'halfpenny club' at the Brents around the time of the First World War. Members paid ½d. the first week, 1d. the second week and so on, increasing each week by a ½d. until they were paying 1s. 1d.; then the process would begin again. This would accumulate 28s. 8d. per person. At the share-out participants would get their 28s. and Matthews kept 8d. in commission.[132] No doubt a range of variants of the same theme have vanished without a trace, dying with the memories of the participants.

Sickness and death were costly businesses. Family reconstitutions for this part of rural Kent suggest that up to the end of the nineteenth century 25 to 30 per cent of labouring marriages were broken by the death of at least one of the partners before the woman reached the age of 45. Of the children of labouring households, one out of every five would not live to see their fifth birthday.[133] The cheapest of burials in the nineteenth century in rural areas, paid for by poor relief, cost about £1 for a baby and £2 for an adult, large sums in a labouring house-hold's terms.[134] Sickness could be expensive too. It was not unknown for medical bills to be as high as £2 or £4. There was also the cost of getting nursing assistance (2s. 6d. a week per patient) and, most important, the loss of earnings if the sick person was bringing in an income.[135]

Membership of a benefit society, friendly society or club was a way of insuring against the impact of these facts of life.[136] Services were provided by what were known as the legally enrolled benefit or friendly societies. For a weekly payment, they provided insurance for

[129]   Hernhill Oral History, H. Wheeler, b. 1912. For the role of shopkeepers in the community, see C. P. Hosgood, 'The "pigmies of commerce" and the working-class community: small shopkeepers in England, 1870–1914', *Journal of Social History*, 22 (1989), pp. 439–60.

[130]   TL, H. Matthews, b. 1890.

[131]   Johnson, *Saving and spending*, pp. 150–2; TL, E. Clark, b. 1885.

[132]   TL, H. Matthews, b. 1890.   [133] See chapter 3.

[134]   See CKS, G/F RA 12–14.   [135] *Ibid.*

[136]   Johnson, *Saving and spending*, ch. 3; M. Winstanley, 'Nineteenth century friendly societies', *Bygone Kent*, 1981; D. Neave, *Mutual aid in the Victorian countryside: friendly societies in the rural East Riding 1830–1914* (Hull, 1991).

sickness or death. There was also a host of unregistered clubs and societies which provided assistance dependent on the amount of cash in the coffer and the demands of sickness and death for any given year. Quite often, these unregistered societies would share out the remaining kitty at an end-of-year dinner at Whitsun. The Sittingbourne Death Club (1872) was one such society. It was not enrolled and had no written rules. Held at the Globe and Engine public house, its policy was to pay at the death of each member £2 10s. for a man, £2 for a woman and £1 10s. for a child. It had about 160 members who paid 2d. a week (payable every three weeks). Its secretary was a labourer.[137] Albert Packman could remember various societies in the Hernhill district early this century. He had heard of the Royal Ancient Order of Buffaloes, nicknamed 'the ragged arse old buggers'. His father was a member of the Oddfellows of Faversham, but he was also the treasurer of the local Hernhill sickness club, which met at the pub. People paid 6d. or 1s. a week, according to Packman, and drew money when they were sick – whatever was left was shared out at a Christmas dinner.[138] Mrs E. Clark, a cordwainer's daughter from Badlesmere, was able to list off the club festivities in her area: Molash 'had a do' on the first Saturday in May, Challock on the second Saturday, Badlesmere on the third, Throwley on the fourth. 'Everybody' belonged to these sickness clubs. Her father was a member of the tradesman's club at Wye, as the local one was for the labourers.[139] Len Austin's father belonged to a 'slate-club' in Boughton village. For 'a tanner a week', sickness benefits were paid to the tune of 10s. a week, if there was money in the club. Members were expected to drink at the pub when they paid their dues. If anything was left at the end of the year, they had a share-out. Harry Ash's father belonged to an identical club in nearby Harbledown; 'they let them draw on it so much, then after that you couldn't have any more'.[140] Matthews was the secretary of the Brents' sickness benefit club (the landlord of the Brents Tavern held the money). The club met every second Monday at the tavern, members paid 1s. 2d. a fortnight and were given a token of 2d. which was spent on a pint of beer. In other words, the contribution was 6d. a week, for which they were eligible for sickness relief of 10s. a week for up to ten weeks of illness. If a member died, contributors would be levied 1s. each to go towards funeral expenses. Matthews said that every pub had its sickness benefit club; 'I belonged to two or three'.[141]

The benefits provided by the clubs were minor. It is clear from the

[137] *Faversham Mercury*, 3 February 1872.   [138] TL, A. Packman, b. 1892.
[139] TL, E. Clark, b. 1885.   [140] TL, L. Austin, b. 1902; H. Ash, b. 1898.
[141] TL, H. Matthews, b. 1890.

poor law records of the 1850s and 1860s, where applicants for relief had to declare club pay-outs, that such payments were small – 10s. to as little as 4s. 6d. a week – and that they reduced in size after a few weeks or were cut out altogether. But every little bit helped. We do not know what percentage of the labouring population were members of such societies. My impression is that contributions of 6d. or more a week on a regular basis would be difficult for the bulk of rural workers. The records of the mid nineteenth century certainly show that some of those claiming assistance under the New Poor Law were receiving club pay-outs. There were few of them. Only a quarter of those from Boughton, Dunkirk and Hernhill, mostly agricultural labourers, seeking sickness or injury relief from the Poor Law Union relieving officer had been in receipt of club benefits.[142] Although one could argue that club members were less likely to be seeking poor relief than those without a club, such figures do not suggest wide-spread affiliation at mid century. The Rowntree and Kendall survey implied stronger club membership among agricultural labourers in the early twentieth century. Yet, as Paul Johnson has pointed out, the low rates of subscription – 3d. per week was common – indicate member-ship of one of the lower-cost clubs rather than the affiliated friendly societies.[143]

IX

Recent work on poverty and charity has suggested that poor relief should be seen as yet another strategy for survival and that we should not assume any sense of shame on the part of the receiver. Viewed from the 'bottom up', charity was a 'neighbourhood resource'.[144] Even though the policy of the New Poor Law was to discourage such strategies, calling upon poor relief was an important part of the social

---

[142] These observations and calculations are based on CKS, G/F RA 12–14.

[143] Johnson, *Saving and spending*, p. 59. Neave has argued against 'the widely held view' that friendly societies 'contributed only marginally to the welfare and economy of the bulk of the working-class in nineteenth-century Britain'. He claims that the evidence of surviving membership lists for the East Riding – which shows that up to 80 per cent of new members to societies were 'agricultural workers' – refutes the pessimistic orthodoxy. However, this still begs the wider and more crucial question: what percentage of the labouring population made use of the societies? It is surely significant that Neave's agricultural worker membership contained a strong con-tingent of young (aged 20 or under), unmarried, male farm servants. See Neave, *Mutual aid*, ch. 5 (the quotes come from pp. 66, 68).

[144] See P. Mandler (ed.), *The uses of charity: the poor on relief in the nineteenth-century metropolis* (Philadelphia, 1990), particularly the chapters by Mandler, Lynn Hollen Lees and Ellen Ross. The phrase 'neighbourhood resource' comes from Ross's chapter, 'Hungry children: housewives and London charity, 1870–1918', p. 166.

economy. One way of gauging the significance of poor relief is through detailed reconstruction of profiles at the local level. If one Kent parish in the 1830s is any guide, some 60 per cent of agricultural labourers and small farmers required poor relief during the winter months. The Old Poor Law of the period before 1835 provided a wide range of welfare payments. The overseers' books record payments for food, clothing, tools, fuel, even tobacco. Doctors' bills were paid; women were hired to nurse, care and wash for the elderly, the infirm and the heavily pregnant. The parish paid for funeral costs, including payments for beer. It provided unemployment relief during the winter. The vast majority of agricultural labourers would have received such assistance during their lives. Over 80 per cent of labouring households listed in the census of 1841 for Hernhill (not counting newcomers to the parish) had received relief at some stage in the life-course of their households. Under the Old Poor Law recourse to relief was a central means of getting a living for large numbers of labouring people. It could add as much as £10 a year to the family economy.[145]

The New Poor Law was less generous, both in the amounts paid and with the range of benefits. Indeed one of the aims in framing it had been to remove such security. But people still approached it for help with the hardship that inevitably accompanied old age, sickness and injury, death, childbirth, widowhood and desertion. For those without friendly society or club subscriptions and, as we have noted, for some of those with club membership, people had little option other than the relieving officer. If, again, local studies are any indication of wider trends, from 10 to 15 per cent of rural households would draw on poor relief during any given year in the 1850s and 1860s.[146] The likelihood that an individual family would need assistance increased over its life-cycle. A Faversham man could remember parents putting their children in the workhouse in the winter in the early part of this century because they could not afford to keep them; when things picked up later in the year they took them home.[147] Twelve-year-old J. W. Manuel was committed to the workhouse for medical assistance when his face was injured in an explosion while bird-scaring: 'There was a certain degree of poverty where you didn't have to pay for much in medical treatment.'[148] Len Austin's father was laid off work in the winter and had to go on poor relief. It was the common practice of his

---

[145] See Reay, *Last rising*, index: 'poor', 'poor-relief'. The figure of 80 percent comes from my total reconstitution files.
[146] I arrived at these figures by calculating the percentage of Boughton, Dunkirk and Hernhill households on poor relief in 1861; that is, by correlating the Faversham Union Relieving Officer's Application and Report Books with the census of 1861.
[147] TL, S. Twist, b. 1899.   [148] TL, J. W. Manuel, b. 1903.

employer, a local landowner, who would make allowance by not demanding his rent until the spring. Austin recalled a couple in his hamlet who would go into the Faversham poorhouse every winter and return again in the spring. 'If you hadn't got anything you hadn't got anything, you had to go somewhere where someone would look after you. That's all there was in it. What else could you do?'[149]

Finally, families could also turn to one another for assistance. Ellen Ross has shown the importance of neighbourhood sharing in London before 1914.[150] Tremeere described a similar situation in Dover: women would stand in the streets, in little groups talking to each other. 'They mostly sat on the steps, on the stairs ... If anybody wanted any help they'd go in and help'. He said that sometimes they would have a new baby 'born and washed and everything before the midwife's come'.[151] Manuel remembered that in his street in Faversham people would borrow small items of food from neighbours – tea or sugar – but not basics like bread or butter, so there may have been some kind of unspoken code.[152] Then there were little acts of kindness. Matthews recalled that in the winter a brickyard foreman at the Brents (Faversham) would boil up half a bullock's head in his copper and give away the stew for nothing to those who needed it. Even something as straightforward as keeping a pig depended on a certain amount of neighbourhood reciprocity. The brick-moulders would usually keep a couple of pigs which they fed on scraps donated by their neighbours. In return, they sold the meat cheap when the pig was killed.[153]

Though perhaps not as strong as for the towns, there is evidence of community support in the rural areas. Violet Turner's father cut wood and his children would sell it by the bushel; he told them that if someone was too poor to pay the 3d. they should leave the wood for them – 'they'll pay me one day'.[154] Harry Wheeler's mother and grandmother would lend their black mourning clothes out to those who could not afford their own when someone died.[155] Other oral history informants have talked of neighbourly acts of kindness or support during times of hardship or crisis.[156] Vincent has argued that such networks may have been more attenuated in rural areas because of the scattered nature of some of the settlements and the size of their populations.[157]

---

[149] TL, L. Austin, b. 1902.
[150] E. Ross, 'Survival networks: women's neighbourhood sharing in London before World War One', *History Workshop*, 15 (1983), pp. 4–27.
[151] TL, S. R. Tremeere, b. 1897.   [152] TL, J. W. Manuel, b. 1903.
[153] TL, H. Matthews, b. 1890.   [154] TL, V. Turner, b. 1896.
[155] Hernhill Oral History, H. Wheeler, b. 1912.
[156] Hernhill Oral History, H. Kay, b. 1921; E. Wade, b. 1908.
[157] Vincent, *Poor citizens*, p. 14.

X

The focus of this chapter is strongly regional; the tempos of brick-making and fruit- and hop-growing dominated the local economy and dictated the rhythms of poverty. It could be argued that the picture that I have presented is highly specific. And yet the economic history of Britain is a history of regional economies. The labouring population was adept at grasping whatever opportunities the local economy had to offer. This study should be seen as part of a growing literature which challenges the econometricians' obsession with 'adult-male, average, full-time earnings'.[158] We have a number of studies from widely differing societies – highly urbanized nineteenth- and early twentieth-century London, the northern towns of Barrow, Lancaster, Manchester, Salford and Preston, dockland Liverpool during the 1930s, and now rural and small-town Kent – which place the adult male wage in a wider perspective.[159]

This raises the possibility of a new agenda where the 'social economy' replaces the icon of the male wage. We can sketch out the essential elements of this economy. The male wage should not be ignored but it should be set firmly in the context of the family economy, where the role of the wife was central and the contribution of children important. Tremeere's motto, 'Yesterday's gone, tomorrow never comes. It's today you've got to think of', held a certain appeal in the milieu of poverty. But few wives and mothers would have been able to share his male bravado; they had to worry about tomorrow and

[158] For example, P. H. Lindert and J. G. Williamson, 'English workers' living standards during the Industrial Revolution: a new look', *Economic History Review*, 36 (1983), pp. 1–25; J. G. Williamson, *Did British capitalism breed inequality?* (London, 1985). However, see the far more promising approach of Sara Horrell and Jane Humphries, 'Old questions, new data and alternative perspectives: families' living standards in the Industrial Revolution', *Journal of Economic History*, 52 (1992), pp. 849–80; and their forthcoming work.

[159] For example, S. Meacham, *A life apart: the English working class 1890–1914* (London, 1977); R. Samuel, *East End underworld: chapters in the life of Arthur Harding* (London, 1981); Ross, 'Survival networks'; E. Roberts, *A woman's place: an oral history of working-class women 1890–1940* (Oxford, 1984); E. Roberts, ' "Women's strategies", 1890–1940', in J. Lewis (ed.), *Labour and love: women's experience of home and family, 1850–1940* (Oxford, 1986), ch. 9; J. White, *The worst street in north London: Campbell Bunk, Islington, between the wars* (London, 1986); C. Chinn, *They worked all their lives: women of the urban poor in England, 1880–1939* (Manchester, 1988); P. Ayers, 'The hidden economy of dockland families: Liverpool in the 1930s', in P. Hudson and W. R. Lee (eds.), *Women's work and the family economy in historical perspective* (Manchester, 1990), ch. 11; Vincent, *Poor citizens*; M. J. Childs, *Labour's apprentices: working-class lads in late Victorian and Edwardian England* (London, 1992); A. Davies, *Leisure, gender and poverty: working-class culture in Salford and Manchester, 1900–1939* (Buckingham, 1992); Ross, *Love and toil*.

making do and budgeting were as vital as the wage in the struggle for survival. The margins between survival and desperation were narrow. 'There was no hope for you, you wouldn't be in abject poverty when you was able to work, but you'd be just above it.' It was a world where if you could afford two sets of clothes 'you were comfortable'; one in which, as Tommy Boorman observed, if 'an old farm chap went in a bank they looked at him'.[160] The vicissitudes of the lives in the pages above, the imperative to 'scheme' a few shillings, undermine the tidy picture provided by those who relentlessly chart the male wage. The adult male wage tells us little about the lives of vast numbers of the labouring population in England's past and should be treated in terms of what it was: a cog in the social economy.

[160] TL, J. W. Manuel, b. 1903; Hernhill Oral History, T. Boorman, b. 1920.

5

Class

I

The concept of class is under attack. Predictably much of the discussion
relates to nineteenth- and early twentieth-century England; but as a
leading critic has suggested, if the centrality of class in nineteenth-
century England can be called into question, this surely has implications for other places and times.[1] It is not surprising that the focus of
this recent discussion is on industrial England: Patrick Joyce's important intervention, *Visions of the people*, is firmly rooted in the northern
town.[2] Yet it makes little sense to banish rural England from the
picture. Until 1901, agriculture was the single largest employer in
England. Whether we have in mind population distribution and
contribution to the GDP in the nineteenth century or the countryside's
identification with Englishness this century, rural England is central.[3]

This neglect of the countryside is particularly ironic given the recent
turn in rural studies. As is so often the case, urban and rural historians
have their separate agendas, but one of the current concerns of the
latter, a reconsideration of the class structure of rural society, has
obvious relevance for urban revisionists. I refer to recent critiques of
the conventional division of rural society into a tri-partite structure of
landlord, tenant farmer and proletarian labourer. This orthodoxy,
pervading such classics as Eric Hobsbawm and George Rudé's *Captain
Swing*, Howard Newby's *The deferential worker* and James Obelkevich's

---

[1] P. Joyce, 'A people and a class: industrial workers and the social order in nineteenth-
century England', in M. L. Bush (ed.), *Social orders and social classes in Europe since
1500: studies in social stratification* (London, 1992), p. 217. See also an important chapter
by William Reddy: 'The concept of class', in Bush (ed.), *Social orders*, ch. 2.

[2] P. Joyce, *Visions of the people: industrial England and the question of class 1848–1914*
(Cambridge, 1991).

[3] A. Howkins, *Reshaping rural England: a social history 1850–1925* (London, 1991), p. 8.

Plate 18 Horseman at Langdon Court Farm, Graveney.

influential study of nineteenth-century rural Lincolnshire, is being challenged by recent work which emphasizes a greater complexity in the class structure and which throws doubt on the ubiquity of landless farm labour.[4] Such attacks on the prominence of the nineteenth-century rural proletariat have obvious affinities with Joyce's demotion of the urban working class.[5]

The aim of this chapter is to explore some aspects of class relations

[4] E. J. Hobsbawm and G. Rudé, *Captain Swing* (London, 1969); J. Obelkevich, *Religion and rural society: south Lindsey 1825–1875* (Oxford, 1976); H. Newby, *The deferential worker: a study of farm workers in East Anglia* (London, 1977). For a developing critique, see M. Reed, 'The peasantry of nineteenth-century England: a neglected class?', *History Workshop*, 18 (1984), pp. 53–76; M. Reed, 'Class and conflict in rural England: some reflections on a debate', in Reed and R. Wells (eds.), *Class, conflict and protest in the English countryside 1700–1880* (London, 1990), ch. 1; A. Hall, *Fenland worker-peasants: the economy of smallholders at Rippingdale, Lincolnshire, 1791–1871* (Agricultural History Review, Supplement Series vol. I, 1992); A. Howkins, 'Peasants, servants and labourers: the marginal workforce in British agriculture, c. 1870–1914', *Agricultural History Review*, 92 (1994), pp. 49–62. J. M. Neeson, *Commoners: common right, enclosure and social change in England, 1700–1820* (Cambridge, 1993), ch. 10 has argued that a peasantry survived into the early nineteenth century.

[5] Joyce, 'A people and a class'.

and perceptions by setting class in rural context (*c.* 1800–1930). At the locality, after all, is where the majority of people experienced class, whether in urban neighbourhood or rural hamlet or village. I intend to examine class as structure and class as culture, with particular reference to agricultural labourers. Was the archetypal farmworker of the nineteenth century 'the only real Marxian proletariat that England ever had'?[6]

II

The structural centrality of landless farm labour in rural society has been attacked on a variety of fronts. Revisionists have stressed the survival both of farm service (workers as servants rather than 'free' labour) and peasant smallholdings (worker peasants), as well as the role of women in the rural work force. The new theme is of 'a complex variety of experiences for those who worked the land'.[7]

The place of the agricultural labourer in the occupational and social structure has been outlined in chapter 1, but it is worth summarizing my argument with the revisionist interpretation in mind. Male farm-workers – in probable increasing numerical order – included regular outdoor labourers (those who did not live in as servants), farm servants and casual labourers. And there were occupational hierarchies within these broad categories. We saw that farm service was an important source of rural labour in this part of Kent and a formative work experience for large numbers of nineteenth-century rural labourers. Chapter 4 showed the prominence of the work of women (and children) in the social economy; there is no reason that the representative farmworker should be male.

It could also be argued that the rural work force included those who held small plots of land (the small-farmer labourers), those who earned a subsidiary living at a craft or trade, and the families of these people, given that their basic economic unit was household production. We saw in chapter 1 that the small farmers maintained a presence in the Blean communities well into this century and how difficult it is to

[6] R. A. E. Wells, 'The development of the English rural proletariat and social protest, 1700–1850', in Reed and Wells (eds.), *Class, conflict and protest*, p. 29. He was quoting J. P. D. Dunbabin. Wells's influential article, originally published in 1979, began with the statement that the English peasantry had virtually disappeared by 1800 and that the 'vast bulk of the inhabitants of the English countryside since the mid-eighteenth century were landless agricultural labourers and their families' (*ibid.*).
[7] A. Howkins, 'The English farm labourer in the nineteenth century: farm, family and community', in B. Short (ed.), *The English rural community: image and analysis* (Cambridge, 1992), p. 102.

separate such worker farmers from the agricultural labourer. A. Austin (born 1889) was the son of a small farmer. His early recollections are of helping his mother look after the family smallholding in the summer because his father was busy working for wages in other farmers' orchards and hop-grounds. His father was both wage-earner and wage-payer. He would hire women to harvest his own fruit crop: blackcurrants, gooseberries, redcurrants, raspberries and strawberries. He rented a few acres in Boughton and a small plot in nearby Dunkirk. He kept pigs; two would be killed each year for the household, the rest were sold to the butcher. Austin's mother took in a lodger, an old lady who paid 18d. a week. Austin stated that the small farmer had one advantage over the ordinary labourer in that the farming family could work their own property during the low-employment winter. None the less, his memories were of poverty and hard work; 'I don't want to see never no more people have to work and go through the times like we had'.[8] Len Austin (born 1902) lived in the area as well. He recalled that 10 acres was considered 'quite a size'. The little farmers 'used to have a little piece of hops, didn't matter how big it was, it was only about a quarter of an acre, or an acre, or two acres':

They used to have anything, practically anything. Whatever came along they'd have. Whatever sort of fruit came along, they'd try to get whatever sort of vegetables ... Some used to sell locally, some used to have a little shop to sell them in or home made sweets. Keep a pig or two. A few chicken. Anything, so they hadn't got all their eggs in one basket, so if they had a failure with one, they'd got something else coming in. Didn't matter what it was ... Some used to go and work in the wood, they were woodmen at different times of the year and then carry on smallholding, perhaps they'd got a son carrying on or a wife could carry it on, then they'd go wooding ... Work one job in with the other. They had to.[9]

Percy Saddleton remembered small farmers in Hernhill in the 1920 and 1930s: men with 4 or 5 acres, 7 or 8 acres, 10 or 12 acres; 'the wife' would work on it, they would keep pigs and poultry, feed their own stock, 'scratch a living'.[10]

This is all grist for the revisionist mill. But the fact still remains that up to about 60 per cent of occupied males in Boughton, Dunkirk and Hernhill (according to the census definition) were labourers, predominantly agricultural workers. If we use the household as our unit of analysis, 50 per cent or more of households were headed by a labourer or agricultural labourer. The census of 1891 provides information on

[8] TL, A. Austin, b. 1889.   [9] TL, L. Austin, b. 1902.
[10] Hernhill Oral History, P. Saddleton, b. 1907. The Hernhill Oral History Tapes are interviews which I carried out in 1991–2.

whether those surveyed were employers or employed, allowing us a glimpse of the class hierarchy in Boughton, Dunkirk and Hernhill at

Table 5.1   *Occupational structure of employers, employed and self-employed, 1891 (percentages)*

Occupational structure	Employers	Employed	Self-employed
Gentry/Professional	11.1	0.0	1.2
Farmers	43.2	3.8	15.1
Trades/crafts	40.7	9.9	69.8
Ag. Lab./Lab.	0.0	75.1	5.8
Others	5.0	11.2	8.1

Heads of households (male and female) in Boughton, Dunkirk and Hernhill in 1891.

Table 5.2   *Employment status of occupational group, combined parishes, 1891 (percentages)*

Status	Gentry/Professional	Farmers[a]	Trades/crafts	Ag.Lab./Lab.
Employers	90.0	52.2	23.2	0.0
Employed	0.0	28.4	34.5	98.6
Self-employed	10.0	19.4	42.2	1.3

[a] Note that the employed farmers are bailiffs; if they were removed from the calculation, the percentage of farmer employers would rise to 73 percent and that of the self-employed to 27 percent.

the end of the nineteenth century. The employers, at the top of the hierarchy, principally farmers and those earning a living in the crafts and trades, made up only 11 per cent of households. The self-employed, in the middle of the hierarchy, again mainly those in the trades and crafts, were also a small section of society – only 12 per cent of households. The employed, the last of the three groups, formed the bulk of households in 1891 – 70 per cent. And most of those were labouring households. Ninety-nine per cent of the households of agricultural labourers and labourers were classified as working for someone else (see tables 5.1 and 5.2 and figures 5.1 and 5.2). The archetypal male employee in the nineteenth-century Blean was an agricultural labourer; just as the typical employer was a farmer or someone who derived a living from a trade or craft. The archetypal female worker in the nineteenth-century Blean either laboured on the land or was a woman from an agricultural labouring household earning a living as a servant. She was probably destined to marry a

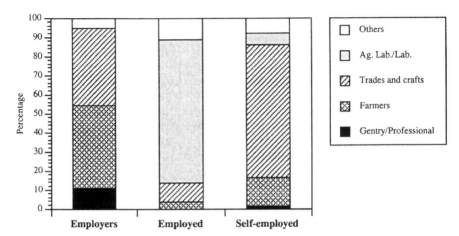

Figure 5.1 Occupational structure of employers, employed and self-employed, 1891 (percentages). Heads of households (male and female) in Boughton, Dunkirk and Hernhill.

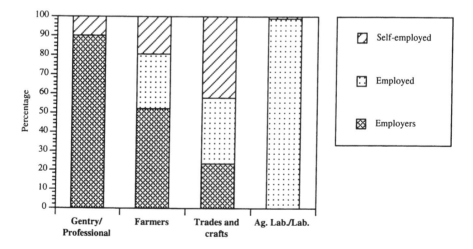

Figure 5.2 Employment status of occupational groups, 1891 (percentages). Heads of households (male and female) in Boughton, Dunkirk and Hernhill.

rural worker and/or to become one herself. Refinements aside, if we are to understand and analyse class in the local context we cannot ignore the households of the agricultural labourers.

III

The advantage of the local study is that it allows a social group to be subjected to close scrutiny. Although historians make assumptions about the conditions of the English farmworker and have discussed occupational variation, there has been little scrutiny of the workers' collective lives. Did agricultural labourers own or rent land? Were they cottagers; or were they rural proletarians in the classic sense of the term? Were they prisoners of occupation and class? Could individuals advance in status over their lifetimes or were they locked into the one occupation until death? Was the labouring class largely self-replicating; is there evidence of what John Goldthorpe has termed 'demographic class formation'.[11] Did agricultural labourers come mainly from a labouring background and did their sons and daughters marry into the same stratum? The technique of total reconstitution permits us to answer some of these questions. We can also make use of a survey carried out after the abortive rising of 1838, when a lawyer from London carried out a unique scrutiny of labouring conditions in Boughton, Dunkirk and Hernhill. The man, Frederick Liardet, surveyed 151 labouring households from our three parishes, approximately 50 from each, although one gets the impression that his sample may also have included some small farmers or dealers.[12]

Let us start with Liardet's survey. The subtle contrast in community conditions is intriguing. In Hernhill and Boughton, agricultural labourers formed a rural proletariat: people who owned only their labour. But Hernhill, with its larger gardens, was better placed as far as the household economy was concerned. 'All the labourers concurred in estimating the value of a garden to them. Without it, they said, they could not get on at all. By its means they contrive to procure sufficient vegetables for their families for a great part of the year.' The gardens attached to the cottages which the lawyer visited in Hernhill varied from 8 to 16 perches; a few had half-acre plots; and two or three had more than half an acre. In Boughton, although forty-one out of fifty of

[11] See the informative review article by Mike Savage, 'Social mobility and class analysis: a new agenda for social history?', *Social History*, 19 (1994), pp. 69–79. The quote comes from p. 71.

[12] F. Liardet, 'State of the peasantry in the county of Kent', in *Central Society of Education, third publication* (London, 1968), pp. 87–139 (first published in 1839).

the households had gardens, most were 'small patches not sufficient to raise half the quantity of vegetables required by a family'. Seventeen of the Hernhill families kept pigs, compared to only four in Boughton. Five Hernhill households from the survey had a horse and cart. But not one labourer, in either Hernhill or Boughton, owned a cow: 'Few, indeed, of the cottagers aspire so high as to the possession of a cow.' Liardet found that local farmers were opposed to their labourers holding land or livestock; there was 'a lurking apprehension that the labourer would become more independent and less manageable'.[13]

We know from the Hernhill tithe survey of 1840, matched against the census of the following year, that of sixty-five agricultural labourers who were heads of households in 1841, only one owned any farmland (which he let). Two (one was William Curling, encountered in an earlier chapter) rented 10 acres; one owned a cottage and garden and rented 1 acre. The rest, for whom there is information, rented cottages or parts of houses, usually with gardens.[14]

In Dunkirk, however, there was some ground to the farmers' fears about labouring independence. Kent was a county of long-established enclosure and was, as the historical geographer Roger Kain has put it, 'singularly void of common'.[15] Dunkirk was one of the few areas opened up in the county in the 1790s and 1800s, when the pressure of war with France put a premium on commons and wastes. Denstrode and Dargate Commons were enclosed and their woodland was cleared. A land survey carried out in the late 1820s reveals that 75 per cent of properties and dwellings had been first settled, enclosed or built after the late 1780s. About 60 per cent of this settlement had occurred during the Napoleonic Wars (1793–1815).[16] This in-migration is confirmed by the census, which records that the population of Dunkirk increased by a third in the first ten years of the nineteenth century.[17]

The story of the family of the labourer, Thomas Ralph, from Kingsdown, near Sittingbourne, provides a brief sketch of what must have been the experience of many Dunkirk settlers. In the 1780s he obtained permission to enclose about an acre of wasteland in Dunkirk at an annual quit rent of 5s. The land was in a bad state; Ralph grubbed it up and converted it to tillage. In the early 1800s he erected a small cottage

[13] *Ibid.*

[14] PRO, IR 29/17/178, Hernhill Tithe Apportionment Award 1840; PRO, HO 107/473/12, Hernhill Census 1841.

[15] R. Kain, 'The land of Kent in the middle of the nineteenth century' (University of London Ph.D., 1973), p. 345.

[16] PRO, MPZ 26, Reference Book or Terrier to the Plan of the Ville of Dunkirk 1827–8.

[17] B. Reay, *The last rising of the agricultural labourers* (Oxford, 1990), p. 11, Table 1.

which cost from £10 to £20. His wife, Susanna, remained in the cottage after the death of Thomas in 1809, although she had to send several of her children to Kingsdown because she could not provide for them.[18]

The labouring population had greater access to land in the Ville of Dunkirk (as it was known) than in adjoining Hernhill. Of forty-eight agricultural labourers, labourers and woodmen actually living in Dunkirk in the late 1820s, twenty-five (52 per cent) were owner-occupiers; and nearly a half of those had properties larger than an acre. In 1841 at least 20 per cent of those described as labourers or agricultural labourers in the census were owner-occupiers of cottages and gardens and, in most cases, of small sections of land ranging from half an acre to 9 acres. Several others rented a few acres each.[19] Liardet noted the presence of freehold cottages, but commented that most of them were 'mortgaged nearly to their full value'. Of the fifty labouring families interviewed, nineteen kept pigs, two kept a cow and six had a horse (or donkey) and cart. Most cottages had a garden. But there was less farm work available in Dunkirk than in the neighbouring parishes, so the cottagers were more dependent upon their tiny holdings.[20]

However, the indications are that these labourer–farmers were a temporary phenomenon and that they were squeezed out fairly rapidly over time. In the 1860s the vast majority of heads of labouring households – 87 per cent – rented a cottage or house and garden. Eight per cent rented pieces of land (and dwellings) ranging from half an acre to 3 acres. And a mere 5 per cent were owner-occupiers (of properties of 1 acre, $1\frac{1}{2}$ acres and $2\frac{1}{2}$ acres respectively).[21] This proletarianization of Dunkirk is born out when the property surveys of the 1820s and the 1860s are compared. Small owners (of less than 1 acre) decreased in number by just over 40 per cent even though the overall population increased; but the number of small occupiers rose by over 90 per cent.[22] Of those families who owned land in Dunkirk and who were living there for the census of either 1861 or 1871, the vast majority were headed not by labourers but by farmers and those in the trades and crafts. For a brief period of time, then, there was a substantial group of landowning workers in Dunkirk (and we have to allow for such local variation) but the majority of the labouring population in the three parishes had only their labour to sell.

How much social mobility was there? Could these workers rise the

[18] *Ibid.*, p. 10.
[19] PRO, MPZ 26; PRO, HO 107/466/5, Dunkirk Census 1841.
[20] Liardet, 'State of the peasantry'.
[21] CKS, U 11772 O24, Dunkirk Land Survey, 1866; PRO, RG 9/525, Dunkirk Census 1861; PRO, RG 10/976, Dunkirk Census 1871.
[22] PRO, MPZ 26; CKS, U 11772 O24.

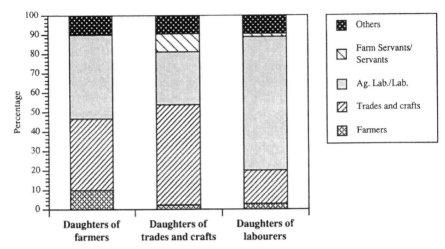

Figure 5.3 Marriages of daughters by occupation of father and husband: family reconstitution cohorts, 1800–80 (based on a total of 247 women: 165 daughters of labourers, 30 daughters of farmers and 52 daughters of tradesmen and craftsmen).

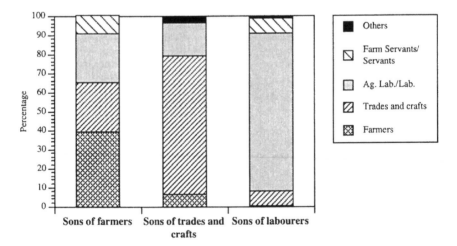

Figure 5.4 Occupations of sons by occupation of father at time of son's marriage: family reconstitution cohorts, 1800–80 (based on a total of 505 men: 358 sons of labourers, 81 sons of tradesmen and craftsmen and 66 sons of farmers).

social or occupational ladder? All the indications are that they were essentially a socially static group. A few daughters of labourers would marry farmers or tradesmen and craftsmen. Women from farming families frequently married men who were described as labourers. But the total number of farmers' daughters was small and would make little impact on the overall structure of labouring households. The majority of women from labouring households married agricultural labourers and labourers (see figure 5.3).

A similar pattern emerges when the occupations of grooms are compared with the occupations of their fathers. Some sons of farmers were earning a living as labourers when they married, but again they would have been a small percentage of the total labouring population. The majority of young labouring men who stood before the altar were the sons of labourers and farmworkers (see figure 5.4). Of those male labouring household heads in the census of 1851 whose backgrounds are known from family reconstitution, 84 per cent had fathers who had earned their living in the same way (see table 5.3). This is convincing evidence for demographic class cohesion among the rural workers.

Nor was there much individual mobility. Total reconstitution makes it possible to trace household heads throughout their life-course to determine upward (or sideways movement) in occupational status. Figure 5.5 suggests little movement. Some labourers became bailiffs, took up a craft or a trade (especially dealing) or, if they were the kin of farmers, inherited a small block of land: roughly a quarter changed occupation or status in some way at some stage. The most noticeable means of movement was into and out of the occupation of dealer. The attractions and possibilities of dealing for the labourer are obvious. He could be his own boss and have control over his own time. With a little capital, perhaps with no capital and just credit, a labourer could do a deal, turn some profit. It might not be enough to get a complete living; labour may still have to be sold. But dealing helped in the struggle for survival and it built on the skills of penny capitalism which (as we saw in chapter 4) were part of labouring culture. There was also a sense of chance, of gambler's luck. You might lose one year, but there was always the lure of a killing the next. Over time, it all probably evened out. These labourer capitalists are an interesting and important phenomenon, but it is important to get their number into perspective. Like the worker farmers they hardly threaten the integrity of the rural proletariat. Only 13 per cent of the sample of household heads were dealers at some stage in their lives. The vast majority – almost 75 per cent of the sample – remained mere wage labourers.

Table 5.3 *Male household heads, 1851, by known occupation of man's father (combined parishes) (percentages)*

Occupation of head	Occupation of father			
	Ag. Lab./Lab.	Trades and crafts	Farmers	Total number
Ag. Lab./Lab.	84	2	14	98
Trades and crafts	38	45	17	29
Farmers	18	0	82	17

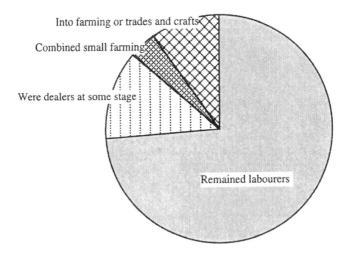

Figure 5.5 Changes in occupation of labouring household heads: family reconstitution cohorts, 1800–80 (based on a total of 203 households where the male head of the family earned a living as a labourer at some stage during his life).

IV

What of class as culture? We saw earlier that service was a common experience for young labouring people of the nineteenth century. How important was service in the culture of class? The class implications of service are the subject of contention. Some historians have argued that the decline of farm service in the nineteenth century meant the erosion of an organic relationship, 'that special relationship between master and man'.[23] The implication of this argument is that farm service represented an identity of interest between farmer and worker in a formative stage of the latter's development and presumably that such common purpose undermined sharp divisions of class.

Yet as Mick Reed has argued, there had always been a degree of distance in what was an inherently unequal relationship.[24] The picture that we get is one of coercion rather than identity of interest. Those young men who went into service in the nineteenth century were socialized in the households of their social superiors: a Sussex commentator in 1834 referred to the custom of 'domesticating' the labourer.[25] 'Master' was the term used to describe the farmer; while the latter described workers on his farm as 'his men'. Later, as farmworkers, they would call their bosses 'Mr' or 'Sir' to their faces, although they had other names for them behind their backs.[26] Employers had the weight of the law to bolster their authority. In a typical case, John Saddleton of Forester's Lodge Farm took one of his servants in husbandry to the Petty Sessions in 1866 (and hence a week's prison) for refusing to feed his horses, a dispute occasioned by the man's lateness one morning. Rules and regulations governed long hours of work. Saddleton's man had been hired for 12 months for wages of £10. He had to be up out of bed at 3.30: the waggoner deposed that it was his job to raise the farm servants at 3.30 a.m. and to call the maidservant a little after 4.00. The servants were allowed out on Sundays but had to be back home by 7.30 p.m.[27] According to an address to the Sittingbourne Agricultural Association in the 1850s, the waggoner's day started at 3.30 a.m. in East Kent and finished at about 6 p.m. His mate began work at 5 a.m., but would work into the evening, and it would be as late as 10 p.m. before the horses were fed and locked up. There was also Sunday work, for the horses still had to be cared for.[28] Furthermore, the relationship of hierarchy was reinforced by a large difference in ages. Farmers were older than their employees, both labourers and servants (see figure 5.6).

Of course there is no guarantee that such 'domestication' was

23 B. Short, 'The decline of living-in servants in the transition to capitalist farming: a critique of the Sussex evidence', *Sussex Archaeological Collections*, 122 (1984), pp. 147–64.
24 M. Reed, 'Indoor farm service in 19th-century Sussex: some criticisms of a critique', *Sussex Archaeological Collections*, 123 (1985), pp. 225–41.
25 Quoted by Short, 'Decline of living-in servants', p. 152.
26 TL, H. Ash, b. 1898.
27 CKS, PS/US 11, Upper Division of the Lathe of Scray Petty Sessions 1864–8, 2 October 1866.
28 *Second Report of the Commissioners on the Employment of Children, Young Persons, and Women in Agriculture*, PP, 1868–9, vol. XIII, p. 281.

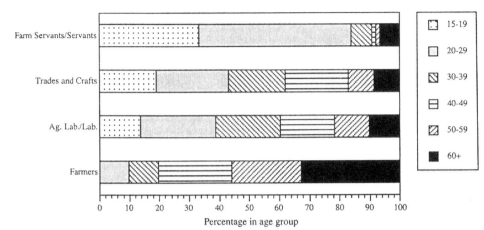

Figure 5.6 Age structure of occupational groups (male and female combined) in Dunkirk and Hernhill 1851 (the trades and crafts include apprentices).

successful. When challenged because he had got out of bed at 4.30 a.m. instead of the required 3.30 a.m., Saddleton's servant said that he 'would be buggered' if he was going to work an extra hour to make up for the delay.[29] Common disputes between farmers and servants over the care of animals and the pilfering of grain (usually to provide extra feed for horses) and arguments over hours worked and the time that servants should be in bed, demonstrate that conditions were far from free of conflict.[30] However, the point is that service bred conflict and coercion rather than community of interest.

It is difficult to work out the class implications of the living arrangements of farm servants because there was so much variation. Some lived on their own, or perhaps with one other, in the household of a small or medium farmer or on the farm of a substantial man who relied mainly on day labour. Others lived with larger groups of fellow workers. The Boughton farms of Brenley, Boughton Court, Wellbrook and Dane Court had hierarchies of servants in husbandry in 1851: waggoner, second man, third man, waggoner's mate, second boy, third boy. Forester's Lodge in Dunkirk had eight farm servants. Some boarded with the bailiff or steward (as at Dargate House Farm, Wellbrook and Dane Court); some were part of the farmer's household

[29] CKS, PS/US 11, 2 October 1866.
[30] Such cases recur in the Petty Sessions and Quarter Sessions records: Reay, *Last rising*, p. 51.

(at Brenley, Boughton Court, Forester's Lodge and Colkins Farms); some lived with the waggoner.[31] But whatever the domestic arrangement, there is scant support for any common farming interest. There was little likelihood that class barriers were lowered by proximity of living when farm servants boarded with the waggoner (a labourer) or the bailiff (often of labouring background, though, as one labourer put it, sometimes worse than the boss).[32] Even when servants lived in the household of a farmer, their relationship was more likely to have been a simple one of authority rather than the fostering of any community of interest. Living conditions were not exactly conducive to any common feeling between master and man either. Two of Saddleton's farm servants slept in the same bed. A report in the 1850s noted the cramped arrangements for farm servants, several men sharing a chamber and 'in most cases a bed'. In winter such quarters must have been cold, damp and smelly.[33]

The cultural implications of female service are equally difficult to pinpoint; the variety of experiences and household situations undermine generalization. In theory, service provided a grounding in the rules of class. A male servant early this century was struck by the replication of hierarchy at the humblest of levels, although 'they were only servants the same as you are'. There are stories of the lady's maid who 'thought she was bigger than the lady she worked for'. There was a pecking order among the chauffeurs: 'if you was driving a Rolls Royce you wouldn't dare speak to a bloke that was only driving a Ford'. We hear of the new servant having to learn his place at the servants' dinner table and that he had to have his jacket on (rather than off) when he ate. He observed that the butler, cook and lady's maid disappeared into another room for their sweet: 'What ruddy game is that ... Even the servants had got the etiquette business.' And there is the first encounter with hors d'oeuvres. 'We used to say, yes, but we don't know what the hell it is and you don't know whether you've got to eat it with a knife, fork or spoon.'[34]

But the education of most servant women would not have been in the finer gradations of hierarchy of the sort experienced by our male informant. The majority worked in small households. Each household was a little school of obedience and deference, it is true. Like their male counterparts, the women serving in farming households worked for

[31] See the Census Enumerators' Books (1841–91) for the parishes of Hernhill, Boughton and Dunkirk: PRO, HO 107/466/5; HO 107/471/11; HO 107/473/12; HO 107/1626; RG 9/525; RG 10/976–7; RG 11/966–7; RG 12/712.
[32] TL, L. Austin, b. 1902.
[33] *PP*, 1868–9, vol. XIII, p. 281.   [34] TL, A. Wise, b. 1894.

social superiors. Yet the social gap between master or mistress and female servant was slight in many trade and craft homes and perhaps it is in gender rather than class that the real implications were felt. Leonore Davidoff has described the experience of these working-class servants and wives as 'mastered for life'; 'the majority of girls moved from parental control, in their parents' home, into service and then into their husband's home – thus experiencing a lifetime of personal subordination in private homes'.[35] As with the men, it is questionable how successful such socialization was. When Mrs Post did not like an employer, she moved on. 'I don't know whether I was a bit of a bolshy or not, but I didn't accept the rules, you know, what had been layed down sort of for generations if you understand me.'[36] Lydia Boorman (born 1916), who worked as a maid at Kemsdale in Hernhill, was trained for service almost from the time she entered a Brixton orphanage at the age of 4. By the time she left Brixton for her first position as general servant at the age of 16, she had spent many hours scrubbing floors, getting up at 5.30 a.m. to light the coppers for washing and waiting on orphanage staff in the dining hall: 'we was trained'. But this did not mean that Lydia was compliant; she argued with her employers and left when conditions were not to her liking, the only real weapon that servants had.[37]

V

It was not just through service that class messages were imparted. Socialization began at an early age. Children at the Hernhill school in the 1880s were taught the 'importance of cheerful obedience to duty'. They had a lesson on a 'special subject': 'To order myself lowly and reverently to all my betters'.[38] Enculturation continued throughout life. The Faversham Agricultural Association (an organization of landlords and farmers) handed out prizes for loyal and productive agricultural labourers and servants. Winners were listed in the *Faversham Gazette* along with their employers. There were awards for hop-drying, rearing the largest number of lambs, continuous service, for raising a family without recourse to poor relief and even for bringing up large numbers of children in wedlock (the man rather than the woman received the

---

[35] L. Davidoff, 'Mastered for life: servant and wife in Victorian and Edwardian England', *Journal of Social History*, 7 (1974), p. 409.
[36] TL, G. Post, b. 1896.
[37] Hernhill Oral History, L. Boorman, b. 1916.
[38] CKS, C/ES 183/1/1, Hernhill Church of England School Log Book, 1872–1959, pp. 94, 105, 106.

acclaim). The Right Hon. Lord Sondes outlined the objectives of the Association:

to provide for the social and moral welfare of the labouring classes, and it depended upon their own conduct how such an object could be met. All they would have to do would be to maintain a strict sense of honour amongst themselves – to do their duty to their employers, and thus raise themselves to independence. By independence he did not mean that they might become independent of their employer, but of parish relief; and, above all, that they might learn to be content with their various stations in life, and thus put an end to that grumbling spirit which is so often observable, and which only tended to make them unhappy. He (the noble chairman) hoped they would instil these principles into the minds of their children, and that they would take care that their houses and gardens were neatly kept, that when they returned from their day's toil they might find comfort around the domestic hearth.[39]

Whether such messages were internalized is a different issue. No doubt many agricultural labourers were persuaded of their own inferiority. A sense of acceptance of the social order is clear from the oral histories, but it was resignation rather than active endorsement. Those towards the bottom of the social hierarchy found it difficult to conceive of any different life situation as far as they were concerned; it was as if their futures were predetermined. It was not that they were all unaware of how the other half lived, for service provided a cultural conduit. 'We just accepted it because we, we didn't, we didn't think we would, you know, be able to ever do anything like that.'[40] J. W. Manuel said that he did not blame anybody for his family's poverty 'because it didn't occur to me, who could I blame. Only God!'[41] A sense of social captivity comes through poignantly in Albert Packman's summary of his Edwardian father's life, 'If he could have had a life in these days, I reckon he would have been very clever.'[42]

The Boughton labourer Len Austin spoke with passion about a narrowness of expectations and of horizons bred of a poverty of options. 'Well you didn't expect nothing better in those days, you knew you wouldn't get anything better.' 'People say why did you put up with it, because you blasted well had to.' 'Well as I say you were born to do it because you knew you'd got to do it or get out ... Most people accepted the fact that they had got to do it. They liked the job, took a pride in it really in a way of doing the job. You was quite a man when you'd got a horse.'[43] (Working-class males could at least seek consolation in their masculinity and work skills.) Austin hinted that he became critical of his given situation through a mixture of discussion

---

[39] *Faversham Gazette*, 13 September 1856.
[40] TL, A. Wise, b. 1894.   [41] TL, J. W. Manuel, b. 1903.
[42] TL, A. Packman, b. 1892.   [43] TL, L. Austin, b. 1902.

(with conscientious objectors who worked in Boughton in the First World War), reading and personal experience:

> the parson would tell you [that each man was in his place], you was always kept humble, always kept down, but then other parts in the religion tell you that all the things in the world are for everyone to share. Love one another and all sorts of things like that, and help one another. But you was starving and they was living on the fat of the land, and it made you begin to rebel a bit didn't it, made you think ... and as I say, I went in to gentleman's service and saw how they lived and the way I lived, I thought well I don't know.[44]

The case of Austin and Sondes' warning about grumblers suggests that we should not assume total labouring passivity. An expert on rural resistance has cautioned against inferring ideological support 'even from the most faithful compliance' on the part of the subordinate group.[45] When nineteenth-century middle-class observers bothered to look, they discovered feelings towards the rich that were 'not merely envious but vindictive'. Hence the 'charities of the [rich] are regarded but as the return of a miserable fraction of the wealth they have extorted from their own labours and are received by them with ingratitude and sullenness'.[46]

VI

Rural voices have not featured in recent discussions of the languages of class. Indeed one analysis of the languages of social description in Victorian Britain referred to rural divisions only to draw a contrast with the sophistication of urban terminology. 'Whether we focus on the bald three categories [landowner, farmer, labourer] which dominated discussion of rural life or these uses of more archaic terms [peasantry, statesmen, yeomen], it is striking how little the class language of social description was used for village society.'[47] As the historian concerned stressed, his account drew on the 'public language' of print and debate and there would undoubtedly have been far greater variation at the level of 'everyday' description.[48] It is extremely difficult to gauge such nineteenth-century vocabularies, but oral history provides a fascinating twentieth-century window into less formal languages of social classification and description.

[44] *Ibid.*
[45] J. C. Scott, *Weapons of the weak: everyday forms of peasant resistance* (New Haven, 1985), p. 325.
[46] Liardet, 'State of the peasantry', pp. 133–4.
[47] G. Crossick, 'From gentleman to the residuum: languages of social description in Victorian Britain', in P. Corfield (ed.), *Language, history and class* (Oxford, 1991), p. 175.
[48] *Ibid.*

When the labourer Len Austin was interviewed in the 1970s he had a strong sense of class, though it is impossible to say with precision when this consciousness developed. It may have owed something to the influence of the conscientious objectors who worked on the farms with him in World War I – an electrician, school teachers, 'some of them with a jolly good education', 'atheists', 'christians' and 'socialists'. As Austin put it, 'they was like another country to us'. Austin, a Methodist, was clear that the clergy were part of the elite. He thought that rural society at the turn of the century had consisted of 'only two classes really, only what you call the snobs as we call them and the workers, that's all there was. One or two in between, such as the village grocer or village blacksmith or the publican, thought they was a little bit better than other people, the bailiff or manager.' He recalled that he used to think that the 'big men' were good because they dispensed charity; later he thought that it would have been better if they had paid people more in the first place.[49]

B. H. Fagg (born 1894), a Harbledown blacksmith, provides a slightly different perspective on the social complexion of the Blean communities.

Q: A delicate question, did you or your father being craftsmen in the village, did you feel you were one above the labourer in the social mix of the village or did you feel on a level?
A: Well we were friendly, but at the same time you had the feeling that you were just a little bit better than them. You would never show it if you could help it. You were always best of friends with them. You would always drink with them. That sort of thing. But as I say, there was always that feeling that you were just a little better than them.

He observed that the farmers' children did not play with the children of labourers. 'Those people didn't mix with the working people. You didn't see any of them that employed labour mix with the people that worked with them.' Fagg explained that his father, a wheelwright, would drink with a farm bailiff in the saloon bar, not with 'the common people in the public bar'. 'No, he used to go in the saloon. It was always hello Tom, hello Dick, but never to get intimate with them.'[50]

It would be foolish, in the light of such comments, to deny any sense of social otherness in the rural world of England's past. But what is interesting about these lives and commentaries is the relative nature of people's perceptions of social ordering. Len Austin talked in terms of two classes; but his social antenna was tuned most acutely to the gradations at his own social level. He did not quite know where to

[49] TL, L. Austin, b. 1902.   [50] TL, B. H. Fagg, b. 1894.

place the crafts, trades and bailiffs, although he was aware that they considered themselves to be a bit above the common labourer. Fagg was a perfect example of what Austin was talking about. He was not divorced from labouring life; culturally he seems indistinguishable from the labourer in all sorts of ways. But he did have that sense of slight social superiority. It is also interesting that what we might call the range of his class knowledge was limited to his own level and below. He had vague notions of a difference between 'the real gentry' (who were nice) and the 'jumped up' lot (who were not so nice) and said that the women were often worse than the men in this respect, but tended, with considerable imprecision, to lump wealthy farmers, some shopkeepers and gentry together. 'You'd had to touch your hat to everybody who was better off than you, and the girls had to curtsy.' 'The Publican?' 'Not the publican, no. All these gentrified people like, you know. Moneyed, if they'd got money.'[51]

It is worth pausing to subject the Austin interview to closer textual scrutiny. Those who would have lined up at his own level in the social scale he described as ordinary workmen, the labourers, farmworkers ordinary people, 'only country people like I was' (a phrase whose context denoted social level rather than geographical origin). It was a fairly limited vocabulary compared to the range of descriptions for his social superiors: employers, the boss, the big man, the squire, governor, master, toffs, real magnates, really rich men, the big house, bosses, big nob (referring to squire or farmer), higher nobs (referring to school-masters), the nobs in the village (referring to craftsmen and small-holders), 'the certain people' (meaning those just above him in the social scale). Indeed Austin's descriptions of fellow working people frequently invoked occupational specificity rather than class position: horsemen, waggoners, shepherds, stockmen, fruitmen, woodmen, those from the brickfields, those in service, those in yearly service, those who worked weekly, casuals.[52]

The finer hierarchies emerge repeatedly in the oral tapes and transcripts. Syd Twist, who grew up in Faversham in the early years of this century, could recount the social complexion of particular streets. The railway workers (who fancied themselves 'slightly superior to the others') lived in 'better class houses'; 'I suppose they were a better class. They were still working class, but probably artesian [*sic*] class, just that fraction above the brickies.' Brickmakers and bargemen were also 'spreading up that way, buying their own houses up that way'. The old houses down by the quays were occupied 'by the lower class

---

[51] *Ibid.*   [52] TL, L. Austin, b. 1902.

of people', the casual labourers who could not have survived without the local pawnshops. But even they were a rung above the itinerants who frequented the casual ward of the workhouse and the poorer quarter's lodging houses.[53]

J. W. Manuel (born 1903), a horseman's son who moved to Faversham and then Ospringe with his mother when his father died, conveyed a similar impression of the class geography of the town.

Wallers Row was a dump where all the really rough people lived, you know, really common. They used to live there. You knew where, and Tanner Street was another slum place in Faversham. Anybody who lived down Tanner Street, yet we was as poor as they were, but we felt that we were above them by living in Water Lane. And that old place in Ospringe. Very fine class distinctions. It didn't always necessarily mean that the more money the higher you rose in class, because there was so little difference in the money anyway.

Manuel's mother worked as a washer-woman in the Faversham workhouse, but she instilled in her children the feeling that they were just that bit better than the run-of-the-mill working class; she 'had a sort of idea that she was above the ordinary common, you know, the lowest working class'.[54]

As Paul Thompson has observed, the British people of the early twentieth century were 'visually divided', their social origins marked by the clothing that they wore.[55] On Sundays, Twist recalled, it was possible to pick out the 'craftsmen that fancied themselves a step above the others' in their blue serge suits, gold watches and chains and bowler hats.[56] Albert Packman, born in Hernhill, remembered his father's transition from worker (agricultural labourer) to boss (bailiff). Packman senior sported brown leggings and boots, breeches with leather inserts and took up cigar smoking. 'He was a boss then with his shiny leggins.' Albert also recounted that when he went into hotel service (c. 1906), the Hernhill farmworkers were taken with his clothing whenever he visited home: 'Cor ... he's got a white shirt on ... on a weekday ... whatever job has he got!'[57]

'Old Wives Lees was a place of only two sets of people. Those that went to the pub and those that went to chapel, and I belonged to a family that went to chapel, and our interest in life was our home, our family and our chapel and Sunday School.'[58] Emily Burgess's characterization was not entirely accurate; her father was active in the Kent Agricultural Workers' Union and used to scrutinize elections to make

[53] TL, S. Twist, b. 1899.   [54] TL, J. W. Manuel, b. 1903.
[55] P. Thompson, *The Edwardians* (London, 1984 edn), p. 312.
[56] TL, S. Twist, b. 1899.   [57] TL, A. Packman, b. 1892.
[58] TL, E. Burgess, b. 1890.

sure that the men were not intimidated by their bosses when they voted. However, her basic division of the village is a reminder that there were various ways of viewing the world and that class was not necessarily paramount.

Len Austin employed a series of binary opposites to describe those who had lived around him. There were boys and girls; men and women; old and young; 'townies' and 'clod hoppers'; those who had 'got' an education (blacksmith, grocer, baker and butcher) and those who had not; locals and outsiders (he refers to other villages as 'a foreign land'); large families (associated with poverty) and small families; those on the land and those not; Liberals and Tories; the rebellious and those who accepted; the Methodist and the non-Methodist; and the rough and the respectable. In other words, while he saw the world in class terms and was continually invoking the polarity of big and little to describe this world – only a few big bosses owned cars: 'They was like aeroplanes ... very scarce' – Austin was by no means limited to this way of explaining and describing his experience and society. Occupation, age, gender and a whole number of other lenses or classifiers were employed by a man who was perhaps more class conscious than many of his contemporaries.[59]

When they did invoke the language of class to describe their environment, we have seen that village people used a variety of categories. Their classifications were continually shifting and the descriptions that they used varied from context to context. This was a world where the 'big man' could be either a shepherd or an aristocrat. However, the description that was favoured was the one used by Emily Wade, daughter of an agricultural labourer, and Ann Bones, a plumber's daughter, who thought in terms of two classes. 'We didn't see many middle class ... You either had it or you didn't. You came down on a level with each other.'[60] Austin most often used the notion of the 'little man' and the 'big man' to describe positions in society: again a two–class society.[61]

In his study of East Anglian farmworkers in the 1970s, Howard Newby discovered 'great diversity' in class images. Although a majority of respondents leaned towards a two-class model, the number of classes distinguished ranged from none to five and those interviewed would slide from one notion of class to another according to situation or context. Newby concluded that for the agricultural labourer class was 'not a fixed property – it is an amorphous, nebulous and fluid

[59] TL, L. Austin, b. 1902.
[60] Hernhill Oral History, E. Wade, b. 1908; A. Bones, b. 1912.
[61] TL, L. Austin, b. 1902.

concept which he feels he recognizes when he is confronted by it, but a clear conception of which is not always necessary for him to engage in his everyday social encounters.'[62] The languages of class in the Blean were very similar.

VII

What can we conclude about class and the agricultural labourer? Is it indeed true, as William Reddy has put it, that 'once the microscope is brought into focus neat class boundaries dissolve'?[63] There is much in the Kent evidence which would support a revisionist interpretation. We have seen a fragmentation both in terms of structure and cultural perception which would sit well with the arguments of Joyce and Reddy. A case could also be made for a slippage between structure and the languages of class: there was no neat, unproblematic correspondence between social division and culture.

We have only considered part of the picture. I have had nothing to say about labouring politics and popular culture; we have not considered attachment to gender, locality or religion. But to replace 'class' with Joyce's notion of 'the people' would make little sense for rural England.[64] The idea of a rural working class, comprised principally of agricultural labourers (men, women and children), remains after all the qualifications have been made. There was a coherent social–occupational group, self-replicating, largely endogamous and, by and large, landless. And 'rural proletariat' is a fair description of this class. Populism, it might be argued, describes the labourer's representation of society in terms of the big man and the little man, but insufficiently describes the feeling of class which permeates the oral evidence. Class may not have dominated nineteenth- and early twentieth-century rural perceptions and structures. However, class was central to the rural world. If historians have had trouble finding a coherent working class in Victorian England, perhaps they should turn their attention to the village.

[62] Newby, *Deferential worker*, pp. 387, 388, 395.
[63] W. M. Reddy, *Money and liberty in modern Europe: a critique of historical understanding* (Cambridge, 1987), p. 9.
[64] The argument of Joyce, 'A people and a class', and his *Visions of the people.*

6

Families

I

There is an influential strand in the history of the English family, casting its shadow over interpretations of the nineteenth century and rapidly becoming sociological orthodoxy, which stresses the centrality of what has been termed the 'autonomous nuclear family'.[1] This representation of English families is best described in the observations of Alan Macfarlane's hypothetical oriental visitor surveying England at the start of the nineteenth century. He or she would have been struck by the 'high rate of geographical mobility' and the 'weakness of

---

[1] I think particularly of P. Laslett, *The world we have lost* (London, 1965); P. Laslett, *The world we have lost – further explored* (London, 1983); P. Laslett and R. Wall (eds.), *Household and family in past time* (Cambridge, 1972); R. Wall, J. Robin and P. Laslett (eds.), *Family forms in historic Europe* (Cambridge, 1983); A. Macfarlane, *The origins of English individualism* (Oxford, 1978); A. Macfarlane, *The culture of capitalism* (Oxford, 1987); J. E. Goldthorpe, *Family life in western societies: a historical sociology of family relationships in Britain and North America* (Cambridge, 1987). The quotation comes from Goldthorpe, *Family life*, p. 6. As with much of this type of social history, the early-modern period dominates the historiography. It should be noted that I refer to influence rather than consensus, for there is disagreement among the early-modernists: see M. Chaytor, 'Household and kinship: Ryton in the late 16th and early 17th centuries', *History Workshop*, 10 (1980), pp. 25–60; K. Wrightson, 'Household and kinship in sixteenth-century England', *History Workshop*, 12 (1981), pp. 151–8; O. Harris, 'Households and their boundaries', *History Workshop*, 13 (1982), pp. 143–52; R. Houston and R. Smith, 'A new approach to family history?', *History Workshop*, 14 (1982), pp. 120–31; R. A. Houlbrooke, *The English family 1450–1700* (London, 1984), ch. 3; D. Cressy, 'Kinship and kin interaction in early modern England', *Past and Present*, 113 (1986), pp. 38–69; D. O'Hara, ' "Ruled by my friends": aspects of marriage in the diocese of Canterbury, *c.* 1540–1570', *Continuity and Change*, 6 (1991), pp. 9–41; A. Mitson, 'The significance of kinship networks in the seventeenth century: south-west Nottinghamshire', in C. Phythian-Adams (ed.), *Societies, cultures and kinship, 1580–1850* (Leicester, 1993), ch. 2. For a critique of the 'immutable English family' from a medieval perspective, see Z. Razi, 'The myth of the immutable English family', *Past and Present*, 140 (1993), pp. 3–44.

156

Plate 19 A Boughton middle-class family, early twentieth century.

kinship'. 'Above all, kinship seemed very weak; people were early independent of parental power and most relied mainly on their own efforts ... The weakness of kinship showed itself in the household structure; this was nuclear, on the whole, with few joint or extended families.'[2]

This view of our past has had important implications for English social history, not always beneficial. The dominance of family forms in the historical agenda, the concentration upon household size and structure – as several critics have pointed out – has meant that relations *between* households, kinship links, have been neglected. Furthermore, the supposed ubiquity of the nuclear family has been taken as an indicator of 'loose kin relations'.[3] In the words of Peter Laslett, the

[2] Macfarlane, *Culture of capitalism*, pp. 145–6, 151. See also, Goldthorpe, *Family life*, pp. 9, 33. This text of historical sociology is a prime example of the permeation of the 'autonomous nuclear family household' thesis.

[3] For criticisms, see Chaytor, 'Household and kinship'; G. Levi, 'Family and kin – a few thoughts', *Journal of Family History*, 15 (1990), pp. 567–78; D. I. Kertzer, 'Household history and sociological theory', *Annual Review of Sociology*, 17 (1991), pp. 155–79; O'Hara, '"Ruled by my friends"'. For some examples of research 'beyond the household' for the nineteenth century, see Kertzer's *Family life in central Italy, 1880–1910* (New Brunswick, 1984), ch. 7: 'Kinsmen beyond the household'; and Kertzer,

most influential of the family history scholars, 'Our disposition has
always been to connect ... kinship consciousness and kinship inter-
change with the complex rather than with the simple family household.'[4] This emphasis on the nuclear family system has also been used
by revisionist historians of nineteenth-century social welfare to argue
for the extra-familial locus of assistance, that the community or state
rather than family and kin was the main source of support for the
needy sections of society, particularly the elderly.[5]

This chapter questions some of the orthodoxies associated with the
'autonomous nuclear family'.

II

On the face of it, the Kent parishes conform to Macfarlane's characterization, with the main ingredients for 'loose kinship'. The population
was highly mobile. In the ten years between the censuses of 1841 and
1851, 44 per cent of the Hernhill population and 56 per cent of people
in Dunkirk had left their parishes. (A further 8 and 9 per cent
respectively had died.)[6] These are figures very similar to those of
Laslett's famous seventeenth-century studies, the first to stress early-
modern geographical mobility.[7]

Moreover, at a given point in time, as tables 6.1 and 6.2 show, the
most common form of family structure was the simple family household and the nuclear family. Table 6.3 corroborates Richard Wall's
argument for occupational variation in household structure. Around
25 per cent of the households of farming and trades/crafts families
were complex (mostly extended) in form in 1851 and 1881, whereas the
corresponding figure for the labouring population was closer to 12 per

D. P. Hogan and N. Karweit, 'Kinship beyond the household in a nineteenth-century Italian town', *Continuity and Change*, 7 (1992), pp. 103–21. See also the important article, C. Wetherell, A. Plakans and B. Wellman, 'Social networks, kinship, and community in Eastern Europe', *Journal of Interdisciplinary History*, 24 (1994), pp. 639–63.

[4] P. Laslett, 'Family, kinship and collectivity as systems of support in pre-industrial Europe: a consideration of the "nuclear-hardship" hypothesis', *Continuity and Change*, 3 (1988), p. 160.

[5] For example: R. M. Smith, 'Fertility, economy, and household formation in England over three centuries', *Population and Development Review*, 7 (1981), pp. 595–622; D. Thomson, 'Welfare and the historians', in L. Bonfield, R. M. Smith and K. Wrightson (eds.), *The world we have gained* (Oxford, 1986), ch. 13. I discuss this issue and provide further references later in the article.

[6] Based on linking the census household listings for 1841 with those for 1851 and correlating them with the registers of burials.

[7] P. Laslett, *Family life and illicit love in earlier generations* (Cambridge, 1977), pp. 50–101.

Table 6.1   *Household structure in Hernhill, 1851–91 (percentages)*

Type	1851	1861	1871	1881	1891
Solitaries	2.3	3.5	6.6	1.9	4.7
No family	–	1.4	0.7	1.3	1.2
Simple	82.9	80.9	73.5	75.9	78.6
Couples	18.6	12.8	14.6	12.0	22.5
Couples and child. (nuclear)	60.5	61.0	51.0	55.7	49.7
Wid. and child.	3.9	7.1	7.9	7.0	5.2
Unmarried and child.	–	–	–	1.3	1.2
Extended	14.7	13.5	17.2	18.3	13.9
Multiple	–	–	0.7	1.3	1.7
Co-resident siblings	–	0.7	1.3	1.3	–
Total number	129	141	151	158	173

Table 6.2   *Household structure in Boughton, Dunkirk and Hernhill, 1851 (percentages)*

Type	Boughton	Dunkirk	Hernhill
Solitaries	8.9	9.9	2.3
No family	–	–	–
Simple	73.6	75.7	82.9
Couples	12.9	13.2	18.6
Couples and child. (nuclear)	53.5	57.9	60.5
Wid. and child.	6.9	4.6	3.9
Unmarried and child.	0.3	–	–
Extended	16.5	13.8	14.7
Multiple	–	–	–
Co-resident siblings	1.0	0.7	–
Total number	303	152	129

Table 6.3   *Complex households by occupational group of household head (combined parishes)*

	1851		1881	
Occupational group	Total number	% complex	Total number	% complex
Farmers	73	23.3	70	24.3
Trades/crafts	132	22.0	150	26.0
Ag. Lab./Lab.	293	10.6	353	12.7
All occupations	584	15.4	671	17.0

cent.[8] Even so, the censuses of the nineteenth century show that only a minority of the area's households – from 14 to 20 per cent according to place and decade – could be categorized as extended or complex in structure.

Yet to finish with this analysis would be to provide a very incomplete picture. Data derived from a single census can be misleading. The individual census provides a frozen structure at a given point, failing to capture movement over time. If we turn to a totally different source, the twentieth-century oral history testimony, we can gain some notion of potential flux. Take the case of the Kays, a small-farming household who have lived in Hernhill since the early nineteenth century. Harold Kay, one of eleven surviving children, who grew up in the 1920s and 1930s in the Forstall, a Hernhill hamlet, explained that their nuclear family (though he did not use this term) occupied a small four-roomed cottage – 'two-up and two-down' – next door to his grandfather, his father's father, who lived with his second wife and stepson in a larger farmhouse (formerly a parish house for the poor). But because conditions were so cramped in the cottage, several of the children slept in his grandfather's house. When Harold's father finally took over the farm, the families swapped residences, with his grandparents moving into the cottage. Harold recalls that his sisters and their husbands moved into the farmhouse to live with his parents at various stages in the family cycle. His wife's mother (who was also his aunt – Harold married a cousin) also lived in the farmhouse with her father when her husband died and left her with a small child. 'That was always used for all sorts of people as you went through life.'[9] Now it is quite probable that a census taken at ten-yearly intervals would have recorded a simple family structure for the Kays, missing the interaction between family cells (more of which later) and the flexibility of structure.

One way around this problem for the nineteenth century is to trace individual families through successive censuses, to obtain slow-moving snapshots at ten-yearly intervals. It does not provide a true chart of family histories – changes in structure within the decade are

---

[8] R. Wall, 'The household: demographic and economic change in England, 1650–1970', in Wall, Robin and Laslett (eds.), *Family forms*, p. 509, Table 16.5. My figures show lower percentages for the labouring population than Wall's (they are more in keeping with his figures for 1750–1821 than 1851); but my percentages for the trades and crafts are higher. Our figures for complex farming households are almost identical, however.

[9] Hernhill Oral History, H. Kay, b. 1921. The Hernhill Oral History Tapes are interviews that I carried out in 1991–2.

irretrievable for any more than a handful of households – but it does provide some sense of process.[10]

Indeed the simple categorization of households into 'simple', 'extended' and 'multiple' does little justice to the range of permutations and changes experienced by these households of the Blean. James Wraight, an agricultural labourer, his wife, Sarah and their six children lived at Dargate Common on the boundary of Hernhill and Dunkirk. In 1841 their household structure was simple, but Sarah died in 1846 and James's widowed mother joined the family until she died in 1861. The other person in the house in 1861 was a son, George, an unmarried 31-year-old agricultural labourer, who had been living away as a farm servant in 1851 but who was now back at home. (Other children lived nearby: Elias, a 17 year old, was a live-in carter at Dargate Farm, practically next door; Edward, a dealer, was a lodger at the Dolphin Inn in Boughton; William was living in Staple Street, Hernhill, with his wife, their two children and her illegitimate child; a daughter, Mercy, was close at hand at Dargate with her small-farmer husband and their family.) By 1871 the household's personnel had changed yet again. Elias was back with a wife and child and was listed in the census as household head and agricultural labourer. James, now aged 71, still a farm labourer and Edward and George, both still unmarried though in their thirties and forties, lived with Elias and his wife and child. (Elias's wife Mary had another child, born when she was still single, but this daughter was living with her grandparents.)[11] It would be possible to provide example after example of these mutating households.

Hans Medick warned long ago against assuming that uniformity in household type represented unity in the economic and social functions of those respective structures. 'The "extended family" of the proletariat primarily functioned as a private institution to redistribute the poverty of the nuclear family by way of the kinship system. The extended family of the peasant, on the other hand, served as an instrument for

[10] See L. Danhieux, 'The evolving household: the case of Lampernisse, West Flanders', in Wall, Robin and Laslett (eds.), *Family forms*, ch. 13; A. Janssens, 'Industrialization without family change? The extended family and the life cycle in a Dutch industrial town, 1880–1920', *Journal of Family History*, 11 (1986), pp. 25–42. See also the helpful comments of T. K. Hareven regarding the 'life-cycle' and 'life-course' approaches, 'The history of the family and the complexity of social change', *American Historical Review*, 96 (1991), pp. 104–8.

[11] Unless otherwise stated, the information relating to the censuses comes from the Census Enumerators' Books (1841, 1851, 1861, 1871, 1881, 1891) for the parishes of Hernhill, Boughton-under-Blean and Dunkirk: PRO, HO 107/466/5; HO 107/471/11; HO 107/473/12; HO 107/1626; RG 9/525; RG 10/976–7; RG 11/966–7; RG 12/712.

the conservation of property and the caring for the older members of the family.'[12]

It was relatively common for farming households to go through an extended phase. Edward and Sophia Curling at Crockham provide a good example of the family history of a well-off farming household. Edward died in 1841 and Sophia became head of the family, listed in the census of 1871 as farmer of 140 acres, employing seven men and three boys. Edward's will had left his estate to Sarah, but his sons Edward and John were to get Crockham after her death. It is possible that the three of them farmed as a unit, though we do not have the details. It is not clear whether Sophia handed over the property to her sons; on two occasions she is listed as the head of the house at Crockham (in 1851 and 1871), but in 1861 she was with her son John and his family at nearby Yorkletts Farm. Whatever the details of the transfer of property, Sophia lived always with one or other of the sons until her death in 1874. Edward did not have any children. But John went through a similar experience, still farming Yorkletts when the census was taken in 1871, and then handing the farm over to his son Albert some time during the 1870s, probably after the death of his wife in 1875. He was living with Albert and his family in 1881.[13]

The family economies of the small farmers and dealers, where all played a role from a very early age, regardless of sex, cobbling together a living through a variety of means, seemed particularly adaptable to the needs of kin. Henry and Mary Tong and their children made a living in Dunkirk and Hernhill from farm work, labouring in the woods, charcoal-burning and wood-dealing. Over time, this household expanded to incorporate Mary's father and brothers, the Tong's married daughter Ellen Ralph and her children, an illegitimate grandchild and a great grandchild (not to mention a lodger). Henry Tong's brother, William, who earned a living in a similar way, lived in Dunkirk with his wife Mary and a variety of offspring. This household also proved remarkably flexible. William's brothers, both dealers in fruit, were living with them in 1861 and 1871. Mary's father, a widower, was with them in 1881. And by 1891 they had been joined by a widowed daughter (a laundress) with her children, as well as another daughter (a dressmaker) and her brick-maker husband.

[12] H. Medick, 'The proto-industrial family economy: the structural function of household and family during the transition from peasant society to industrial capitalism', *Social History*, 3 (1976), p. 295.

[13] CKS, PRC 32/70/479, Will of Edward Curling, 1841. The rest of the information comes from the census and family reconstitution.

Table 6.4   *Complex households over the life-course by occupational group of household head, 1841–91 (combined parishes)*

Occupational group	Total number	% complex
Farmers	27	55.6
Trades/crafts	54	59.3
Ag. Lab./Lab.	185	47.6
All occupations	267	50.6

It is possible to proceed beyond the qualitative evidence to provide some quantification. Of those couples married in Boughton, Dunkirk and Hernhill and whose households – 267 in all – were present in the immediate area for three or more censuses during the period 1841–91, 51 per cent experienced an extended phase at some stage in the histories of their family structures (see table 6.4). There was both social and local variation, though not to a marked degree. The maximum per centage of extended households was Dunkirk's 55 per cent; and the extended family was slightly more common among farmers and those earning a living at a trade or craft than it was at the level of the labourer. The relatively high percentage for labouring households compared to the low figures for the stationary household structures of table 6.3 probably indicates that extension was more likely to be a short-term arrangement for the impoverished rural proletariat. The better resources of farming and trading and craft households, together with the ties of inheritance, would have encouraged longer-term residence.

Over time, then, at least as many households in the area went through an extended phase as experienced only the simple family structure and for some socio-occupational groups the complex household was more common. This does not undermine any interpretation which stresses the importance of the simple family structure in English social history, but it does have implications for what David Cressy has termed a 'fixation with the nuclear family'.[14] The extended family was not unimportant in nineteenth-century England if these Kent communities are any indication.[15]

[14] Cressy, 'Kinship', p. 41.
[15] More important even than Steven Ruggles has suggested: S. Ruggles, *Prolonged connections: the rise of the extended family in nineteenth-century England and America* (Madison, 1987). My labouring figures do not support his argument about the social complexion of the shift to the extended family.

III

However, household structure is merely one aspect of family history. Giovanni Levi has argued that we need to get away from the 'sterile' debate on the nuclear versus the complex family and to focus instead on kinship relations.[16] The remainder of this chapter will address this issue. How 'loose' were kinship links in the nineteenth-century rural world?

David Levine and Keith Wrightson have used the technique of family reconstitution to chart kinship links in the early-modern Essex parish of Terling.[17] I have followed their technique, using the census of 1851 as a focal point to calculate the percentage of households in Hernhill with kinship links to other households. The kin of each household head was traced along with the relatives of their partner if they were or had been married. The links included grandparents, parents, children, siblings, aunts, uncles and cousins (second cousins were not traced). There is a separate calculation of first-order kinship links through parents, children and siblings. Like those of Levine and Wrightson, my figures provide an underestimation of total household links (see table 6.5).

Sixty per cent of households were related to other households. If we were to include those who had no kin in Hernhill but with relatives in neighbouring Dunkirk or Boughton, then the percentage of kin-related households would rise to 65. Furthermore, several of those with no demonstrable kinship links in the parish had kin (other than nuclear family) residing in the house; if they were included in the calculation we would arrive at a figure of 70 per cent. Even if we stick with the lower per centage (60 per cent), it is still considerably higher than Terling's 39 per cent, so influential in establishing the 'looseness' of pre-industrial kinship links. Fifty-five per cent of Hernhill households in 1851 had first-order links to other households, compared to 33 per cent in Terling in 1671. The sheer extent of interlinkage is tabulated in table 6.5. Twenty-three per cent of households were related to four or more others in the parish (if we include those with links to Boughton and Dunkirk, the figure becomes 27 per cent): in Terling a mere 2 per cent at maximum had relatives in four households. None in Terling were related to more than four, whereas in Hernhill links with twice that number of families were common. No Terling household had first-

---

[16] Levi, 'Family and kin', p. 567.
[17] K. Wrightson, 'Kinship in an English village: Terling, Essex 1500–1700', in R. M. Smith (ed.), *Land, kinship and life-cycle* (Cambridge, 1984), ch. 9. The article was written by Wrightson but drew on family reconstitution for the book by Wrightson and David Levine, *Poverty and piety in an English village: Terling, 1525–1700* (London, 1979).

Table 6.5   *Kinship links in Hernhill, 1851*

Households	All kinship links		First-order kinship links	
	Number	%	Number	%
Related to 1	31	24.0	36	27.9
Related to 2	11	8.5	11	8.5
Related to 3	6	4.6	8	6.2
Related to 4+	30	23.3	16	12.4
Total related	78	60.5	71	55.0
Unrelated	51	39.5	58	45.0

order links with more than two other households, yet in Hernhill 19 per cent of households enjoyed such links. If first-order links in the two adjoining parishes are included, the figure rises to 25 per cent.[18]

These findings correspond to Charles Phythian-Adams' recent work on the Leicestershire parish of Claybrooke Parva, which used 1841 as a focal point, linking it to family reconstitutions covering a similar period, 1771–1841. Again 'without much generational depth' in his data, he was able to establish that nearly 50 per cent of households were linked by kinship within the parish and that 40 per cent of the connected households were related to more than four others (the corresponding figure for Hernhill is 38 per cent).[19]

Because the census returns for 1851 list each household throughout the parish, it is possible to go a little further with the data than the early-modern studies. The geographical origins of heads and wives are set out in table 6.6. The results for place of birth are predictable. Those with kin in other Hernhill, Boughton or Dunkirk families in 1851 had strong local origins, born either in the parish or within five miles of Hernhill. Those without kin came from further afield; they were more likely to have come from another county or from more than twenty miles away. And yet the 'kinless' as a group were surprisingly localized in their roots. Over 60 per cent were less than ten miles from their place of birth; some 80 per cent had home parishes less than twenty miles away. Even the 'kinless' were likely to have had kin relatively close at hand in surrounding villages.

Table 6.7 indicates clear social differences in the headship of households with and without kin. Labouring households, the bulk of the population, are over-represented among those with kin links; 74 per

[18] The Terling figures come from Wrightson, 'Kinship', pp. 317–20.
[19] C. Phythian-Adams, *Re-thinking English local history* (Leicester, 1987), p. 41. See also, Phythian-Adams (ed.), *Societies, cultures and kinship*.

Table 6.6　*Place of birth of household heads and spouses with kin and no kin*
in other households in area (percentages)

Place of birth	Whole parish	Heads and spouses with kin in area[a]	Heads and spouses without kin in area[a]
Hernhill	32.8	42.5	13.6
Less than 5 miles	37.8	40.0	33.3
5–10 miles	11.2	8.1	17.3
10–20 miles	9.5	5.0	18.5
Greater than 20 miles	7.0	1.9	17.3
Unknown	1.7	2.5	–

[a] Area is defined here as Boughton, Dunkirk and Hernhill.

Table 6.7　*Kinship links by occupational group of household head*

Occupational group	Total number	% with kin in area[a]
Gentry/elite	5	0.0
Farmers	27	48.2
Trades/crafts	11	90.9
Ag. Lab./Lab.	73	74.0
All occupations	129	65.1

[a] Area is defined here as Boughton, Dunkirk and Hernhill.

cent had relations in other Hernhill, Boughton and Dunkirk households. There is not much support here for John Gillis's observation
about the lack of close kin ties among the southern and eastern rural
proletariat.[20] The profiles of farmers were divided fairly evenly
between those with long parish histories and complex links with other
local families (on the one hand) and (on the other) those presumably
with marriage and kinship ties further afield in the district or county –
Alan Everitt has drawn attention to intermarriage among the farming
elite in Victorian east Kent.[21] The craft and trade families, although
unfortunately thin on the ground in Hernhill at that time, seem to have
been more uniformly integrated into the immediate kinship community, possibly the result of a willingness to marry locally. Ten out of
eleven such households had kin in the area. Of course this does not
preclude wider links on their part: although he was only going by
surnames in the county directories, Everitt has written of the 'dynas-
ties' of blacksmiths in Kent, 'sons, brothers, fathers, uncles, nephews,

[20] J. R. Gillis, *For better, for worse: British marriages, 1600 to the present* (New York, 1985),
pp. 116–17.
[21] A.M. Everitt, *Transformation and tradition: aspects of the Victorian countryside* (Norwich,
1984), pp. 10–11.

and cousins are often found to be at work in a group of nearby parishes or in the back-streets of local market towns'.[22]

The picture, then, is far from that of households 'isolated within the village in terms of kinship'.[23] There is a warning here for those who would read early-modern conditions into the nineteenth-century rural world. The structures of kinship were in place in Hernhill; families had kin all about them. This has rather significant implications for a historiography which in its discussions of kinship, the elderly and poverty draws a somewhat rigid distinction between kin and community (or 'collectivity' or neighbourhood) as if they were easily isolable entities.[24] This separation would have been meaningless in nineteenth-century Hernhill where, at least in terms of structures, kinship was part of neighbourhood.

We can enter this milieu with a simple case study, the family connections of James Wraight, the agricultural labourer encountered earlier in the discussion of household structures. By again using the census list of households as a point of reference and correlating the census book with family reconstitutions, it is possible to calculate just how many kin Wraight had in the three Blean parishes in 1851. Wraight was one of eleven children, only six of whom had survived childhood, and 1851 (we may recall) saw him widowed, with three children and his widowed mother, Mary Wraight, living together in his Dargate house. There were kin all around. First, at the Forstall (or Bessborough), there were his married brothers, William, an agricultural labourer, and Edward, a higgler and labourer. They were near an uncle, Noah Miles, and a married cousin, Edward Miles, who lived together on Noah's farm. Staple Street contained more kin: Wraight's cousins Matilda Jackson, wife of a carpenter and the publican of the Three Horse Shoes, and Harriet Curling, married to a blacksmith (a nephew of Wraight was also an apprentice in this household in 1851). Still in Staple Street, were two nieces (both married) and his daughter Martha Spratt, a blacksmith's wife. Next, in the small settlement around Hernhill Church, lived an uncle, the farmer John Butcher, and a cousin, Noah Miles junior, publican of the Red Lion. There were other relations scattered in the immediate vicinity – farmer uncles at Way Street and High Street, a married son in Dunkirk, a niece at Boughton Common.

However, it is the kin living right at his front door in Dargate that are of the most interest and we can chart their proximity by their household entry-numbers in the census book (Wraight's number was no. 36). Here he had two married sisters, Mary Ann Goodwin (no. 24)

---

of the Dove beerhouse and Harriet Packman (no. 25) who was married
to an agricultural labourer; a married niece (no. 28); an uncle, William
Wraight (no. 26), small farmer of 11 acres; and cousins George Wraight
(no. 22), greengrocer and fruit dealer and Frederick Wraight (no. 27),
farm labourer. Finally, James Wraight's late wife's sister, Dinah Kay,
lived at Dargate Farm (no. 17) with William Kay, the farm bailiff. (A
son of one of Wraight's cousins lived at Dargate with his dressmaker
wife (no. 15), but we will not include him as kin.) Even though this was
a family network traced for a fleeting moment of time – those kin
present when the census of 1851 was taken – it provides a glimpse of
the rural kinship environment. James Wraight had at least twenty
families of kin in Hernhill, more if we include neighbouring parishes.
His case is not a random selection, but the structure of Wraight's
kinship network was far from unique and it would have been easy to
have mapped out similar linkages for other inhabitants of the Blean.

IV

It is a giant step from structure to sentiment and some will argue that
even if kinship ties were 'dense' there is no guarantee that people
made use of them. Indeed the fact that they were all around may have
meant that they were taken for granted and rarely exploited. This is
unlikely. In a convincing study, the American historian Nancy Grey
Osterud has mapped out networks of kin-based reciprocity in nineteenth-century rural New York; the people of this valley farming
community certainly did not ignore their family connections.[25] There is
some qualitative evidence that a similar situation prevailed in Hernhill.
   Once again twentieth-century oral history from this part of rural
Kent can provide some insights into the sort of kinship interaction
which may well lurk behind the sparser nineteenth-century quantitative data. Let us return to the family of Harold Kay. Although parents
and grandfather lived in separate households, the family had close
economic links. The 45 acres that they farmed together provided a
living (meagre most of the time) for the two families and his grandfather's brother and his sons also worked on the farm occasionally.
One could not describe the situation as common ownership, for
Harold's father (and his sons after him) were paid wages, but the
families did operate as an integrated economic unit and the expectation
was that the sons would inherit part (or perhaps all) of the farm.[26] Or

[25] N. G. Osterud, *Bonds of community: the lives of farm women in nineteenth-century New
      York* (Ithaca, 1991), esp. ch. 2: 'The power of kinship'.
[26] Hernhill Oral History, H. Kay, b. 1921.

we could take the case of Albert Packman (born 1892), son of the bailiff at Crockham Farm. There were six in the house: his mother and father, three children and his mother's sister's illegitimate child. His mother's parents lived less than a mile away and his grandfather was employed by Albert's father (in his capacity of bailiff) as a ditcher. The Packmans lived in a tied cottage and were not allowed to keep pigs, so Albert's father kept them at his in-law's place. He would ride his bicycle up each night to tend to the pigs, while Albert's grandmother looked after them during the day. When young Albert wanted to escape farming life, he made use of wider kinship links, writing to a relative in Folkestone (his 'father's sister's son') and asking him to find a job in the town.[27]

Although the nineteenth-century documentary sources are somewhat less forthcoming, there is some evidence that people turned to their relations for help. Few discussions of Victorian welfare deal with the issue of illegitimate children, but 27 per cent of those in nineteenth-century Boughton, Dunkirk and Hernhill lived in the houses of their grandparents (either alone or with their mothers). The majority of children born out of wedlock were raised by their mothers, but a significant number depended upon relatives for support.[28] As Cressy has said, kin were 'like a reserve account to be drawn upon as the need arose'.[29] When the elderly wife of a Boughton labouring man needed opium, she borrowed a penny from her daughter-in-law.[30] A farm servant who wanted to go harvesting arranged with his master for his brother to take his place so that he would not breach his hiring agreement.[31] When a charcoal burner and his wife fought in the middle of the night and neighbours responded to 'screams of murder', they were told that the man and his wife had quarrelled and that she had taken her son out of bed to go to her sister's house to sleep. (They discovered the child out in the street, naked except for a coat which the man's brother had thrown over his shoulders.)[32] And when Eliza Jane Tappenden was deserted by her husband in 1865, three years into their marriage, she placed her elder child with her parents in Staple Street while she and the younger went into the workhouse. The census return for 1871 records that the child was still in the house of his grandparents and that by then his mother was living there as well.[33]

[27] TL, A. Packman, b. 1892.   [28] See p. 206 below.
[29] Cressy, 'Kinship', p. 69.   [30] *Faversham Mercury*, 18 May 1861.
[31] CKS, PS/US 7, Upper Division of the Lathe of Scray Settlement Examinations 1812–16, p. 208.
[32] *Faversham Mercury*, 5 January 1878.
[33] CKS, PS/US 11, Upper Division of the Lathe of Scray Petty Sessions 1864–8, 12 August 1865.

An interaction between kinship and economy surfaces from time to time, usually when such arrangements went wrong. In the case of Holmes vs. Rook in 1861 it transpired that a Boughton builder was paying his workers through credit (truck) at his brother-in-law's shop.[34] In 1878 a wood-dealer's widow, Mary Tong, sued her late husband's brother for £2 13s. 9d. for 'goods supplied and work done'. The court was told that there 'were a great many dealings between her husband and the defendant', both dealers; 'They used to work for each other and set off accounts against one another.'[35] When the parish census listings are linked with family reconstitutions it is possible to detect young people working for their kin: farmers employing grandchildren, nephews or a cousin's children as farm or household servants; uncles with a craft or trade taking on kin as apprentices or servants.

It has become fashionable of late to emphasize the role of the community rather than kin and the family in the support of the disadvantaged in England's past, particularly in the care of the elderly. In his attack on the 'simple-minded premise that families cared for their disadvantaged members', David Thomson has argued that geographical mobility and mortality would have removed many potential supporters, that the prevalent household structure does not suggest co-residential support and that the elderly have been long considered the responsibility of the community rather than relatives.[36] Thomson's theme is of community rather than familial responsibility for the elderly. But the evidence from Hernhill and its neighbouring parishes raises the possibility of the importance of family and kin. From 45 per cent to 56 per cent of elderly women and men in nineteenth-century Hernhill, Boughton and Dunkirk were living with a child or other kin according to the censuses of 1851 and 1881. A further 28 to 37 per cent were living alone with a spouse. When we look at the elderly widowed and never married, the picture is much the same. A high percentage of widowers and unmarried men lived alone or in lodgings in 1881, but the predominant pattern was for the widowed to live with a child or kin: up to 73 per cent did so. The pattern, in short, was for residence with family or for independence in a kin-based environment – around 80 per cent of the over 65-year-old males in these Kent parishes were listed as employed.[37]

[34] *Faversham Mercury*, 24 August 1861.   [35] *Faversham Mercury*, 18 May 1878.
[36] In a series of brilliant articles. The best summaries of his research are to be found in: Thomson, 'Welfare and the historians'; and 'The welfare of the elderly in the past: a family or community responsibility?', in M. Pelling and R. M. Smith (eds.), *Life, death, and the elderly: historical perspectives* (London, 1991), ch. 7. The quotation comes from Thomson, 'Welfare and the historians', p. 358.
[37] The figures are for men and women of 65 years and over living in Boughton, Dunkirk

Nor did being old involve a total reliance upon the Poor Law. Of 174 elderly and their partners in Boughton, Dunkirk and Hernhill in 1861, only 30 (17 per cent) had been or were on poor relief during the period 1859–61.[38] The role of family and kinship is further underlined when the fates of couples are traced over time. There were 241 household heads and their partners in Hernhill in 1851 and I have traced their movements until the end of the century.[39] Seventy had left the parish by 1901 (usually with their families) and seven were still alive at the end of the survey period. Of the remaining 164 adults, 81 (49 per cent) died when they were with a partner. This left eighty-three widows and widowers. Of this final group, thirty-two (38 per cent) died in the house of an adult child; twenty-five (30 per cent) died in the area – Boughton, Dunkirk or Hernhill – although their household arrangements are unclear; fifteen (18 per cent) died outside the area and were brought back to the parish for burial; seven (8 per cent) remarried; and only four (5 per cent) died in the workhouse. A little less than 40 per cent of the widowed certainly ended their days amidst kin, but the final number would include some of those who had died outside the parish. We must also remember that many of the 30 per cent who died in our three parishes would have had kin near at hand. At the very least, my findings raise a question mark over Thomson's claim that 'moves to incorporate an ageing parent into the home of a child were not widespread'.[40]

V

John Mack Faraghar has said of the nineteenth-century American farming community of Sugar Creek, Illinois, that it was 'a rural community that adhered through the bonds of kinship – subtly turning neighbours into family and anchoring community into something

and Hernhill for the censuses of 1851 and 1881. Each census was treated separately, as were males and females and widowed and married. The totals are for the combined parishes.

[38] Calculated from CKS, G/F RA 12–14, Faversham Union Relieving Officer's Application and Report Books 1859–61.

[39] I have followed them through successive censuses and checked them against the reconstitutions and the parish registers.

[40] Thomson, 'Welfare and the historians', p. 364. The work of Jean Robin also sits uncomfortably with Thomson's interpretation. She traced (for the Devonshire parish of Colyton) a cohort of men and women aged 50–59 through successive censuses from 1851 to 1871, concluding that 'children, and particularly daughters, played a considerable part in caring for their elderly parents': 56 percent of the cohort still in Colyton in 1871, and by then in their seventies, were living with their children. See J. Robin, 'Family care of the elderly in a nineteenth-century Devonshire parish', *Ageing and Society*, 4 (1984), p. 515.

more firm than merely a desire to belong somewhere'.[41] We catch
something of the same sentiment in the recollections of Leonard
Austin, a farmworker who grew up and worked in the hamlet of South
Street in Boughton early this century, when he discussed the social and
economic implications of getting the sack and the calculations that a
labourer and his wife and children had to make before they decided to
move to better conditions of work.

> Horsemen used to move nearly every year. Stockmen and horsemen. But
> labourers didn't used to move so much. They moved more for, well, little
> better conditions of work. Not much more wages. Perhaps the boss was a little
> better where they went to, that's all, a little more lenient, but wages no more
> different perhaps. It's just that the ground was better to work, you see it was
> all hard work, so if you've got very stiff clay old ground over there and you
> could get a job on a farm with better soil, well you went if you could. If the
> conditions were suitable. Well you might want to go somewheres where you'd
> got a few relatives. You see that's what it was. If you got the sack this week,
> you've got to get where you could, so you had to go and break all your ties
> with relatives or clubs or whatever you belonged to and go wherever you
> could get a job. That meant you was in a foreign land straight away didn't it. It
> all depends where you had to go, perhaps it would be four or five miles away
> and you didn't know anyone there perhaps at all. You had to start afresh. Kids
> all had to start a fresh school. It was all fresh you see.[42]

Austin's phrase about a 'foreign land', coming immediately after his
reference to relatives as a vital component in the social equation,
reinforces my argument about the centrality of kin to community.

Austin's other consideration when he talked about labouring mobility, whether forced or voluntary, was the loss of the benefits of those
pub-based, community welfare agencies, the clubs, which in return for
regular weekly contributions would insure against loss of income
through sickness and cover the costs of a dignified burial.[43] This dual
consideration of the 'collectivity' and kin is significant. And lest my
case is misinterpreted as an emphasis on the role of kinship to the
exclusion of all else, I would like to elaborate my argument.

The tendency in the revisionist history of nineteenth-century social
welfare is to combine the observation (1) that England had a highly
developed poor relief system with (2) the 'implications of the discovery
of the nuclear family system in preindustrial England'.[44] In such work
there is a rather rigid distinction drawn between family and commu-

---

[41] J. M. Faragher, 'Open-country community: Sugar Creek, Illinois, 1820–1850', in
S. Hahn and J. Prude (eds.), *The countryside in the age of capitalist transformation*
(Chapel Hill, 1985), p. 251.
[42] TL, L. Austin, b. 1902.   [43] See chapter 4.
[44] Smith, 'Fertility', p. 606. See also, Thomson, 'Welfare and the historians' and 'Welfare
of the elderly'.

nity, with the emphasis on the latter as the main source of welfare or support. Some of the discussion relates to the early-modern period, but there is the connecting theme of what Richard Smith has described as the 'remarkable continuity in patterns from the late sixteenth through the first half of the nineteenth century' and 'remarkable consistency in the *extra-familial* locus of welfare institutions'.[45] The thesis has been best summarized in a recent article by Laslett:

> Living in simple-family households (nuclear families) leaves many individuals without familial support. The nuclear-hardship hypothesis states that the more dominant simple-family households are in a society, the more important will be support for such individuals from the collectivity – that is, charitable organisations such as the Church, municipalities and the State. Considerable attention has been paid to support coming from kin outside the family in which an individual resides and to the extent of transfer through the collectivity. It is concluded that in England and North-West Europe, where the simple-family household was dominant, transfers through the collectivity were indeed of great importance for these purposes in pre-industrial times, and transfers from kin of little significance.[46]

There is much in the revisionist canon that I can agree with. It is true that community support in the form of the Poor Law was a long-accepted part of English social life, although not all revisionists sufficiently confront the changes in rules after 1834. I can agree that in periods of our past there were fewer kin actually alive to be potential helpers.[47] I am aware that large numbers of the population were in no financial position to support their ailing or less fortunate kin. But I have considerable reservations about revisionist assumptions on the inexorability and isolation of the nuclear household. Couples formed new 'independent' households but most did so amidst a community of kin. What a French anthropologist has said of a village in nineteenth-century France could be applied to Hernhill: 'nuclear is not independent'. The concept of a nuclear family was 'strongly embedded in wider social networks'.[48] Nor did mobility

---

[45] Smith, 'Fertility', p. 608; R. M. Smith, 'Transfer incomes, risk and security: the roles of the family and the collectivity in recent theories of fertility change', in D. Coleman and R. S. Schofield (eds.), *The state of population theory* (Oxford, 1986), p. 200. See also, his 'The structured dependence of the elderly as a recent development: some sceptical historical thoughts', *Ageing and Society*, 4 (1984), pp. 409–28.

[46] Laslett. 'Family, kinship and collectivity'. The quotation comes from the abstract on p. 137.

[47] Laslett. 'Family, kinship and collectivity', pp. 161–3; J. Bongaarts, T. Burch and K. Wachter (eds.), *Family demography, methods and their applications* (Oxford, 1987).

[48] M. Segalen, 'Nuclear is not independent: organization of the household in the Pays Bigouden Sud in the nineteenth and twentieth centuries', in R. McC. Netting, R. R. Wilk and E. J. Arnould (eds.), *Households: comparative and historical studies of the domestic group* (Berkeley, 1984), p. 172.

lead inevitably, as too many historians have assumed, to weak kinship networks.[49] Households were not immutable structures in any case; and they adapted to meet the demands of family and kinship. There is a danger that in an effort to trounce old assumptions about family-based welfare, the new interpretation will rule out kinship as a significant factor at all.[50] I have been at pains to emphasize the family as process and the need to place it in the wider context of kin networks. Life was seldom a simple choice between family and Poor Law or collectivity; instead we should think of life-course strategies, of a constant negotiation which drew upon available resources.[51] Our informant, Austin, was quite clear on this for early twentieth-century Boughton. People turned to relatives, neighbours and poor relief in their quest for survival. Some depended on the good will or self-interest (they were not always mutually exclusive) of employers: one old couple went into the workhouse in the winter and returned to their rented cottage in the spring so that the man could work on the farm. Some out-of-work labourers and their sons remained in Boughton in the winter, living in the farmers' flimsy hop-huts, while their women-folk went to Faversham to stay with kin. Some of the poor were totally on their own. Austin had no illusions about the restrictions of poverty. Those who fell on hard times could turn to relatives or neighbours for a while; 'but not for long because they couldn't afford to keep them for long'. He continued, with the welfare state in mind, 'You either had to stand on your own feet or die out of

---

[49] English historians would do well to read an important article by Gerard Bouchard, 'Mobile populations, stable communities: social and demographic processes in the rural parishes of the Saguenay, 1840–1911', *Continuity and Change*, 6 (1991), pp. 59–86.

[50] It should be said that Richard Smith pulls back from such an interpretation in a more recent discussion: Pelling and Smith, 'Introduction', in Pelling and Smith (eds.), *Life, death, and the elderly*, esp. pp. 12–17. For an interesting and nuanced study of the roles of family and state in support for the elderly in the twentieth century (which does not rule out kinship), see C. Gordon, 'Familial support for the elderly in the past: the case of London's working class in the early 1930s', *Ageing and Society*, 8 (1988), pp. 287–320.

[51] This kind of interaction comes through strongly (in an urban context) in P. Mandler (ed.), *The uses of charity: the poor on relief in the nineteenth-century metropolis* (Philadelphia, 1990), particularly in the chapters by Mandler, Lynn Hollen Lees and Ellen Ross. See also the discussions in J. Quadagno, *Aging in early industrial society: work, family, and social policy in nineteenth-century England* (New York, 1982), ch. 3: 'Household and kin'; R. Wall, 'Relationships between the generations in British families past and present', in C. Marsh and S. Arber (eds.), *Families and households: divisions and change* (London, 1992), ch. 4; and S. O. Rose, 'Widowhood and poverty in nineteenth-century Nottinghamshire', in J. Henderson and R. Wall (eds.), *Poor women and children in the European past* (London, 1994), ch. 13.

Families 175

the way in those days.' People, he thought – although this was in 1975 – are 'in heaven today'.[52]

VI

This argument may have implications for views of the early-modern period, but it is not the intention to use nineteenth-century sources to rewrite the history of seventeenth-century England. Indeed one of the aims of this chapter has been to counter a sociological tendency to merge the rural worlds of the two centuries. The nineteenth-century Blean was not characterized by the 'loose kin relations' of sixteenth- and seventeenth-century Essex. There is a contrast between what might have been expected, based on Macfarlane's precis at the beginning of this article and what was actually discovered.

When Michael Anderson wrote his path-breaking monograph *Family structure in nineteenth century Lancashire*, he began by noting a paradox: the contrast between the nuclear family patterns of pre-industrial England and the kinship-based, working-class communities of twentieth-century Britain. The key to this change lay, he thought, in the nineteenth century.[53] Yet this study forms part of growing evidence that kinship was already a significant factor in both rural and urban communities in the first half of that century.[54] Assuming that the interpretation of 'loose kin relations' during the early-modern period is correct, the transition to dense kinship patterns was earlier than Anderson anticipated and has yet to be explained.

[52] TL, L. Austin, b. 1902.
[53] M. Anderson, *Family structure in nineteenth century Lancashire* (Cambridge, 1971), pp. 1–3. For an introduction to twentieth-century kinship, see M. Segalen, *Historical anthropology of the family* (Cambridge, 1986), ch. 3: 'Kin relationships in urban society'. For rural kinship, see M. Strathern, 'The place of kinship: kin, class and village status in Elmdon, Essex', in A. P. Cohen (ed.), *Belonging: identity and social organization in British rural cultures* (Manchester, 1982), ch. 4.
[54] Apart from this study, see Anderson, *Family structure*, including ch. 7 on Ireland and rural Lancashire; D. Jenkins, *The agricultural community in south-west Wales at the turn of the twentieth century* (Cardiff, 1971), ch. 7; D. R. Mills, 'The residential propinquity of kin in a Cambridgeshire village, 1841', *Journal of Historical Geography*, 4 (1978), pp. 265–76; Phythian-Adams, *Re-thinking English local history*, pp. 40–2; D. Symes and J. Appleton, 'Family goals and survival strategies: the role of kinship in an English upland farming community', *Sociologia Ruralis*, 26 (1986), pp. 345–63; E. Lord, 'Communities of common interest: the social landscape of south-east Surrey, 1750–1850', in Phythian-Adams (ed.), *Societies, cultures and kinship*, ch. 4. W. M. Williams's famous study, *A west country village, Ashworthy* (London, 1963), concluded that kinship in nineteenth-century Ashworthy was 'relatively narrow in range and shallow in depth' (p. 144); but Williams was misled by household structure and mobility, and he did not reconstitute his families. Hernhill seems closer to twentieth-century Gosforth, another village studied by Williams: *The sociology of an English village: Gosforth* (London, 1956), ch. 4: 'Kinship'.

PART III

Cultures

Plate 20 Richard Redgrave's *The Outcast*, 1851.

1

Sexuality

I

More bad history has been written about sex than any other subject. Our ignorance about the sexual attitudes and behaviour of people in the past is matched only by a desire to rush to generalization.[1] This is unfortunate, for (consciously or not) our perceptions of the present are shaped by our assumptions about the past. Britain's preoccupation with 'Victorian values' in the 1980s was but a politically visible example of a more general phenomenon.[2] Nor, more specifically, do we know a great deal about lower-class sexuality in nineteenth-century England. There are studies of bourgeois desires and sensibilities, but little on the mores of the vast bulk of the population.[3]

This chapter covers an aspect of nineteenth-century sexuality – the social context of illegitimacy. More particularly, this analysis will question the usefulness of the concept of a 'bastardy-prone sub-society', a term that has been influential in historical sociology and which has curious similarities to the current political theory of an

---

[1] For example, E. Shorter, *The making of the modern family* (London, 1977); L. Stone, *The family, sex and marriage in England 1500–1800* (London, 1977). For critiques, see, respectively, R. T. Vann, 'The making of the modern family', *Journal of Family History*, 1 (1976), pp. 106–17; A. Macfarlane, 'The family, sex and marriage', *History and Theory*, 18 (1979), pp. 103–26. Shorter has written an even worse book: *A history of women's bodies* (London, 1982).

[2] See 'Victorian values', *New Statesman*, 27 May 1983; J. Walvin, *Victorian values* (London, 1988).

[3] Michael Mason's *The making of Victorian sexuality* (Oxford, 1994) provides the most comprehensive, multi-layered approach to the general subject, although his argument is not always easy to follow. For courtship (with some sensible comments on sexuality), see J. R. Gillis, *For better, for worse: British marriages, 1600 to the present* (Oxford, 1985). For the lower classes, see F. Barret-Ducrocq, *Love in the time of Victoria* (London, 1991). For the bourgeoisie, see P. Gay, *The bourgeois experience, Victoria to Freud* (2 vols., Oxford, 1984, 1986).

179

underclass.[4] The experience of rural Kent suggests that bearing children outside marriage should be seen not as a form of deviancy but rather as part of normal sexual culture.

II

The first point that needs to be made about illegitimacy in nineteenth-century England is that it was set in a general context of high rates of premarital sexual activity. As Jean Robin has remarked, the large proportion of brides who were pregnant when they stood before the altar makes it rather difficult to think of sexual activity before marriage as some kind of nonconformism.[5] Statistically, the population in this part of Kent – as in Robin's Colyton – was more or less evenly divided between those who manifestly had intercourse before marriage and those who may not have (see table 7.1). Fifty per cent of brides in Boughton, Dunkirk and Hernhill in the nineteenth century were either pregnant when they stood in front of the altar, or had actually given birth before their marriage. In this part of Kent most baptisms occurred 1–2 months[6] after the birth of the child and prenuptial pregnancy intervals are based on the time from marriage to first *baptism*. To compensate for what amounts to an underestimation of the true rate of prenuptial pregnancies by this two-month delay, those children baptized 9–10 months after marriage could be included in the prenuptial

4 Illegitimacy is one of the defining characteristics of the 'underclass': see C. Murray, 'Underclass', *Sunday Times*, 26 November 1989; and for a critique, A. Walker, 'A poor idea of poverty', *Times Higher Education Supplement*, 17 August 1990.
5 J. Robin, 'Prenuptial pregnancy in a rural area of Devonshire in the mid-nineteenth century: Colyton, 1851–1881', *Continuity and Change*, 1 (1986), p. 114.
6 The civil registers of births (under the control of the Registrar General) are effectively closed to use by historical demographers, but I was able to calculate the ages of baptism in Dunkirk and Hernhill by matching the registers of baptisms against the dates of birth given in the vaccination registers for the Boughton District 1853–1871 (CKS, G/F NPv1/1, 5–6). The Boughton church registers provide both the date of birth and baptism for several years during the 1870s and 1880s, so it is possible to calculate intervals for this parish too. The results are set out below.

Interval between birth and baptism: Dunkirk and Hernhill, 1853–5, 1861–2, 1866–72

Interval	<1 month	1–2 months	2–3 months	>3 months	Total
Number	62	129	49	25	265
%	23.4	48.7	18.5	9.4	

Interval between birth and baptism: Boughton, 1869–76, 1887–9

Interval	<1 month	1–2 months	2–3 months	>3 months	Total
Number	59	123	62	47	291
%	20.3	42.3	21.3	16.1	

Table 7.1 *Prenuptial and postnuptial pregnancies and births, 1780–1871*

Type	Boughton %	Dunkirk %	Hernhill %	Combined parishes Number	%
Prenuptial births[a]	11.4	9.1	5.9	66	9.0
Prenuptially conceived	39.8	34.8	46.6	299	40.7
Postnuptially conceived	48.8	56.1	47.5	370	50.4
Total number	299	198	238	735	

[a] Children born to couples before their marriage.

category, taking the figures as high as 64 per cent for Hernhill, 63 per cent for Boughton and 54 per cent for Dunkirk. And when the historian takes into account the likelihood that an act of sexual intercourse will result in pregnancy – a monthly probability of from 15–50 per cent for women who have regular intercourse – and the survival rate of a fertilized ovum (a 50 per cent chance of survival to the end of 9 months), these bridal pregnancies are truly the tip of an iceberg of sexual activity. In the words of Richard Smith, it is possible 'that periods of regular sexual relations or cohabitation of up to a year and a half could precede an eventual church marriage on the part of many of those who were pre-nuptially pregnant'.[7] The parish register figures also hide a number of casual liaisons which did not result in pregnancy. Many of those claiming maintenance from the fathers of their illegitimate children in Kent in the 1860s mentioned prolonged sexual activity before the resultant pregnancy; several had been intimate with other men too.[8] Pre-marital sex was not a form of deviant behaviour. As John Knodel has observed of nineteenth-century Germany, it is likely that the majority of women experienced their first sexual intercourse outside of marriage.[9] Such activity was socially biased but not socially specific. The daughters and sons of labourers were more likely to indulge in premarital intercourse, but about a third of the brides and grooms from farming backgrounds and over 40 per cent of those from the trades and crafts were pregnant when they married (see table 7.2).

The overall age profile of pregnant brides was very similar to brides in general. Although we may need to slightly modify P. E. H. Hair's

[7] R. M. Smith, 'Marriage processes in the English past: some continuities', in L. Bonfield, R. M. Smith and K. Wrightson (eds.), *The world we have gained* (Oxford, 1986), p. 92.
[8] CKS, PS/US 21, Upper Division of the Lathe of Scray Petty Sessions Bastardy Examinations 1860–71.
[9] J. Knodel, *Demographic behavior in the past* (Cambridge, 1988), p. 219.

Table 7.2   *Prenuptial pregnancies by known occupational group of bridegroom and bride's father, 1780–1871 (combined parishes)*

	Bridegroom		Bride's father	
Occupational group	Number at risk	% pregnant	Number at risk	% pregnant
Farmers	77	29.9	63	38.1
Trades/crafts	121	46.3	59	42.4
Ag. Lab./Lab.	474	55.3	270	54.8
Total	672	50.7	392	50.3

claim that there is no statistical evidence for teenage promiscuity – just under a third of pregnant brides in Hernhill were 16, 17 and 18 years old – the burden of his point remains. The bulk of single women and men were sexually active at about the age at which they married rather than the age at which they reached sexual maturity[10] (see tables 7.3 and 7.4). Seventy-five per cent of pregnant brides were aged from 18 to 24 years; 70 per cent of their grooms were aged 21 to 27.

We also have figures for the degree of pregnancy, which hint at two types of prenuptial intercourse: that where sexual activity resulting in pregnancy led to marriage and that where anticipation of marriage led to sexual activity (and pregnancy).[11] Nearly 80 per cent of pregnant brides in Boughton and Dunkirk and 74 per cent in Hernhill were at least three months pregnant when they stood in front of the minister, indicating sexual activity some time before marriage. The remainder – 23 per cent for the combined parishes – presumably had intercourse once marriage had been agreed (see table 7.5).

In her work on Swedish illegitimacy, Ann-Sofie Kälvemark has reasoned that if pregnancy before marriage was considered to be shameful there would be pressure for marriage at an early stage of the pregnancy; in other words, it would be unlikely that the seasonal pattern for the marriages of pregnant brides would be the same as that for non-pregnant women. As figure 7.1 indicates, the patterns are in fact remarkably similar. The vast majority of pregnant brides were able to postpone their marriage until the conventional marriage month of October. This Kent evidence supports Kälvemark's findings that 'social pressure was not such as to force a pregnant bride to marry quickly to

[10] P. E. H. Hair, 'Bridal pregnancy in earlier rural England further examined', *Population Studies*, 24 (1970), p. 65; E. A. Wrigley, 'Marriage, fertility and population growth in eighteenth-century England', in R. B. Outhwaite (ed.), *Marriage and society* (London, 1981), p. 161.

[11] See also Knodel, *Demographic behavior*, pp. 216–18; Wrigley, 'Marriage', p. 158.

Table 7.3 *Mean ages at marriage and illegitimacy bearing, 1780–1871*

Age	Boughton		Dunkirk		Hernhill		Combined	
	Bride	Groom	Bride	Groom	Bride	Groom	Bride	Groom
At first marriage of all brides and grooms in parish 1800–80[a]	23.3	25.7	22.4	25.5	22.4	26.2	22.8	25.8
At marriage of pregnant brides and spouses	23.4	26.7	23.1	26.0	21.3	24.9	22.6	25.9
At marriage of non-pregnant brides and spouses	23.4	26.4	22.6	26.0	22.8	25.7	23.0	26.0
Of single women bearing first known illegitimate child	22.4	–	21.4	–	21.3	–	21.8	–
Of 'bastard-bearing sub-society'	22.3	–	21.5	–	21.5	–	21.8	–
Of 'sparrows'	22.8	–	22.5	–	20.5	–	22.1	–
At marriage of illegitimate-bearers	24.8	–	24.0	–	23.4	–	24.1	–

[a] Based on family reconstitution: marriage ages of 356 Boughton women, 224 Dunkirk women, 278 Hernhill women, 316 Boughton men, 223 Dunkirk men and 246 Hernhill men: 858 women and 785 men in all. The figures for women bearing illegitimate children do not include widows.

Table 7.4 *Proportions of prenuptial and postnuptial pregnancies within each age group, 1780–1871 (combined parishes)*

Age at marriage	Bride				Groom			
	Prenuptial		Postnuptial		Prenuptial		Postnuptial	
	Number	%	Number	%	Number	%	Number	%
15–20	115	41.5	107	42.5	25	9.8	25	9.9
21–25	124	44.8	93	36.9	142	55.5	123	48.8
26–30	21	7.6	33	13.1	56	21.9	69	27.4
31–35	13	4.7	15	5.9	17	6.6	19	7.5
36–40	2	0.7	4	1.6	4	1.6	12	4.8
41+	2	0.7	–	–	12	4.7	4	1.6
Total number	277		252		256		252	

Cultures

Table 7.5   *Relative distribution of first births occurring within nine months of marriage, 1780–1871*

Marriage duration (complete months)	Boughton Number	Dunkirk Number	Hernhill Number	Combined parishes Number	Combined parishes Cumulative %
0	4	3	5	12	4.0
1	5	6	5	16	9.4
2	12	8	7	27	18.4
3	33	15	19	67	40.8
4	14	10	12	36	52.8
5	13	7	18	38	65.5
6	13	5	16	34	76.9
7	17	12	16	45	92.0
8	8	3	13	24	100.0
Total number	119	69	111	299	

avoid a scandal'.[12] Perhaps 40 per cent of pregnant brides in these Blean parishes were visibly with child when they entered the church.[13]

III

Because it appears to be so easily measurable, illegitimacy is a category much favoured by historians.[14] Yet the simplicity of the descriptions –

12   A.-S. Kälvemark, 'Illegitimacy and marriage in three Swedish parishes in the nineteenth century', in P. Laslett, K. Oosterveen and R. M. Smith (eds.), *Bastardy and its comparative history* (Cambridge, Mass., 1980), p. 332.
13   That is those whose children were baptized 0–3 months after marriage (see table 7.5), still probably an underestimation of the visibly pregnant (see footnote 6 above). Compare Smith's survey for sixteen English parishes 1550–1799: Smith, 'Marriage processes', pp. 84–6 (esp. Tables 3.1 and 3.2).
14   For a sample of the range of studies – apart from those already mentioned – see J. Frykman, 'Sexual intercourse and social norms: a study of illegitimate births in Sweden 1831–1933', *Ethnologia Scandinavica*, 3 (1975), pp. 111–50; I. Carter, 'Illegitimate births and illegitimate inferences', *Scottish Journal of Sociology*, 1 (1977), pp. 125–35; D. Levine, *Family formation in an age of nascent capitalism* (New York, 1977), ch. 9; C. Fairchilds, 'Female sexual attitudes and the rise of illegitimacy: a case study', *Journal of Interdisciplinary History*, 8 (1978), pp. 627–67; G. N. Gandy, 'Illegitimacy in a handloom weaving community: fertility patterns in Culcheth, Lancs., 1781–1860' (University of Oxford D. Phil. thesis, 1978); J. R. Gillis, 'Servants, sexual relations, and the risks of illegitimacy in London, 1801–1900', *Feminist Studies*, 5 (1979), pp. 142–73; K. Oosterveen, R. M. Smith and S. Stewart, 'Family reconstitution and the study of bastardy: evidence from certain English parishes', in Laslett, Oosterveen and Smith (eds.), *Bastardy*, ch. 3; A. Newman, 'An evaluation of bastardy recordings in an east Kent parish', in Laslett, Oosterveen and Smith (eds.), *Bastardy*, ch. 4; D. Levine and K. Wrightson, 'The social context of illegitimacy in early modern England', in Laslett, Oosterveen and Smith (eds.), *Bastardy*, ch. 5; R. Davies, '"In a broken dream": some aspects of sexual behaviour and the dilemmas of the unmarried mother in south west

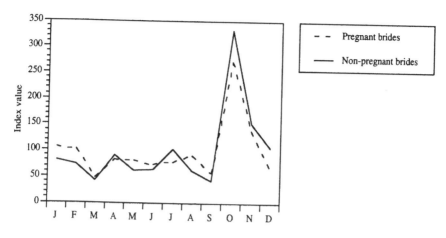

Figure 7.1 Seasonality of marriages in combined parishes, 1780–1871.

illegitimacy, 'bastard-bearing' – should not be permitted to mask the complexity of the social scenarios and human relationships which they claim to classify.[15] There was a variety of illegitimates and illegitimacies in Boughton, Dunkirk and Hernhill in the nineteenth century, as there was elsewhere in the country. First there was what Knodel has called 'legitimized' illegitimacy, where the parents later married, a phenomenon akin to prenuptial pregnancy (indeed the category is

Wales, 1887–1914', *Llafur*, 3 (1983), pp. 24–33; J. J. Brumberg, ' "Ruined" girls: changing community responses to illegitimacy in upstate New York, 1890–1920', *Journal of Social History*, 18 (1984–5), pp. 247–72; N. J. Tranter, 'Illegitimacy in nineteenth century rural Scotland: a puzzle resolved?', *International Journal of Sociology and Social Policy*, 5 (1985), pp. 33–46; P. P. Viazzo, 'Illegitimacy and the European marriage pattern', in Bonfield, Smith and Wrightson (eds.), *World we have gained*, ch. 4; J. A. D. Blaikie, 'Illegitimacy in nineteenth-century north-east Scotland' (University of London Ph.D. thesis, 1987); J. Robin, 'Illegitimacy in Colyton, 1851–1881', *Continuity and Change*, 2 (1987), pp. 307–42; G. Nair, *Highley: the development of a community 1550–1880* (Oxford, 1988), index: 'illegitimacy'; A. Wilson, 'Illegitimacy and its implications in mid-eighteenth-century London: the evidence of the Foundling Hospital', *Continuity and Change*, 4 (1989), pp. 103–64; R. Mitchison and L. Leneman, *Sexuality and social control: Scotland 1660–1780* (Oxford, 1989); J. A. D. Blaikie, 'The country and the city: sexuality and social class in Victorian Scotland', in G. Kearns and C. W. J. Withers (eds.), *Urbanising Britain: essays on class and community in the nineteenth century* (Cambridge, 1991), ch. 4; G. Pomata, 'Unwed mothers in the late nineteenth and early twentieth centuries: clinical histories and life histories', in E. Muir and G. Ruggiero (eds.), *Microhistory and the lost peoples of Europe* (Baltimore, 1991), ch. 8; H. Marks, 'On the art of differentiating: proletarianization and illegitimacy in northern Sweden, 1850–1930', *Social Science History*, 18 (1994), pp. 95–126.

[15] Note Wrigley's comment: 'illegitimacy is better regarded as embracing a wide range of situations rather than as a simple, categorical alternative to legitimacy' (Wrigley, 'Marriage', p. 155).

included with my figures for bridal pregnancy in table 7.1 above). Then there were those illegitimacies where the mother of the child did not marry the child's father. Sometimes she would marry another man a year or so later. Sometimes she would remain single. Such non-legitimized illegitimacies would include intended, though interrupted, marriages (possibly on more than one occasion for individual women), cases where a woman lived in a permanent, unmarried relationship with a man, and instances where women bore illegitimate children (again sometimes more than one) to men they had no intention of marrying. (Married women would also bear children to men other than their husbands but they are difficult to detect.)

A few examples give some indication of the scope of social arrangements. Some women lived in what amounted to common-law marriages. The 1881 census for Hernhill listed the Staple Street household headed by Isabella Newman, unmarried, aged 37, a needleworker with three sons, Alfred W. B., age 8, Herbert E., 5 and John C., 2. Also in the house was Herbert Butcher, 'boarder', single, a 40-year-old agricultural labourer. We know that the relationship was more than that of 'head' and 'border' because the Dunkirk baptisms for 1872 (the year of 8-year-old Alfred's birth) list Alfred William Butcher son of Isabel Ann Newman of Dunkirk and because the marriage entry for a daughter of Newman (born in 1882) lists Butcher as the father.[16] Lucy Wills, wife of William Wills, one of the leaders of the rising of agricultural labourers in 1838, transported to Tasmania for his transgression, was living in Chartham in 1851. The census refers to Lucy Wills, housekeeper, 'widow' (she was no such thing), aged 35, born in Hernhill and living in what was obviously a common-law marriage with Daniel Cozens, a 42-year-old widowed agricultural labourer and their children Jane and Harriet Cozens (his children by a previous marriage), Daniel Wills (her child born after the departure of William but before the relationship with Daniel?) and an infant Mary Cozens Wills (the offspring of Wills and Cozens).[17] Our third example, Harriet Dunkin, was what some historians call a 'repeater', bearing no less than eight illegitimate children from 1858 to 1879 (that is, from the age of 24 to 45). Most of the baptisms (the majority of her children were baptized) refer only to

---

[16] PRO, RG 11/966, Hernhill Census 1881. Unless otherwise indicated, this case and these which follow are based on my family reconstitution files for Boughton, Dunkirk and Hernhill, which include material from the parish registers and the census returns, 1841–91.

[17] PRO, HO 107/1623, Chartham Census 1851. Daniel Cozens' wife, Elizabeth (Arnold), died in 1848. The Chartham parish register records the baptism of Daniel Wills, 'son of Lucy Wills, Chartham', on 2 September 1849; but there is no entry for the infant Mary Cozens Wills. CCA, Chartham Registers of Burials and Baptisms.

the mother, but in 1863 there is mention of the father of the child, Alfred Tong, whom we know from the census was living with his brother and his family in a cottage at Horse Lees (a settlement which straddled Dunkirk and Boughton). Harriet, who is listed in the census of 1861 as a general servant, lived most of her life in her father's cottage on the border of Hernhill and Boughton parishes, just across the road from Tong's brother's cottage. She was still there in 1881, still unmarried (her father died in 1873), with a 'boarder', Alfred Tong, a wood-dealer from Dunkirk. When Tong died in the 1890s, he left money to Herbert, Robert and William Dunkin, referred to in the will as 'the sons of the late Harriet Dunkin'.[18] Finally, Harriet Branchett, another single woman and repeater, bore a total of ten children out of wedlock. She lived at Hickman's Green, Dunkirk, and is listed in the census returns for 1861 and 1871 as housekeeper to Abram (*sic*) Setatree, a wheelwright. The census and Church of England baptisms never acknowledge him as the father of her children born from 1858 to 1872, although one of them is called 'Abram', but the Primitive Methodist registers record the birth of William Setatree, son of Abraham Setatree and Harriet Branchett 'not married'.[19] It is likely that here too was a long-term relationship. Women like these had fertility profiles identical to those of their married neighbours. Some 'repeaters', then, seem to have been in long-term relationships, although this tells us nothing of the emotional or the power structures or strategies of their households. In the case of Newman and Dunkin the social arrangements which lay behind their unmarried motherhood may have afforded them more power – as household heads – than marriage would have brought and a better income than if they had lived alone.

Other 'repeaters', nearly always those with smaller numbers of children, progressed through a succession of relationships. The three children of Sarah Wraight, a 20-year-old from a Hernhill small-farming household, had as many different fathers, all labourers, before she married yet another agricultural labourer, John James, in 1832. As we will see, few mothers of illegitimate children lived on their own. Emma Eve did, at Boughton Common in the 1860s, supporting her three children through dressmaking and field work (her 12-year-old son also worked in the fields). It was more common for what we would call single-parent families to live with the woman's parent or parents. Eliza Branchett, an agricultural labourer, was living with her son and her mother and father (both of whom were agricultural labourers) at Boughton Street in 1861 and in 1871 with her widowed mother and

[18] Somerset House, London, Will of Alfred Tong 1898.
[19] CKS, M8/1D/5/1, Primitive Methodist Register of Baptisms.

another two children. In the hamlet of Staple Street in Hernhill, two laundress sisters, Hester and Jemima Hadlow, both of whom remained single and both of whom lived with their mother Frances, also a laundress, produced a total of six illegitimate children to unknown fathers. (When two of the children married in Hernhill in 1888 and 1890 there were blanks in the register where the father's name was usually recorded.)

Statistically, however, most of the unmarried mothers, about 80 per cent in each parish, were responsible for a single illegitimate birth (see table 7.9). And in many respects the profiles of the mothers of illegitimate children were similar to those of pregnant brides, or indeed to those of the general female population of the same age group. Of the total 151 women, 16 (10.6 per cent) were widows, 1 was a deserted wife and the rest were unmarried. Most were local women – from Boughton, Dunkirk, Hernhill or adjoining parishes (see table 7.6). They were sexually active at about the same age as pregnant brides (see table 7.3). They were more likely to marry eventually than to remain single (although some left the parish) (see table 7.7). They came from, or lived in, most of the parishes' hamlets. They belonged to the parishes' principal social groups, although the fathers and mothers of illegitimates were drawn disproportionately from labouring families (see table 7.8).

IV

Many English historical demographers, following the work of Peter Laslett, are wedded to the notion of a 'bastard-bearing sub-culture'. In Laslett's formulation, the 'bastardy-prone sub-society' (as he called it) consisted of 'a series of bastard-producing women, living in the same locality, whose activities persisted over several generations and who tended to be related by kinship or marriage'. He suggested that the tendency to illegitimacy might have been inherited. Laslett divided 'bastard-bearers' into two basic types: 'singletons', who had one illegitimate child only and 'repeaters', who had two or more children out of wedlock and who were looked upon as deviant by the rest of society (an assumption we shall question). These 'repeaters', by defini-tion, formed the nucleus of the 'sub-society' as Laslett saw it, but he also included 'singletons' who had links with other illegitimate-bearers or illegitimates through kinship or marriage. Those singletons who stood outside the sub-society, who can be linked only with a solitary birth out of wedlock, are known as 'sparrows'. Although Laslett admitted that the sub-society is 'somewhat complex as a concept,

Table 7.6 *Mothers of illegitimate children by place of birth, combined parishes, 1821–71*

Place of birth	Mothers of illegitimate children		Census of 1851: all single women aged 15–45	
	Number	%	Number	%
In parish	90	59.6	104	45.6
Less than 5 miles away	32	21.2	61	26.7
5–10 miles	5	3.3	18	7.9
10–20 miles	3	2.0	21	9.2
20+ miles	1	0.7	20	8.8
Not known[a]	20	13.2	4	1.7
Total number	151		228	

[a] It is likely that these women were born outside the parish.

Table 7.7 *Life-courses of mothers of illegitimate children, 1821–71 (combined parishes)*

Life-course		Number	%
Marrying before 1871		75	49.7
Married father of illegitimate child	28		
Married man who was not father of child	26		
Not clear	21		
Leaving, marital status unchanged before 1871		37	24.5
Remaining in parish, marital status unchanged		25	16.6
Not clear		13	8.6
Died immediately		1	0.7
Total number		151	

Table 7.8 *Social background of mothers and known fathers of illegitimate children by occupational group, 1821–71 (combined parishes)*

Occupational group	Fathers of illegitimate-bearers		All male household heads, 1851		Fathers of illegitimates		All male occupations, 1851	
	Number	%	Number	%	Number	%	Number	%
Farmers	14	11.3	73	12.5	2	3.3	87	10.2
Trades/crafts	19	15.3	132	22.6	14	23.3	173	19.9
Ag. Lab./Lab.	91	73.4	293	50.2	37	61.7	469	54.0
Servants	–	–	–	–	7	11.7	89	10.2
Others	–	–	86	14.7	–	–	50	5.8
Total number	124[a]		584		60		868	

[a] Excludes 27 not known.

disconcertingly blurred at the edges', his hypothesis of 'a sub-society of illegitimacy prone' has been influential. Jean Robin's microstudy, while modifying some aspects of Laslett's work, confirmed the usefulness of the 'sub-society' for the nineteenth century: 'such a society certainly existed, its members living together in close proximity, and bound by ties of kinship and marriage'.[20]

It is perfectly possible to impose the classifications of Laslett and Robin on the Kent material. The proportion of women who bore two or more illegitimate children is almost identical for the three parishes: 18–20 per cent (see table 7.9). The relative number of single illegitimate births is greater in Dunkirk than in Hernhill, though this may merely reflect the more detailed family reconstitution files for the latter. For the 'sub-society' itself the strongest link with other illegitimate-bearers, as Robin found of Colyton, was through siblings: 40 per cent of women in the 'sub-society' had sisters who bore children out of wedlock.[21] However, the figures also provide some support for Laslett's theme of direct descent – 'bastard-bearing' handed down from mother to daughter[22] (see table 7.10). The 'sub-society' represented the main social groups in the combined parishes and the noticeable presence of Hernhill farmers is an interesting contrast to Robin's findings for Colyton[23] (see table 7.11).

And yet the Laslett–Robin classification is rather unsatisfactory. The terms employed are problematic. At best, the labels are bizarre: 'sparrows', 'singletons'. At worst, the language is ideologically loaded, treating the women concerned either negatively, as deviants ('repeater', 'bastard-bearing', 'sub-society'), or as powerless and passive ('illegiti-macy-prone', 'bastardy-prone'). In order to engage with current histor-iography it is sometimes necessary to use these words. But the historian and the reader, should be aware that though moralizing is not intended in this chapter, 'bastard' is hardly a neutral word. The very use of terms such as 'repeater' and 'sub-society', even 'illegiti-mate', is to adopt categories with value-laden meanings which, as I trust will become clear, may do an injustice to the historical context.[24] It is as if social attitudes have been pronounced before they have been

---

20 P. Laslett, 'The bastardy prone sub-society', in Laslett, Oosterveen and Smith (eds.), *Bastardy*, pp. 217, 219; Robin, 'Illegitimacy', p. 339.

21 Robin, 'Illegitimacy', pp. 328–9, 339.

22 Laslett, 'Bastardy prone sub-society', pp. 217–18.

23 Eleven of Hernhill's thirty-one-strong 'sub-society' came from farming families (i.e. 35 percent). Cf. Robin, 'Illegitimacy', pp. 312, 330. However, she did find that the highest percentage of prenuptial pregnancies was initiated by farmers: Robin, 'Prenuptial pregnancy', p. 117.

24 I have benefited greatly from Meg Arnot's analysis of this whole question.

Table 7.9 *Mothers of illegitimate children by category of illegitimacy, 1821–71*

Type	Boughton %	Dunkirk %	Hernhill %	Combined parishes %	Number
(A) 'sparrows' (single illegitimate birth)	43.1	51.3	36.7	43.0	65
(B) 'singletons' connected to other bastard-bearers through kinship or marriage	36.9	29.7	44.9	37.7	57
(C) 'repeaters' (two or more illegitimate births)	20.0	18.9	18.4	19.2	29
'Bastardy-prone sub-society' (B + C)	56.9	48.6	63.3	56.9	86
Single illegitimate births (A + B)	80.0	81.0	81.6	80.8	122

Table 7.10 *Connections of 'bastardy-prone sub-society', 1821–71 (combined parishes)*

Connections of women with illegitimate children	Number	%
Self illegitimate	4	4.6
Maternal connections	17	19.8
Sister an illegitimate-bearer	34	39.5
Other links (marriage/kin)	17	19.8
No known connection	14	16.3
Total number	86	

Table 7.11 *Social background of 'sub-society', 1827–71 (combined parishes)*

Occupational group	Number	%
Farmers	13	15.1
Trades/crafts	10	11.6
Ag. Lab./Lab.	52	60.5
Others	–	–
Not known	11	12.8
Total number	86	

unravelled: a 'deviancy', which may in fact have never existed, is being
foreshadowed by the classification and ordering of the historical data.
    Moreover, such neat pigeon-holing can hide as much as it reveals
and arguably forces people into inappropriate categories. How useful
is a category which includes women who bore a single illegitimate
child (who indeed may represent legitimized illegitimacy) alongside
women who bore several children out of wedlock to several different
fathers or who had affairs with married men – merely because the
'singleton' had a sister or mother who bore an illegitimate child? To
understand the social context of illegitimacy and to test the usefulness
of the notion of a sub-society, we need to move beyond the typology of
Laslett and Robin.
    As figure 7.2 indicates, there was a bewildering skein of links
between some of the illegitimate-bearing households.[25] The scattered
black circles and triangles and the lines which join them, show links
between 'illegitimacy-prone' families and individuals. There were
certainly households which could be described as 'illegitimacy-prone'.
Harriet Branchett, whom we have already encountered, had one sister
who was an unmarried mother and another, Caroline, who married
into a family of six illegitimates (the result, incidentally, of a single
union). She also had three aunts who bore children out of wedlock and
an uncle who married an illegitimate woman (see figure 7.2(b)). The
household of the Hernhill small farmer William Curling, at Sluts Hole
(*sic*: the name may not be coincidental), contained three illegitimate
children in the 1860s, the offspring of three of his daughters. It appears
that Curling and his wife Sarah Butcher – one of the Butcher clan (see
figures 7.2(a) and 7.2(b)) – lived together before they married in 1831:
the parish register for 1830 refers to the baptism of Caroline, 'daughter
of William and Sarah Curling' (*sic*). He may well have been the
William Curling who, according to a servant, had sex with her in the
late 1840s in the Hernhill church porch.[26]
    There were, it is important to note, 'illegitimacy-prone' males as well
as females. Charles Luckhurst, who was probably related to James
Luckhurst, the father of Emma Godden (illegitimate), fathered two
bastards to different women in the 1820s. The brothers Amos and
Othello Rook, Boughton bricklayers, were responsible for at least three
illegitimate children. Emily Tong, the 17-year-old daughter of a

[25] For an extremely useful study of illegitimacy networks in the Kent parish of Ash-next-
Sandwich, 1654–1840, see Newman, 'Evaluation of bastardy recordings', esp. pp. 154–
5, Fig. 4.3(a) and (b).
[26] Family reconstitution data. For the church porch episode, see CKS, Fa/JP 9/1,
Borough of Faversham Proceedings in Bastardy, Hammond vs. Jackson.

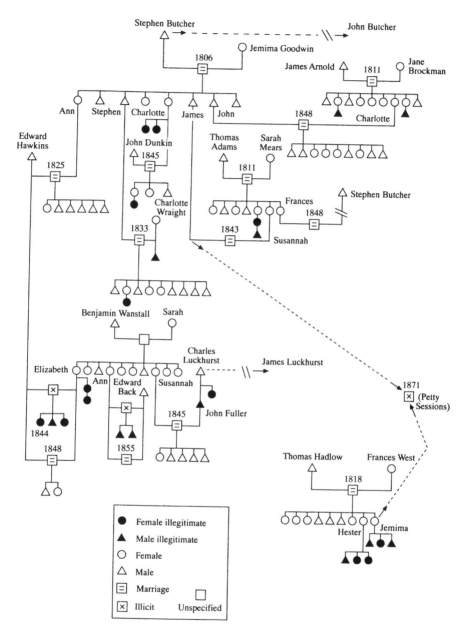

Figure 7.2(a)

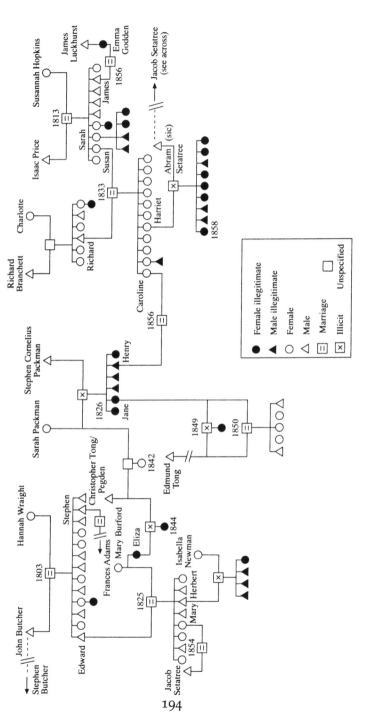

Figure 7.2(b)

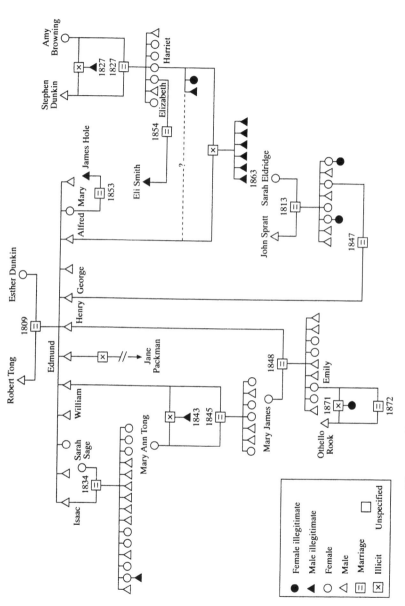

Figure 7.2(c) Illegitimacy links in Boughton, Dunkirk and Hernhill.

195

Dunkirk charcoal burner, had a child as a result of a liaison with 20-year-old Othello and Amos was the father of two of Eliza Branchett's children.[27]

Some of these households fall into the 'rough' rather than the 'respectable' section of the labouring population. Othello Rook appeared before the Petty Sessions in 1872 for being 'drunken and riotous' at Boughton; he was 'in the Street with his coat off he was shoving his fists in peoples faces'. He had been charged previously with a similar offence at the Three Horse Shoes Inn at Hernhill. He was violent towards his wife too. In 1874 and 1875 Emily Rook brought complaints of assault against her husband but then either declined to prosecute or did not appear.[28] Christopher Tong (alias Pegden), father of an illegitimate child to a woman who was herself illegitimate, living in what was almost certainly a common-law marriage to a woman who had been involved in a similar relationship with another man, was continually falling foul of the law. He was prosecuted for theft, poaching and for sexually assaulting his step-daughter.[29]

Superficially, these examples may seem further grist for the Laslett–Robin thesis. And yet, like David Levine and Keith Wrightson in their study of illegitimacy in the early-modern Essex parish of Terling, I would hesitate to describe my findings as support for an illegitimacy-prone sub-society.[30] The black geometric shapes stand out in the diagrams in figure 7.2; but more significant are all those boxes which indicate church marriages and the fact that most births (black and white) are derived from the church registers.[31] The 'illegitimacy-prone', if that is what we should persist in calling them, do not form a genealogical ghetto but are scattered throughout conventional unions and legitimate progeny.

Several of the strings of illegitimates, we have seen (and can see from the diagrams), were the product of *de facto* marriages or long-term consensual relationships. We know about such relationships, it is worth pointing out, because of the existence of detailed marriage registers and census data for the nineteenth century. This has important implications for work on earlier centuries. For the early-modern

27 CKS, PS/US 21, Tong vs. Rook, Branchett vs. Rook.
28 CKS, PS/US 12, Upper Division of the Lathe of Scray Petty Sessions 1868–71, 6 July 1871; CKS, PS/US 13, Upper Division of the Lathe of Scray Petty Sessions 1871–6, 5 December 1872, 5 November 1874, 3 December 1874, 24 November 1875.
29 Family reconstitution files; CKS, PS/US 14, Upper Division of the Lathe of Scray Petty Sessions 1820–33, pp. 142, 155; CKS, Q/S Be 191, East Kent Quarter Sessions, January 1848.
30 Levine and Wrightson, 'Social context of illegitimacy'. Anthea Newman seemed similarly ambivalent: Newman, 'Evaluation of bastardy recordings', pp. 154–6.
31 A point also made by Newman, 'Evaluation of bastardy recordings', p. 156.

period, where such material is not available and where investigations of illegitimacy are based solely on family reconstitution or aggregative analysis, the presence of a male partner could easily pass undetected and a woman living in a stable relationship with one man and having his illegitimate children would be classified as a 'repeater' and part of the core of the 'sub-society'. Studies of illegitimacy which are not based on close contextual research are likely to contain such disguised common-law marriages.

Those who produced illegitimate children seem to have lived near one another in Colyton;[32] but they were scattered throughout the community in the Blean hamlets and villages. There were what could be described as 'bastardy-prone' households and women like Eliza Branchett in Boughton and Jemima Hadlow in Hernhill, who, as we will see, were treated with suspicion by other women and with little respect by the men. There were men who fathered bastards, poached, drank and fought. It seems that there were even one or two women who engaged in casual, village prostitution. A Hernhill servant (and mother of an illegitimate child) was accused in 1849 of taking money for sex. She had shown 2s. 6d. to a fellow servant, saying that it was her 'morning's work'. Some of her partners were married men and one, a Boughton miller whom she said was the father of her daughter, had claimed that he paid her money 'as he did any other prostitute'.[33] But such cases are extremely rare. There is no evidence of any *sub-culture* or *sub-society*. The illegitimacy-prone intermarried with all but a very small parish elite. The violence, drinking and petty crime cannot really be classified as deviancy in a society for which such behaviour was part of everyday neighbourhood interaction.[34] A 'sub-society' implies a cultural or social coherence which did not exist.

V

It is possible to obtain a more nuanced picture of the social and cultural context of illegitimacy by making use of the examinations of unmarried mothers in the Petty Sessions records. These remarkable dossiers cast their net wider than Hernhill, Dunkirk and Boughton but all involve cases from that part of the county. Under the Acts 7 and 8 Victoria cap. ci (1844) and 8 Victoria cap. x (1845) women who bore an illegitimate child could apply for the alleged father to be summoned before a magistrate who could then – according to his findings – award

[32] Robin, 'Illegitimacy', pp. 331–5.
[33] CKS, Fa/JP 9/1, Hammond vs. Jackson.
[34] See B. Reay, *The last rising of the agricultural labourers* (Oxford, 1990), ch. 3.

maintenance, in practice 1s. 6d. to 2s. a week until the child was 13,
and often, though not always, 10s. for the costs of a midwife. The
result, for the Lathe of Scray in Kent, is a file of bastardy examinations
for the 1860s.[35] Like all primary documents, these sources are biased.
The woman had to have a good case before making such an allegation.
According to 7 and 8 Victoria cap. ci, the claimant was required to
have proof that the man alleged to be the child's father had paid
money for its maintenance at some stage. In most of the dossiers the
woman either had evidence of a verbal promise to marry or acceptance
of responsibility on the part of the man concerned, or else he had
demonstrated his liability by some exchange of money – that is,
support for his child. There were seventy-six illegitimacies in
Boughton, Dunkirk and Hernhill during the period 1860–71. In six
cases the child died as an infant, in eleven cases the parents (two
couples) were in long-term relationships and in eight cases the parents
married. This leaves fifty-one instances where a claim could have been
made, yet only twelve (23.5 per cent) appear in the Petty Sessions.
About 75 per cent of cases, then, never found their way to the courts:
the women concerned did not take advantage of the Acts. In some
cases the woman supported herself and her child or her parents
assumed responsibility; in others maintenance arrangements were
settled informally out of court. So the dossiers represent but a small
segment of actual illegitimacies. A woman was unlikely to pursue
maintenance – about a day's wage every week – from an impoverished
labourer. The social bias of the files is reflected in the fact that over a
half of the reputed fathers called before the Petty Sessions in the 1860s
earned their living in the crafts or trades. Less than a third were
labourers (compare table 7.8). Women must also have been aware that
when they appeared in court their morality would come under
scrutiny and that the maintenance claim could become an occasion for
the trial of a woman's own sexual probity. This aside, the examinations
provide a marvellous entry into the world of popular courtship and
sexuality in the nineteenth-century hamlet and village.

The dossiers certainly lend support to Levine and Wrightson's
suggestion that illegitimacy should be seen as part of wider courtship
patterns in popular culture.[36] Spring and summertime festivity are
frequently mentioned as the context for sexual encounters. Whitsun
celebrations (May–June), the Boughton Feast (early July), local friendly
society club days (May–July), hopping festivities (September) recur in

---

[35] CKS, PS/US 21. For the context of these Acts, see U. R. Q. Henriques, 'Bastardy and
the New Poor Law', *Past and Present*, 37 (1967), pp. 103–29.
[36] Levine and Wrightson, 'Social context of illegitimacy', pp. 168–9.

women's statements about the circumstances of their pregnancies. Maria Knight, a 19-year-old woman from Boughton, daughter of an agricultural labourer, had been seen dancing with a Faversham blacksmith (the father of her illegitimate child) at Boughton Feast one year and in another year at Whitsun in a Hernhill public house.[37] When she brought a case against a Doddington baker, Elizabeth Payn had to face the counter-accusation that she had been seen having intercourse with another man in late May, on the night of the Newnham Club Feast at the George Inn. To strengthen her case, the woman produced a witness who testified that she was with the defendant, Reuben Sellen, on a Saturday night during hopping time (September) and in Doddington one evening during Whitsun.[38] Less commonly mentioned, though still significant, was the period between Christmas and New Year, when servants were allowed time off, or when the master or mistress would leave them unsupervised. One witness recalled seeing Ellen Sherlock of Throwley, a miller's servant, and William Aylett of Faversham, a draper's porter, playing 'kiss in the ring' in her master's house at Oare; the woman could not remember whether it was Christmas Day or New Year's Day. Sherlock claimed that she and Aylett had sex on both occasions.[39]

It makes little sense to stress either control or laxity when one describes sexual mores of the past. In nineteenth-century Kent there is evidence for both. The community did exert control. There was a framework of moral vigilance and comment. Courting couples came under neighbourhood scrutiny, as is clear from the number of witnesses able to comment on the courtship practices and the various liaisons of complainant and defendant. When the Dargate (Hernhill) woman Susan Hole saw Emma Smith and Alfred Butcher together in a meadow, 'several times by themselves between 8 and 9 at night', she told them to 'mind what they got about'.[40] Maria Knight and William Smith had been observed dancing at a public house and 'about the street' in Boughton. They had been sitting on a stile about '10 and 11 at night'; 'it was rather dark and I could not see what they were doing till I got close to them'. But Knight also had to face accusations that she had 'walked out' on other occasions with Henry Godden, Henry Beale and William Beale: 'I have seen her walking out of an evening with different young Men'.[41] Community opinion (usually divided) was called upon to sway the case in favour of complainant or defendant, to

---

[37] CKS, PS/US 21, Knight vs. Smith.
[38] CKS, PS/US 21, Payn vs. Sellen, May 1868, June 1868.
[39] CKS, PS/US 21, Sherlock vs. Aylett.   [40] CKS, PS/US 21, Smith vs. Butcher.
[41] CKS, PS/US 21, Knight vs. Smith.

demonstrate, or deny, the sort of visible, close social contact which could be construed as leading ultimately to what the examinations describe, clinically, as 'connexion' or 'connection'. As the shoemaker Walter Wraight testified on behalf of Mary Curling, an unmarried mother from Hernhill, 'I have never seen her with any other young man. I have seen Mary Curling and Deft. several times together. I saw them together at Graveney Tea party. He had his arm around her waist then'.[42] Elizabeth Payn lost her case when a Doddington constable testified that he had seen her about with more than one man: 'it was of an evening. Peter Read, Reuben Croucher, Little Joe the Keeper and John Jury I have seen her with walking together. I think she is not a moral steady well conducted girl'.[43]

If the scrutiny and comment of the neighbourhood formed one constraint upon the conduct of courting couples, the intervention of parents formed another. Interestingly, such intervention came after rather than before 'connection' and its consequences. If the bastardy files are any indication, the parents of courting couples were remarkably free in their attitudes. Recourse to the court was clearly a last-ditch attempt to secure maintenance from recalcitrant sexual partners. Before things reached this stage, parents or siblings, or sometimes friends, put pressure on the fathers of illegitimate children in an effort to make them meet what were perceived as their responsibilities. Eighteen-year-old Emma Milgate's father, a farm labourer, went to see George Bass about his daughter's allegation of paternity. 'I went to Deft and told him he had got my daur in trouble. I sd I suppose you have had connexion with her. He replied Yes I have and so have others.'[44] When she was in Boughton for the hopping, Eliza Branchett's married sister tackled the bricklayer Amos Rook about Eliza's pregnancy. 'I saw the Deft at the Dolphin Inn Boughton. He came up to me and said Well Emma and called for a pot of Ale and asked me to drink and asked me to have a dance and we danced. I sd what do you intend doing for my sister. He sd he meant marrying her and he had intended giving her money if he could have met with her.'[45] So sometimes it was a sister, sometimes a father, who put pressure on the recalcitrant male. But more commonly it seems to have been the task of the woman's mother. Susan Wood went to see Daniel Rook, the father of the child that her daughter was carrying. 'I saw him up at the Forstall about the state my Daur. was in. He sd it was a bad job. I told him she

[42] CKS, PS/US 21, Curling vs. Kay.
[43] CKS, PS/US 21, Payn vs. Sellen (May 1868).
[44] CKS, PS/US 21, Milgate vs. Bass.
[45] CKS, PS/US 21, Branchett vs. Rook (December 1867).

must go into the Union [workhouse] as soon as her father in law [stepfather] found out her state.'[46] Elizabeth Nicholls asked John Black three times if he would support her daughter's child, and he replied '3 times' that if he had 'money enough he would keep it'.[47]

The final pointer to a certain order and structure in sexual relations during this period is the fact that most of this activity was predicated on the assumption of future marriage. Often – although not always – the man was alleged to have promised marriage: 'she asked me if she was in the family way would I make her a home' (Nicholls vs. Black); 'I heard Deft say he would marry complainant as soon as he had the means. She was then quite large and visibly in the family way' (Branchett vs. Rook); 'He sd he would maintain me at home and marry me' (Foster vs. Cole); 'he promised to marry me as soon as he could' (May vs. Lovell); 'he had promised me marriage. The Banns had been published in Preston Church' (Coveney vs. Hughes); 'The Deft promised me marriage' (Tong vs. Rook). Usually the promise occurred after pregnancy was detected: 'she asked me if she was in the family way would I make her a home. I said Yes certainly she then sd she was in the family way and I told her to go away.'[48] But such responsibilities, evaded or not, must indicate unspoken assumptions when intercourse took place. Sexual intercourse occurred and the understanding, articulated or not, was that if the result was an unwanted pregnancy, marriage would follow. The bulk of these maintenance actions in the Petty Sessions represented a breach or misuse of that code. There were restraints or controls upon the sexual behaviour of the unmarried, then, and a recognition that sexual intercourse carried certain responsibilities.

Yet given this general moral framework of anticipated marriage and neighbourhood supervision, there was – indeed there had been for centuries – considerable room for manoeuvre.[49] Couples had intercourse in meadows, up against stiles, in the kitchen of a master's house, in the woods, at the back of the house, at the side of the house, behind hedges, in shrubs, at the side of the road and 'in the road'. Maria Knight testified that she had connection with William Smith 'near Mr Squire Ladds Meadow, just out of the street between 12 and 1 in the morning – it is not an uncommon thing for me to be out at that time ... I had connexion with him also near Mr Barnes Hop Oast.'[50]

[46] CKS, PS/US 21, Silcock vs. Rook.   [47] CKS, PS/US 21, Nicholls vs. Black.
[48] *Ibid.*
[49] See M. Ingram, 'The reform of popular culture? Sex and marriage in early modern England', in B. Reay (ed.), *Popular culture in seventeenth-century England* (London, 1985), ch. 4; M. Ingram, *Church courts, sex and marriage in England, 1570–1640* (Cambridge, 1987), ch. 4.
[50] CKS, PS/US 21, Knight vs. Smith.

Couples would sit up together long after the woman's parents or brothers or sisters had gone to bed. Mary Curling explained her relationship with Edward Kay, who, although she did not know it, was several years her junior. 'He frequently visited me at my father's house. Sometimes at 10 or 11 at night and sometimes later. I was left alone with him some times – only him and me left up'. 'My father has handed me the key of the bedroom door out of his window about 11 o'clock. Kay was with me.' Mary's sister, Susan Clark, confirmed her story. 'I left him with my sister. None of my family were left up and he stayed up after we had all gone to bed ... I have frequently seen her sitting on his knee.' What is interesting is that despite the freedom for courtship both sisters were adamant that no impropriety had occurred in their parents' house. Intercourse took place 'on the road from our house to Hernhill'. Mary denied rumours of sex with other men on 'the rug before the fire' and in her sister's bed.[51] In another case, Kate Lefever and her lover were 'often left alone' at her home in Throwley Forstal; as Kate's mother swore, 'I was in the habit of leaving them sitting up together. He has stayed in the house all night.'[52]

One couple took tea with the woman's mother and then had intercourse in the woods shortly after chatting to her father.[53] Elizabeth Payn was visiting her sister, a nurse in the home of a Doddington farmer, when she first had intercourse with Reuben Sellen. Payn recalled that she left her sister inside while she and Sellen went into some shrubs at the side of the house. The sister remembered that they were gone for about ten minutes.[54] Eliza Branchett and Amos Rook, neighbours at Boughton Street, first had intercourse at the back of her father's house – on a Sunday evening, after they had been to church together.[55] As we saw earlier, there were encounters after parish festivities, tea parties and pub dances. Mary Curling described a 'tea party' at the Three Horse Shoes in Hernhill where she 'danced with a young Gentlemen who did not act in a gentlemanly manner. He offered me money to go for a walk with him. I refused.'[56]

VI

Perhaps 'freedom' is an inappropriate word to use when discussing sexuality, for from the women's point of view the situation was more

[51] CKS, PS/US 21, Curling vs. Kay.   [52] CKS, PS/US 21, Lefever vs. Harris.
[53] CKS, PS/US 21, Silcock vs. Rook.
[54] CKS, PS/US 21, Payn vs. Sellen (June 1868).
[55] CKS, PS/US 21, Branchett vs. Rook (July 1865).
[56] CKS, PS/US 21, Curling vs. Kay.

problematic. As Cissie Fairchilds found in her work with French sources, there is evidence of exploitative sex.[57] The very existence of the maintenance claims demonstrates that some men attempted to evade the responsibilities referred to earlier. Some had no intention of marrying. Elizabeth Branchett had three illegitimate children, two of them to the same man, Rook. In 1865 the court awarded maintenance of 1s. 6d. a week for Rook's child, although he denied paternity. After that he continued to see Branchett, visiting her at her lodgings, staying with her overnight, promising marriage. In early 1867 she had another child to him and presumably continued to believe his lies for she took action against him only when she discovered that he had married someone else 'secretly'. 'I applied to Deft on the morning of his marriage.'[58] John Harper told a pregnant Sarah Johncock to lay her child to someone else or to 'take something and kill it'.[59] John Black gave Elizabeth Nicholls 'some stuff to take'.[60] While some women clearly chose to terminate their pregnancies for reasons of their own and may have welcomed male advice, others experienced unwanted pressure from their partners. Elizabeth Payn testified that when she informed Reuben Sellen that she was pregnant he gave 'me some stuff to take to do away with the child. He sd it was tincture of Steel and I was to take 3 drops night and morning and that would take off the Child. I did not take any.'[61] One or two men were already married. Harper was a 54-year-old married farm bailiff.[62] Sophia Drewry of Eastling claimed that Richard Wakefield, a Lenham innkeeper, was the father of her daughter. Wakefield said that she was 'a great fool for laying it to him as he was a married man. She knew a Miller and had been with him and she ought to have laid it to him.' (The magistrate adjudged Wakefield to be the father and ordered him to pay 2s. a week until the child was 13 years old.)[63]

There is evidence of a certain amount of male violence, of a meanness of spirit and predatoriness in male sexuality. The phraseology used by some of the women to describe their experiences – 'mauled in the brickyards', 'he got the better of me' – gives an indication of the

[57] Fairchilds, 'Female sexual attitudes'. For an interesting analysis of attitudes towards women which makes use of the criminal records for nineteenth-century Kent, see C. A. Conley, 'Rape and justice in Victorian England', *Victorian Studies*, 29 (1985–6), pp. 519–36; and her *The unwritten law: criminal justice in Victorian Kent* (New York, 1991), esp. ch. 3.

[58] CKS, PS/US 21, Branchett vs. Rook, July 1865, December 1867, January 1868.

[59] CKS, PS/US 21, Johncock vs. Harper. [60] CKS, PS/US 21, Nicholls vs. Black.

[61] CKS, PS/US 21, Payn vs. Sellen (May 1868).

[62] See PRO, RG 9/525, Throwley Census 1861.

[63] CKS, PS/US 21, Drewry vs. Wakefield.

tenor of some relationships.[64] The servant Johncock was harassed by
Harper until she gave in to his wishes. Though it never resulted in a
formal charge, the experience of Emma Smith was rape rather than
seduction. The connection took place out of doors, she stated in her
claim upon Alfred Butcher. 'I told him I should not have any of that. I
struggled and called out. He used considerable violence and eventually
effected his purpose against my will. On returning home I did not tell
my mother or ever told anybody.'[65] The rough behaviour of the
Boughton men who pulled up the skirts of a woman at the Ship Inn
and tried to kiss her and the offerings of money for sex (alluded to in
Curling's description above), speak volumes for male attitudes to
women.[66] Such incidents should be seen as part of what was almost
certainly wider practice of male violence. Accepting a drink from a
man could be interpreted as consent for sex. A man bought gins for a
young woman at St Dunstans (Canterbury) and Harbledown and then
attempted to rape her. The woman's response – 'I said, if he insulted
me because of my drinking his gin, I would pay him for it' – suggests
such an unwritten code for some men.[67] Females of all ages were at
risk (just as they are today). Nine-year-old Ann Milgate was alone in
the house while her parents were out working when two Dunkirk
youths attempted to rape her. John Smith, a 38-year-old bricklayer,
sexually assaulted two Boughton children in broad daylight at the side
of Nash Court hill.[68]

Depressing too is the language of the illegitimacy files, as men
attempted to wriggle out of maintenance by proving the promiscuity
of their former sexual partners. 'You knew I was a Married Man', John
Harper said to Sarah Johncock, so 'why should you lay yourself out for
me'.[69] Robert Wise, a Faversham thatcher, recalled a conversation that
he had had with the alleged father of an illegitimate child. 'He said the
child was not his more than any body else. I expect he suggested other
people had been there – but I don't think there had'.[70] The Doddington
baker, Sellen, told a friend that he (Sellen) could do 'just as he likes'
with Elizabeth Payn.[71] 'I am not the father of that child', said Amos
Rook of his illegitimate offspring, 'and there's plenty to prove it'.[72]

[64] CKS, PS/US 21, Parks vs. Hyland, Smith vs. Butcher.
[65] CKS, PS/US 21, Smith vs. Butcher.
[66] CKS, PS/US 11, Upper Division of the Lathe of Scray Petty Sessions 1864–8, 29
September 1865.
[67] CKS, Q/SBe 176, East Kent Quarter Sessions, Easter 1844.
[68] CKS, PS/US 10, Upper Division of the Lathe of Scray Petty Sessions 1839–45, 13 July
1844; CKS, Q/SBe 228, East Kent Quarter Sessions, April 1857.
[69] CKS, PS/US 21, Johncock vs. Harper.   [70] CKS, PS/US 21, Knight vs. Smith.
[71] CKS, PS/US 21, Payn vs. Sellen (May 1868).
[72] CKS, PS/US 21, Branchett vs. Rook (July 1865).

Sometimes attitudes are revealed in the court records. Jane Martin had intercourse with Henry Ralph, she said, because he forced her. 'I have had connection with her', Ralph bragged, 'and she cannot deny it – she was always running about after me and gave me tobacco for me to go along with her'.[73] When Alfred Brunger threw Mary Tong to the ground and unbuttoned his trousers, he said 'he meant having a piece tonight'.[74] Thomas Smith grabbed Jane Johnson, a married woman from Hernhill; he 'put indecent questions to me' and then said 'let's have a bit there's no one near us'.[75]

Some women undoubtedly internalized such attitudes, or at least could see no alternative to the male sexual agenda. Despite the violence of Butcher's advances, Smith continued to see him. 'I thought it better to keep it quiet and continued to walk with him.'[76] However, we should be wary of interpreting individual cases of resignation or vulnerability as evidence for a more general female passivity. Women fought back. When Tong was harassed by Brunger she told him to go home to his wife. He 'said "he had a Bob in his pocket I could have" I replied I did not want it he could take it home to his wife'. He offered her half a crown to 'lay still'. She said 'I have not come to that yet I don't intend to be your whore you bloody scamp and lugged into his Hair he cried out you have made my Nose bleed'.[77] Women also showed determination in securing maintenance for their children when they thought that they had a legitimate claim. Branchett and Payn had their cases dismissed by the Petty Sessions but they persevered, pressing fresh claims and eventually winning.[78]

VII

The pronouncements of middle-class, Victorian moralists were unambiguous as far as illegitimacy was concerned. Albert Leffingwell wrote of the 'history of shame and sorrow' revealed by the table of illegitimate births returned by the Registrar General of Births, Deaths and Marriages in the 1880s.

Here is an event, involving in forty thousand English homes a certain degree of social ruin and disgrace ... let us try for a moment to bring before the mind some conception of the suffering and sorrow; of the apprehension and dread; of the sense of immeasurable disgrace, felt not only by mothers themselves, but

[73] CKS, PS/US 11, 29 May 1865.
[74] CKS, Q/SBe 238, East Kent Quarter Sessions, October 1859.
[75] CKS, PS/US 13, 1 August 1876.   [76] CKS, PS/US 21, Smith vs. Butcher.
[77] CKS, Q/SBe 238.
[78] CKS, PS/US 21, Branchett vs. Rook, July 1865, December 1867, January 1868; Payn vs. Sellen, May 1868, June 1868.

by relatives and friends, which the vast number of unlawful and unblessed births occasioned on every side.

He called it 'this annual harvest of sorrow and shame'.[79] The fallen woman, clasping an infant, the visible evidence of her sin, was a powerful icon in Victorian art and literature.[80] Characters in Elizabeth Gaskell's *Ruth* (1853) spoke of the sin, shame, disgrace, depravity, disgust and degradation of unmarried motherhood. The children of such women – 'the badge of her shame' – were 'miserable offspring of sin', heirs of shame, 'stained and marked with sin from their birth', whose very presence could pollute or contaminate 'innocent children'. When he discovered his origins, Ruth Hilton's son Leonard shunned public contact, 'stealing along by the back streets – running with his head bent down – his little heart panting with dread of being pointed out as his mother's child'.[81] Yet it is in fact extremely difficult to determine the extent of the stigma attached to the bearers of illegitimate children, or indeed to the children themselves. How does one test Leffingwell's 'harvest of shame'?

Certainly if there was any stigma attached to bastard-bearing it was not sufficient to prevent the woman's marriage. It is true that they married later than other brides (see table 7.3). But a majority of women in both Hernhill and Dunkirk and 40 per cent of those in Boughton were able to marry after the birth of their children and, of those, just under a third married men who were not the child's father. (See table 7.7.)

The fate of their illegitimate offspring varied, as table 7.12 suggests. About 12 per cent died – reconstitutions indicate that infant mortality was higher among illegitimates than legitimates.[82] Some (27.1 per cent) were absorbed into their grandparents' families (either with or without their mothers). These would be recorded as 'grandchild' in the censuses of the nineteenth century. Presumably they could be reared and described as grandchildren rather than illegitimates, though the local community would doubtless remember their origins. A large percentage of illegitimates, however, 46.2 per cent of those in our three parishes, remained with their mothers. Of the minority – 5.2 per cent – who were with their mothers and their new partners, most would

---

[79] A. Leffingwell, *Illegitimacy and the Influence of the Seasons upon Conduct* (London, 1892), pp. 5–7.
[80] See L. Nead, *Myths of sexuality: representations of women in Victorian Britain* (Oxford, 1988), Plates 48–50.
[81] E. Gaskell, *Ruth* (Oxford, 1986), pp. 90, 106, 119, 120, 121, 337, 340, 355, 373. The book was first published in 1853. The attitudes of the author and other characters in the book were more sympathetic.
[82] Oosterveen, Smith and Stewart, 'Family reconstitution', p. 103.

Table 7.12   *Immediate fate of illegitimate*
children, 1821–71 (combined parishes)

Fate	Number	%
Died	26	12.4
Left parish	22	10.5
With grandparents	24	11.4
With mother and grandparents	33	15.7
With mother alone	22	10.5
With mother and father (common-law union)	9	4.3
With mother and father (married)	22	10.5
With mother and husband	11	5.2
With other kin	1	0.5
Not known	40	19.0
Total number	210	

Inclues multiple illegitimacies.

usually retain the mother's single name. When the census was taken they would be described as 'wife's daughter', 'wife's daughter before marriage', or (less commonly) 'son-in-law' or 'daughter-in-law'. But those illegitimates who were in households where their parents legitimized their relationship through marriage – 10.5 per cent – nearly always assumed the man's name; in other words, they were extreme examples of prenuptiality.

The language of the courts, inscribed on the white and blue forms and examination certificates of the Petty Sessions, refers to illegitimate children as 'bastards' – in the 1860s as in the 1820s. But the other records of church and state are by no means as condemnatory. Rarely was the word 'bastard' or even 'illegitimate' used as a description in the census – in these parts at least. Nor is it common to find the word 'illegitimate' in the parish registers. While the names of both parents were sometimes given when a child born out of wedlock was baptized, it was far more usual simply to record the name of the mother with the addition 'single woman'. If the illegitimate children themselves married, the registrar would sometimes leave a blank (or write 'unknown' or ' – ') in the space for the name and occupation of the bride or groom's father, sometimes give a surname different to that of the child and very occasionally provide the name of the mother instead.

Though it scarcely suggests a simple division of society into 'bastards' and 'bastard-bearers' (on the one side) and the legitimate and sexually pure (on the other), it is difficult to know what else to make of this kind of information. The blanks, 'unknowns' and differing second names recorded when illegitimates married, may reflect legal precision rather than moral censure. Wills would occasionally refer to a 'natural son' or 'a child born out of wedlock' and then go on to treat the child in the same way as his or her legitimate brothers or sisters. William Kay's will stated that his illegitimate granddaughter 'shall participate therein [in the legacy] ... as if she had been born in lawful wedlock'.[83] Precision was combined with caring and affection. We must also remember that a census form or parish register is no guarantee of individual identity. James Tong, the illegitimate son of Stephen Hole, was described as James Tong when he married in Boughton in 1853, but he signed the register 'James *Hole*'.

Another approach to attitudes is through depositions in the court records, for they provide us with access to statements from less exalted levels of society than the likes of Albert Leffingwell. Edward Cole, a butcher from Milton near Sittingbourne, was alleged to have promised the pregnant Emma Foster that he would 'marry her for the sake of her character and that of her Mother and Father in less than 3 months for the sake of himself and hers and friends and he would keep her at her Mother's house till the time', which certainly suggests a concern for reputation and a certain stigma attached to unmarried motherhood.[84] Much depended upon the social milieu. The bricklayer Rook said that his two illegitimate children 'were no disgrace to him whatever'.[85] A Boughton woman who had been deserted by her husband many years before and who was living with another man, attended a meeting of the Poor Law Union guardians in 1870 when they suspended relief to her widowed and elderly mother who lived with them. The officials wanted the widow removed to 'some respectable lodging', but the woman 'boldly told the guardians the fact of her having bastard children was nothing to them as she did not ask the guardians to maintain them'.[86] Experience was governed by gender too. The mother of Rook's children, Branchett, was treated with suspicion by her landlady who kept an eye on the comings and goings of her own male relatives.[87] Attitudes must have varied according to the type of

[83] Somerset House, Will of William Kay 1879.
[84] CKS, PS/US 21, Foster vs. Cole.
[85] CKS, PS/US 21, Branchett vs. Rook (December 1867).
[86] PRO, MH 12/5061, Ministry of Health Poor Law Papers, Faversham Correspondence, Letter of Francis Wrighte of Boughton, 26 October 1870, and reply of Faversham Guardians, 4 November 1870.
[87] CKS, PS/US 21, Branchett vs. Rook (January 1868).

illegitimacy. The woman who bore an illegitimate child to a single man and the woman who was in a long-term relationship (even if she had several children), were no doubt treated differently to those who fell pregnant to married men or who had a variety of liaisons. Jemima Hadlow, a Staple Street laundress and mother of three illegitimate children, was attacked by Susannah Butcher who spat in her face and called her a 'nasty wanton whore'. She accused Jemima of having an affair with her husband, referring to her as 'her husband's whore', 'a filthy whore'.[88] As we saw, Mary Tong told her would-be, married, seducer that she did not want to be his 'whore'.

VIII

It is important to remember that the institution of church marriage loomed large in the cultural and sexual horizons of the people of the nineteenth-century Blean. Most pregnant brides did indeed marry. Few women lived alone with their illegitimate children. Only a handful of households contained couples living openly in a declared, unmarried state. There is another group which we have not yet touched on: those who lived together as man and wife and who were accepted as such in the census and by the vicar when he registered the baptisms of their children (if they had any) but for whom there is no evidence of church marriage. Perhaps from 10 to 15 per cent of couples at mid century lived in such common-law arrangements, but it is significant that they presented themselves, and were accepted, as married – man and wife and daughter and son – with no imputation of illegitimacy. They were treated in the same way as those whom we know from reconstitutions were married in the church and we have only learned of their existence because it has been impossible to find record of their marriages. That they presented themselves as married does not suggest widespread tolerance of illegitimacy.[89]

[88] CKS, PS/US 12, 1 June 1871.

[89] Anthea Newman calculated a figure of between 15 and 20 percent for the Kent parish of Ash in the first half of the nineteenth century (Newman, 'Evaluation of bastardy recordings', pp. 150–1). My estimation for the Blean is based on the extremely time-consuming process of linking Dunkirk and Hernhill couples listed in the census of 1851 (a focal point) with the Kent registers of marriages held in the CKS and the CCA for the parishes of birth for those couples and the places of birth for their first children (both of which are given in the census) to see if they were married in church. Thus of 239 couples in Dunkirk and Hernhill, 72 were not confirmed as married. Seven of those were discounted because they were gentry/professional and either married outside the area or were likely to have been married by licence. This left 65 not confirmed, but 29 were difficult to check because they were either from outside the county or from a large parish or town. The remaining 36 were possibly living in common-law marriage – 15 percent of the original 239 couples, or 17 percent if we

And yet illegitimacy was a risk that virtually all women ran until they were married, and afterwards as well if they were widowed. As was noted at the beginning of this chapter, illegitimacy has to be set first in the wider context of premarital sexual activity. Of 202 known first births in Hernhill from 1780 to 1851, 86 (42.6 per cent) were conceived before marriage, 22 (10.9 per cent) were illegitimate and 94 (46.5 per cent) – a minority – were conceived in wedlock. This is a conservative estimate; it may be necessary to adjust extra-marital conceptions to a figure of over 60 per cent.[90] The similarity with Colyton is striking. There, as in Hernhill, 'only four out of ten women conceived their first-born child after marriage'.[91] If these two parishes in Kent and Devon are at all representative of rural life in nineteenth-century England, it makes nonsense of claims that sex before marriage was unusual at this time.[92]

If we consider the illegitimacy rates and ratios, the usual measurements for illegitimacy, the ratio for Hernhill, 5.0, was much the same as for the nation at large (that is, the proportion of illegitimate births to total births). Hernhill's illegitimacy rate, 20.0 (number/1,000 unmarried or widowed women aged 15–45), was only slightly higher than that for England and Wales (18.1) at mid century.[93] But such figures tell us little of collective experience over time. Of 129 households in Hernhill in 1851, 45, that is more than a third, contained family members who were either illegitimate themselves or whose father, mother, sister or brother had been born out of wedlock or had (or would have) an illegitimate child. If we were to exclude those who were in the parish for a short time (for whom we have insufficient background), the number would increase to 42 per cent. If we included households who had less direct kinship links to bastard-bearers, the proportion would be even higher.[94] Put into this perspective, the social experience of illegitimacy was not a phenomenon limited to a small section of society.

discount the 29 non-confirmable couples. Another way of estimating is to limit the sample to those couples who were actually born in the area (that is, in Boughton, Dunkirk and Hernhill). There were 77 such couples in Dunkirk and Hernhill in 1851 and I have been able to trace church marriages for 69 of them. That is, only 8 (10 percent) were possibly in a common-law arrangement.

90 See pp. 180–1 above.
91 Robin, 'Illegitimacy', pp. 337–8.
92 For example: Walvin, *Victorian values*, p. 126.
93 P. Laslett, 'Introduction', in Laslett, Oosterveen and Smith (eds.), *Bastardy*, p. 17. The figures for Hernhill were arrived at by aggregative analysis of the parish registers of baptisms; the population of unmarried women aged 15–45 was calculated from the 1851 census for Hernhill.
94 Family reconstitution data. Compare Gwyneth Nair's very similar comments for the nineteenth-century Shropshire village of Highley: Nair, *Highley*, p. 239.

Nor, as we have seen, was it confined to any one social group. Those in labouring families were most likely to indulge in premarital intercourse, it is true. But illegitimate-bearers also included the respectable farming family of William Kay of Hernhill, farm bailiff at Dargate House Farm for a Canterbury banker, and then a small farmer on his own account at Snowdown Farm. One of Dinah and William Kay's sons became a farmer, another a bailiff and one a craftsman; their daughters married into farming and craft families. One of their daughters, Jane, had an illegitimate child, Laura, in 1871. A son, Edward, fathered Mary Curling's illegitimate child (see above) shortly before he joined the county police. (It is also worth mentioning that although they went as husband and wife, there is no actual evidence that Dinah and William Kay were married.)[95] I wrote in an earlier version of this chapter that the only families not affected, who seem to have kept their households – including their servants – free from association with prenuptial pregnancy or illegitimacy, were those of a narrow, parish elite: the gentleman Edward Stone at the manor house, Hernhill; the vicar Charles Handley at Mount Ephraim; the mercer and haberdasher Henry Woolright at Berkeley Lodge on Boughton Hill; and a handful of farmers and craftsmen who dominated the Hernhill vestry – men such as Edward Curling, bailiff and farmer, Poor Law guardian, parish overseer and landlord, and John Foreman, wheelwright and carpenter, farmer, undertaker and landlord of several labourers' cottages.[96] But I have since discovered that a Faversham woman, a servant in the household of Edward Stone (the first on the list), was alleged to have offered sex for money and to have entertained her partners in the Stone's wash-house and in the porch of the nearby parish church. The result was an illegitimate child.[97] It should also be pointed out that Edward Curling (fourth on the list) was the uncle of William Curling of Sluts Hole, who has featured so prominently in this chapter. So even those households initially singled out for their sexual probity are not as free from contact with the experience of illegitimacy as I first thought. It is still likely that some members of village and hamlet felt the need to make their households examples to society; sexual transgression would, as the vicar of Dunkirk put it (although he was actually referring to theft and drunkenness), slander the character of a household.[98] But actual behaviour suggests that such attitudes

---

[95] Family reconstitution data.
[96] B. Reay, 'Sexuality in nineteenth-century England: the social context of illegitimacy in rural Kent', *Rural History*, 1 (1990), p. 242.
[97] CKS, Fa/JP 9/1, Hammond vs. Jackson.
[98] CKS, U2394 Z1, Family Scrap Book of Reverend J. W. Horsley.

were not shared unequivocally by fellow parishioners. If there was any 'sub-society' in the nineteenth-century Blean, it was a society of the sexually 'pure'.

The neat demarcation between legitimate and illegitimate implied by some historical demography does not correspond to the complexity revealed by microhistory. Bastardy, as Levine and Wrightson have observed for an earlier period of English history, was indeed a 'compound phenomenon'.[99] Our historical understanding of this phenomenon is not well served by the sociology of deviancy: Laslett's influential typology of the 'bastard-bearing sub-society' has little value in understanding the context or meaning of illegitimacy.[100] 'Bastard-bearers' included a few families which could perhaps be described as 'deviant', but for the most part illegitimacy should be seen as part of the normal sexual culture of the hamlets of the past. This is not to argue for a widespread tolerance of illegitimacy, nor to claim that attitudes to unmarried mothers and children born out of wedlock were as benign as those towards pregnant brides. Social attitudes were complex and varied. But the social stigma of illegitimacy was certainly not as pronounced as one might infer from the declamations of Victorian middle-class moralists and from the later, more unwitting, classifications and categories favoured by some historical demographers.

[99] Levine and Wrightson, 'Social context of illegitimacy', p. 169.
[100] This is not to deny the tremendous value of Peter Laslett's work as a stimulus to research and discussion; it is rather to suggest that we now move beyond the language and terminology of the 'Laslett thesis'.

Literacies

I

There are numerous studies of literacy and education in the past. A vast apparatus of scholarship has been erected on a simple measurement of 'literacy': a person's ability to sign his or her name.[1] The general contours of 'signature literacy' have been established, despite some disagreement about the causes of the observable trends. Yet some of the most intriguing work on the subject has taken the form of detailed examinations of the actual context and meaning of some of the basic assumptions of this scholarly edifice. How useful is the historian's functional definition based on that ability to sign or make a mark? What did 'literacy' actually mean at a grass-roots level? To what extent did oral culture persist in the face of popular literacy?[2] One way of

[1] For just a sample, see L. Stone, 'Literacy and education in England, 1640–1900', *Past and Present*, 42 (1969), pp. 69–139; R. S. Schofield, 'Dimensions of illiteracy, 1750–1850', *Explorations in Economic History*, 10 (1973), pp. 437–54; D. Cressy, *Literacy and the social order: reading and writing in Tudor and Stuart England* (Cambridge, 1980); F. Furet and J. Ozouf, *Reading and writing: literacy in France from Calvin to Jules Ferry* (Cambridge, 1982); R. A. Houston, *Scottish literacy and the Scottish identity: illiteracy and society in Scotland and northern England, 1600–1800* (Cambridge, 1985); H. J. Graff, *The legacies of literacy: continuities and contradictions in Western culture and society* (Bloomington, 1987); W. B. Stephens, *Education, literacy and society, 1830–70: the geography of diversity in provincial England* (Manchester, 1987); D. Vincent, *Literacy and popular culture: England, 1750–1914* (Cambridge, 1989); W. B. Stephens, 'Literacy in England, Scotland, and Wales, 1500–1900', *History of Education Quarterly*, 30 (1990), pp. 545–71; F. W. Grubb, 'Growth of literacy in colonial America: longitudinal patterns, economic models, and the direction of future research', *Social Science History*, 14 (1990), pp. 451–82; D. F. Mitch, *The rise of popular literacy in Victorian England* (Philadelphia, 1992).

[2] See K. Thomas, 'The meaning of literacy in early modern England', in G. Baumann (ed.), *The written word: literacy in transition* (Oxford, 1986), pp. 97–130; Houston, *Scottish literacy*, chs 5–6; D. Cressy, 'The environment for literacy: accomplishment and context in seventeenth-century England and New England', in D. P. Resnick

Cultures

Plate 21 Hernhill school, 1906.

approaching these issues is through the use of the local study. The
microstudy cannot be used to establish broad trends – although it has
been remarked that the diversity of elementary education in nineteenth-century England makes it almost nonsensical, in any case, to
talk of a 'national condition'[3] – but the detailed case study can speak
volumes on the actual 'nature and meaning of popular literacy'.[4] This
chapter is an attempt to ground literacy studies in a firmer context.

The chapter has two main aims. The first is to enter, through a
focused study, the cultural environment of nineteenth-century rural
England. The second, rather more implicit agenda, is to test some of
the assumptions of the dominant historiography of literacy. I will
argue that although quantitative studies of literacy based on signatures

(ed.), *Literacy in historical perspective* (Washington, 1983), pp. 23–42; T. W. Laqueur,
'Toward a cultural ecology of literacy in England, 1600–1850', *ibid.*, pp. 43–57;
Vincent, *Literacy and popular culture*; D. Cressy, 'Literacy in context: meaning and
measurement in early modern England', in J. Brewer and R. Porter (eds.), *Consumption
and the world of goods* (London, 1993), ch. 15. For France, see R. Chartier, 'The practical
impact of writing', in R. Chartier (ed.), *A history of private life: passions of the Renaissance*
(Cambridge, Mass., 1989), pp. 111–59.
3 Stephens, *Education, literacy and society*, p. 2.
4 T. C. Smout, 'Born again at Cambuslang: new evidence on popular religion and
literacy in eighteenth-century Scotland', *Past and Present*, 97 (1982), p. 116.

have much to offer, there is (as Keith Thomas has suggested for the early-modern period) a real danger that the complexities of popular literacy are being hidden by the quantifier's all too easy division into 'literate' and 'illiterate'.[5] Hence, I hope to demonstrate, the importance of the local study.

This study draws on a unique document generated by the Hernhill rising of 1838, England's last millenarian revolt and the last rising of its agricultural labourers. The Central Society of Education carried out a survey in the wake of the conflict. The investigator, a barrister named Liardet, moved through the affected parishes, questioning people in beershops, in their cottages and in the fields. How many rooms per family were there and what were the sleeping arrangements for the children? How clean were the dwelling places? How many wives could bake and sew? How did people spend their leisure hours? (Few admitted to resorting to the beershop.) How many gardens had flowers, a sign of civilization? Did cottagers keep livestock? And, more important for our purposes, how many households possessed books? Were there any prints on the walls (like flowers, a gauge of 'cultivation in the cottager')? How many children attended school; how many could write and/or read?[6] Journalists also descended upon the area to observe the ways of 'the peasantry'.[7] I draw upon this important source for cultural historians, together with family reconstitution, to provide rare contextual information on literacy and education.

II

It is easy to trace the contours of 'signature literacy' for this part of Kent. As figure 8.1 shows, male literacy was relatively stable for the period 1750–1850, hovering either just above or below the 50 per cent mark. It was the second half of the nineteenth century which saw a marked improvement in adult male literacy (those marrying from the 1850s onwards or schooled – if they were schooled – from the mid 1830s on), with the rates roughly doubling over a fifty-year period. At mid century only about a half of the grooms were able to sign the marriage register; by the end of the nineteenth century almost all could. These findings are remarkably similar to Roger Schofield's data

[5] Thomas, 'Meaning of literacy', p. 99.
[6] F. Liardet, 'State of the peasantry in the county of Kent', in *Central Society of Education, third publication* (London, 1968), pp. 87–139 (first published in 1839). Liardet's survey was used in David Vincent, 'Reading in the working-class home', in J. K. Walton and J. Walvin (eds.), *Leisure in Britain, 1780–1939* (Manchester, 1983), ch. 11.
[7] B. Reay, *The last rising of the agricultural labourers* (Oxford, 1990), ch. 7.

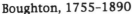

Boughton, 1755-1890

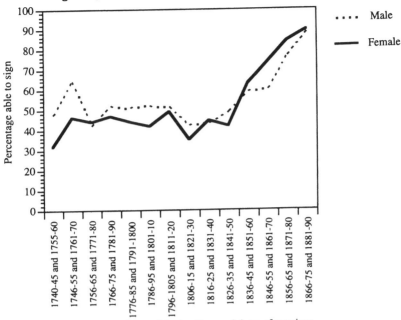

Estimated years of potential schooling, and dates of marriage

Dunkirk, 1801-90

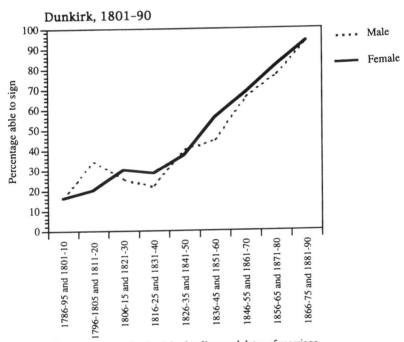

Estimated years of potential schooling, and dates of marriage

Figure 8.1

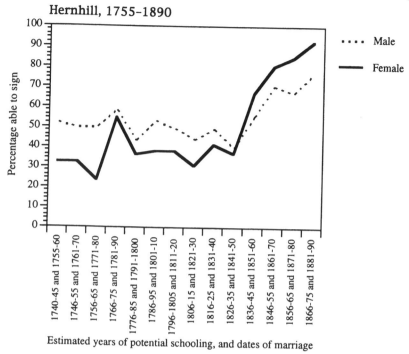

Hernhill, 1755-1890

.... Male

—— Female

Estimated years of potential schooling, and dates of marriage

Figure 8.1 Signature literacy, 1755–1890.

at a macro level for nineteenth-century England.[8] Female literacy followed a similar course, lagging just below that of men (around the 40 per cent mark) until the middle of the nineteenth century, then improving dramatically, indeed overtaking male rates in the 1850s in all three parishes and maintaining an edge on to the end of the century. This female superiority runs counter to national trends, but is in keeping with the experience of many rural areas during this period. David Vincent has established that by the 1860s women were ahead of men 'in almost all the counties south of a line from the Wash to Dorset'.[9]

Signature literacy in Boughton, Dunkirk and Hernhill was graded

[8] Schofield, 'Dimensions of illiteracy'. See also Stephens, *Education, literacy and society*, p. 9, Table 1.2.

[9] Stephens, *Education, literacy and society*, pp. 11, 18, 192; Vincent, *Literacy and popular culture*, pp. 24–5.

218   *Cultures*

Table 8.1   *Signature illiteracy by occupational group, 1801–90 (combined parishes*

Occupational group	Male (%)			Female (%)		
	1801–50	1851–70	1871–90	1801–50	1851–70	1871–90
Gentry	0.0	0.0	0.0	14.3	0.0	0.0
Farmer	43.9	5.0	0.0	50.0	5.0	0.0
Craft	12.7	2.2	2.0	32.7	13.3	2.0
Trade	33.3	11.1	6.1	48.1	7.4	6.1
Ag. Lab./Lab.	77.2	60.5	38.5	80.1	44.4	22.0
Total number	501	339	299	501	339	299

Marriages in Boughton, Dunkirk and Hernhill. From 1837 the marriage registers provide details of the occupations of grooms; the occupational information before that date is derived from my family reconstitution files. The groupings for female signature illiteracy refer to the occupation of the woman's husband and not that of her father.

according to social and economic status and gender.[10] As table 8.1 indicates, for the first half of the nineteenth century a man was less likely to be 'illiterate' if he earned his living in the crafts or at a trade than if he was a labourer. The gentry were 100 per cent literate. Women were more 'illiterate' (or less literate) than men at all social levels before 1850. Thereafter the picture is not so clear-cut. Farmers' brides achieved parity with their partners, while labouring wives were halving their signature illiteracy every two decades. Male labourers marrying in the period 1871–90 were (statistically) almost twice as 'illiterate' as their female partners (see also plate 22). The social structure of signature illiteracy also reveals that while farmers, craftsmen and those engaged in trades were predominantly literate by the 1870s and 1880s (see also plate 23), just under 40 per cent of labouring men were not able to sign their own names. The decrease in the 'illiteracy' of labouring men was not as spectacular as that of other social or occupational groups, or indeed that of their own wives.

These averages disguise some interesting local variations. In the first half of the nineteenth century Dunkirk farmers, predominantly small-holding peasants, had an 'illiteracy' rate twice that of the more substantial Hernhill farmers (see tables 8.2 and 8.3). Dunkirk farming

[10] For other studies of the social structure of 'illiteracy', see Schofield, 'Dimensions of illiteracy', p. 450, Table 1; D. Cressy, 'Levels of illiteracy in England, 1530–1730', in H. J. Graff (ed.), *Literacy and social development in the West* (Cambridge, 1981), ch. 6; W. B. Stephens (ed.), *Studies in the history of literacy* (Leeds, 1983); Houston, *Scottish literacy*, ch. 2; Vincent, *Literacy and popular culture*, pp. 96–104.

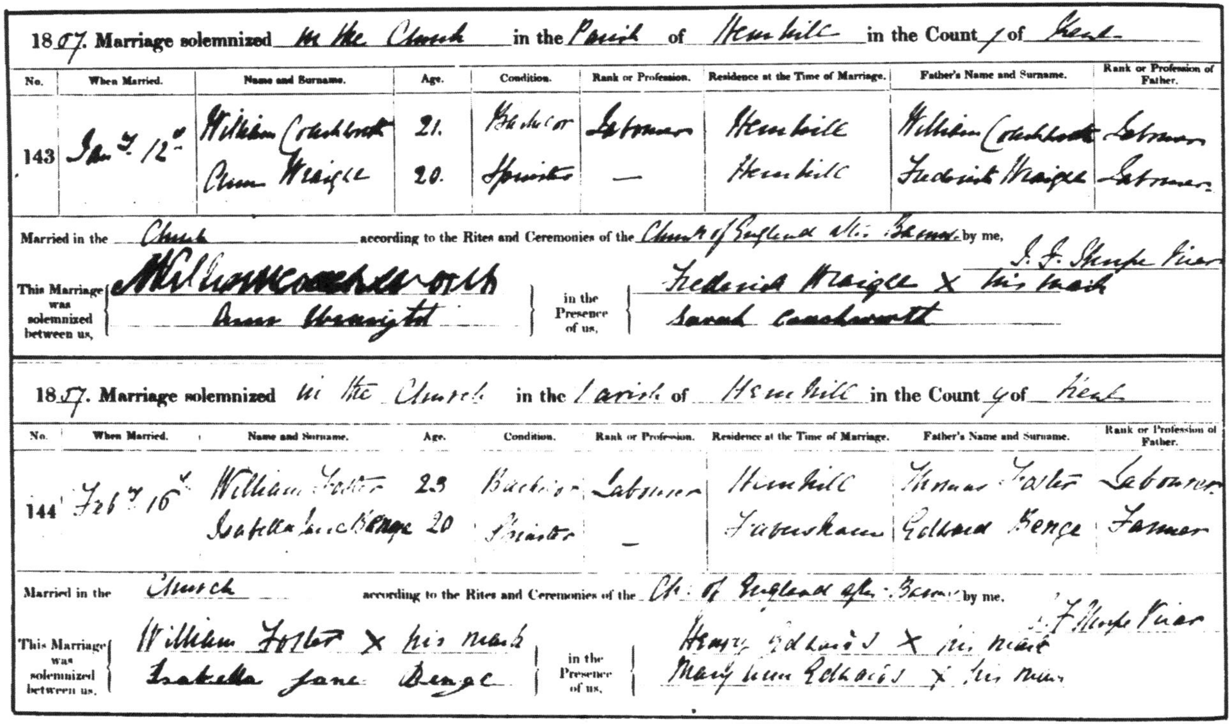

Plate 22 Hernhill marriage certificates, 1867. These entries encapsulate the advances in the signature literacy of labouring women during the second half of the nineteenth century. Note the tortured signature of William Coachworth and the marks of William Foster and Frederick Wraight (the men). Contrast the tidy signatures of the sister and the bride (Sarah Coachworth and Ann Wraight).

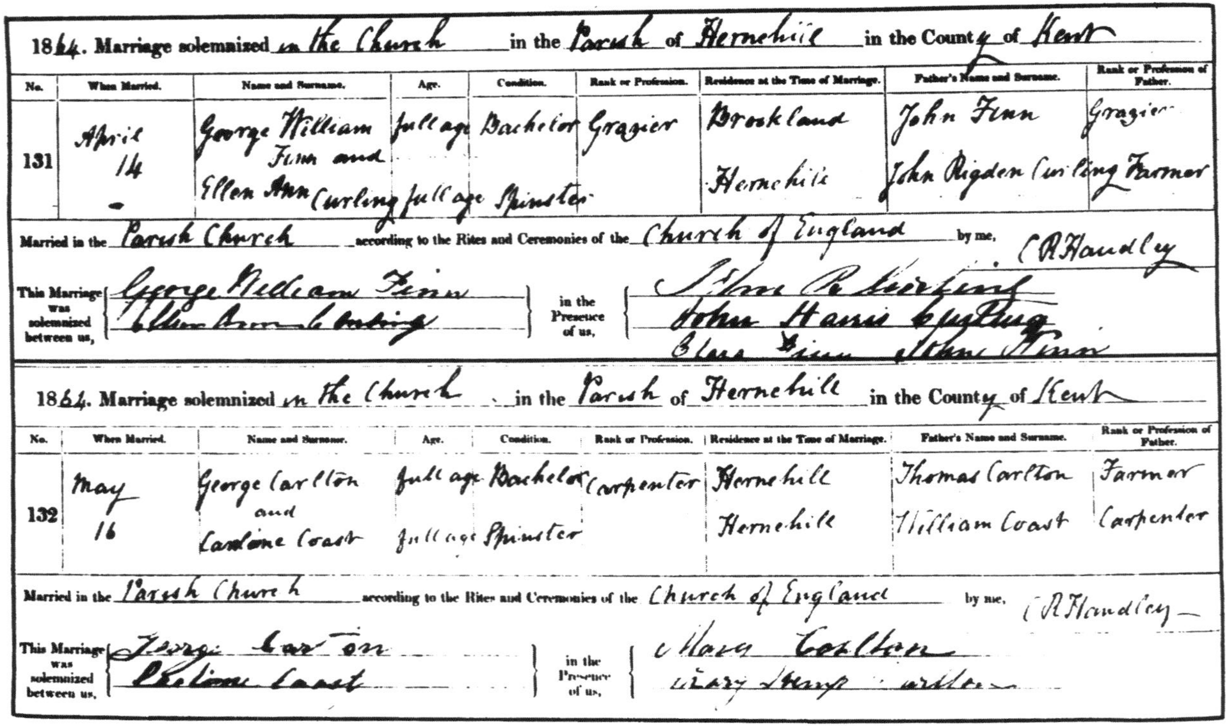

1864. Marriage solemnized in the Church in the Parish of Hernhill in the County of Kent

No.	When Married	Name and Surname	Age	Condition	Rank or Profession	Residence at the Time of Marriage	Father's Name and Surname	Rank or Profession of Father
131	April 14	George William Finn	full age	Bachelor	Grazier	Brook land	John Finn	Grazier
		Ellen Ann Curling	full age	Spinster		Hernhill	John Stephen Curling	Farmer

Married in the Parish Church according to the Rites and Ceremonies of the Church of England by me, (A Hulett) Cy.

This Marriage was solemnized between us, George William Finn / Ellen Ann Curling — in the Presence of us, John Robertson / John Honnes Curling / Blass Finn Honnes Fenn

1864. Marriage solemnized in the Church in the Parish of Hernhill in the County of Kent

No.	When Married	Name and Surname	Age	Condition	Rank or Profession	Residence at the Time of Marriage	Father's Name and Surname	Rank or Profession of Father
132	May 16	George Carlton	full age	Bachelor	Carpenter	Hernhill	Thomas Carlton	Farmer
		Caroline Coast	full age	Spinster		Hernhill	William Coast	Carpenter

Married in the Parish Church according to the Rites and Ceremonies of the Church of England by me, (A Hulett) Cy.

This Marriage was solemnized between us, George Carlton / William Coast — in the Presence of us, Mary Coslton / Mary Sharp

Plate 23 Hernhill marriage certificates, 1864. These entries reflect the signature literacy of farming households: observe the lack of crosses and marks.

Table 8.2 *Hernhill signature illiteracy by occupational group, 1801–50*

Occupational group	Male		Female	
	Total number	% unable to sign	Total number	% unable to sign
Farmer	34	32.3	34	50.0
Craft	21	0.0	21	42.9
Trade	12	50.0	12	58.3
Ag. Lab./Lab.	125	75.2	125	80.8

See note for table 8.1.

Table 8.3 *Dunkirk signature illiteracy by occupational group, 1801–50*

Occupational group	Male		Female	
	Total number	% unable to sign	Total number	% unable to sign
Farmer	28	64.3	28	53.6
Craft	16	25.0	16	31.2
Trade	9	33.3	9	55.5
Ag. Lab./Lab.	145	79.3	145	79.3

See note for table 8.1.

women were more literate than their husbands. Dunkirk is also interesting for the lack of differentiation between male and female signature literacy at the labouring level during this half of the century: the figure for both is 20 per cent literate (80 per cent 'illiterate'). The Dunkirk literacy figures are in fact extremely low. Of 254 couples either married in Dunkirk or Dunkirk people marrying in adjoining parishes in the period 1801–50, only 30 per cent of men and 29 per cent of women signed the register. This was considerably lower than the county averages (for 1838–41) of 71 per cent and 60 per cent respectively;[11] in fact more in keeping with seventeenth-century literacy rates! Although it caught up with the other parishes after 1850, early nineteenth-century Dunkirk represents a pocket of hitherto unknown rural 'illiteracy'.

The figures hide important local variations, but the basic contours remain: signature literacy in this part of Kent, as in the nation at large, was socially and gender selective. It showed little sign of improvement during the period 1750–1850, but improved dramatically in the second half of the nineteenth century, particularly for women at the labouring level.

[11] *Fourth Annual Report of the Registrar General of Births, Deaths and Marriages in England*, PP, 1842, vol. XIX, p. 456.

The timing of these changes is much harder to explain. The initial rise in literacy in Boughton, Dunkirk and Hernhill may be connected to the establishment of elementary schools in these parishes, just as the achievement of mass literacy at the end of the century may be linked to the replacement of these private schools (which taught only reading) with a national system which stressed the three Rs – though the chronological correlation (for both) is imprecise.[12] Dunkirk's extremely low levels of signature literacy certainly seem to correspond to the lack of educational facilities in that parish before 1831. But it would be foolhardy to try to isolate such single factors to account for change in individual parishes. The population of the hamlets of this area was highly mobile, so an education could be acquired, or missed, in any one of many nearby parishes: the people whose literacies are charted in the figures were not necessarily schooled (if they were schooled) in Boughton, Dunkirk or Hernhill.

Alternatively, it is likely that a rudimentary literacy could have been gained with the help of family or neighbours, outside the walls of a school. William Branchett, a Boughton labourer, told a court in 1838 that when he was young there was no day school in his parish and that he was 'put to work before I was well able to do it, and not sent to school'. He could not write, but he could read, despite the lack of schooling.[13] Other studies have stressed the importance of informal means of education. The data for Boughton, Dunkirk and Hernhill suggest that this was particularly true for females. Those males listed as 'scholars' in the censuses of 1851 for whom we have subsequent information on literacy were more likely to be able to sign their names than those who were working in the fields or woods or who were at home when the surveys were taken. But the future signature-literacy profiles of female non-scholars were almost the same as those who were at school in 1851 (see table 8.4).

There was, then, as other historians of literacy have discovered, 'no mechanical connection between literacy and schooling'.[14] Schooling is

---

[12] For the chronology of schooling in the local area, see below. For a national perspective, see J. S. Hurt, *Elementary schooling and the working classes, 1860–1918* (London, 1979); P. Gardner, *The lost elementary schools of Victorian England* (London, 1984); A. Digby and P. Searby, *Children, school and society in nineteenth-century England* (London, 1981); J. Purvis, 'The experience of schooling for working-class boys and girls in nineteenth-century England', in I. F. Goodson and S. J. Ball (eds.), *Defining the curriculum* (London, 1984), pp. 89–115; Vincent, *Literacy and popular culture*, pp. 73–94; G. Sutherland, 'Education', in F. M. L. Thompson (ed.), *The Cambridge social history of Britain 1750–1950*, vol. III, *Social agencies and institutions* (Cambridge, 1990), ch. 3.

[13] *The Times*, 10 August 1838.

[14] Houston, *Scottish literacy*, p. 111. See also the comments of Stephens, *Education, literacy and society*, p. 13; Laqueur, 'Toward a cultural ecology of literacy', pp. 47–8.

Table 8.4   *Children aged 5–14 in 1851 for whom there is subsequent information on signature literacy (combined parishes)*

Sex	Scholars		At home or working	
	Total number	% able to sign	Total number	% able to sign
Male	25	72.0	36	44.4
Female	40	85.0	43	81.4
Total	65	80.0	79	64.6

Based on parish census returns for 1851 and family reconstitution files.

probably necessary, though it seems scarcely sufficient, to explain the trends in signature literacy. The figures, it is worth noting, show that improvements in literacy were well and truly established before the impact of the Education Acts of the 1870s.[15]

Perhaps the improvements reflected a general desire to educate the young, though most of the evidence, as we will see later, points to a contrary sentiment at the labouring level. The nature of – and changes in – child employment, female and male, may also account for some of the observable trends. Again it is hard to come by precise information. Boys were certainly much employed in agriculture and girls were relatively under-utilized in work outside the home, which may help to explain the marked differential in male/female rates at the labouring level after the mid century. The general rise in male literacy may reflect a decline in the use of child labour. But there is precious little evidence at the micro level for any such change, or indeed for any alteration in the structure of employment which would correspond to the configurations of the figures.

III

Let us now turn to the educational environment in our Kentish hamlets. We have quite a detailed picture of educational provisions in the area at mid century, thanks to the efforts of Liardet. There were three schools in Hernhill in 1838 (as well as a Sunday school). One was what Liardet termed 'the high school of the place', kept by a man 'who, being from physical infirmity incapable of labour, was obliged to adopt this mode of life'.[16] It was the only one in the parish which taught writing, a skill acquired after reading in the elementary

---

[15] Compare Vincent, *Literacy and popular culture*, p. 54.
[16] Liardet, 'State of the peasantry', p. 111.

schooling of the first half of the century. It had only eighteen scholars, half of whom came from outside Hernhill. The fees were 6d. a week for reading; 13s. 5d. a quarter (or about 1s. a week) for reading, writing and arithmetic. Few scholars availed themselves of the latter. Liardet described the instruction as old-fashioned and of the 'simplest kind'; he noted also the use of the Bible to teach reading and the absence of history, geography and grammar. The other schools were what he described as 'dame schools', taught by women. These establishments offered nothing but 'sewing and reading'. Again, religious material was used for instruction. One of these schools, the larger and in fact the first school in the parish, had been set up by the Rev. C. R. Handley in 1817 shortly after he arrived in the area. He provided accommodation for a school mistress in return for guaranteed places for some of the poorer children of the neighbourhood, whom he sponsored. Others who attended paid 3d. a week per child. Numbers at the school fluctuated from about thirty to fifty. Classes were held in the late afternoons in recognition of the needs of labourers; when a reporter from *The Times* visited Hernhill in 1838 he noted that there were eight children at school in the day, but thirty-two during the evenings. Presumably these kinds of facilities served Hernhill until the Church of England school was established in 1872.[17]

Schooling came later to Dunkirk, in 1831, once again due to the efforts of Handley. The Ville's school was a day school, teaching reading and sewing at the cost of 3d. a week for each scholar (as in Hernhill there were some free places for the poor). The Education Returns for 1833 refer to a 'daily school', limited to an intake of fifty and consisting of twenty-three males and twenty-seven females. A handful of Dunkirk children attended a school in Boughton which offered writing: this cost them 6d. a week. A new National School for boys and girls was set up in Dunkirk in the 1840s in an effort to civilize the inhabitants, blamed – wrongly – for the unrest of 1838.[18] Night classes were also offered in Dunkirk – we know this because four·

---

[17] For schooling in Hernhill, see *Answers and Returns Relative to the State of Education in England and Wales*, I (hereafter *Abstract of Education Returns, 1833*), PP, 1835, vol. XLI, p. 402; Liardet, 'State of the peasantry', pp. 111–13; CKS, U951 C37/34, Charles Handley, vicar of Hernhill, to Archbishop of Canterbury, 11 June 1838; *The Times*, 9 June 1838; Lambeth Palace Library, London, VG/3/3a, fos. 343–4, Visitation Returns, 1864.

[18] *Abstract of Education Returns, 1833*, p. 396; Liardet, 'State of the peasantry', p. 119; CKS, U951 C37/34; S. Bagshaw, *History, Gazetteer, and Directory of the County of Kent* (Sheffield, 1847): 'Dunkirk Ville'; National Society Archives, Church House, Dean's Yard, Westminster, *Ninth Annual Report of the Canterbury Diocesan Board of Education* (Maidstone, 1848), p. 29.

Dunkirk youths were prosecuted for damaging a hedge in 1845 as they were on their way to school at 6.30 p.m.[19]

Boughton offered a greater number of educational facilities: two boarding schools, which also took day pupils, four day schools and a Wesleyan Methodist Sunday school. As in so many English country towns, the boarding schools were patronized by people from other villages and towns. A few Boughton children attended as day scholars, from the families, mainly, of farmers and tradesmen. Samuel Bagshaw's gazetteer of 1847 listed two 'genteel Boarding Schools for young gentlemen, and one for young ladies' and a Wesleyan academy (under the new Wesleyan chapel). One of the gentlemen's academies was Tenterden House, a 'classical, mathematical, and commercial boarding establishment'.[20] According to Liardet, the day schools confined their teaching to reading and sewing; writing was taught in only one. All the day schools (dame schools?) were kept by women: the average number of scholars in each in 1838 was fourteen. The vicar of Boughton, like his counterpart in Hernhill, assumed some responsibility for the education of his parishioners. One of his children recalled in the 1850s that the parish paid for the schooling of about twenty students at a time. They were taught reading and 'work' by a widow; 'some of them were at our house [that is, the vicarage] part of each day, to learn household work from our servants and when they left school they were considered valuable servants every one glad to take them'.[21] However, the majority of Boughton children who were exposed to any kind of formal education must have received it at the Wesleyan Sunday school which provided instruction in reading and religious knowledge. Eighty boys and sixty girls attended this school according to Liardet's information, though he commented on the large number of labouring children in Boughton who were unable to read. By the 1860s Boughton had a Church of England school with over a hundred students on the books. The curriculum, in the early years, was heavily religious.[22]

Apart from a few sons and daughters of farmers and Hernhill's lone gentleman, who we know from the census of 1851 went as boarders to schools in Boughton and Faversham, the bulk of those who were

---

[19] CKS, PS/US 10, Lathe of Scray Petty Sessions Depositions 1839–45, 18 January 1845.
[20] Bagshaw, *Gazetteer*: 'Boughton next Faversham'.
[21] PRO, MH 12/5059, Ministry of Health Poor Law Papers, Faversham Correspondence, 1855–61.
[22] For schooling in Boughton, see *Abstract of Education Returns, 1833*, p. 389; Liardet, 'State of the peasantry', p. 123; *The Times*, 9 June 1838; Lambeth Palace Library, VG/3/3a, fos. 83–4; CCA, U3/221/25/13, Boughton-under-Blean School Log Book, 1864–95.

Table 8.5   *Children aged 5–14 at school as percentage of total population of*
that age group

	Boughton		Dunkirk		Hernhill		Combined parishes	
Year	Male	Female	Male	Female	Male	Female	Male	Female
1851	53.5	54.5	54.4	57.0	32.9	42.4	48.5	51.9
1861	59.1	52.3	40.2	42.3	69.7	67.0	57.1	54.2
1871	63.4	72.0	63.9	63.4	68.9	74.1	65.0	70.5
1881	79.3	76.0	62.0	70.8	73.4	80.0	73.2	75.5
1891	78.9	75.9	75.6	76.2	79.1	81.3	78.1	77.2

Calculated from the census returns for 1851–91. There were 642 children aged
5–14 in the three parishes in 1851, and 845 in 1891. The percentages do not
include scholars at boarding school in Boughton.

educated institutionally in our area attended locally. Few labouring
families chose (or were able) to pay for the education of their children:
of fifty Dunkirk families interviewed by Liardet only ten paid for the
schooling of their young.[23] As figure 8.2 and table 8.5 show, those who
attended school were a minority (or a bare majority) of the eligible
population in 1851, a substantial majority after 1871. Among Hernhill
boys, 33 per cent of the 5–14-year-old age group were described as
'scholars' in the census of 1851: in 1891 the figure was 79 per cent.
Among Hernhill girls, 42 per cent were at school in 1851 compared to
81 per cent in 1891 (see table 8.5). There was both gender and social
variation. Only 13 per cent of agricultural labourers' sons were at
school in Hernhill in 1851 compared to 40 per cent of their daughters;
65 per cent of the daughters of farmers were scholars and 58 per cent of
their sons.[24]

The fact that 87 per cent of Hernhill agricultural labourers' sons were
not at school when the census of 1851 was taken, and that even in 1881
nearly 30 per cent of parish boys were not described as 'scholars',
suggests that a significant section of the population was not making
use of local facilities. Literacy, W. B. Stephens has observed, 'was not a

---

[23]   Liardet, 'State of the peasantry', p. 119.
[24]   The cases of female supremacy run counter to national and county figures (see
       Stephens, *Education, literacy and society*, pp. 18, 351), but correspond to the findings of
       several other studies of nineteenth-century rural communities: see B. J. Davey,
       Ashwell, 1830–1914: the decline of a village community (Leicester, 1980), pp. 18–19; J.
       Robin, *Elmdon: continuity and change in a north-west Essex village, 1861–1964* (Cam-
       bridge, 1980), p. 21. Meg Gomershall has pointed out that while there were more boys
       than girls at school in the nation as a whole, girls had superior access to education in
       a number of rural districts: M. Gomershall, 'Ideals and realities: the education of
       working-class girls, 1800–1870', *History of Education*, 17 (1988), pp. 39–42.

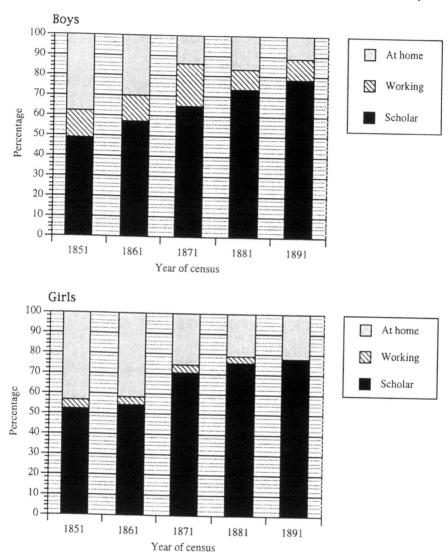

Figure 8.2 Children at school, at home and in the work force as percentage of total population of that age group, 1851–91 (combined parishes).

functional essential for a high proportion of working people'.[25] There was a feeling that school education, book-learning, did little to mould a potential agricultural labourer. School might be a budding agriculturalist's 'general education', but labour was his 'special education'. The farm labourer, 'before he can claim work throughout the year, as an able-bodied labourer, must, especially in these counties, where the cultivation is so varied, honestly profess the use of very many implements, which require a peculiar mode of handling … The spade, the scythe, the hoe, the axe, the sickle, the flail, the beck, the bagging-hook and the other implements of husbandry, – all require a cunning and handicraft of their own'.[26] This skill was acquired at a father's side and not in a school room. Presumably it was in response to sentiments such as these that 'work' – domestic service, one assumes mainly for girls – formed part of the curriculum in one of the Boughton day schools.[27]

Education should be viewed in the context of local economic and employment patterns. Figure 8.2 indicates that school attendance absorbed an ever-increasing proportion of the potential child work force, but that these scholars were drawn disproportionately from the ranks of the young 'unemployed' (those 'at home' or without an occupation) rather than the children and young people described as working when the decadal censuses were taken. Although the census disguises its full extent, child labour was an established cog in the rural economy. Apart from the constraints of skill and physical strength, there was little that a boy could not undertake or assist with: ' "At eight years old", says a farmer in East Kent, "a boy is fit to help his father in the barn a little at threshing" '.[28] Figures 8.2 and 8.3 map out some of the contours of school education and work. The dominant age group for scholars in 1871 was 5 to 9 years; whereas those in the 10 to 14-year-old category were most likely to be working, unemployed (and not at school), or helping around the home. As Hugh Cunningham has demonstrated, most English child workers (in the census definition of the term) were aged 10 and over.[29] Children in Boughton, Dunkirk and Hernhill were unlikely to be in waged work until they were in their early teens: the vast bulk of those described as agricultural labourers, labourers, servants, nurses, carters, errand boys and so on were aged from 12 to 14.

---

[25] Stephens, *Education, literacy and society*, p. 50.
[26] *Reports of Special Assistant Poor Law Commissioners on the Employment of Women and Children in Agriculture*, PP, 1843, vol. XII, p. 171.
[27] See p. 225 above.
[28] PP, 1843, vol. XII, p. 148.
[29] H. Cunningham, 'The employment and unemployment of children in England *c.* 1680–1851', *Past and Present*, 126 (1990), pp. 115–50.

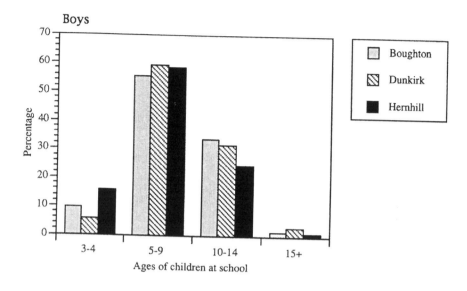

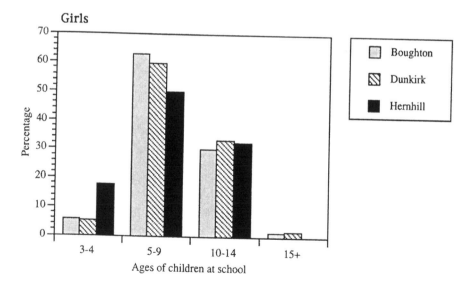

Figure 8.3 Age distribution of scholars, 1871.

Figure 8.2 also suggests gender variation. Few girls were described
as 'working'; they were more likely to be listed as at home, or to be
ascribed no occupation whatsoever. The notoriously gender-biased
censuses are a poor guide to the work of women (and the very young),
but they provide some indication of work patterns in the formal wage
economy. Although they assisted their mothers in the hop-grounds,
were often kept at home to look after younger children and would
leave school and family to go into service, girls were not employed in
outside work to the same extent as their brothers. Thus it is that the
economic structure is thought to have influenced the differential levels
of male and female literacy (eventually in favour of the women or girls
in this part of the country). Indeed, pursuing a utilitarian argument, it
must have made sound economic sense for agricultural labourers,
when able, to keep their daughters at school where they could be
looked after while the mother worked and where they would at least
learn sewing. One observer described Kent schools as a 'kind of
nursery' for the children of labouring women.[30] Hence, one assumes,
the 3- and 4-year-old scholars of figure 8.3.

Even when children did go to school, their attendance was spas-
modic. Boys would be taken from the classroom to earn money, girls to
attend to domestic chores – as late as 1895 a Hernhill teacher
complained that 'many of the children' were 'occasionally away to suit
their parents' convenience'.[31] The school fees of 3d. or 6d. a week may
seem trifling to us, but this was no small amount for the penny
economies of labouring households. It was easy to get behind with
payments, particularly when several children were involved, and those
pennies soon became shillings – the log books refer to arrears of as
much as 6s.[32] There were lost earnings to take into account quite apart
from the matter of fees: Liardet pointed out a boy's wage, 6d. a day,
could cover the weekly rent. Not surprisingly, Liardet found that the
child was 'removed whenever a job of work can be found for him ...
Many of the children attend so irregularly, and are so often absent for
such long periods, that they forget all they have learned.'[33] It was not
just children from labouring families who were affected. The labour of
the children of smallholders – the true peasantry – was vital to the
running of the farm, crucial for family subsistence. Stephens has noted
the association of small farmers with poor educational standards.[34]

[30] *PP*, 1843, vol. XII, p. 208.
[31] CKS, C/ES 183/1/1, Hernhill Church of England School Log Book, 1872–1959, p. 219.
[32] CCA, U3/221/25/13, p. 221.
[33] Liardet, 'State of the peasantry', pp. 109, 111.
[34] Stephens, *Education, literacy and society*, p. 41.

Local school log books of the 1870s and 1880s provide a perspective on children's work which can never be obtained from the qualitatively barren census returns.[35] They also reveal the erratic attendance of Kent village children, even after the Education Acts of the 1870s and 1880 made attendance compulsory from the age of 5 until the age of 10. The Boughton school log book has frequent references to 'numbers away working with their parents illegally'; 'Many away in the fields at work contrary to law.' Girls stayed home all day to help their mothers with the washing: on Fridays in Canterbury and on Wednesdays in Harbledown. Sometimes Boughton youngsters remained at home on the day before a market so that they could pick produce in their parents' gardens. April and May saw Harbledown scholars away bark-stripping and Boughton children occupied in the hop-grounds ('most of the girls are at work'). There were over a hundred children enrolled at the Boughton-under-Blean Church of England school in 1872, yet in May of that year attendance slumped to less than half that number due to 'the effects of hop-tying': 'Hop-tying has now really begun', reads a log book entry for 18 April, and 'several boys & girls are away helping their parents'. In June, Graveney boys were out minding sheep, Boughton children at work in the cherry orchards. Canterbury and Boughton boys and girls were absent at times in July because of the pea-picking, and in Boughton because their parents took them to Seasalter for haymaking on the marshes. By August the harvest was making its mark on school numbers in Graveney and Harbledown: 'School has been very thinly attended during the week. Several boys and girls Harvesting. Some under 8 years of age.' Attendance 'is diminished sufficiently to tell us Harvest is here'. Schools broke up from August until early October, in recognition of the harvests, but even then children stayed away in October in Canterbury, Harbledown and Graveney because of field work or to attend local fairs. The teacher at Graveney bemoaned the backwardness of the scholars who returned to school after the harvest break: 'They appear to have forgotten all they had learned previous to hopping, so that we have had to go back to the beginning again.' 'Several children in the upper standards are away at work in the fields', a Boughton teacher noted in late October (in 1876). 'Those children in the lower standards who are not at school are kept away to nurse the younger ones while the mothers are at work in the fields.'[36]

[35] For an excellent account of child labour, which draws upon Kent school log books, see J. Kitteringham, 'Country work girls in nineteenth-century England', in R. Samuel (ed.), *Village life and labour* (London, 1975), pp. 75–138.
[36] CCA, U3/221/25/13; CKS, C/ES 54/7/1, Canterbury Broad Street Diocesan School

The Hernhill Church of England school log book provides a detailed picture of the impact of employment on education in that parish from 1872 onwards. Children were away at field work in April, in the hop-grounds in May (the girls tying hops), pea-picking and haymaking in June, at pea-picking and field and orchard work in July. Anticipating school closure, the 'elder children' were already at work on the harvest in the first week of August. School returned in October, but 'fieldwork', including the harvest of root crops, was 'still occupying the elder children'. Some boys were kept away from school in the winter too, rook-scaring and shaving hop-poles. A Hernhill teacher complained of the unruliness of the rook boys once they had returned to school ('so I exhibited a piece of cane').[37]

When labour and the various harvests did not interfere with attendance, illness intervened. Mumps, ague, influenza, colds, sore throats, bronchitis, whooping cough, chickenpox, sore feet, sores and recurring epidemics of diphtheria, scarlet fever and measles depleted school numbers.[38] The snow and wet weather were consistent seasonal problems. The coughing, sneezing and wheezing of those who attended school – as the Hernhill log book noted in January 1888 – made school work very difficult.[39]

The census of 1871 described 70 per cent of Hernhill 5- to 14-year-olds as scholars, but the school log book shows that in fact on good days or weeks only about 60 per cent of the eligible section of the parish population were actually at school and attendance could be as low as 20 or 30 per cent.[40]

Horrified commentators encountered what they described as gross ignorance. 'It is quite common to meet with boys engaged in farms who cannot read or write', one man reported in 1843. 'The unity of God, a future state, the number of months in the year, are matters not universally known.' Another complained in 1838 that he had been unable to find a waggoner able to read the directions on parcels to be sent to London.[41] Liardet came across pupils in Hernhill in the same year who could not read even though they had been attending school for two or three years. The barrister surveyed forty-two children under

Infants Department Log Book, 1863–83; CKS, C/ES 54/9/1, Canterbury Broad Street Diocesan School Girls Department Log Book, 1863–82; CKS, C/ES 158/2/1, Graveney Mixed and Infants School Log Book, 1876–89; CKS, C/ES 170/1, Harbledown Church of England School Log Book, 1868–93.
[37] CKS, C/ES 183/1/1.   [38] See chapter 3.
[39] CKS, C/ES 183/1/1, p. 153.
[40] Calculated from the Hernhill Census of 1871 and the attendance entries in the Hernhill School Log Book during the early 1870s.
[41] PP, 1843, vol. XII, p. 169; *Minutes of Evidence before the Select Committee Appointed to Inquire into the Administration of Relief to the Poor*, PP, 1837–8, vol. XVIII, pt 3, p. 135.

the age of 14 who attended school, mostly the children of labourers. Only six (14 per cent) could read and write; thirteen (31 per cent) could read fluently; nine (21 per cent) could read very little. The remainder (33 per cent) could not read at all.[42] Even those who could read had learned to read in the [New] Testament so they floundered when forced to read out of context, or when confronted with another book. 'When asked if they could read, a common answer was, "Yes, a little in the Testament".' They 'have read, and heard read, the same thing so often, that the sound of one word suggests the following one. They even remember some words from their length or form and the position they occupy in the page, which they would not know in another book.' Consequently it was 'not very uncommon' for children to lose the skill once they left school.[43] The Kent man who had trouble with his parcels was told by some men that they had learned a little reading at Sunday school 'but could never get further than spelling painfully through a chapter of the New Testament; that had been entirely forgotten'.[44] Family reconstitution studies sometimes reveal individuals whose skills deteriorated over time. When 19-year-old Hannah Matson married in 1826 she was able to write her name in the parish register; when she remarried as Hannah Foster in 1843, she made a mark. Seventeen-year-old Matilda Miles was able to sign her sister Ann's marriage certificate in 1840, but she used a cross at her own wedding five years later.[45]

IV

The historian's functional definition of 'literacy' is the ability of a person to sign his or her name. The attraction of using recorded signatures or marks (usually crosses) as a gauge of literacy is that they permit measurement through time and across gender, class and occupational groups. Writing, for much of recorded western history, was treated as a rather technical skill, acquired after a person had learned to read. Many children – for the sorts of economic reasons outlined earlier – would have left school before they learned to write. Today there is a social stigma attached to illiteracy and people who can neither read nor write may well be capable of signing. But as Schofield has argued, this was unlikely in pre-industrial England, 'given the phasing of instruction in reading and writing, the lack of writing materials in most homes, and the very few occasions in a lifetime in which a signature or mark was required'. There was little point in a person learning to sign

[42] Liardet, 'State of the peasantry', pp. 109, 110. [43] *Ibid.*, p. 112.
[44] *PP*, 1837–8, vol. XVIII, pt 3, p. 135. [45] Family reconstitution files.

just his or her name. Although it will overestimate those able to write
with facility, the presence or absence of a signature gives a crude
indication of the presence or absence of the ability to write. It is what
Schofield has termed a 'middle range' measurement. It will also give a
minimum figure of those able to read. Those who cannot sign may be
able to read, but they will not be able to write.[46]

There are several problems with the use of signatures as a gauge of
literacy. What does this brief movement of the pen actually signify?[47] It
tells us that the individuals concerned could or could not sign their
names: it does not, strictly speaking, despite our assumptions, inform
us whether that person could read and write. Indeed it is rare for
historians to have information on individual educational attainment as
well as an indication of signature literacy. This can come only with the
detailed reconstruction of a local community. In the case of Hernhill,
the insurrectionists of 1838 provide a unique opportunity to make this
link between literacy skills and signature and to thereby test some of
the assumptions which lie behind the historian's functional definition
and measurement of literacy, for the vicar of Hernhill, who knew most
of the men personally, provided short summaries of the educational
levels of the rioters of 1838, individual by individual, commenting on
whether or not they could write and/or read.[48] It has been possible to
match these verdicts – for twenty-eight men – against family reconstitution data for individual signature literacies.

Seventeen of the twenty-eight were able to read (60 per cent), but
only eleven were able to sign their names (40 per cent): that is, the
proportion able to read was one and a half times the proportion able to
sign. Of those who made a mark (seventeen), seven (41 per cent) were
able to read and ten were illiterate – evidence again that those defined
as illiterate include some readers. When Liardet visited the cottages of
two of these readers, William Burford and William Foster, he discovered Testaments and religious books, although both men and their
wives were unable to write their names.[49] Of those eleven who signed,
seven (64 per cent) were able to read and write, three to read only and
one was described as illiterate (unable to read or write). This indicates
that the functional definition of literacy, as well as underestimating
hidden readers, overestimates those who could actually write. The
study of the rioters also underlines the well-known social selectivity of

[46] Schofield, 'Dimensions of illiteracy', pp. 440–1.
[47] For a sensible discussion, see R. A. Houston, *Literacy in early modern Europe: culture and education, 1500–1800* (London, 1988), ch. 6.
[48] PRO, HO/40/36/435–41, Home Office Papers, 'List of persons concerned in the late riot near Canterbury'.
[49] Liardet, 'State of the peasantry', pp. 95–6.

literacy. Apart from one shepherd, those who could read and write and sign their names were all farmers, small farmers, bailiffs or craftsmen. Those who could sign their names, but who could read only, were all agricultural labourers. The illiterates who signed with a cross were mostly agricultural labourers, but they included a farmer/publican, a petty dealer and a beershop-keeper. Those who could read, but who used a mark, were farm labourers (including a beershop-keeper who was also a labourer).

Our sample is extremely small, but the results are interesting. They confirm what many historians have long suspected: the 'middle-range' measurement is truly middle range, a rough guide. If the experience of the rioters of 1838 was at all representative, the simple signature substantially underestimates the number of men and women able to read and significantly overestimates the number of people with writing ability. As Roger Chartier has stated, literacy figures 'constitute a kind of rough, composite index, which does not precisely measure the diffusion of either writing skills (which the percentages exaggerate) or reading skills (which they underestimate)'.[50]

As the example of the rioters indicates, the main problem with this middle-range measurement is that it will underestimate those able to read; Thomas has referred to a 'spectacular' underestimation.[51] It is difficult to actually measure the extent of this group of hidden readers, but other nineteenth-century studies suggest that the proportion able to read was about the same as the sample above: one and a half to two times the proportion able to sign.[52] In his survey of 123 young people over the age of 14 in Hernhill, Dunkirk and Boughton, Liardet found that only a quarter could read and write, but over half could read. If the ability to sign had been used as the criterion for literacy, 75 per cent of his young sample would have been classified as illiterate, when in fact only 45 per cent could not read or write.[53] If this measurement of literacy underestimates those able to read, it has been suggested that it is a more accurate representation of those able to read fluently. As Liardet put it, 'Whenever a poor man is in the habit of reading, you may be sure he can write.'[54]

There is a further problem with the functional definition. It is likely that women are disproportionately under-represented in the 'middle range'. The very low proportions of female signatures and large

[50] Chartier, 'Practical impact of writing', p. 112.
[51] Thomas, 'Meaning of literacy', p. 103.
[52] R. K. Webb, *The British working class reader, 1790–1848* (New York, 1971), p. 22; Laqueur, 'Toward a cultural ecology of literacy', pp. 45–6.
[53] My calculations from Liardet, 'State of the peasantry', pp. 109, 118, 122–3.
[54] Schofield, 'Dimensions of illiteracy', p. 440; Liardet, 'State of the peasantry', p. 112.

number of marks made by women may well hide a high percentage of
women able to read, but not write. T. C. Smout found that of a group
of women involved in a religious revival in an eighteenth-century
Scottish village only one in ten could write, but all of them could
read.[55] Writing was not considered necessary for women: at all social
levels, well into the nineteenth century, it was usual for higher
percentages of women to sign their names with a cross or mark.[56] And
yet we have noted a tendency for more females than males in the area
to attend schools which taught reading. Obviously it is difficult to
prove the existence of these invisible readers; they are not susceptible
to measurement, truly hidden from history. We catch glimpses of
individuals, however. The homes of Emily Burford and Hannah Foster
contained religious books and yet neither they or their husbands could
write their names.[57] Sarah Wraight, wife of the rioter Wraight junior,
who when she married signed the register with a cross, described how
she had stayed up all night *reading the Bible* after 'poor Edward was
taken prisoner'.[58] So there may well have been some foundation to the
claim in 1838 that the reading facility of the women had helped to
mobilize the insurrectionaries. It was said that in Hernhill

the proportion of women who can read is greater than that of the men, and it is
thus that they have been enabled to do so much mischief ... they availed
themselves of their power of reading the Scriptures, which to them or their
husbands was a book they could not open, to distort tenets, not very clear in
themselves, into proofs that Thom [Courtenay: the leader of the rising] was the
promised Messiah.[59]

If this was indeed the case, it has intriguing implications. The
spectacular increase in signature literacy in the second half of the
nineteenth century, traced in figure 8.1, may merely reflect women's
acquisition of an additional skill, that of writing, rather than a dramatic
leap from illiteracy to literacy. Their reading facility may have been a
constant; female attendance at school may have been a constant. What
changed, feasibly, was the curriculum and the type of school.[60]

[55] Smout, 'Born again at Cambuslang', pp. 121–3.
[56] Cressy, *Literacy and the social order*, pp. 128–9; R. O'Day, *Education and society, 1500–1800* (London, 1982), ch. 10; Purvis, 'Experience of schooling'; Gomershall, 'Ideals and realities'.
[57] Family reconstitutions.
[58] Liardet, 'State of the peasantry', p. 91.   [59] *The Times*, 9 June 1838.
[60] The existence of a hidden female reading literacy also has implications for some of David Levine's assumptions and findings on family literacy, where he equates 'maternal literacy' with the ability of a woman to write her name and then goes on to make various deductions about the transmission of knowledge. See D. Levine, 'Education and family life in early industrial England', *Journal of Family History*, 4 (1979), p. 375.

When James Jacob married in Hernhill in 1824 he made a mark in the parish register; yet when his daughter married almost thirty years later, he was (as a witness) able to write his own name. Jacob, a small farmer, had improved his literacy in the intervening years. The case of Jacob, and the examples of the women, mentioned earlier, who lost their signature literacy, present something of a problem. How typical were these people? Their existence highlights one final shortcoming of the conventional measurement of literacy: it provides only a snapshot view, a measurement at a single point in a person's life. The local study, however, based on family reconstitution, can actually chart individual progress over time. It cannot measure changes in reading ability, of course, but by tracing remarriages it is possible to detect whether or not the signature literacy of individuals deteriorated or improved over time.[61]

Did those who signed or made a mark at the time of their first marriage, usually in their late teens to mid twenties, still sign or make a mark if they remarried later? Of thirty-two remarriages traced in Dunkirk and Hernhill in the nineteenth century, fifteen signed at their first marriage and seventeen made a mark. Of the fifteen who were signature literate, fourteen (93 per cent) were still able to write when they remarried – only one person (a woman) lost the ability to write. Of the seventeen who made a mark at the time of first marriage, sixteen (94 per cent) were still using a cross when they remarried – again only one person (also a woman) had changed their signature literacy, having learned to write her name.[62] The sample, once more, is small, but it suggests that the snapshot measurement of signature literacy is not a distortion of the reality of the life-cycle. Those who were able to write their names in their teens or early twenties tended, by and large, to retain that skill. Alternatively, few of those without writing skills at the time of marriage would acquire them later. The pattern in the towns, however, may have been different.

V

What were the reading habits of the labouring population? What did they read (or not read) with facility or difficulty? When the middle-class observers came to Boughton, Dunkirk and Hernhill in the wake of the abortive rising of 1838, they were struck by the literary deprivation of the agricultural labourer. Liardet visited 151 labouring homes and found that in less than 10 per cent of them did parents claim to

[61] See Houston's comments, in his *Literacy in early modern Europe*, p. 126.
[62] Family reconstitutions.

open a book in the evening. To the enquiry as to how they passed this time, most replied 'About home, doing sometimes one thing sometimes another; but, most times, going early to bed for want of something to do'. Over 40 per cent of those interviewed possessed absolutely no reading material whatsoever. The lawyer was astonished by the lack of literature other than the Bible, Testament and prayer- or hymn-books. Only twelve houses contained non-religious books. There were traces of more secular influences. Some of the prints on the walls of labouring cottages looked to Liardet as though they had been 'cut off the heads of ballads purchased from some travelling hawker'. But 'Not a Penny Magazine, nor any of the other cheap publications of the day, which convey so much useful instruction and amusement to the working classes in the towns, was to be seen'.[63] In short, the one book that a bare majority of labourers' homes contained was the Bible or Testament. Sometimes it must have been one of the few movable items of value in a home. When a labourer went into an open cottage on the turnpike road at Dunkirk, the two items he stole were a Testament and a prayer-book.[64] The owner of the books, an agricultural labourer, was described in an earlier Quarter Sessions document as an 'imperfect reader'; his wife signed her deposition with a cross.[65]

Even the majority of prints were of a religious kind. They were also 'of the poorest kind, and were usually such as might have been seen in cottages half a century back. The productions of modern graphic art have not as yet found their way into these rural districts.'[66] This was in an area situated a few miles from Canterbury and less than fifty miles from London. The culture of print was relatively undeveloped in this part of Kent and, I suspect, in many mid nineteenth-century rural villages and hamlets.

The twentieth-century academic mind tends to draw neat demarcations between literate and non-literate societies, including various assumptions about 'mind-sets' and rationality.[67] Rab Houston and Thomas have advocated a more subtle approach when dealing with early-modern Britain. They argue for the complexity of the situation, for interaction rather than hard-and-fast cultural division. 'Early-modern England ... was not an oral society ... neither was it a fully

63 Liardet, 'State of the peasantry', 108, 118, 122, 128.
64 CKS, Q/SBe 193, Midsummer 1848.
65 CKS, Q/SBe 148, Easter 1837; CKS, Q/SBe 193, Midsummer 1848.
66 Liardet, 'State of the peasantry', p. 109. For the expansion of mass-circulation, illustrated literature from the 1830s (including the *Penny Magazine*), see P. Anderson, *The printed image and the transformation of popular culture 1790–1860* (Oxford, 1991).
67 For a critique of such assumptions, see B. V. Street, *Literacy in theory and practice* (Cambridge, 1984), chs. 1–2.

literate one.'[68] If our part of Kent is any indication, the same was true of rural England for much of the nineteenth century. When the absentee landowner James Lambert wanted to check the accuracy of his estate map and establish liability for tithes, he consulted two men who had been resident in Hernhill for forty to sixty years and they in turn confirmed their opinions with old people living in the parish.[69] When the village censuses were taken in the nineteenth century, the variety of spelling, the phonetics of naming, suggests a resilient orality: people were used to hearing and saying their personal names and place names rather than having them written down. The significance of those examples is that they demonstrate interaction between the oral and the written. The census enumeration forms were written out; Lambert's informants gave affidavits – their memory, oral evidence, was set down in writing.

This cultural mix can be demonstrated in other ways. Those who were able to read could read aloud to the non-literate. After the rising of 1838 a reporter from *The Times* encountered a labouring man who 'took from his breast a few pages of the Testament containing the whole of the Revelations; a mark was made at the 6th chapter; and the man told me that he could neither read nor write himself, but that his wife read the book to him every night, and said that some such person as Sir William Courtenay', the labourers' leader, 'was spoken of in it'.[70] Courtenay and his followers employed mobilizing techniques which showed an awareness of the cultural heterogeneity of potential recruits. The use of symbols and songs, the iconography of the loaf of bread on a pole, the dramatic message of incendiarism, would ensure communication to illiterate as well as literate. The would-be rebels of 1838, and other protesters in Kent, also employed graffiti, which implies recognition of at least some ability to read – unless the messages were intended solely for their social superiors.[71] With their varied literacies, the rioters themselves are interesting representatives of this cultural milieu. It may seem somewhat perverse (as Houston once remarked) for a study of literacy to stress the prevalence of orality,[72] but it is a fact that in the rural areas of nineteenth-century England orality was still important.

There is, then, little evidence at mid century for any great separation of the cultures.[73] Table 8.6 sets out three different profiles of literacy in individual households during the nineteenth century, and table 8.7 summarizes patterns at the parish and occupational level. As table 8.7

[68] Thomas, 'Meaning of literacy', p. 98; Houston, *Scottish literacy*, ch. 6.
[69] CKS, U521 E2/159–63, Lambert Estate Papers.
[70] *The Times*, 9 June 1838. [71] See Reay, *Last rising*, pp. 77, 85, 100, 102.
[72] Houston, *Scottish literacy*, p. 209. [73] Cf. Levine, 'Education and family life'.

Cultures

Table 8.6 *Literacy within selected families*

(a) Total 'illiteracy': a labouring family

Names of parents	Names of children	Literacy	Spouse's literacy	Occupation or occupation of spouse
William and Elizabeth Edwards		X	X	Agricultural lab.
	William	X	–	Agricultural lab.
	Henry	X	X	Agricultural lab.
	Frances	X	X	Labourer
	Elizabeth	X	X	Labourer
	Edward	X	X	Labourer
	John	X	X	Labourer

Time span: 1821–61

(b) Total literacy: a craft family

Names of parents	Names of children	Literacy	Spouse's literacy	Occupation or occupation of spouse
John and Ann Foreman		S	S	Wheelwright/farmer
	Edmund	S	S	Wheelwright
	Olivia	S	S	Draper
	Harriet	S	S	Carpenter
	Emma	S	S	Hairdresser

Time span: 1810–52

(c) Mixed literacy: a peasant family

Names of parents	Names of children	Literacy	Spouse's literacy	Occupation or occupation of spouse
James and Olive Hadlow		X	S	Small farmer
	Edward	X	–	Labourer
	Ann	X	X	Labourer
	William	X	X	Labourer
	Frances	S	X	Labourer
	Frederick	X	X	Agricultural lab.
	Alfred	X	S	Agricultural lab.
	Edwin	S	X	Agricultural lab.
	Osborne	X	X	Agricultural lab.
	Emma Jane	S	X	Labourer

Time span: 1821–61

(d) Mixed literacy: household producer

Names of parents	Names of children	Literacy	Spouse's literacy	Occupation or occupation of spouse
Henry and Mary Tong		X	X	Woodman/charcoal-burner/wood-dealer

Table 8.6 *(contd)*

(d) Mixed literacy: household producer *(contd)*				
Names of parents	Names of children	Literacy	Spouse's literacy	Occupation or occupation of spouse
	Acts of the Apostles			
	(Henry)	S	X	Woodman
	Hester	X	S	Agricultural lab.
	Emily	S	X	Agricultural lab.
Time span: 1848–79	William	S	S	Woodman/ag. lab.

All profiles are based on family reconstitution files. S = able to sign; X = not able to sign. These profiles include information on the literacy of the children's spouses, whereas the profiles in table 8.7 refer to the literacies of parents and children only.

Table 8.7 *Known signature literacy of families in 1851 (as percentage of total families)*

	Totally literate	Illiterate	Mixed	Total number
By place				
Dunkirk	9.8	31.5	58.7	92
Boughton	22.5	23.6	53.9	89
Hernhill	16.3	21.7	62.0	92
By occupation				
Farmers	32.5	2.5	65.0	40
Trades/crafts	38.0	12.0	50.0	50
Ag. Lab./Lab.	6.2	34.8	59.0	178
All households	16.1	25.6	58.2	273

These figures are based on the 273 families in the three parishes in 1851 for which there is information on the signature literacy of both parents (when they married) and the future literacy of their children (if they had any). It includes households where we know the signature literacy of the parents only, as well as those households with incomplete information on the future literacy of their offspring. 1851 is intended as a focal point only, a way of selecting a cohort of households. In other words, the sample does not capture literacy in 1851, but the family profile over time – it is a measure of life-course signature literacy stretching over the nineteenth century. The 'totally literate' are defined as those families where all members (for whom there is information on literacy) could sign their names. The 'illiterate' are those where no-one in the family (for whom there is information on literacy) could write his or her name. The 'mixed' families contain both the signature literate and the signature illiterate. Note that the 'all households' total includes five households with occupations other than those included in the main occupational categories.

shows, there were few households in Boughton, Dunkirk and Hernhill in 1851 where all members of the family could sign their names like those in the Foreman household in table 8.6(b). The proportion of 'totally literate' households in 1851 ranged from just 6 per cent of labouring families to 38 per cent of those where the household head was employed in the trades or crafts: the combined total for the three parishes was 16 per cent. But 'illiterate' families were also a minority group. Only just over a quarter of the 1851 sample contained parents and children who were all signature illiterate as they were in the family of William and Elizabeth Edwards in table 8.7(a). The proportions of signature illiterate families varied from 2.5 per cent for farmers to 35 per cent for labourers and agricultural labourers. Most households (58 per cent) contained a combination of those who signed and those who made a mark – the percentage for each occupation and place was never less than 50. The proportion of families which contained a parent or a child able to read would have been higher.[74]

The most representative profile of literacy, then, is that in table 8.7(c) and (d). Literacy and 'illiteracy' were present within most families. This is captured perfectly in the case of the Tongs – see table 8.7(d) – where we know from additional information in a court case that the children could write, the woman could read but not write (although she kept her husband's accounts) and the man of the house was (presumably) illiterate.[75] Occasional references in oral histories suggest that examples of mixed literacy could still be found at the end of the nineteenth and in the early twentieth centuries. Frank Kemsley (born 1887) said that his father, a dealer, 'couldn't read his own name, couldn't write his own name. I can remember when I was a little boy, the Boer War was on ... my father used to come home from Canterbury market or from town with a little old paper he give a 1d. for, so that I could read out to him what happened in the Boer War.'[76] Harold Kay (born 1921) recalled that his father, a Hernhill small farmer, had never learned how to read or write. His wife read the newspaper to him. Kay's mother also read stories to the children on Sunday evenings after church and his father would sit and listen.[77]

But we can take our discussion further than the issue of the separation or lack of separation between oral and literate. There was in

---

[74] Phil Gardner cites a survey of Ramsbottom in Lancashire, 'with a reported illiteracy rate of over 50 per cent in 1839, [where] only 11 families of a total of 309 had no single reader among their number': Gardner, *Lost elementary schools*, p. 179.

[75] *Faversham Mercury*, 18 May 1878.   [76] TL, F. Kemsley, b. 1887.

[77] Hernhill Oral History, H. Kay, b. 1921. The Hernhill Oral History Tapes are interviews that I carried out in 1991–2.

fact a diversity of literacies in the nineteenth-century rural world.[78] Given a cultural environment where few labouring people could 'write their own names' and where 'those who could read, rarely ventured upon any other book than the Testament or Bible', Liardet claimed that people with even a modicum of education – for example, the school-mistress Lydia Hadlow and her brother William Wills – were 'regarded as prodigies of learning by their simple neighbours'.[79] He conversed with a charcoal burner who, when the lawyer remarked that only the most ignorant could have been taken in by Courtenay, retorted: 'Why ... there was Edward Wraight, a man who held his own land, and William Wills, who has the best of education, quite a learned man, *beleft* him; and, besides them, there was Foad, and Griggs, and others, who had all had a Bible education ... *beleft* him.'[80] The charcoal burner, who was presumably illiterate (though not inarticulate), clearly con-sidered that he inhabited a different intellectual world to that of the small farmers Wills, Wraight and Lydia Hadlow. The irony is that the narrator of the story tells it with the self-assurance of a man who knows that he inhabits yet another cultural plane. Wills, Liardet scoffed, had merely 'had the benefit of the common instruction given in the middling class of schools in country towns'; Hadlow, the 'oracle of the community', was 'scarcely more enlightened than her ignorant neighbours'.[81]

If we can dispense with the value judgements and assumptions of superiority and inferiority, this vignette provides a tidy illustration of the different cultures of literacy in one small rural area in the mid nineteenth century.[82] Plates 24 and 25 provide a further visual dimen-sion. There was a world of difference between the literacy of a farmer like Edward Curling, who signed his name with ease, and that of a labourer such as William Coachworth, who made a mark in the marriage register, and who could neither read nor write; or that of his son (and namesake) who could manage a tortured scrawl of a signature when he married in 1867 (see plate 22). Curling was at ease with a pen because he had to write up farm accounts and, like other farmers and craftsmen of substance, keep the records of local office. In the eighteenth century some of these men made a mark instead of signing their name in the Hernhill churchwardens' accounts, but by the mid nineteenth century most of this class were able to write (see plates

---

[78] I have benefited greatly from the discussion of literacy in C. Lankshear, *Literacy, schooling and revolution* (Lewes, 1987), ch. 2. I have also had the opportunity to discuss such issues with the author.
[79] Liardet, 'State of the peasantry', p. 96.   [80] *Ibid.*, p. 90.   [81] *Ibid.*, pp. 93, 96.
[82] For a valuable account of the early-modern context, see Cressy, 'Environment for literacy' and his 'Literacy in context'.

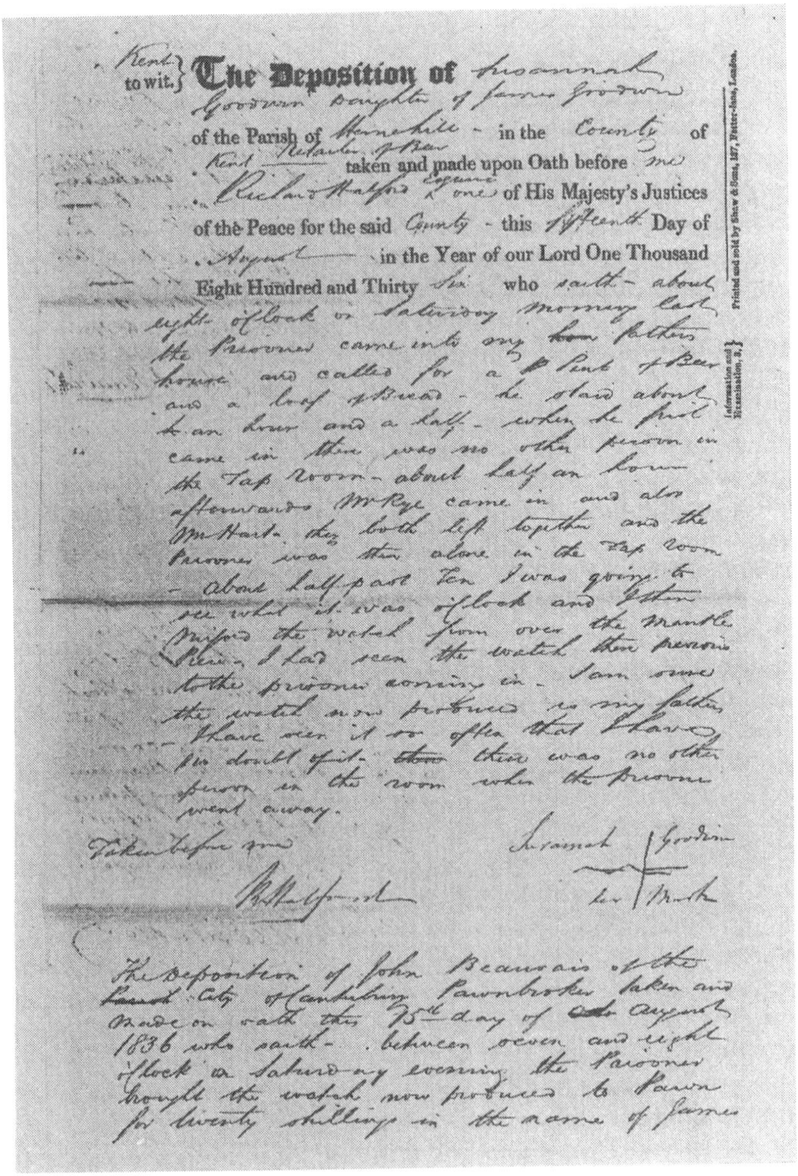
Kent to wit. } **The Deposition of** Susannah Goodwin Daughter of James Goodwin of the Parish of Hernehill in the County of Kent Retailer of Beer taken and made upon Oath before me Richard Halford Esquire one of His Majesty's Justices of the Peace for the said County this fifteenth Day of August in the Year of our Lord One Thousand Eight Hundred and Thirty Six who saith — about eight o'clock on Saturday morning last the Prisoner came into my father's house and called for a Pint of Beer and a loaf of Bread — he staid about an hour and a half — when he first came in there was no other person in the Tap room — about half an hour afterwards Mr Rye came in and also Mr Hart — they both left together and the Prisoner was then alone in the Tap room — About half past Ten I was going to see what it was o'clock and I then missed the watch from over the Mantle Piece, I had seen the watch there previous to the prisoner coming in — I am sure the watch now produced is my father's I have seen it so often that I have no doubt of it — there was no other person in the room when the prisoner went away.

Taken before me

R Halford

Susannah + Goodwin
her Mark

The Deposition of John Beauvais of the City of Canterbury Pawnbroker taken and made on oath this 15th day of August 1836 who saith — between seven and eight o'clock on Saturday evening the Prisoner brought the watch now produced to Pawn for twenty shillings in the name of James

Printed and sold by Shaw & Sons, 137, Fetter-lane, London.

[Information and Examination, 2.]

Plate 24 The deposition and mark of Susannah Goodwin, 1836. Clearly she is ill at ease with a pen, as she would be over a decade later (see plate 25). Contrast the ease with which the JP drafted the deposition. Susannah was the 14-year-old daughter of the labourer and beershop-keeper, James Goodwin; the family kept the Dove beershop at Dargate. Both Goodwin and his wife were unable to sign their names; of their children, two boys were signature literate, and three girls were not.

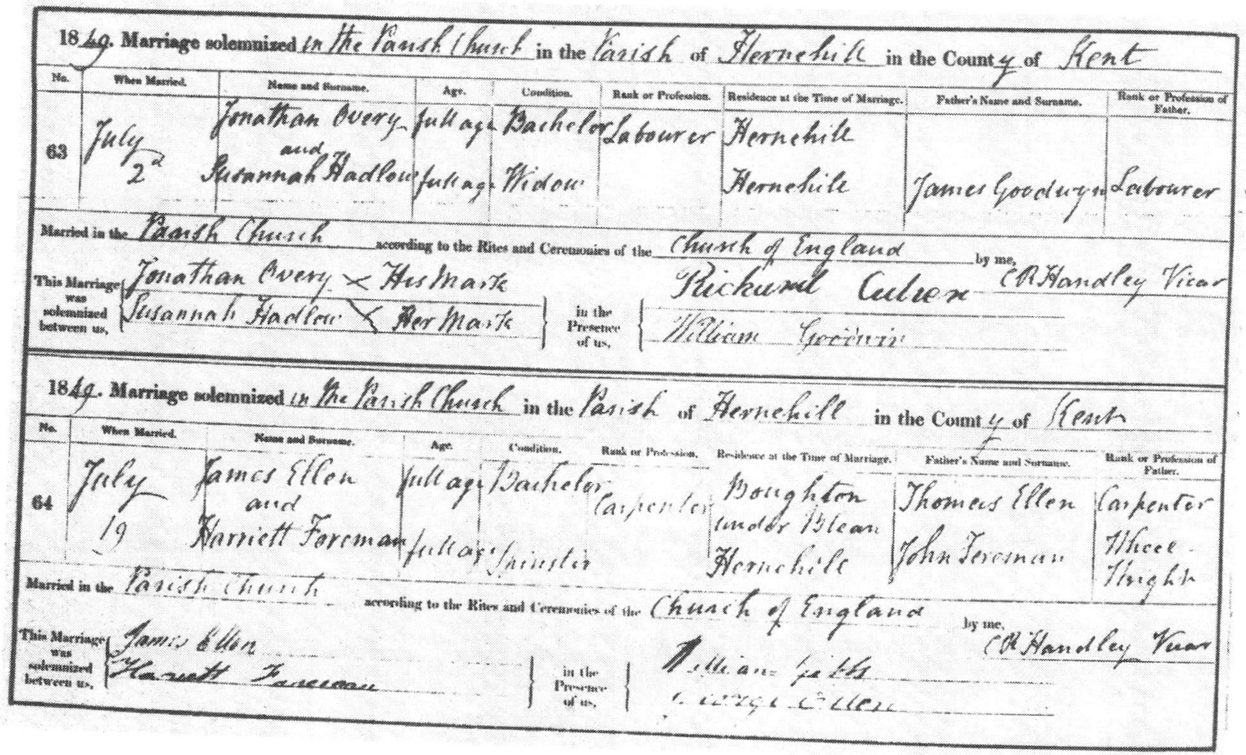

18*49*. Marriage solemnized *in the Parish Church* in the *Parish* of *Hernehill* in the County of *Kent*

No.	When Married.	Name and Surname.	Age.	Condition.	Rank or Profession.	Residence at the Time of Marriage.	Father's Name and Surname.	Rank or Profession of Father.
63	July 2d	Jonathan Overy	full age	Bachelor	Labourer	Hernehill		
		and Susannah Hadlow	full age	Widow		Hernehill	James Goodwyn	Labourer

Married in the *Parish Church* according to the Rites and Ceremonies of the *Church of England* by me, *C R Handley Vicar*

This Marriage was solemnized between us, *Jonathan Overy × His Mark* / *Susannah Hadlow × Her Mark* in the Presence of us, *Richard Culver ×* / *William Goodwin*

18*49*. Marriage solemnized *in the Parish Church* in the *Parish* of *Hernehill* in the County of *Kent*

No.	When Married.	Name and Surname.	Age.	Condition.	Rank or Profession.	Residence at the Time of Marriage.	Father's Name and Surname.	Rank or Profession of Father.
64	July 19	James Ellen	full age	Bachelor	Carpenter	Boughton under Blean	Thomas Ellen	Carpenter
		and Harriett Foreman	full age	Spinster		Hernehill	John Foreman	Wheelwright

Married in the *Parish Church* according to the Rites and Ceremonies of the *Church of England* by me, *C R Handley Vicar*

This Marriage was solemnized between us, *James Ellen* / *Harriett Foreman* in the Presence of us, *William Fells* / *George Ellen*

Plate 25 Two Hernhill marriage certificates, 1849. These entries mirror varying cultures of literacy: note the different signature abilities of the labouring and craft families, and of the vicar of Hernhill. Susannah Hadlow, who had difficulty making a mark, is Susannah Goodwin (see plate 24), now in her twenties and on to her second marriage.

26 and 27). The literacy of this 'village elite', farmers, craftsmen and a few shopkeepers, would have been a functional literacy – enough to perform the duties required by the parish vestry, to fill in a land-tax form, to write a bill, understand the terms of a rental or mortgage agreement, and (possibly) to make a will (see plates 27 and 28). We can assume that almost all of these men (and women) could read. They could usually pen a letter – as a draper's porter did in 1871 to his pregnant woman friend:

Dear Nellie,
Excuse me for not writing more. I will see you on Sunday and praphs will come till then Believe me to be Yours.
William Aylett[83]

They could, if angered, write a threat. William Wills was said to have written the following, found in 1838 on the door of the Hernhill tithe barn:

> If you new ho was on earth your harts Wod turn
> But dont Wate to late
> They how R
> O that great day of gudgement is close at hand
> it now peps in the dor
> every man according to his woks
> Our rites and liberties We Will have[84]

As the above examples demonstrate, a steady signature hand did not necessarily imply equal skills of composition, or that the writer had imbibed the increasingly standardized rules of grammar, punctuation, syntax and spelling. Liardet considered Curling worthy but 'uncultivated', and he noted that few of the farming class knew anything other than agricultural affairs; they were not in the position, 'even if they were willing, to assist much in the moral improvement of the people'.[85]

Those at the bottom of the social scale, the agricultural labourers, varied in their literacies and non-literacies. Some, particularly in the second half of the century, could sign their names with confidence (see plates 22 and 25) and presumably could read, if only in the Bible. Others, like the rat-catcher Charles Hadlow, one of the rioters of 1838, were unable to write but could read.[86] Many, we have seen, until the end of the century, could only make a mark in the marriage register. Even the marks of these 'illiterates' seem to indicate some hierarchy of facility, ranging from the confident Xs on plate 22 to the pained

---

[83] CKS, PS US 21, Upper Division of the Lathe of Scray Petty Sessions Bastardy Examinations, 1860–71, Sherlock vs. Aylett.
[84] *The Times*, 6 June 1838.
[85] Liardet, 'State of the peasantry', p. 99.   [86] Family reconstitutions.

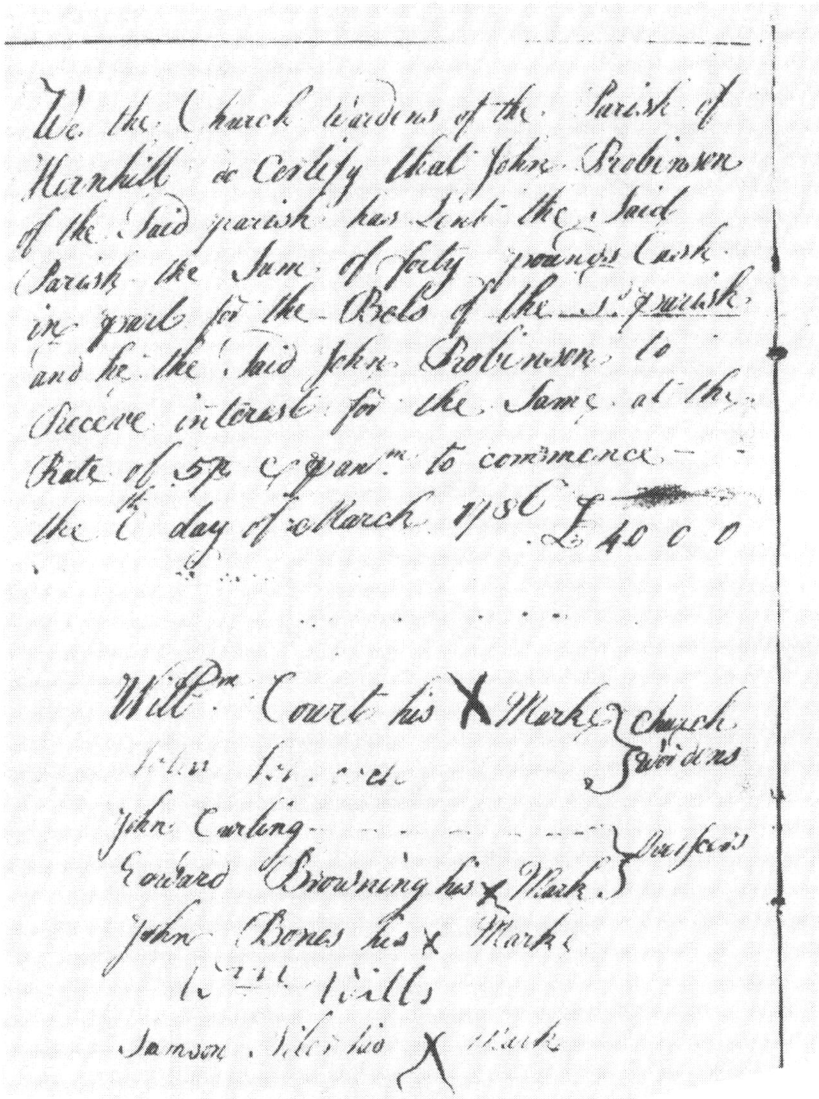
We the Church wardens of the Parish of
Hernhill do Certify that John Robinson
of the Said parish has Lent the Said
Parish the Sum of forty pounds Cash
in part for the Debts of the sd parish
and he the said John Robinson to
Receive interest for the Same at the
Rate of 5p Cent p ann.m to commence
the 6th day of March 1786 £ 40 0 0

Willm Court his X Mark } Church wardens
John ...
John Carling } Overseers
Edward Browning his X Mark
John Bones his X Mark
Wm Wills
Samson ... his X Mark

Plate 26 Hernhill churchwardens' Accounts, 1786. Observe the number of crosses, indicating the signature illiteracy of the village elite: signature illiteracy did not preclude the exercise of local office in the eighteenth century. Such office-holding 'illiteracy' was rare by the mid nineteenth century.

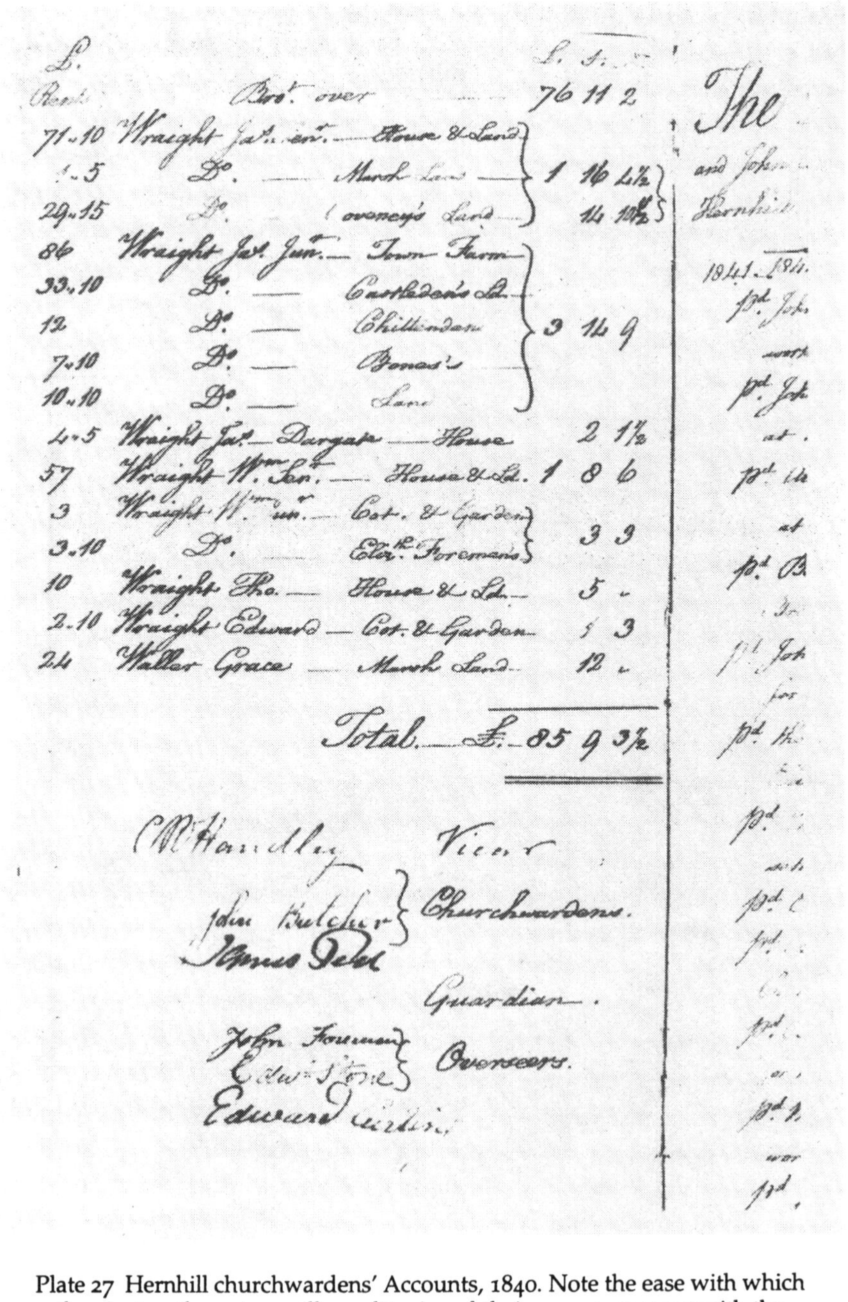

Plate 27 Hernhill churchwardens' Accounts, 1840. Note the ease with which the nineteenth-century village elite signed their names: contrast with the literacy of their eighteenth-century counterparts in plate 26. John Butcher was a farmer; James Pell was a cattle dealer and landlord of several cottages; Edward Curling was a farmer; John Foreman was a wheelwright and farmer; Edward Stone was a minor gentleman; and Charles Handley, who lived in Hernhill's 'big house' in 1840, was the parish vicar.

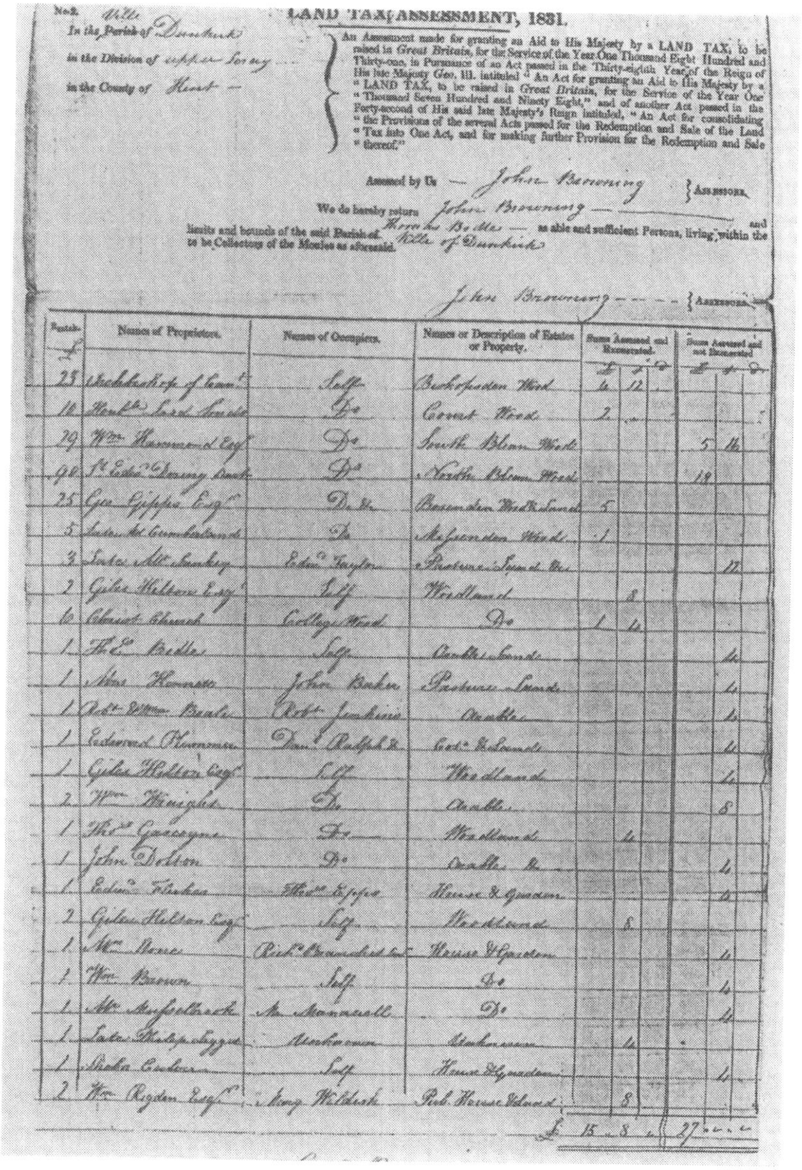

No. 2. Ville
In the Parish of Dunkirk
in the Division of upper Scray
in the County of Kent

LAND TAX ASSESSMENT, 1831.

An Assessment made for granting an Aid to His Majesty by a LAND TAX, to be raised in *Great Britain*, for the Service of the Year One Thousand Eight Hundred and Thirty-one, in Pursuance of an Act passed in the Thirty-eighth Year of the Reign of His late Majesty Geo. III. intituled "An Act for granting an Aid to His Majesty by a "LAND TAX, to be raised in *Great Britain*, for the Service of the Year One "Thousand Seven Hundred and Ninety Eight," and of another Act passed in the Forty-second of His said late Majesty's Reign intituled, "An Act for consolidating "the Provisions of the several Acts passed for the Redemption and Sale of the Land "Tax into One Act, and for making further Provision for the Redemption and Sale "thereof."

Assessed by Us — John Browning } Assessors.

We do hereby return John Browning
Thomas Bedle — as able and sufficient Persons, living within the limits and bounds of the said Parish of Ville of Dunkirk and to be Collectors of the Monies as aforesaid.

John Browning } Assessors.

Rentals £	Names of Proprietors.	Names of Occupiers.	Names or Description of Estates or Property.	Sums Assessed and Exonerated. £	s	d	Sums Assessed and not Exonerated. £	s	d
25	Archbishop of Cantr	Self	Bishopsden Wood	4	12				
10	Honble Lord Sondes	Do	Court Wood	2	–				
29	Wm Hammond Esqr	Do	South Blean Wood				5	16	
90	Sr Edwd Dering Bart	Do	North Blean Wood				18		
25	Geo Gipps Esqr	Do &c	[illegible] Wood & Land	5					
5	Late Mr Cumberland	Do	[illegible] Wood	1					
3	Late Mr Sankey	Edwd Taylor	Pasture Land &c					12	
2	Giles Hilton Esqr	Self	Woodland		8				
10	Christ Church	College Wood	Do	1	4				
1	Thos Bedle	Self	Arable Land					4	
1	[illegible]	John Baker	Pasture Land					4	
1	Robt Wm Beale	Robt Jenkins	Arable					4	
1	Edward Plummer	Danl Ralph &c	Cottg & Land					4	
1	Giles Hilton Esqr	Self	Woodland					4	
2	Wm Wright	Do	Arable					8	
1	Thos Gascoyne	Do	Woodland		4				
1	John Dolton	Do	Arable &c					4	
1	Edwd [illegible]	[illegible]	House & Garden					4	
2	Giles Hilton Esqr	Self	Woodland		8				
1	[illegible]	Richd [illegible] &c	House & Garden					4	
1	Wm Brown	Self	Do					4	
1	[illegible]	[illegible]	Do					4	
1	Late [illegible]	Unknown	Unknown		4				
1	[illegible]	Self	House & Garden					4	
2	Wm Ryder Esqr	Mary Wildish	Pub. House & Land		8				
			£	15	8	–	27	–	–

Plate 28 Land-tax assessment for the Ville of Dunkirk, 1831. An example of functional literacy at the middle levels of society. The assessor, John Browning (who wrote clearly), was a farmer: his will in 1837 described him as a 'husbandman'.

scratches on plates 24 and 25. For some labouring men and women holding a pen was an alien experience. These were hands which could wield a sickle or flail with skill, which were supple enough to tie hops, but manoeuvring a pen was a different matter, even if only to make a mark.

David Cressy has drawn a distinction between 'passive literacy' (reading without writing) and 'active literacy' (those who are able to write as well as read).[87] Yet we should be wary of pursuing this ascription too far. People can read actively; they do not need to write (or even read widely) before they can think in a non-passive way. Liardet talked to a man in Dunkirk who, in response to the former's observation that it was 'a pity there was no gentry in the neighbourhood', replied that he could not see what good they were: 'all they do is to make hard laws to grind us down'. The man also told the lawyer that poaching was not a crime and that because God gave the land to all 'a few can't have no right to the whole of it'. Liardet's informant had not seen a *Penny Magazine*, had never read a newspaper, 'but I read a little in the Testament'.[88]

Above farmworkers, farmers and the crafts and trades – in terms of ease and facility with the pen – stood the gentry, clergy and large landowners of Boughton, Dunkirk and Hernhill, those of Liardet's class. They could keep registers, notebooks and accounts, write frequent letters, draft affidavits and depositions, and more. The vicar of Hernhill, Charles Handley, wrote a memoir of the Courtenay affair.[89] The mother-in-law of John Horsley, Handley's counterpart at Dunkirk, produced a beautifully written, water-colour illustrated, manuscript account of the family's early years in that parish. Horsley himself kept a journal and designed a chandelier, altar cloth and altar rails for his church.[90] Such people inhabited a different cultural world.

VI

The substantial levels of signature illiteracy and the findings of Liardet's cultural survey suggest that literacy was not a *sine qua non* for the day-to-day existence of many of the inhabitants of our communities and not just those in labouring households. Louisa Pay, wife of the proprietor of Woodman's Hall (on the boundary of Dunkirk and

[87] Cressy, 'Levels of illiteracy', p. 105.
[88] Liardet, 'State of the peasantry', pp. 134–5.   [89] CCA, Hernhill Tithe Book, 1853.
[90] 'The history of John William Horsley' (a nineteenth-century handwritten book in the possession of J. W. Horsley, Steyning, Sussex); CKS, U2394 Z1, Family Scrap Book of Revd J. W. Horsley.

Boughton) was unable to write, but she could serve in a public house well enough – in 1851 when a customer tried to pass a counterfeit shilling for a glass of porter she put the coin in her mouth, bit it and declared it 'a bad one'. Her husband too could not sign his own name.[91] The higgler Edward Wraight junior, the beershop-keeper James Goodwin and the publican/farmer Noah Miles were unable to sign their names and were described as illiterate when they were listed in 1838 for their part in the Hernhill rising; there is no evidence that their 'imperfect education' prevented the exercise of their trades.[92] Kemsley, son of a Molash small farmer and dealer, recalled that his illiterate father – an archetypal penny capitalist entrepreneur with a finger in every pie – never kept any written record of his dealings. 'Only here. In his head.' Kay's father likewise 'ran the farm in his head. He was marvellous at figures.'[93]

And it was always possible to draw upon the skills of others, in household or neighbourhood. Mary Tong, the wife of a Boughton wood-dealer – whose family signature-literacy profile is set out in table 8.7(d) – 'managed the business of her late husband and kept the books'. 'She could not write herself. The entries in the books were made by her children. She could read such writing as her children did.' When she had to take court action over a disputed transaction, 'the account which [was] ... filed in court was made out for her by her grocer'.[94] Mrs E. Clark (born 1885) said that her father, a shoemaker and 'the only man in the village, besides the parson, who could write', wrote letters and made wills for people in Badlesmere and its adjoining parishes.[95]

Writing seemed particularly irrelevant to the agricultural and wood-land workers who comprised the bulk of the population in this part of Kent. When Boughton labourers wanted to subscribe to the local coal club which provided fuel for its members in the winter season, the treasurer (the landlord of a public house) signed for them. Labourers relied on their sense of smell, touch and sight to function in their world and upon their skill and strength. They had to wield a bagging or bill hook rather than a pen. Writing was a skill beyond their realm of expectation. 'Master ... if I could do that [meaning write], I would not use the flail and the shovel.'[96] It should be recognized that the inability to read and write – as the examples of Kemsley and Kay suggest – did not preclude basic numeracy. Harry Matthews, brought up in turn-of-

---

[91] CKS, Q/SBe 207, East Kent Quarter Sessions, January 1852; family reconstitutions.
[92] Information from family reconstitution and the list of rioters in PRO, HO/40/36/435–41.
[93] TL, F. Kemsley, b. 1887; Hernhill Oral History, H. Kay, b. 1921.
[94] *Faversham Mercury*, 18 May 1878.
[95] TL, E. Clark, b. 1885.   [96] *The Times*, 9 June 1838.

the-century Faversham, said that neither of his parents could read or write; he had to write their letters for them. 'But my father, if you were to say to him, say, how much would fifty hop-poles come to, $4\frac{1}{2}$d. each, or something like that, he'd tell you before you could hardly look round.'[97]

The evidence from the Blean fully supports David Levine's work on the nineteenth-century Midland village of Shepshed. In only a minority of Boughton, Dunkirk and Hernhill families – as we saw earlier – could both parents and all the children (if they had them) sign their names. Most of the totally literate families were to be found among the farmers and craftsmen, but even in these groups they were in a minority. As Levine has pointed out, 'the very haphazardness with which this skill was handed down from generation to generation seems to question the value which parents (and their children) placed on it ... it does not seem that literacy was inordinately prized'.[98]

It may be objected that the weight of my argument is unduly negative, so let me stress that the nineteenth century was a time of transition to predominant literacy. The figures and tables demonstrate impressive gains in signature literacy. England, David Vincent has written, 'for the first time in history achieved a literate society ... literacy spread into every interstice of English society'.[99] If I have lingered on those least affected by the transition, it is because of their relative absence from the historiography. It is certainly ironic that when one deals with the labouring population it is far easier to account for their non-acquisition of literacy and lack of schooling than it is to explain why a farmworker might want to read and write.

It is unlikely that historians will ever abandon their functional definition of literacy – indeed I have used it myself to chart trends and to note differences according to gender and class. But the implicit argument of this chapter is that although this measurement of literacy has its value, it has to be employed with a great deal of circumspection. Graphs can be misleading. The decline of the so-called 'illiteracy' of labouring women in the rural areas of nineteenth-century England may merely reflect the acquisition of an additional skill, that of writing, rather than any spectacular leap from illiterate to literate.[100] The rising curve of the graph of male literacy hides the less than dramatic improvement for agricultural labourers.

---

[97] TL, H. Matthews, b. 1890.
[98] Levine, 'Education and family life', p. 378. For an example of haphazardness, see table 8.6(c) above.
[99] Vincent, *Literacy and popular culture*, p. 1.
[100] A conclusion also reached by Vincent: *ibid.*, p. 104.

Signatures and marks tell us little of educational skills, of reading ability or levels of comprehension. Yet we should certainly not follow Michael Sanderson in simply dismissing those who cannot write their own names as illiterate: 'In no sense can they be regarded as literate'.[101] Those who made a mark included large numbers of readers and to exclude them from the category 'literate' would be to fundamentally misunderstand the cultural context of nineteenth-century England, where, for the labouring population, reading was literacy. The simple dichotomy between 'literate' and 'illiterate' implied by much of the statistical work on literacy in the past masks the complexities of popular culture. As we have seen, we should think of a range of cultures, of *literacies* rather than literate and non-literate or illiterate. As Cressy once put it, the ability or inability to write a signature may be one of the less significant, and least interesting, aspects of literacy.[102]

[101] M. Sanderson, *Education, economic change and society in England, 1780–1870* (London, 1983), p. 10.
[102] Cressy, 'Levels of illiteracy', p. 106

Conclusion

Plate 29 Boughton Street at the turn of the century.

9

Microhistories

I

Nineteenth- and early twentieth-century commentators on rural England have shown little understanding of the men and women who worked the land. 'I was like a man travelling in a foreign country.' 'If one could get down to understand village life! I have reached that initiatory stage in which one is convinced of ignorance ... It were as easy to write of the Chinese.' 'No-one knows the labourer.'[1] Rural workers have fared little better at the hands of some later twentieth-century historians who tend to see them (much as Thomas Hardy had) through the eyes of farmers.[2] While it does not ignore other sections of society, this book focuses on those firmly part of the labouring community: the craftsmen and petty traders, the woodcutters and charcoal burners of Dunkirk, the brick and tile makers of Boughton, laundresses, beershop-keepers, domestic servants, the dealers, those who eked out a living on one- or two-acre plots, and the bulk of the population, women and children as well as men, who worked in the fields and orchards and hop-grounds as agricultural labourers or farmworkers.

The environments that they inhabited were as varied as their means of subsistence. There were landscapes within the landscape – marsh, forest, orchard, corn-land, hop. Those who lived in the marshes suffered the summer ravages of mosquitoes; while pockets of pollution

[1] C. Holdenby, *Folk of the Furrow* (London, 1913), pp. 26–7; G. Sturt, *Change in the Village* (1912) and *Journals of George Sturt, 1890–1927* (1967), quoted in K. D. M. Snell, *Annals of the labouring poor: social change and agrarian England 1660–1900* (Cambridge, 1985), p. 6.

[2] I am thinking of A. Armstrong, *Farmworkers: a social and economic history 1770–1980* (London, 1988). For a wider critique, see K. D. M. Snell, 'Agrarian histories and our rural past', *Journal of Historical Geography*, 17 (1991), pp. 195–203.

257

in Boughton and Hernhill cut a deadly swath through the lives of the very young.

The advantage of placing a small community under the microscope is that it becomes possible to see and explore the complexity of social interaction and social and economic processes. The settlements of the Blean were not static, isolated communities but highly geographically mobile. As we have seen, over a given ten years about half the population would have left their parishes. A few went as far as North America, Australia and New Zealand. There was compensatory movement into the area as well: censuses between 1851 and 1881 show that between 60 and 70 per cent of the population aged 15 years and over came from outside the parish. And yet the majority of movement was localized, within walking distance, the rural worker's five-mile radius. Of several hundred emigrants from Dunkirk and Hernhill living in parishes within a ten-mile arc in 1851, nearly 90 per cent had moved less than five miles away. Every census between 1851 and 1881 shows that as many as 45 per cent of the inhabitants aged 15 and over were born outside the parish but in a place less than five miles away. In other words, from 64 to 77 per cent of the adult population lived less than five miles from their place of birth.[3]

Contrary to the claims of some historians, mobility did not disrupt the ties of kinship. This pattern of dynamic localism occurred in societies where kin were all around, where kinship was part of neighbourhood.

The family is central to understanding these communities of our past, but a focus on the nuclear family, headed by a male breadwinner, will not get us far. Histories of farmworkers which stress the role of the adult male wage earner to the neglect of the contributions that women and children made to the family economy sit oddly in the Blean, where what Andrew August has called 'the culture of female work' was strong – whatever the middle-class norm.[4] Families were adaptive and flexible too. They expanded as the need arose to care for an illegitimate grandchild, a deserted daughter or an elderly parent.

Most people married young and had large families. But we have seen that labouring couples did not await some late nineteenth-century, middle-class lead in fertility control. There is demographic evidence that labouring families were practising forms of family limitation after the 1830s, perhaps in response to the New Poor Law.

---

[3] Based on detailed work with the Census Enumerators' Books.
[4] August was referring to working-class London. See A. August, 'How separate a sphere? Poor women and paid work in late-Victorian London', *Journal of Family History*, 19 (1994), p. 305.

Twentieth-century oral informants refer to withdrawal and abstinence (one talked of the 'push him off' method of birth control!) and to a local woman who performed abortions.[5] Presumably similar methods were used in the nineteenth century.

Class was central to this rural world, although I have been at pains to describe the complexities of workers' social identities. There were fine hierarchies at the labouring level. Self-perceptions changed with situation and context. But demographic class cohesion, socialization and patterns of land ownership maintained a rural working class, in culture as well as structure.

The culture of the Blean was as complex as its economy and society and there are interesting gaps between the dominant discourses of the nation's middle class and practice in the village. Illegitimacy and bridal pregnancy were commonplace, indicating a sexual culture – while not without its own controls and mores – far removed from that of middle-class prescriptions. England became a 'literate society', yet the Blean provides important evidence for cultural mixes, of multiple literacies and persisting orality. Literacy (as we think of it) did not hold high priority for rural working people.

II

The title of this book is rather un-English and some practitioners of local history may object to having their subject renamed in this way. So let me emphasize that I have drawn on a long and highly developed tradition of English local history, ranging from Alan Everitt's sense of landscape to Charles Phythian-Adams' exploration of the link between local and national societies. The work of Jean Robin has been influential, for example; and I can still recall the time I first read Margaret Spufford's *Contrasting communities* (1974). It would require a chapter in itself to explain such debts.[6]

While firmly situated within this English tradition, I depart from it in several ways. Twenty years ago, in a review article which dealt with village studies, Keith Wrightson discussed two major research strategies open to local historians. The first, he termed the approach of 'total history', 'the assembly of every discoverable record relating to a particular locality and the attempt to obtain as full a picture of local life as the sources permit'. The second approach was that of 'village sampling', the selection of a particular subject or issue which is then

---

5   Hernhill Oral History, D. Tong, b. 1912.
6   For a thought-provoking summary of such work, see C. Phythian-Adams, *Re-thinking English local history* (Leicester, 1987).

explored or tested in a variety of local studies. The danger of 'total history', warned Wrightson, was that it could end up as the history of trivia; while the problem of sampling was that, blinded by a single issue, it could be oblivious to the complexity of the local context.[7]

Strictly speaking, *Microhistories* falls into neither category. Although there are elements of 'total history' in the sense that it employs 'total reconstitution', the book is not a comprehensive history of the Blean or even of one village or hamlet. Although it uses the local to explore wider issues, my book is certainly not a 'village sampling' and is acutely aware of the complexity of the local context.

The title *Microhistories* is a declaration of both methodological direction and theoretical conviction. The local is the site for exploring significant social change and for teasing out important historiographical issues. As Giovanni Levi has commented (paraphrasing Clifford Geertz) microhistorians 'do not study villages, they study in villages'.[8] The guiding principle of microhistory is historical research on a reduced scale, under the microscope so to speak, with the conviction that detailed observation and analysis will not only uncover unknown complexities and reveal 'new meanings' in structures, processes, belief systems and human interaction, but sometimes even – as Italian practitioners have pointed out – render macrohistorical analyses irrelevant. Although the focus in much microhistory has been on the subaltern, the 'lost peoples of Europe', its subject matter is virtually limitless: a community, social group, family or individual, a trial, battle, ritual, riot, a work of art, an encounter or a gesture.[9]

The interrelationship between the specific and the general is crucial to my work. The subject matter of the book's chapters – fertility, mortality, work (widely defined), class, family and kinship, sexuality, orality and literacy – benefits from a marked awareness of local context. The importance of context is one of the dominant themes of the book. As David Sabean has explained, the '*local* is interesting precisely because it offers a *locus* for observing relations ... Once we center our attention on relationships, we are forced into research

[7]   K. Wrightson, 'Villages, villagers and village studies', *Historical Journal*, 18 (1975), pp. 632–9.
[8]   G. Levi, 'On microhistory', in P. Burke (ed.), *New perspectives on historical writing* (Oxford, 1991), p. 96.
[9]   For the merits and methodologies of microhistory, see Levi, 'On microhistory'; D. W. Sabean, *Property, production, and family in Neckarhausen, 1700–1870* (Cambridge, 1990), pp. 7–12; E. Muir. 'Introduction: observing trifles', in E. Muir and G. Ruggiero (eds.), *Microhistory and the lost peoples of Europe* (Baltimore, 1991), pp. vii–xxviii; C. Ginzburg and C. Poni, 'The name and the game: unequal exchange and the historiographical marketplace', in Muir and Ruggiero (eds.), *Microhistory*, ch. 1; C. Ginzburg, 'Microhistory', *Critical Inquiry*, 20 (1993), pp. 10–35.

strategies which favor the local and the particular.'[10] And yet all the topics covered in *Microhistories* depend on analysis of wider economic, social and cultural developments. It is not local history written in isolation from wider processes.

They rarely use the term, but there are English practitioners of microhistory. David Levine and Keith Wrightson's detailed studies of small rural, proto-industrial and industrial communities have changed our ways of thinking about the population, economy and society of England's past.[11] This book would never have appeared without the stimulus of their work.

If my geographical focus is narrow, I trust that this is more than compensated by its methodological range. *Microhistories* can be read as an experiment in combining the oral, demographic and social-structural, an incursion across borders into territories and traditions of historical research which – to their collective and individual poverty – have too long maintained artificially separate agendas, strategies and personnel. Although I am conscious of some originality of approach here (such holism is rare in the writing of English local history), I am also aware of a strong affinity to what has been termed the 'new rural history', advocated and practised by Keith Snell and others connected with the journal *Rural History*. *Microhistories* likewise aims to replace the older 'agricultural history' ('plough and cow' history) with a more widely defined and methodologically adventurous rural social history.[12]

III

Reviews of the local study invariably become embroiled in rather facile discussion about the respective merits of macro and micro analysis. The intention behind this small study is to engage with big questions, to challenge received opinion. But it is not part of any empirical project to piece together a cumulative picture, community by community, for the whole of the nation; or to arrive at some ultimate, definitive solution to a historical question. Although historians continually generalize and provide broad sweeps (often, ironically, on the basis of a few microstudies), I have no great faith in the attainment of the

[10] Sabean, *Property, production, and family*, pp. 10–11.
[11] D. Levine, *Family formation in an age of nascent capitalism* (New York, 1977); K. Wrightson and David Levine, *Poverty and piety in an English village: Terling, 1525–1700* (London, 1979); Wrightson and Levine, *The making of an industrial society: Whickham 1560–1765* (Oxford, 1991).
[12] See the first issue of *Rural History: Economy, Society, Culture* (1990). See also Snell's review of Armstrong's *Farmworkers*, in *Social History*, 15 (1990), pp. 120–2.

definitive account, the 'big picture'. By the time the first few empirical studies appear in print, the agenda has usually changed and new questions are being asked. There is no last word in the writing of history.

There is a sense in which this book is a series of essays situating what have been described as 'knowable communities' in the wider worlds of demographic, social and cultural change. It is what could be termed 'strategically situated' social history.[13] But the cultural flow is not one way. The aim has been not just to explore the working out of wider social and cultural processes at a local level, but to use the local to challenge our view of the very nature of these processes. The issues that we are dealing with are neither trivial nor peripheral: the decline in fertility, the mortality transition, the making of class, the shift to total literacy, are among the great transformations in European history. The message of this book is that it is impossible to understand society and culture without examining local contexts. We will never unravel the meanings of class and the structures of kinship, challenge 'the adult male wage' as the main unit of analysis for economic and labour historians, explore the 'multiple paths' of Europe's demographic revolution, comprehend the complexities of the cultures of popular literacy or locate the slippages between the condemnatory discourse of Victorian moralists and popular sexuality, other than by detailed work at the level of the locality.

But I want to go even further than this in my argument. For it seems to me that the local is central to the nature of the historical process. In the end, all history is microhistory. I have applied the methodology of microhistory to a limited number of subjects, but my argument for the centrality of the local could equally apply, say, to histories of gender, migration, ethnicity, politics, religion, war and crime. Indeed it is difficult to think of any fraction of the historical process which is not sited in the locality. Histories which exclude the 'knowable community' are histories half written. We will never fully understand the social and cultural processes of our past (and our present) until we recognize them as microhistories.

---

[13] G. E. Marcus and M. M. J. Fischer, *Anthropology as cultural critique: an experimental moment in the human sciences* (Chicago, 1986), ch. 4.

Bibliography

(Place of publication is London unless otherwise stated.)

Akerman, S., Johansen, H. C. and Gaunt, D. (eds.), *Chance and change* (Odense, 1978)

Alexander, S., Davin, A. and Hostettler, E., 'Labouring women', *History Workshop*, 8 (1979), pp. 174–82

Allen, R. C., *Enclosure and the yeoman: the agricultural development of the south Midlands 1450–1850* (Oxford, 1992)

Anderson, M., *Family structure in nineteenth century Lancashire* (Cambridge, 1971)

'The study of family structure', in E. A. Wrigley (ed.), *Nineteenth-century society* (Cambridge, 1972), ch. 2

'Marriage patterns in Victorian Britain: an analysis based on registration district data for England and Wales 1861', *Journal of Family History*, 1 (1976), pp. 55–78

'The relevance of family history', in C. Harris (ed.), *The sociology of the family* (Sociological Review Monograph, 28, 1979), pp. 49–73

Approaches to the history of the western family 1500–1914 (1980)

'The emergence of the modern life cycle in Britain', *Social History*, 10 (1985), pp. 69–87

The 1851 census: a guide to the national sample of the enumerators' returns (Cambridge, 1987)

'Households, families and individuals: some preliminary results from the national sample from the 1851 census of Great Britain', *Continuity and Change*, 3 (1988), pp. 421–38

Population change in north-western Europe, 1750–1850 (1988)

'The social implications of demographic change', in F. M. L. Thompson (ed.), *The Cambridge social history of Britain 1750–1950*, vol. II, *People and their environment* (Cambridge, 1990), ch. 1

Anderson, P., *The printed image and the transformation of popular culture 1790–1860* (Oxford, 1991)

Anderton, D. L. and Bean, L. L., 'Birth spacing and fertility limitation', *Demography*, 22 (1985), pp. 169–83

Armstrong, [W.] A., 'The use of information about occupation', in E. A. Wrigley (ed.), *Nineteenth-century society* (Cambridge, 1972), ch. 6

263

Farmworkers: a social and economic history 1770–1980 (1988)
'Labour I', in G. E. Mingay (ed.), *The agrarian history of England and Wales*, vol. VI, *1750–1850* (Cambridge, 1989), ch. 7
'Labour II', in G. E. Mingay (ed.), *The agrarian history of England and Wales*, vol. VI, *1750–1850* (Cambridge, 1989), ch. 8
'The countryside', in F. M. L. Thompson (ed.), *The Cambridge social history of Britain 1750–1950*, vol. I, *Regions and communities* (Cambridge, 1990), ch. 2
Arnold, R., *The farthest promised land: English villagers, New Zealand immigrants of the 1870s* (Wellington, 1981)
August, A., 'How separate a sphere? Poor women and paid work in late-Victorian London', *Journal of Family History*, 19 (1994), pp. 285–309
Ayers, P., 'The hidden economy of dockland families: Liverpool in the 1930s', in P. Hudson and W. R. Lee (eds.), *Women's work and the family economy in historical perspective* (Manchester, 1990), ch. 11
Baker, A. R. H. and Gregory, D. (eds.), *Explorations in historical geography* (Cambridge, 1984)
Banks, J. A., *Victorian values: secularism and the size of families* (1981)
Barber, J., '"Stolen goods": the sexual harassment of female servants in west Wales during the nineteenth century', *Rural History*, 4 (1993), pp. 123–36
Barker, T. and Drake, M. (eds.), *Population and society in Britain 1850–1980* (New York, 1982)
Barret-Ducrocq, F., *Love in the time of Victoria* (1991)
Beckett, J. V., *A History of Laxton: England's last open-field village* (Oxford, 1989)
Bell, R. M., *Fate and honor, family and village: demographic and cultural change in rural Italy since 1800* (Chicago, 1979)
Bengtsson, T., Fridlizius, G. and Ohlsson, R. (eds.), *Pre-industrial population change: the mortality decline and short-term population movements* (Stockholm, 1984)
Benson, J., *The penny capitalists* (Dublin, 1983)
(ed.), *The working class in England 1875–1914* (1985)
The working class in Britain 1850–1939 (1989)
Blaikie, J. A. D., 'The country and the city: sexuality and social class in Victorian Scotland', in G. Kearns and C. W. J. Withers (eds.), *Urbanising Britain: essays on class and community in the nineteenth century* (Cambridge, 1991), ch. 4
Bongaarts, J., 'A method for the estimation of fecundability', *Demography*, 12 (1975), pp. 645–60
'The proximate determinants of natural marital fertility', in R. A. Bulatao and R. D. Lee (eds.), *Determinants of fertility in developing countries*, vol. I (New York, 1983), ch. 4
and Burch, T. and Wachter, K. (eds.), *Family demography, methods and their applications* (Oxford, 1987)
Bouchard, G., 'Mobile populations, stable communities: social and demographic processes in the rural parishes of the Saguenay, 1840–1911', *Continuity and Change*, 6 (1991), pp. 59–86
and de Pourbaix, I., 'Individual and family life courses in the Saguenay region, Quebec, 1842–1911', *Journal of Family History*, 12 (1987), pp. 225–42
Bouquet, M., *Family, servants and visitors: the farm household in nineteenth and twentieth century Devon* (Norwich, 1985)
Bowley, A. L., *Wages in the United Kingdom in the nineteenth century* (Cambridge, 1900)

Bradley, H., *Men's work, women's work* (Cambridge, 1989)

Bradley, L., 'An enquiry into seasonality in baptisms, marriages and burials. Part 3: burial seasonality', in M. Drake (ed.), *Population studies from parish registers* (Matlock, 1982), ch. 12

Bradley, T. and Lowe, P. (eds.), *Locality and rurality: economy and society in rural regions* (Norwich, 1984)

Brandon, P. and Short, B., *The south east from AD 1000* (1990)

Brandstrom, A., 'The impact of female labour conditions on infant mortality: a case study of the parishes of Nedertornea and Jokkmokk, 1800–96', *Social History of Medicine*, 1 (1988), pp. 329–58

and Sundin, J. (eds.), *Tradition and transition: studies in microdemography and social change* (Umea, 1981)

Brumberg, J. J., ' "Ruined" girls: changing community responses to illegitimacy in upstate New York, 1890–1920', *Journal of Social History*, 18 (1984–5), pp. 247–72

Buchanan, I., 'Infant feeding, sanitation and diarrhoea in colliery communities 1880–1911', in D. J. Oddy and D. S. Miller (eds.), *Diet and health in modern Britain* (Dover, New Hampshire, 1985), ch. 8

Burke, P., *Popular culture in early modern Europe* (1978)

Burnett, J., *Plenty and want: a social history of diet in England from 1815 to the present day* (1979 edn)

A social history of housing 1815–1985 (1986 edn)

Carter, I., 'Class and culture among farm servants in the north-east, 1840–1914', in A. A. MacLaren (ed.), *Social class in Scotland* (Edinburgh, 1976), ch. 6

'Illegitimate births and illegitimate inferences', *Scottish Journal of Sociology*, 1 (1977), pp. 125–35

Farm life in north-east Scotland (Edinburgh, 1979)

Chamberlain, M., *Fenwomen: a portrait of women in an English village* (1975)

Chartier, R., 'The practical impact of writing', in R. Chartier (ed.), *A history of private life: passions of the Renaissance* (Cambridge, Mass., 1989), pp. 111–59

Chartres, J. A., 'Country tradesmen', in G. Mingay (ed.), *The Victorian country-side* (1981), ch. 22

and Turnbull, J. A., 'Country craftsmen', in G. Mingay (ed.), *The Victorian countryside* (1981), ch. 23

Chaytor, M., 'Household and kinship: Ryton in the late 16th and early 17th centuries', *History Workshop*, 10 (1980), pp. 25–60

Childs, M. J., *Labour's apprentices: working-class lads in late Victorian and Edwardian England* (1992)

Chinn, C., *They worked all their lives: women of the urban poor in England, 1880–1939* (Manchester, 1988)

Christie, A. B., *Infectious diseases* (1980)

Cleland, J. and Wilson, C., 'Demand theories of the fertility transition: an iconoclastic view', *Population Studies*, 41 (1987), pp. 5–30

Coale, A. J. and Demeny, P., *Regional model life tables and stable populations* (New York, 1983)

Cohen, A. P., *The symbolic construction of community* (1985)

(ed.), *Symbolising boundaries* (Manchester, 1986)

Collins, E. J. T., 'The agricultural servicing and processing industries', in G. E. Mingay (ed.), *The agrarian history of England and Wales*, vol. VI, *1750–1850* (Cambridge, 1989), ch. 5

Conley, C. A., 'Rape and justice in Victorian England', *Victorian Studies*, 29 (1985–6), pp. 519–36
The unwritten law: criminal justice in Victorian Kent (New York, 1991)
Coontz, S., *The social origins of private life: a history of American families, 1600–1900* (1988)
Cosgrove, D. and Daniels, S. (eds.), *The iconography of landscape* (Cambridge, 1988)
Crafts, N. F. R., 'Average age at first marriage for women in mid-nineteenth-century England and Wales: a cross-section study', *Population Studies*, 32 (1978), pp. 21–5
'Duration of marriage, fertility and women's employment opportunities in England and Wales in 1911', *Population Studies*, 43 (1989), pp. 325–35
Creighton, C., *A history of epidemics in Britain* (2 vols., 1965 edn), vol. II
Cressy, D., *Literacy and the social order: reading and writing in Tudor and Stuart England* (Cambridge, 1980)
'Levels of illiteracy in England, 1530–1730', in H. J. Graff (ed.), *Literacy and social development in the West* (Cambridge, 1981), ch. 6
'The environment for literacy: accomplishment and context in seventeenth-century England and New England', in D. P. Resnick (ed.), *Literacy in historical perspective* (Washington, 1983), pp. 23–42
'The seasonality of marriage in old and New England', *Journal of Interdisciplinary History*, 16 (1985), pp. 1–21
'Kinship and kin interaction in early modern England', *Past and Present*, 113 (1986), pp. 38–69
'Literacy in context: meaning and measurement in early modern England', in J. Brewer and R. Porter (eds.), *Consumption and the world of goods* (1993), ch. 15
Crossick, G., 'From gentleman to the residuum: languages of social description in Victorian Britain', in P. Corfield (ed.), *Language, history and class* (Oxford, 1991), ch. 7
Crow, G. and Allan, G., *Community life: an introduction to local social relations* (1994)
Cunningham, H., 'The employment and unemployment of children in England c. 1680–1851', *Past and Present*, 126 (1990), pp. 115–50
Danhieux, L., 'The evolving household: the case of Lampernisse, West Flanders', in R. Wall, J. Robin and P. Laslett (eds.), *Family forms in historic Europe* (Cambridge, 1983), ch. 13
Davey, B. J., *Ashwell, 1830–1914: the decline of a village community* (Leicester, 1980)
Davidoff, L., 'Mastered for life: servant and wife in Victorian and Edwardian England', *Journal of Social History*, 7 (1974), pp. 406–28
'The family in Britain', in F. M. L. Thompson (ed.), *The Cambridge social history of Britain 1750–1950*, vol. II, *People and their environment* (Cambridge, 1990), ch. 2
and Hall, C., *Family fortunes: men and women of the English middle class 1780–1850* (1987)
Davies, A., *Leisure, gender and poverty: working-class culture in Salford and Manchester, 1900–1939* (Buckingham, 1992)
and Fielding, S., *Workers' worlds: cultures and communities in Manchester and Salford, 1880–1939* (Manchester, 1992)

Davies, R., ' "In a broken dream": some aspects of sexual behaviour and the dilemmas of the unmarried mother in south west Wales, 1887–1914', *Llafur*, 3 (1983), pp. 24–33

Davin, A., 'Child labour, the working-class family, and domestic ideology in 19th century Britain', *Development and Change*, 13 (1982), pp. 633–52

'Working or helping? London working-class children in the domestic economy', in J. Smith, I Wallerstein and H.-D. Evers (eds.), *Households and the world economy* (Beverly Hills, 1984), ch. 14

'When is a child not a child?', in H. Corr and L. Jamieson (eds.), *Politics of everyday life* (1990), ch. 3

Digby, A. and Searby, P., *Children, school and society in nineteenth-century England* (1981)

Dobson, M., ' "Marsh fever" – the geography of malaria in England', *Journal of Historical Geography*, 6 (1980), pp. 357–89

Donajgrodzki, A. P., 'Twentieth-century rural England: a case for "peasant studies"?', *Journal of Peasant Studies*, 16 (1989), pp. 425–42

Drake, M., 'The census, 1801–1891', in E. A. Wrigley (ed.), *Nineteenth-century society* (Cambridge, 1972), ch. 1

(ed.), *Population studies from parish registers* (Matlock, 1982)

(ed.), *Time, family and community: perspectives on family and community history* (Oxford, 1994)

and Finnegan, R. (eds.), *Sources and methods for family and community historians: a handbook* (Cambridge, 1994)

Driver, F., *Power and pauperism: the workhouse system 1834–1884* (Cambridge, 1993)

Dupree, M., 'The community perspective in family history: the Potteries during the nineteenth century', in A. L. Beier, D. Cannadine and J. M. Rosenheim (eds.), *The first modern society* (Cambridge, 1989), ch. 16

Dyson, T. and Murphy, M., 'The onset of fertility transition', *Population and Development Review*, 11 (1985), pp. 399–440

Eriksson, I. and Rogers, J., (eds.), *Rural labor and population change: social and demographic developments in east-central Sweden during the nineteenth century* (Uppsala, 1978)

Evans, G. E., *The horse in the furrow* (1960)

The pattern under the plough (1966)

The farm and the village (1969)

Where beards wag all: the relevance of the oral tradition (1970)

Everitt, A., *Transformation and tradition: aspects of the Victorian countryside* (Norwich, 1984)

Landscape and community in England (1985)

Eversley, D. E. C., 'Exploitation of parish registers by aggregative analysis', in E. A. Wrigley (ed.), *Introduction to English historical demography* (New York, 1966), ch. 3

Fairchilds, C., 'Female sexual attitudes and the rise of illegitimacy: a case study', *Journal of Interdisciplinary History*, 8 (1978), pp. 627–67

Faragher, J. M., 'Open-country community: Sugar Creek, Illinois, 1820–1850', in S. Hahn and J. Prude (eds.), *The countryside in the age of capitalist transformation* (Chapel Hill, 1985), ch. 8

Fentress, J. and Wickham, C., *Social memory* (Oxford, 1992)

Finnegan, R. and Drake, M. (eds.), *From family tree to family history* (Cambridge, 1994)

Fliess, K. H., 'Fertility, nuptiality, and family limitation among the Wends of Serbin, Texas, 1845 to 1920', *Journal of Family History*, 13 (1988), pp. 251–63

Floud, R., Wachter, K. and Gregory, A., *Height, health and history: nutritional status in the United Kingdom, 1750–1980* (Cambridge, 1990)

Frykman, J., 'Sexual intercourse and social norms: a study of illegitimate births in Sweden 1831–1933', *Ethnologia Scandinavica*, 3 (1975), pp. 111–50

Furet, F. and Ozouf, J., *Reading and writing: literacy in France from Calvin to Jules Ferry* (Cambridge, 1982)

Gardner, P., *The lost elementary schools of Victorian England* (1984)

Garrett, E. M., 'The trials of labour', *Continuity and Change*, 5 (1990), pp. 121–54

and Reid, A., 'Satanic mills, pleasant lands: spatial variation in women's work, fertility and infant mortality as viewed from the 1911 census', *Historical Research*, 67 (1994), pp. 156–77

Gaunt, D., 'Family planning and the pre-industrial society: some Swedish evidence', in K. Agren and others, *Aristocrats, farmers, proletarians* (Uppsala, 1973), pp. 28–59

Gay, P., *The bourgeois experience, Victoria to Freud* (2 vols., Oxford, 1984, 1986)

Gerard, J., *Country house life: family and servants, 1815–1914* (Oxford, 1994)

Gillis, J. R., 'Servants, sexual relations, and the risks of illegitimacy in London, 1801–1900', *Feminist Studies*, 5 (1979), pp. 142–73

For better, for worse: British marriages, 1600 to the present (New York, 1985)

and Tilly, L. A. and Levine, D. (eds.), *The European experience of declining fertility: a quiet revolution, 1850–1970* (Oxford, 1992)

Ginzburg, C., 'Microhistory', *Critical Inquiry*, 20 (1993), pp. 10–35

and Poni, C., 'The name and the game: unequal exchange and the historiographical marketplace', in E. Muir and G. Ruggiero (eds.), *Microhistory and the lost peoples of Europe* (Baltimore, 1991), ch. 1

Gittins, D., 'Between the devil and the deep blue sea: the marriage and labor markets in nineteenth-century England', in J. Friedlander, B. W. Cook, A. Kessler-Harris and C. Smith-Rosenberg (eds.), *Women in culture and politics: a century of change* (Bloomington, 1986), pp. 18–31

'Marital status, work and kinship, 1850–1930', in J. Lewis (ed.), *Labour and love* (Oxford, 1986), ch. 10

Golby, J. (ed.), *Communities and families* (Cambridge, 1994)

Goldstone, J. A., 'The demographic revolution in England: a re-examination', *Population Studies*, 49 (1986), pp. 5–33

Goldthorpe, J. E., *Family life in western societies: a historical sociology of family relationships in Britain and North America* (Cambridge, 1987)

Gomershall, M., 'Ideals and realities: the education of working-class girls, 1800–1870', *History of Education*, 17 (1988), pp. 37–53

Graff, H. J., *The legacies of literacy: continuities and contradictions in western culture and society* (Bloomington, 1987)

Groneman, C. and Norton, M. B. (eds.), *"To Toil the Livelong Day"* (Ithaca, 1987)

Grey, E., *Cottage life in a Hertfordshire village* (Harpenden, 1977)

Grigg, D., 'Farm size in England and Wales from early Victorian times to the present', *Agricultural History Review*, 35 (1987), pp. 179–89

Grubb, F. W., 'Growth of literacy in colonial America: longitudinal patterns, economic models, and the direction of future research', *Social Science History*, 14 (1990), pp. 451–82

Gutmann, M. P., 'Denomination and fertility decline: the Catholics and

Protestants of Gillespie County, Texas', *Continuity and Change*, 5 (1990), pp. 391–416

Haines, M. R., 'Social class differentials during fertility decline: England and Wales revisited', *Population Studies*, 43 (1989), pp. 305–23

'Western fertility in mid-transition: fertility and nuptiality in the United States and selected nations at the turn of the century', *Journal of Family History*, 15 (1990), pp. 23–48

'Conditions of work and the decline of mortality', in R. Schofield, D. Reher and A. Bideau (eds.), *The decline of mortality in Europe* (Oxford, 1991), ch. 10

Hair, P. E. H., 'Bridal pregnancy in earlier rural England further examined', *Population Studies*, 24 (1970), pp. 59–70

Hall, A., *Fenland worker-peasants: the economy of smallholders at Rippingdale, Lincolnshire, 1791–1871* (Agricultural History Review, Supplement Series, vol. I, 1992)

Hammerton, A. J., *Cruelty and companionship: conflict in nineteenth-century married life* (1992)

Hardy, A., 'Rickets and the rest: child-care, diet and the infectious children's diseases, 1850–1914', *Social History of Medicine*, 5 (1992), pp. 389–412

The epidemic streets: infectious disease and the rise of preventive medicine 1856–1900 (Oxford, 1993)

Hareven, T. K., 'The history of the family and the complexity of social change', *American Historical Review*, 96 (1991), pp. 95–124

Harris, O., 'Households and their boundaries', *History Workshop*, 13 (1982), pp. 143–52

Head-Konig, A.-L., 'Demographic history and its perception of women from the seventeenth to the nineteenth century', in K. Offen, R. R. Pierson and J. Rendall (eds.), *Writing women's history: international perspectives* (1991), ch. 2

Hélias, P.-J., *The horse of pride: life in a Breton village* (New Haven, 1978)

Henderson, J. and Wall, R. (eds.), *Poor women and children in the European past* (London, 1994), ch. 13

Henriques, U. R. Q., 'Bastardy and the New Poor Law', *Past and Present*, 37 (1967), pp. 103–29

Higgs, E., 'Domestic servants and households in Victorian England', *Social History*, 8 (1983), pp. 201–10

'Domestic service and household production', in A. V. John (ed.), *Unequal opportunities: women's employment in England 1800–1918* (Oxford, 1986), ch. 4

'Women, occupations and work in the nineteenth-century censuses', *History Workshop*, 23 (1987), pp. 59–80

Making sense of the census: the manuscript returns for England and Wales, 1801–1901 (London, 1989)

Hill, B., 'The marriage age of women and the demographers', *History Workshop*, 28 (1989), pp. 129–54

Hinde, P. R. A., 'Household structure, marriage and the institution of service in nineteenth-century rural England', *Local Population Studies*, 35 (1985), pp. 43–51

'The population of a Wiltshire village in the nineteenth century: a reconstitution study of Berwick St James, 1841–71', *Annals of Human Biology*, 14 (1987), pp. 475–85

'The marriage market in the nineteenth century English countryside', *Journal of European Economic History*, 18 (1989), pp. 383–92

and Woods, R. I., 'Variations in historical natural fertility patterns and the measurement of fertility control', *Journal of Biosocial Science*, 16 (1984), pp. 309–21

Hobsbawm, E. J. and Rude, G., *Captain Swing* (1969)

Holderness, B. A., 'Rural tradesmen, 1660–1850: a regional study in Lindsey', *Lincolnshire History and Archaeology*, 7 (1972), pp. 77–83

'The Victorian farmer', in G. Mingay (ed.), *The Victorian countryside* (1981), ch. 17

Holley, 'The two family economies of industrialism: factory workers in Victorian Scotland', *Journal of Family History*, 6 (1981), pp. 57–69

Horn, P., *Victorian countrywomen* (Oxford, 1991)

Horrell, S. and Humphries, J., 'Old questions, new data, and alternative perspectives: families' living standards in the Industrial Revolution', *Journal of Economic History*, 52 (1992), pp. 849–80

Hosgood, C. P., 'The "pigmies of commerce" and the working-class community: small shopkeepers in England, 1870–1914', *Journal of Social History*, 22 (1989), pp. 439–60

Hostettler, E., '"Making do": domestic life among East Anglian labourers, 1890–1910', in L. Davidoff and B. Westover (eds.), *Our work, our lives, our words* (1986), ch. 2

Houlbrooke, R. A., *The English family 1450–1700* (1984)

Houston, R. A., *Scottish literacy and the Scottish identity: illiteracy and society in Scotland and northern England, 1600–1800* (Cambridge, 1985)

Literacy in early modern Europe: culture and education, 1500–1800 (1988)

and Smith, R., 'A new approach to family history?', *History Workshop*, 14 (1982), pp. 120–31

Howkins, A., 'Economic crime and class law: poaching and the game laws, 1840–1880', in S. Burman and B. E. Harrell-Bond (eds.), *The imposition of law* (New York, 1979), ch. 15

'In the sweat of thy face: the labourer and work', in G. Mingay (ed.), *The Victorian countryside* (1981), ch. 36

Reshaping rural England: a social history 1850–1925 (1991)

'The English farm labourer in the nineteenth century: farm, family and community', in B. Short (ed.), *The English rural community: image and analysis* (Cambridge, 1992), ch. 5

'Peasants, servants and labourers: the marginal workforce in British agriculture, c. 1870–1914', *Agricultural History Review*, 92 (1994), pp. 49–62

Hudson, P. and Lee, W. R., 'Women's work and the family economy in historical perspective', in P. Hudson and W. R. Lee (eds.), *Women's work and the family economy in historical perspective* (Manchester, 1990), ch. 1

Hufton, O., 'Women and the family economy in eighteenth-century France', *French Historical Studies*, 9 (1975–6), pp. 1–22

Humphries, S., *A secret world of sex* (1988)

and Mack, J. and Perks, R., *A century of childhood* (1989)

Hunt, E. H., *Regional wage variations in Britain 1850–1914* (Oxford, 1973)

British labour history 1815–1914 (1988)

Hunt, L. (ed.), *The new cultural history* (Berkeley, 1989)

Hurt, J. S., *Elementary schooling and the working classes, 1860–1918* (1979)

Imhof, A. E., 'Historical demography as social history: possibilities in Germany', *Journal of Family History*, 2 (1977), pp. 305–32

'Man and body in the history of the modern age', *Medical History*, 27 (1983), pp. 394–406

Ingram, M., 'The reform of popular culture? Sex and marriage in early modern England', in B. Reay (ed.), *Popular culture in seventeenth-century England* (1985), ch. 4

Church courts, sex and marriage in England, 1570–1640 (Cambridge, 1987)

Innes, J. W., *Class fertility trends in England and Wales 1876–1934* (Princeton, 1938)

Ittmann, K., 'Family limitation and family economy in Bradford, west Yorkshire 1851–1881', *Journal of Social History*, 25 (1991–2), pp. 547–73

Janssens, A., 'Industrialization without family change? The extended family and the life cycle in a Dutch industrial town, 1880–1920', *Journal of Family History*, 11 (1986), pp. 25–42

Jenkins, D., *The agricultural community in south-west Wales at the turn of the twentieth century* (Cardiff, 1971)

'Rural society inside outside', in D. Smith (ed.), *A people and a proletariat: essays in the history of Wales 1780–1980* (1980), pp. 114–26

Jensen, J. M., *Loosening the bonds: mid-Atlantic farm women 1750–1850* (New Haven, 1986)

Promise to the land: essays on rural women (Albuquerque, 1991)

John, A., *Unequal opportunities: women's employment in England 1800–1918* (Oxford, 1986)

Johnson, P., *Saving and spending: the working-class economy in Britain 1870–1939* (Oxford, 1985)

Jones, R., 'Voices of Kentmere: a Lakeland hill farm community', *Oral History Journal*, 15 (1987), pp. 35–41

Jordan, E., 'Female unemployment in England and Wales 1851–1911', *Social History*, 13 (1988), pp. 175–90

Joyce, P., 'Work', in F. M. L. Thompson (ed.), *The Cambridge social history of Britain 1750–1950*, vol. II, *People and their environment* (Cambridge, 1990), ch. 3

Visions of the people: industrial England and the question of class 1848–1914 (Cambridge, 1991)

'A people and a class: industrial workers and the social order in nineteenth-century England', in M. L. Bush (ed.), *Social orders and social classes in Europe since 1500: studies in social stratification* (1992), ch. 11

Kälvemark, A.-S., 'Illegitimacy and marriage in three Swedish parishes in the nineteenth century', in P. Laslett, K. Oosterveen and R. M. Smith (eds.), *Bastardy and its comparative history* (Cambridge, Mass., 1980), ch. 14

Kertzer, D. I., *Family life in central Italy, 1880–1910* (New Brunswick, 1984)

'Household history and sociological theory', *Annual Review of Sociology*, 17 (1991), pp. 155–79

and Hogan, D. P. and Karweit, N., 'Kinship beyond the household in a nineteenth-century Italian town', *Continuity and Change*, 7 (1992), pp. 103–21

King, P., 'Customary rights and women's earnings: the importance of gleaning to the rural labouring poor, 1750–1850', *Economic History Review*, 44 (1991), pp. 461–76

Kintner, H. J., 'Trends and regional differences in breastfeeding in Germany from 1871–1937', *Journal of Family History*, 10 (1985), pp. 163–82
Kitteringham, J., 'Country work girls in nineteenth-century England', in R. Samuel (ed.), *Village life and labour* (1975), part 3
Knodel, J., 'Infant mortality and fertility in three Bavarian villages: an analysis of family histories from the 19th century', *Population Studies*, 22 (1968), pp. 297–318
'Family limitation and the fertility transition: evidence from the age patterns of fertility in Europe and Asia', *Population Studies*, 31 (1977), pp. 219–49
'Natural fertility in pre-industrial Germany', *Population Studies*, 32 (1978), pp. 481–510
'Natural fertility: age patterns, levels and trends', in R. A. Bulatao and R. D. Lee (eds.), *Determinants of fertility in developing countries*, vol. 1 (New York, 1983), ch. 3
'Demographic transitions in German villages', in A. J. Coale and S. Cotts Watkins (eds.), *The decline of fertility in Europe* (Princeton, 1986), ch. 9
'Starting, stopping, and spacing during the early stages of fertility transition: the experience of German village populations in the 18th and 19th centuries', *Demography*, 24 (1987), pp. 143–62
Demographic behavior in the past (Cambridge, 1988)
and Wilson, C., 'The secular increase in fecundity in German village populations', *Population Studies*, 35 (1981), pp. 53–84
Kussmaul, A., *Servants in husbandry in early modern England* (Cambridge, 1981)
'Time and space, hoofs and grain: the seasonality of marriage in England', *Journal of Interdisciplinary History*, 15 (1985), pp. 755–79
A general view of the rural economy of England, 1538–1840 (Cambridge, 1990)
Landers, J., *Death and the metropolis: studies in the demographic history of London, 1670–1830* (Cambridge, 1993)
Lankshear, C., *Literacy, schooling and revolution* (Lewes, 1987)
Laqueur, T. W., 'Toward a cultural ecology of literacy in England, 1600–1850', in D. P. Resnick (ed.), *Literacy in historical perspective* (Washington, 1983), pp. 43–57
'Sexual desire and the market economy during the Industrial Revolution', in D. C. Stanton (ed.), *Discourses of sexuality: from Aristotle to Aids* (Ann Arbor, 1992), pp. 185–215
Laslett, P., *The world we have lost* (1965)
Family life and illicit love in earlier generations (Cambridge, 1977)
'The bastardy prone sub-society', in P. Laslett, K. Oosterveen and R. M. Smith (eds.), *Bastardy and its comparative history* (Cambridge, Mass., 1980), ch. 8
The world we have lost – further explored (1983)
'The family as a knot of individual interests', in R. McC. Netting, R. R. Wilk and E. J. Arnould (eds.), *Households: comparative and historical studies of the domestic group* (Berkeley, 1984), ch. 14
'The character of familial history, its limitations and the conditions for its proper pursuit', in T. Hareven and A. Plakans (eds.), *Family history at the crossroads* (Princeton, 1987), pp. 263–84
'Family, kinship and collectivity as systems of support in pre-industrial Europe: a consideration of the "nuclear-hardship" hypothesis', *Continuity and Change*, 3 (1988), pp. 153–75

and Wall, R. (eds.), *Household and family in past time* (Cambridge, 1972)

Lawton, R. and Pooley, C. G., *Britain 1740–1950: an historical geography* (1992)

Lee, C. H., *British regional employment statistics 1841–1971* (Cambridge, 1971)

'Regional inequalities in infant mortality in Britain, 1861–1971: patterns and hypotheses', *Population Studies*, 45 (1991), pp. 55–65

Lees, L. H., 'Getting and spending: the family budgets of English industrial workers', in J. M. Merriman (ed.), *Consciousness and class experience in nineteenth-century Europe* (New York, 1979), ch. 8

Levi, G., 'Family and kin – a few thoughts', *Journal of Family History*, 15 (1990), pp. 567–78

'On microhistory', in P. Burke (ed.), *New perspectives on historical writing* (Oxford, 1991), ch. 5

Levine, D., *Family formation in an age of nascent capitalism* (New York, 1977)

'Education and family life in early industrial England', *Journal of Family History*, 4 (1979), pp. 368–80

'"For their own reasons": individual marriage decisions and family life', *Journal of Family History*, 10 (1982), pp. 255–64

Reproducing families (Cambridge, 1987)

'Recombinant family formation strategies', *Journal of Historical Sociology*, 2 (1989), pp. 89–115

'Moments in time: a historian's context of declining fertility', in J. R. Gillis, L. A. Tilly and D. Levine (eds.), *The European experience of declining fertility: a quiet revolution, 1850–1970* (Oxford, 1992), pp. 326–38

and Wrightson, K., 'The social context of illegitimacy in early modern England', in P. Laslett, K. Oosterveen and R. M. Smith (eds.), *Bastardy and its comparative history* (Cambridge, Mass., 1980), ch. 5

Lewis, J., (ed.), *Labour and love: women's experience of home and family 1850–1940* (Oxford, 1986)

Lewis, M. (ed.), *Old days in the Kent hop gardens* (Maidstone, 1981)

Lindert, P. H. and Williamson, J. G., 'English workers' living standards during the Industrial Revolution: a new look', *Economic History Review*, 36 (1983), pp. 1–25

Lord, E., 'Communities of common interest: the social landscape of south-east Surrey, 1750–1850', in C. Phythian-Adams (ed.), *Societies, cultures and kinship, 1580–1850* (Leicester, 1993), ch. 4

Lummis, T., *Occupation and society: the East Anglian fishermen 1880–1914* (Cambridge, 1985)

Listening to history (1987)

Macfarlane, A., 'History, anthropology and the study of communities', *Social History*, 5 (1977), pp. 631–52

The origins of English individualism (Oxford, 1978)

'The family, sex and marriage', *History and Theory*, 18 (1979), pp. 103–26

The culture of capitalism (Oxford, 1987)

and Harrison, S. and Jardine, C., *Reconstructing historical communities* (Cambridge, 1977)

Malcolmson, P. E., 'Getting a living in the slums of Victorian Kensington', *London Journal*, 1 (1975), pp. 28–51

English laundresses: a social history, 1850–1930 (Urbana, 1986)

Mandler, P. (ed.), *The uses of charity: the poor on relief in the nineteenth-century metropolis* (Philadelphia, 1990)

Marcus, G. E. and Fischer, M. M. J., *Anthropology as cultural critique: an experimental moment in the human sciences* (Chicago, 1986)

Marks, H., 'On the art of differentiating: proletarianization and illegitimacy in northern Sweden, 1850–1930', *Social Science History*, 18 (1994), pp. 95–126

Markus Hall, F., Stevens, R. and Whyman, J., *The Kent and County Hospital* (Canterbury, 1987)

Marshall, J. D., 'The Lancashire rural labourer in the early nineteenth century', *Transactions of the Lancashire and Cheshire Antiquarian Society*, 71 (1963), pp. 90–128

Martin, J. M., 'Village traders and the emergence of a proletariat in south Warwickshire, 1750–1851', *Agricultural History Review*, 31 (1983), pp. 179–88

Masnick, G. S., 'The demographic impact of breastfeeding: a critical review', *Human Biology*, 51 (1979), pp. 109–25

Mason, M., *The making of Victorian sexuality* (Oxford, 1994)

McKibbin, R., *The ideologies of class: social relations in Britain, 1880–1950* (Oxford, 1990)

McLaren, A., *Birth control in nineteenth-century England* (New York, 1978)

A history of contraception (Oxford, 1990)

Meacham, S., *A life apart: the English working class 1890–1914* (1977)

Medick, H., 'The proto-industrial family economy: the structural function of household and family during the transition from peasant society to industrial capitalism', *Social History*, 3 (1976), pp. 291–315

and Sabean, D. W. (eds.), *Interest and emotion: essays on the study of family and kinship* (Cambridge, 1984)

Miles, A. and Vincent, D., 'A land of "boundless opportunity"?: mobility and stability in nineteenth-century England', in S. Dex (ed.), *Life and work history analyses: qualitative and quantitative developments* (1991), pp. 43–72

(eds.), *Building European society: occupational change and social mobility in Europe 1840–1940* (Manchester, 1993)

Miller, C., 'The hidden workforce: female field workers in Gloucestershire, 1870–1901', *Southern History*, 6 (1984), pp. 139–55

Mills, D. R., 'The quality of life in Melbourn, Cambridgeshire, in the period 1800–50', *International Review of Social History*, 23 (1978), pp. 382–404

'The residential propinquity of kin in a Cambridgeshire village, 1841', *Journal of Historical Geography*, 4 (1978), pp. 265–76

Aspects of marriage: an example of applied historical studies (Open University Social Science Publications, Milton Keynes, 1980)

'The nineteenth-century peasantry of Melbourn, Cambridgeshire', in R. M. Smith (ed.), *Land, kinship and life-cycle* (Cambridge, 1984), ch. 15

and Pearce, C., *People and places in the Victorian census* (Historical Geography Research Series, vol. XXIII, Cheltenham, 1989)

Mingay, G. (ed.), *The vanishing countryman* (1989)

'The rural slum', in M. Gaskell (ed.), *Slums* (Leicester, 1990), ch. 2

Mitch, D. F., *The rise of popular literacy in Victorian England* (Philadelphia, 1992)

Mitchell, B. R., *British historical statistics* (Cambridge, 1988)

Mitchison, R. and Leneman, L., *Sexuality and social control: Scotland 1660–1780* (Oxford, 1989)

Mitson, A., 'The significance of kinship networks in the seventeenth century: south-west Nottinghamshire', in C. Phythian-Adams (ed.), *Societies, cultures and kinship, 1580–1850* (Leicester, 1993), ch. 2

Mooney, G., 'Did London pass the "sanitary test"? Seasonal infant mortality in London, 1870–1914', *Journal of Historical Geography*, 20 (1994), pp. 158–74

Muir, E. and Ruggiero, G. (eds.), *Microhistory and the lost peoples of Europe* (Baltimore, 1991)

Murray, C., 'Underclass', *Sunday Times*, 26 November 1989

Mutch, A., *Rural life in S. W. Lancashire 1840–1914* (Centre for North-West Regional Studies, occasional paper no. 16, Lancaster, 1988)

'The "farming ladder" in north Lancashire, 1840–1914: myth or reality?', *Northern History*, 27 (1991), pp. 162–83

Nair, G., *Highley: the development of a community 1550–1880* (Oxford, 1988)

Nead, L., *Myths of sexuality: representations of women in Victorian Britain* (Oxford, 1988)

Neave, D., *Mutual aid in the Victorian countryside: friendly societies in the rural East Riding 1830–1914* (Hull, 1991)

Neeson, J. M., *Commoners: common right, enclosure and social change in England, 1700–1820* (Cambridge, 1993)

Netting, R., *Balancing on an alp* (Cambridge, 1981)

Newby, H., *The deferential worker: a study of farm workers in East Anglia* (1977)

Newman, A., 'An evaluation of bastardy recordings in an east Kent parish', in P. Laslett, K. Oosterveen and R. M. Smith (eds.), *Bastardy and its comparative history* (Cambridge, Mass., 1980), ch. 4

Obelkevich, J., *Religion and rural society: south Lindsey 1825–1875* (Oxford, 1976)

O'Day, R., *Education and society, 1500–1800* (1982)

Oddy, D. J., 'Food, drink and nutrition', in F. M. L. Thompson (ed.), *The Cambridge social history of Britain 1750–1950*, vol. II, *People and their environment* (Cambridge, 1990), ch. 5

O'Hara, D., ' "Ruled by my friends": aspects of marriage in the diocese of Canterbury, c. 1540–1570', *Continuity and Change*, 6 (1991), pp. 9–41

Olney, R. J. (ed.), *Labouring life on the Lincolnshire Wolds* (Sleaford, 1975)

O'Neill, G., *Pull no more bines: an oral history of east London women hop pickers* (1990)

Oosterveen, K., Smith, R. M. and Stewart, S., 'Family reconstitution and the study of bastardy: evidence from certain English parishes', in P. Laslett, K. Oosterveen and R. M. Smith (eds.), *Bastardy and its comparative history* (Cambridge, Mass., 1980), ch. 3

Oren, L., 'The welfare of women in labouring families: England, 1860–1950', *Feminist Studies*, 1 (1973), pp. 107–25

Osterud, N. G., *Bonds of community: the lives of farm women in nineteenth-century New York* (Ithaca, 1991)

and Fulton, J., 'Family limitation and age at marriage: fertility decline in Sturbridge, Massachusetts 1730–1850', *Population Studies*, 30 (1976), pp. 481–94

Pahl, R. E., *Divisions of labour* (Oxford, 1984)

(ed.), *On work* (Oxford, 1988)

Payne, C., *Toil and plenty: images of the agricultural landscape in England, 1780–1890* (New Haven, 1993)

Pearce, C. G., 'Expanding families: some aspects of fertility in a mid-Victorian community', *Local Population Studies*, 10 (1973), pp. 22–35

Peel, J., 'The manufacture and retailing of contraceptives in England', *Population Studies*, 17 (1963–4), pp. 113–25

Pelling, M. and Smith, R. M. (eds.), *Life, death, and the elderly* (1991)

Phythian-Adams, C., 'Rural culture', in G. Mingay (ed.), *The Victorian countryside* (1981), ch. 45

Re-thinking English local history (Leicester, 1987)

(ed.), *Societies, cultures and kinship, 1580–1850* (Leicester, 1993)

Pina-Cabral, J. de, *Sons of Adam, daughters of Eve* (Oxford, 1986)

Pooley, C. G. and Whyte, I. D. (eds.), *Migrants, emigrants and immigrants: a social history of migration* (1991)

Porter, J. H., 'The development of rural society', in G. E. Mingay (ed.), *The agrarian history of England and Wales*, vol. VI, *1750–1850* (Cambridge, 1989) ch. 9

Portelli, A., *The death of Luigi Trastulli and other stories: form and meaning in oral history* (New York, 1991)

Potter, R. G., 'Birth intervals: structure and change', *Population Studies*, 17 (1963–4), pp. 155–66

Pressat, R., *The dictionary of demography*, ed. C. Wilson (Oxford, 1985)

Purvis, J., 'The experience of schooling for working-class boys and girls in nineteenth-century England', in I. F. Goodson and S. J. Ball (eds.), *Defining the curriculum* (1984), pp. 89–115

Hard lessons (Oxford, 1989)

Quadagno, J., *Aging in early industrial society: work, family and social policy in nineteenth-century England* (New York, 1982)

Rawding, C., 'The iconography of churches: a case study of landownership and power in nineteenth-century Lincolnshire', *Journal of Historical Geography*, 16 (1990), pp. 157–76

'Society and place in nineteenth-century north Lincolnshire', *Rural History*, 3 (1992), pp. 59–85

Razi, Z., 'The myth of the immutable English family', *Past and Present*, 140 (1993), pp. 3–44

Reay, B., *The last rising of the agricultural labourers* (Oxford, 1990)

'Sexuality in nineteenth-century England: the social context of illegitimacy in rural Kent', *Rural History*, 1 (1990), pp. 219–47

'The context and meaning of popular literacy: some evidence from nineteenth-century rural England', *Past and Present*, 131 (1991), pp. 89–129

'Before the transition: fertility in English villages', *Continuity and Change*, 9 (1994), pp. 91–120

'Kinship and neighbourhood in nineteenth-century rural England: the myth of the autonomous nuclear family', *Journal of Family History*, 21 (1996), pp. 87–104

Reddy, W., *Money and liberty in modern Europe: a critique of historical understanding* (Cambridge, 1987)

'The concept of class', in M. L. Bush (ed.), *Social orders and social classes in Europe since 1500: studies in social stratification* (1992), ch. 2

Reed, M., 'The peasantry of nineteenth-century England: a neglected class?', *History Workshop*, 18 (1984), pp. 53–76

'Indoor farm service in 19th-century Sussex: some criticisms of a critique', *Sussex Archaeological Collections*, 123 (1985), pp. 225–41

'Class and conflict in rural England: some reflections on a debate', in M.

Reed and R. Wells (eds.), *Class, conflict and protest in the English countryside 1700–1880* (1990), ch. 1

' "Gnawing it out": a new look at economic relations in nineteenth-century rural England', *Rural History*, 1 (1990), pp. 83–94

Rendall, J., *Women in an industrializing society: England 1750–1880* (Oxford, 1990)

Riley, J. C., *Sickness, recovery and death: a history and forecast of ill health* (1989)

Roberts, E., *A woman's place: an oral history of working-class women 1890–1940* (Oxford, 1984)

' "Women's strategies", 1890–1940', in J. Lewis (ed.), *Labour and love: women's experience of home and family, 1850–1940* (Oxford, 1986), ch. 9

Robin, J., *Elmdon: continuity and change in a north-west Essex village, 1861–1964* (Cambridge, 1980)

'Family care of the elderly in a nineteenth-century Devonshire parish', *Ageing and Society*, 4 (1984), pp. 505–16

'Prenuptial pregnancy in a rural area of Devonshire in the mid-nineteenth century: Colyton, 1851–1881', *Continuity and Change*, 1 (1986), pp. 113–24

'Illegitimacy in Colyton, 1851–1881', *Continuity and Change*, 2 (1987), pp. 307–42

Rollison, D., *The local origins of modern society: Gloucestershire 1500–1800* (1992)

Rose, W., *Good neighbours* (Cambridge, 1942; reprinted Green Books, Bideford, 1988)

Ross, E., ' "Fierce Questions and Taunts": married life in working-class London, 1870–1914', *Feminist Studies*, 8 (1982), pp. 575–602

'Survival networks: women's neighbourhood sharing in London before World War One', *History Workshop*, 15 (1983), pp. 4–27

' "Not the Sort that Would Sit on the Doorstep": respectability in pre-World War I London neighbourhoods', *International Labour and Working Class History*, 27 (1985), pp. 39–59

Love and toil: motherhood in outcast London 1870–1918 (New York, 1993)

Rudé, G., *Criminal and victim: crime and society in early nineteenth-century England* (Oxford, 1985)

Ruggles, S., *Prolonged connections: the rise of the extended family in nineteenth-century England and America* (Madison, 1987)

Rule, J. G., 'Social crime in the rural south in the eighteenth and early nineteenth centuries', *Southern History*, 1 (1979), pp. 135–53

'Regional variations in food consumption among agricultural labourers, 1790–1860', in W. Minchinton (ed.), *Agricultural improvement: medieval and modern* (Exeter Papers in Economic History, 1981), pp. 112–37

The labouring classes in early industrial England 1750–1850 (1986)

Rutstein, S. O., *Infant and child mortality* (World Fertility Survey Comparative Studies, vol. XLIII, 1984) (pamphlet)

Sabean, D. W., *Property, production, and family in Neckarhausen, 1700–1870* (Cambridge, 1990)

Samuel, R. (ed.), *Village life and labour* (1975)

East End underworld: chapters in the life of Arthur Harding (1981)

and Thompson, P. (eds.), *The myths we live by* (1990)

Sanderson, M., *Education, economic change and society in England, 1780–1870* (1983)

Bibliography

Savage, M., 'Social mobility and class analysis: a new agenda for social history?', *Social History*, 19 (1994), pp. 69–79

Schellekens, J., 'Wages, secondary workers, and fertility: a working-class perspective of the fertility transition in England and Wales', *Journal of Family History*, 18 (1993), pp. 1–17

Schneider, J. and P., 'Demographic transitions in a Sicilian rural town', *Journal of Family History*, 9 (1984), pp. 245–72

Schofield, R. S., 'Dimensions of illiteracy, 1750–1850', *Explorations in Economic History*, 10 (1973), pp. 437–54

'English marriage patterns revisited', *Journal of Family History*, 10 (1985), pp. 2–20

'Did the mothers really die?', in L. Bonfield, R. M. Smith and K. Wrightson (eds.), *The world we have gained* (Oxford, 1986), ch. 9

and Wrigley, E. A., 'Infant and child mortality in England in the late Tudor and early Stuart period', in C. Webster (ed.), *Health, medicine and mortality in the sixteenth century* (Cambridge, 1979), ch. 2

Scott, J. C., *Weapons of the weak: everyday forms of peasant resistance* (New Haven, 1985)

Scott, J. W., *Gender and the politics of history* (New York, 1988)

Seccombe, W., 'Starting to stop: working-class fertility decline in Britain', *Past and Present*, 126 (1990), pp. 151–88

Weathering the storm: working-class families from the industrial revolution to the fertility decline (1993)

Segalen, M., 'The family cycle and household structure: five generations in a French village', *Journal of Family History*, 2 (1977), pp. 223–36

'Nuclear is not independent: organization of the household in the Pays Bigouden Sud in the nineteenth and twentieth centuries', in R. McC. Netting, R. R. Wilk and E. J. Arnould (eds.), *Households: comparative and historical studies of the domestic group* (Berkeley, 1984), ch. 7

Historical anthropology of the family (Cambridge, 1986)

Shammas, C., *The pre-industrial consumer in England and America* (Oxford, 1990)

Sharpe, P., 'The total reconstitution method: a tool for class specific study', *Local Population Studies*, 44 (1990), pp. 41–51

'Literally spinsters: a new interpretation of local economy and demography in Colyton in the seventeenth and eighteenth centuries', *Economic History Review*, 44 (1991), pp. 46–65

Sheppard, J. A., 'Small farms in a Sussex Weald parish', *Agricultural History Review*, 40 (1992), pp. 127–41

Short, B., 'The decline of living-in servants in the transition to capitalist farming: a critique of the Sussex evidence', *Sussex Archaeological Collections*, 122 (1984), pp. 147–64

The geography of England and Wales in 1910: an evaluation of Lloyd George's 'Domesday' of landownership (Historical Geography Research Series, vol. XXII, Cheltenham, 1989)

(ed.) *The English rural community: image and analysis* (Cambridge, 1992)

Smith, D. S., 'A homeostatic demographic regime: patterns in west European family reconstitution studies', in R. D. Lee (ed.), *Population patterns in the past* (New York, 1977), pp. 19–51

'The curious history of theorizing about the history of the western nuclear family', *Social Science History*, 17 (1993), pp. 325–53

Smith, F. B., *The people's health 1830–1910* (1979)

Smith, H., 'Family and class: the household economy of Languedoc wine-growers, 1830–1870', *Journal of Family History*, 9 (1984), pp. 64–87

Smith, J. E., 'Widowhood and ageing in traditional English society', *Ageing and Society*, 4 (1984), pp. 429–49

Smith, R. M., 'Fertility, economy, and household formation in England over three centuries', *Population and Development Review*, 7 (1981), pp. 595–622

'The structured dependence of the elderly as a recent development: some sceptical historical thoughts', *Ageing and Society*, 4 (1984), pp. 409–28

'Marriage processes in the English past: some continuities', in L. Bonfield, R. M. Smith and K. Wrightson (eds.), *The world we have gained* (Oxford, 1986), ch. 3

'Transfer incomes, risk and security: the roles of the family and the collectivity in recent theories of fertility change', in D. Coleman and R. S. Schofield (eds.), *The state of population theory* (Oxford, 1986), pp. 188–211

Smout, T. C., 'Born again at Cambuslang: new evidence on popular religion and literacy in eighteenth-century Scotland', *Past and Present*, 97 (1982), pp. 114–27

Snell, K. D. M., *Annals of the labouring poor: social change and agrarian England 1660–1900* (Cambridge, 1985)

'Agrarian histories and our rural past', *Journal of Historical Geography*, 17 (1991), pp. 195–203

'Deferential bitterness: the social outlook of the rural proletariat in eighteenth- and nineteenth-century England and Wales', in M. L. Bush (ed.), *Social orders and social classes in Europe since 1500: studies in social stratification* (1992), ch. 9

Songer, S., '"... a prudent wife is from the Lord": the married peasant woman of the eighteenth century in a demographic perspective', *Scandinavian Journal of History*, 9 (1984), pp. 113–33

Stansell, C., *City of women: sex and class in New York, 1789–1860* (Urbana, 1987)

Stephens, W. B. (ed.), *Studies in the history of literacy* (Leeds, 1983)

Education, literacy and society, 1830–70: the geography of diversity in provincial England (Manchester, 1987)

'Literacy in England, Scotland, and Wales, 1500–1900', *History of Education Quarterly*, 30 (1990), pp. 545–71

Stone, L., 'Literacy and education in England, 1640–1900', *Past and Present*, 42 (1969), pp. 69–139

Strathern, M., 'The place of kinship: kin, class and village status in Elmdon, Essex', in A. P. Cohen (ed.), *Belonging: identity and social organization in British rural cultures* (Manchester, 1982), ch. 4

Street, B. V., *Literacy in theory and practice* (Cambridge, 1984)

Sutherland, G., 'Education', in F. M. L. Thompson (ed.), *The Cambridge social history of Britain 1750–1950*, vol. III, *Social agencies and institutions* (Cambridge, 1990), ch. 3

Symes, D. and Appleton, J., 'Family goals and survival strategies: the role of kinship in an English upland farming community', *Sociologia Ruralis*, 26 (1986), pp. 345–63

Szreter, S., 'The importance of social intervention in Britain's mortality decline c. 1850–1914: a re-interpretation of the role of public health', *Social History of Medicine*, 1 (1988), pp. 1–37

Taylor, P., 'Daughters and mothers – maids and mistresses: domestic service between the wars', in J. Clarke, C. Critcher and R. Johnson (eds.), *Working class culture* (1979), ch. 5

Tebbutt, M., *Making ends meet: pawnbroking and working-class credit* (Leicester, 1983)

Teitelbaum, M. S., *The British fertility decline* (Princeton, 1984)

Temkin-Greener, H. and Swedlund, A. C., 'Fertility transition in the Connecticut valley: 1740–1850', *Population Studies*, 32 (1978), pp. 27–41

Thomas, K., 'The meaning of literacy in early modern England', in G. Baumann (ed.), *The written word: literacy in transition* (Oxford, 1986), pp. 97–130

Thompson, F., *Lark Rise to Candleford* (Harmondsworth, 1977 edn)

Thompson, F. M. L., *The rise of respectable society: a social history of Victorian Britain, 1830–1900* (1988)

Thompson, P., *The Edwardians* (1984 edn)

(ed.), *Our common history* (1982)

The voice of the past (1988 edn)

Thompson, T., *Edwardian childhoods* (1981)

Thomson, D., 'Welfare and the historians', in L. Bonfield, R. M. Smith and K. Wrightson (eds.), *The world we have gained* (Oxford, 1986), ch. 13

'The welfare of the elderly in the past: a family or community responsibility?', in M. Pelling and R. M. Smith (eds.), *Life, death, and the elderly: historical perspectives* (1991), ch. 7

Tranter, N. J., 'Illegitimacy in nineteenth century rural Scotland: a puzzle resolved?', *International Journal of Sociology and Social Policy*, 5 (1985), pp. 33–46

Turner, M., 'The land tax, land, and property', in M. Turner and D. Mills (eds.), *Land and property: the English land tax 1692–1832* (Gloucester, 1986)

van de Walle, E. and Knodel, J., 'Europe's fertility transition: new evidence and lessons for today's developing world', *Population Bulletin*, 34 (1979), pp. 1–43

Vann, R. T., 'The making of the modern family', *Journal of Family History*, 1 (1976), pp. 106–17

and Eversley, D., *Friends in life and death* (Cambridge, 1992)

Viazzo, P. P., 'Illegitimacy and the European marriage pattern', in L. Bonfield, R. M. Smith and K. Wrightson (eds.), *The world we have gained* (Oxford, 1986), ch. 4

'Victorian values', *New Statesman*, 27 May 1983

Vincent, D., 'Reading in the working-class home', in J. K. Walton and J. Walvin (eds.), *Leisure in Britain, 1780–1939* (Manchester, 1983), ch. 11

Literacy and popular culture: England, 1750–1914 (Cambridge, 1989)

Poor citizens: the state and the poor in twentieth-century Britain (1991)

Walker, A., 'A poor idea of poverty', *Times Higher Education Supplement*, 17 August 1990

Wall, R., 'Regional and temporal variations in English household structure from 1650', in J. Hobcraft and P. Rees (eds.), *Regional demographic development* (1979), ch. 4

'The household: demographic and economic change in England, 1650–1970', in R. Wall, J. Robin and P. Laslett (eds.), *Family forms in historic Europe* (Cambridge, 1983), ch. 16

'Work, welfare and the family: an illustration of the adaptive family economy', in L. Bonfield, R. M. Smith and K. Wrightson (eds.), *The world we have gained* (Oxford, 1986), ch. 10

'Relationships between the generations in British families past and present', in C. Marsh and S. Arber (eds.), *Families and households: divisions and change* (1992), ch. 4

and Robin, J. and Laslett, P. (eds.), *Family forms in historic Europe* (Cambridge, 1983)

Waller, P. J., 'Democracy and dialect, speech and class', in P. J. Waller (ed.), *Politics and social change in modern Britain* (Brighton, 1987), ch. 1

Walter, J., 'The social economy of dearth in early modern England', in J. Walter and R. Schofield (eds.), *Famine, disease and the social order in early modern society* (Cambridge, 1989), ch. 2

Walvin, J., *Victorian values* (1988)

Watkins, S. C. and McCarthy, J., 'The female life cycle in a Belgian commune: La Hulpe, 1847–1866', *Journal of Family History*, 5 (1980), pp. 167–79

Webb, R. K., *The British working class reader, 1790–1848* (New York, 1971)

Weir, D. R., 'Rather never than late: celibacy and age at marriage in English cohort fertility, 1541–1871', *Journal of Family History*, 9 (1984), pp. 340–54

Wells, R. A. E., 'The development of the English rural proletariat and social protest, 1700–1850', in M. Reed and R. Wells (eds.), *Class, conflict and protest in the English countryside 1700–1880* (1990), ch. 2

Wetherell, C., Plakans, A. and Wellman, B., 'Social networks, kinship, and community in Eastern Europe', *Journal of Interdisciplinary History*, 24 (1994), pp. 639–63

White, J., *The worst street in north London: Campbell Bunk, Islington, between the wars* (1986)

Williams, N., 'Death in its season: class, environment and the mortality of infants in nineteenth-century Sheffield', *Social History of Medicine*, 5 (1992), pp. 71–94

Williams, W. M., *The sociology of an English village: Gosforth* (1956)

A west country village, Ashworthy (1963)

Williamson, J. G., *Did British capitalism breed inequality?* (1985)

Wilson, A., 'Illegitimacy and its implications in mid-eighteenth-century London: the evidence of the Foundling Hospital', *Continuity and Change*, 4 (1989), pp. 103–64

Wilson, C., 'Natural fertility in pre-industrial England, 1600–1799', *Population Studies*, 38 (1984), pp. 225–40

'The proximate determinants of marital fertility in England 1600–1799', in L. Bonfield, R. M. Smith and K. Wrightson (eds.), *The world we have gained* (Oxford, 1986), ch. 8

and Oeppen, J. and Pardoe, M., 'What is natural fertility? The modelling of a concept', *Population Index*, 54 (1988), pp. 4–20

and Woods, R., 'Fertility in England: a long-term perspective', *Population Studies*, 45 (1991), pp. 399–410

Winstanley, M., *Life in Kent at the turn of the century* (Folkestone, 1978)

'Voices from the past: rural Kent at the close of an era', in G. Mingay (ed.), *The Victorian countryside* (1981), ch. 46

Wohl, A. S., *Endangered lives: public health in Victorian Britain* (1983)

Woods, R., 'The structure of mortality in mid-nineteenth century England and Wales', *Journal of Historical Geography*, 8 (1982), pp. 373–94

Bibliography

'Mortality patterns in the past', in R. Woods and J. Woodward (eds.), *Urban disease and mortality in nineteenth-century England* (New York, 1984), ch. 2

'Approaches to the fertility transition in Victorian England', *Population Studies*, 41 (1987), pp. 283–311

'Working-class fertility decline in Britain', *Past and Present*, 134 (1992), pp. 200–7

The population of Britain in the nineteenth century (1992)

and Woodward, J., 'Mortality, poverty and the environment', in R. Woods and J. Woodward (eds.), *Urban disease and mortality in nineteenth-century England* (New York, 1984), ch. 1

and Hinde, P. R. A., 'Nuptiality and age at marriage in nineteenth-century England', *Journal of Family History*, 10 (1985), pp. 119–44

and Hinde, P. R. A., 'Mortality in Victorian England: models and patterns', *Journal of Interdisciplinary History*, 18 (1987), pp. 27–54

and Watterson, P. A. and Woodward, J. H., 'The causes of rapid infant mortality decline in England and Wales, 1861–1921. Part I', *Population Studies*, 42 (1988), pp. 343–66

and Watterson, P. A. and Woodward, J. H., 'The causes of rapid infant mortality decline in England and Wales, 1861–1921. Part II', *Population Studies*, 43 (1989), pp. 113–32

Wrightson, K., 'Household and kinship in sixteenth-century England', *History Workshop*, 12 (1981), pp. 151–8

'Kinship in an English village: Terling, Essex 1500–1700', in R. M. Smith (ed.), *Land, kinship and life-cycle* (Cambridge, 1984), ch. 9

and Levine, D., *Poverty and piety in an English village: Terling, 1525–1700* (1979)

and Levine, D., 'Death in Whickham', in J. Walter and R. Schofield (eds.), *Famine, disease and the social order in early modern society* (Cambridge, 1989), ch. 3

and Levine, D., *The making of an industrial society: Whickham 1560–1765* (Oxford, 1991)

Wrigley, E. A., 'Family reconstitution', in Wrigley (ed.), *An introduction to English historical demography* (New York, 1966), ch. 4

'Mortality in pre-industrial England: the example of Colyton, Devon, over three centuries', *Daedalus*, 97 (1968), pp. 546–80

'Births and baptisms', *Population Studies*, 31 (1977), pp. 281–312

'Marriage, fertility and population growth in eighteenth-century England', in R. B. Outhwaite (ed.), *Marriage and society* (London, 1981), ch 7

'Population growth: England, 1680–1820', *ReFresh*, 1 (1985), pp. 1–4

'Men on the land and men in the countryside: employment in agriculture in early-nineteenth-century England', in L. Bonfield, R. M. Smith and K. Wrightson (eds.), *The world we have gained* (Oxford, 1986), ch. 8

and Schofield, R. S., 'English population history from family reconstitution: summary results 1600–1799', *Population Studies*, 37 (1983), pp. 157–84

and Schofield, R. S., *The population history of England 1541–1871* (Cambridge, 1989 edn)

Yasumoto, M., 'Industrialisation and demographic change in a Yorkshire parish', *Local Population Studies*, 27 (1981), pp. 10–23

Index

Index

Cambridge Studies in Population, Economy and Society in Past Time

Titles available in paperback are marked with an asterisk